An Abridgment Of Sir Walter Raleigh's History Of The World: In Five Books

Walter Raleigh

In the interest of creating a more extensive selection of rare historical book reprints, we have chosen to reproduce this title even though it may possibly have occasional imperfections such as missing and blurred pages, missing text, poor pictures, markings, dark backgrounds and other reproduction issues beyond our control. Because this work is culturally important, we have made it available as a part of our commitment to protecting, preserving and promoting the world's literature. Thank you for your understanding.

A N
ABRIDGMENT
OF
Sir *Walter Raleigh's*
HISTORY of the WORLD,
In Five B O O K S.

1. From the Creation to *Abraham.*
2. From *Abraham* to the Deſtruction óf the Temple of *Solomon.*
3. From the Deſtruction of *Jeruſalem* to *Philip* of *Macedon.*
4. From *Philip* of *Macedon* to the Race of *Antigonus.*
5. From the Eſtabliſhment of *Alexander* until the Conqueſt of *Aſia* and *Macedon* by the *Romans.*

Wherein the particular Chapters and Paragraphs are ſuccinctly Abridg'd according to his own Method, in the larger Volume.

To which is Added,
His Premonition to Princes.

LONDON,
Printed for *Mat. Gillyflower,* and Sold by *Andrew Bell,* at the *Croſs-Keys* and *Bible* in *Cornhill* near *Stocks-Market,* 1698.

THE

PUBLISHER's

Advertisement

TO THE

READER.

I Need not give any Account of the Excellency of Sir *Walter Raleigh's* History of the World, of which this is an Abridgment: The great Knowledge and Learning, the accurate Skill and Penetration, the sublime Wisdom and Piety, together with the curious Remarks and Observations which so signally appear in that History, have sufficiently recommended to the Judicious part of the World. Yet notwithstanding these Excellencies,

A 3   Sir

Sir *Walter* has not been without ſome conſiderable Imperfections in reſpect to Hiſtory, which he has ſhewn in his too frequent and long Digreſſions, and Obſervations; and tho' ſeveral of them are very fine and Ingenious, yet too many of them are wholly Foreign to his Subject: But his Moral and Religious Reflections tho ſometimes long, are generally too Excellent to need a Vindication. The above-mention'd Faults of this Great Man which were the general Faults of the Age in which he liv'd, have made many Curious Perſons wiſh for an Epitomy of that large Volume, wherein his Excellencie might in a great meaſure be retain'd, and his Errors be wholly expung'd. This wa attempted near Fifty Years ſince by A lexander *Roſs*, but with ſmall Skill an Succeſs; for he has injudiciouſly fill'd hi Epitomy with the moſt trifling and tra ſhy parts of the Original, and omitted too much of what was moſt material and ſubſtantial. For which Reaſon I have ventur'd to Publiſh this Abridgment, o

whic

which I shall give the Reader this Brief Account.

Above a Year and an half since it was given me by an Ingenious and Judicious Friend, who knew nothing of the Author; but finding it to be done with singular Care and Judgment, he desir'd me to View it and Publish it. Upon Examination, I found my Friend's Character to be rather short of the Author's Deserts, both as to his Skill and Accuracy in Extracting the Essence of the Original; so that I could do no less than expose so choice a Piece to the view of the Publick. All that I have done, besides the Expunging and shortning some Passages, is the Correcting and Altering of the Style, which in most places was too obsolete.: But in that I have still preserv'd its first Resemblance to the Original, which was almost as remarkable for the Style as the Matter; so that the Reader is not to expect all the Purity of a New Written History, for that would have

been

been too unlike Sir *Walter.* Besides, the Reader may here find an Excellent A-bridgment of Sir *Walter*'s Preface, which is a most sublime Piece of Morality and Divinity, and a most Noble Lesson and Instruction to all Princes and great Persons; being by many esteem'd of more Worth than all his History besides.

Louth in *Lincolnshire.*
Octob. 25. 1697.

Laurence Echard.

SIR

Sir *Walter Raleigh's*

Premonition to

PRINCES

MY own weak Reaſon convinc'd me, how unfit a choice I made of my Self, to undertake a Work of this mixture. For had it been generated in my younger Years, before any Wound received either by Fortune or Time, yet I might well have feared that the Darkneſs of Age and Death would have covered both me and it, long before its performance :. It had better ſuited with my Diſability, to have confined my Diſcourſe within our renowned Iſland of Britain, and to have ſet together the disjointed Frame of our Engliſh Affairs, than in the Evening of a Tempeſtuous Life, thus to begin with an Hiſtory of the World from the Creation. But the deep piercing Wounds, which while uncured, are ever aking ; with the deſire to ſatisfy thoſe few Friends, tryed by the Fire of Adverſity (the former inforcing, the latter perſuading) have cauſed me to make my Thoughts legible, and my ſelf the Subject of every Man's Opinion, wiſe or weak.

To the World I preſent them, to which I am nothing indebted ; neither have others that ſucceeded me ſped much better in the change of Fortune ; Proſpe-

rity

rity and Adversity ever tying and untying vulgar Affections. And as Dogs bark at those they know not, and accompany one another in their Clamours, so is it with the unthinking Multitude; which led by uncertain Reports, condemn without hearing, and wound without Offence given; contrary to the Counsel of Syracides. *Against this vanity of Vulgar Opinion,* Seneca *giveth a good Rule;* Let us satisfie our own Consciences, and not trouble our selves about the Censures of others, be it never so ill, as long as we deserve well.

Ecclesiasticus 11. 7.

Touching my self, if in any thing I have preferred the service of my Country, the general acceptation can yield me now no other profit, than a fair Day does after Ship-wrack; and the contrary, no other harm than as a Tempest in the Port. I know I lost the love of many, for my Fidelity to Her, whom I must still honour in the Dust; though farther than the defence of her excellent Person, I never persecuted any. To labour other satisfaction were the effects of Frenzy, not of Hope; seeing it is Truth, *not* Opinion *which can travel the World without a Passport. Equity alone might persuade, if there were not as many Forms of the Mind, as there are external Figures of Men; and that as every Man hath received a several Picture as to Face, so hath he a diverse Picture as to Mind: Every one a Form by himself; every one a Fancy and Cogitation differing; there being nothing in which Nature so much triumpheth, as in Dissimilitude. From hence it cometh that there is found so great a diversity of Opinions; so strong a contrariety of Inclinations; so many natural and unnatural,*

natural, wise and foolish, manly and childish Affections and Passions in mortal Men. For it is not the visible fashion or shape of Plants, or reasonable Creatures, that makes the difference of working in the one, or of Condition in the other, but the internal Form.

And though God has reserved the reading of mens Thoughts to himself; yet as the Fruit tells the name of the Tree, so do the outward Works of men (so far as their Cogitations are acted) give us a Light to guess at the rest. Nay, it were not hard to express the one by the other very near the Life, did not the Craft of many, Fear in most, and the Worlds Love in all, teach every Capacity, according to the compass it has, to qualify and mask over inward Deformities for a time. Yet no man can long continue masked in a counterfeit Behaviour: The things which are forced for pretences, having no ground of Truth, cannot long dissemble their own nature; and the Heart will be seen at the Tongues end.

In this great dissimilitude of reasonable Creatures, the common People are ill Judges of honest things, and their Wisdom is to be despised, said Eccles. As for the better sort, every Understanding has a peculiar Judgment, by which it both censureth others, and valueth it self; and therefore I will not think it strange, if my worthless Papers be torn by Ratts, since in all Ages Censurers have not spar'd to tax the Reverend of the Church with Ambition; the severe to themselves, with Hypocrisie; lovers of Justice, with Popularity; and Men of the truest valour with Vain-glory: For nothing is so easie as to Reprove and Censure.

I will not trouble the Reader with repeating the deserv'd Commendations of History; yet true it is, that among many other Benefits, for which it has been honour'd, it triumphs in this over all Human Knowledge, that it gives Life to our Understanding, since the World it self has Life even to this day: And it has triumphed over Time, which nothing else but Eternity has done; for it has carried our Knowledge over the vast devouring space of many Thousand Years, and has opened the piercing Eyes of our Mind, that we plainly behold living now, as if we lived then, that wise Work of the great God, *saith* Hermes. *By it (I say) we live in* the very time *when it was* Created; *behold how it was* govern'd, *how cover'd with Water, and again* repeopl'd: *How* Kings *and* Kingdoms *flourished and fell, and for what* Virtues *or* Vices God *made the one* prosperous, *and the other* wretched. *Neither is it the least of our Debt to* History, *that it has made us acquainted with our dead Ancestors, and raised them out of Darkness to teach us no less wise, than eternal Policy, by comparing former Miseries with our own ill Deservings. But neither the lively Instructions of Example, the Words of the wisest, nor Terror of future Torments, have yet so wrought upon our stupid Minds, as to make us remember, That the infinite Eye, and Wisdom of God doth pierce through all our Pretences: Nor to make us remember, That the Justice of God requires no other* Accuser *than our own* Consciences, *which by no false Beauty of our apparent actions, nor all the formality, which we (to gull Mens Opinions) put on, can be covered from him.*

Examples

Examples of God's Judgments *in particulars upon all* Degrees, *that have played with his* Mercies, *would fill Volumes.* For *the Sea of Examples hath no Bottom; though Marks, set on private Men, are (when their Bodies are cast into the Earth) written only in their Memory which lived with them; so that the Persons succeeding, who saw not their Fall, fear not their own Faults.* God's Judgments on the Greatest *have been Recorded to Posterity, either by those happy Hands, which the Holy Ghost guided, or by others. Now to point as far as the Angels Fall, for* Ambition; *at* Kings *eating Grass with Beasts for* Pride *and* Ingratitude; *at* Pharaoh's *wise Action when he slew the* Infants; *at* Jesabel's *Policy in covering* Naboth's *Murder, with many Thousands of the like, were but a Proof, that Example should be rejected at a distance. For who hath not observed what* Labour, Practice, Peril, Blood-shed, *and* Cruelty *the* Kings *and* Princes *of the World have undergone and exercised, taken upon them, and committed, to make themselves, and their Issues Masters of the World? yet hath* Babylon, Persia, Macedon, Rome, *or the rest, no Fruit, Flower or Leaf springing upon the face of the Earth: Nay, their very Roots and Ruins do hardly remain; for all that the Hand of Man can make, is either over-turned by the Hand of Man, or Consumed by Time. Politicians say, States have fallen, either by* Foreign Force, *or* Domestick Negligence *and* Dissention; *or by a third Cause rising from both: Others observe, That the greatest have sunk under their own weight; others, That Divine Providence hath set a Period to every State before the first Foundation thereof ; as* Cratippus *objected in* Pompey.

But *seeing the Books following undertake the Discourse of the first Kings and Kingdoms, and that a short Preface cannot run very far back to the Ancients ; I will for the present examine what Advantage has been gain'd by our own Kings and their Neighbour Princes, who having beheld both in Divine and Humane Letters, the success of Infidelity, Injustice and Cruelty, have (notwithstanding) Planted after the same Pattern. Mens Judgments agree not ; and no mans Affection is stirred up alike, with Examples of the like nature ; but is either touched with that which seemeth to come nearest to his own private Opinion, or else best fits his Apprehension. But the Judgments of God are unchangeable ; no Time can weary him, or obtain his Blessing to that in one Age, which he Cursed in another. Those therefore which are Wise, will be able to discern the bitter Fruits of* irreligious Policy, *as well in old Examples as new ; for ill Actions have always been attended with* ill Success, *as will appear by the following Examples.*

We *have then no sooner passed over the* violence *of the* Norman Conquest, *but we encounter that remarkable* Example of God's Justice *upon the Children of* Henry I. *who having by* Force, Craft, *and* Cruelty, *over-reached his Brother* Robert D. of Normandy, *Usurped the Crown of* England, *and dispossessed him of his Dukedom, and barbarously deprived him of his Sight, to make his own Sons* Lords *of all ; but* God cast *them all,* Male *and* Female, Nephews *and* Neeces *(*Maud *excepted) into the bottom of the Sea.*   Edward

Edward II. *being Murdered, a Torrent of Blood followed in the Royal Race, so that all the Masculine Princes (few excepted) dyed of the* Bloody-Flux. *And though* Edward III. *in his young Years, made his* knowledge of that horrible Fact, *no more than* suspicious ; *yet his putting to death his Unkle the* Earl of Kent, *made it manifest he was not ignorant of what had past, nor greatly desirous to have had it otherwise. But this* Cruelty, *the unsearchable Judgment of God revenged on his* Grandchild ; *and so it fell out even to the last of the Line; That in the Second or Third Descent, they were all* buried *under the* Ruins *of those* Buildings *whose Mortar had been tempered with* innocent Blood. For Richard II. *having Murdered his Unkle of* Glocester, *was himself Murdered by* Henry IV.

Henry IV. *having broken Faith to his Lords, and by* Treason *obtained the Crown, Entailed it by Parliament upon his Issue ; and by many* Treacheries *left all* Competitors *defenseless, as he supposed, leaving his Son* Henry V. *full of Valour and signal Victories; yet was his Grand-child* Henry VI. *and his Son the Prince, without Mercy Murdered, and his Crown transferred to the Houses of his Enemies. It was therefore a true Passage of* Caussabon ; *a* Day, *an* Hour, *a* Moment, *is* enough to overthrow what seemeth founded in Adamant.

Henry VI. *overwhelmed with the Storm of his Grandfathers grievous Crimes, generally esteemed an innocent* Prince, *yet refused the Daughter of* Armaignac, *of the House of* Navarre, *to whom he was Ally'd, and Married a Daughter of* Anjou, *and*

a 4   so

fo loft all that he had in France : *He alfo condefcended to the* unworthy Death of *his Unkle of* Glocefter, *the main Pillar of the Houfe of* Lancafter. Buckingham *and* Suffolk *contrived the* Duke's *death, by the* Queen's *procurement* ; *but the Fruit was anfwerable to the Plantation, and they and their Adherents were deftroy'd by* York ; *whofe Son* Edward *depriv'd* Henry *the Father, and* Edward *the Son, of Life and Kingdom. The Politick Lady, the* Queen, *lived to fee the miferable End of her Husband, Son, and all her Adherents* ; *her felf plunder'd, and Father beggar'd to Ranfom her.*

Edward IV. *hath his turn to Triamph, when all the Plants of* Lancafter, *except the Earl of* Richmond, *were extirpated* ; *whom he had alfo bought of the D. of* Britain, *but could not keep him. But what ftability can* Edward's *Plantation promife, when he had feen and approved* Prince Edward's *Murder, by* Glocefter, Dorfet, Haftings, &c. *which efcaped not the Judgment of God in the fame kind?* He inftructed Glocefter *to Murder* Henry VI. *and taught him the Art to kill his own Sons, and to Ufurp the* Crown.

Richard III. *The greateft Mafter in Villany, of all that went before him* ; *who by neceffity of his Tragedy, being to play more Parts in his own Perfon than all the reft, yet fo well fitted every Mans Humour that join'd with him, as if each had acted his own Intereft.* Buckingham *and* Haftings, *Enemies to the* Queen, *and her* Kindred, *are eafily allured to condefcend, that* Rivers *and* Grey *(the* King's *maternal Unkle, and half Brother) fhould firft be feparated*

parated

parated from him ; then imprisoned ; and for avoiding future Inconveniences, to lose their Heads. Having brought them to the practice of that common Precept which the Devil has written on every Post, To deprefs whom they have injur'd, and to deftroy whom they have deprefs'd. *Then* Buckingham *has it form'd in his Head, That when the* King *and his* Brother *shall be of sufficient Age, they will take severe Revenge of the Wrong to* Rivers *and* Gray, *and therefore of necessity, the* King *and his* Brother *must be made away.* Haftings *being founded by* Catesby, *and found not fordable, by reason of his Fidelity to his Masters Sons, after an attempt to kill him, fitting in the Council, the Hangman must get the Tyrant an Appetite to his Dinner, by striking off his Head ; a greater Judgment of God than this upon* Haftings *I never obferv'd : For the fame* Hour, *and in the fame* lawlefs manner, *by his Advice the Execution of* Rivers *and* Gray *was performed.* Buckingham *has yet a part to play for* Richard, *in perfuading the* Londoners *to Elect him* King, *and to be rewarded with the Earldom of* Hereford : *But after much vexation of Mind, and unfortunate attempts, being betrayed by his truftieft Servant, he loft his Head at* Salisbury, *without troubling his* Peers. Richard, *after other Murders, and* Mifchievous Policies, *having deftroy'd his* Nephews and Natural Lords, *by the great Outcry of innocent Blood, became an infamous fpectacle of Shame and Difhonour both to his Friends and Foes.*

Henry

Henry VII. (*the Instrument of Gods Justice in cutting off the* Cruel King) *Succeeded*; *a Politick Prince, if ever there was any, who by the Engine of his Wisdom beat down as many strong Oppositions both before and after he wore the* Crown, *as ever any* King *of* England *did: For as his Profits held the Reins of his Affections, so he wayed his Understanding by his Abilities, leaving no more to hazard, than what cannot be denyed in all Human Actions.* This King *never indured Mediation in rewarding Servants, and was therein exceeding wise; for what himself gave, himself received both* Thanks and Love : *Knowing that the Affections of Men (purchased no way so ready as by Benefits,) were Trains which better became* Great Kings *than* Great Subjects. *On the contrary, in whatsoever he grieved his Subjects, he wisely put it off to those that he found fit Ministers of such Actions. He used not to begin their Processes, whom he* hated or feared *by the Execution, as* Lewis XI. *did: Yet he somewhat follow'd the Errors of his Ancestors, as the* Head *of* Stanley, (*who set the Crown on his*) *and the* Death *of the young* E. of Warwick, *Son to* George D. *of* Clarence *do shew, and likewise the Success of his Grandchildren of the first Line,* &c.

Henry VIII. (*the Pattern of a* merciless Prince) *Succeeded: One who precipitately advanced many, (but for what Virtue no Man could imagine) and with change of his Fancy ruined them, no Man knowing for what Offence. To how many others gave he abundant Flowers from whence to gather* Ho-ny;

ny, *and in the end of Harvest* burnt *them in the* Hive? *How many* Wives *did he* cut *off, or* cast *off, as his* Fancy *or* Affection *changed? How many* Princes *of the Blood, with many o-thers of all Degrees, did he* Execute? *What causeless cruel* Wars *did he make upon his own Nephew* King James V ? *What* Laws *and* Wills *did he invent to establish the* Kingdom *in his own* Family, *using his sharpest Weapons to cut off the* Branches *which sprang from the same* Root *that himself did? Yet God took away all his own without increase; though for themselves in their several Kinds, all* Princes *of eminent* Virtues: *And that Blood which King* Henry *affirmed that the cold Air of* Scotland *froze up in the* North, *God hath diffused by the Sun-shine of his Grace; from whence his Majesty now living, (and long may,) is Descended: Of whom I may say truly, that Malice her self can-not charge him justly with any of those* foul Spots, *by which the* Consciences *of all the fore-named* Princes *were defiled; or the Sword of his Justice stained with any Drops of that innocent Blood which had stained their* Hands *and Fame. And for the Crown of England, it may truly be avowed, He received it from the Hand of God; neither hastning the Time upon any provo-cation; nor* taking Revenge *upon any that sought to put him by it: And refused Assistance of her Enemies, that wore it long with as great Glory, as ever* Princess *did. He entred neither by* Breach *nor* Blood, *but by the ordinary Gate, which his own Right had set open; and was received in*

in at it by an universal Love and Obedience.
Thus the Northern *parts of* Britany *infinitely*
severed from the South *in Affection for a long*
time (whereof grew deadly Wars with much Cru-
elty) were at length happily united. For which
Blessing *of God, never to be forgotten, as we*
are bound to much Thankfulness; so the Fruit
of this Concord maketh all petty Grievances to
appear but as a Mole-Hill to a Mountain. And
if the uniting of the Red Rose *with the* White
were the greatest Happiness, next Christian Religion, *that ever the* Kingdom *received from*
God to that Day; certainly the Peace between
the Two Lions of Gold *and* Gules *doth by many*
Degrees exceed, both by sparing our Blood and
assuring the Land.

As it pleased God to punish the Usurpation
and unnatural Cruelties *of our own* Kings; *so*
do we find he dealt with the Sons of Lewis Debonair, *Son of* Charlemain. *For after* Debonair *had put out his Nephew* Bernard's *Eyes,*
the Son of Pipin *the Eldest of* Charlemain,
King of Italy *and Heir of the Empire, and af-*
ter that caused him to die *in Prison; there fol-*
lowed such Murder *and* Bloodshed, Poisonings,
and Civil Wars, *till the whole Race of that fa-*
mous Emperor was extinguished. Debonair
further to secure himself, put his Bastard Bro-
thers into a Monastery: *But God rais'd up*
his own Sons to vex, invade, imprison, *and*
depose *him, alledging the former Violences to*
his Nephew *and* Brothers: *Yet he did that*
which few Kings do; he publickly acknowledg'd
and

1

and recanted *his* Cruelty *against* Bernard *in the Assembly of the States.* But *Blood* unjustly spilt *is not* easily expiated *by Repentance:* And *such Medicines to the Dead, have but dead Rewards.* He *having also given* Aquitain *to* Pipin *his Second Son,* sought *after that 'to cast him out, as indeed he did his Son after him, of the same Name, at the Persuasion of* Judith *to raise her Son* Charles.

Lothair, *his eldest Son, he left King of* Italy, *and Emperor, against whom his Nephew* Pipin *of* Aquitain, Lewis *of* Bavier, *and* Charles *the Bald made War; between whom was fought the most Bloody Battel that ever was known in* France, *in which the Loss of the Nobility and Men of War encouraged the* Sarazens *to invade* Italy, *the ——— to fall upon* Almain, *and the* Danes *upon* Normandy. *After being invaded by* Lewis, *and by his own* Conscience *for rebelling against his Father, and other Cruelties, he quits the Empire, and dyes in a Monastery.*

Charles *the Bald seizeth on* Pipin *his Nephew, and kills him in a Cloyster, oppresses the Nephews, the Sons of* Lothair, *and usurps the Empire. His Son* Caroloman *rebells, and hath his Eyes burnt out by his Father :* Lewis *of* Bavier *and his Son* Caroloman *are overthrown by* Charles ; *and* Lewis *dies of Grief, as* Charles *doth of Poison by* Zedekias *his Phisician, a* Jew : *Whose Son also* Lewis *le* Begne, *dy'd of the same Potion, and* Charles *the Simple succeeded : whose Natural Brothers* Lewis *and* Charlemain *rebell'd ; The*
Younger

Younger is slain by a wild Boar, the Elder brake his Neck, as did also the Son of Bavier.

Charles *the Gross became Lord of what De-*bonair's *Sons had held in* Germany, *who in-vading* Charles *the Simple, is forsaken of* No-bles, Wife, *and* Wit, *dying a distracted Beg-gar.*

Charles *the Simple held in Wardship by* Eu-des, *Mayor of the* Palace, *and after by* Robert *his Brother; lastly is surprised by the* E. *of* Ver-mandois, *and dyed in Prison.*

Lewis *his Son succeeded, and brake his Neck; one of his Sons dyes of* Poyson, *the other in* Prison.

Francis I. *was one of the worthiest Kings that ever* France *had, except his exposing the* Protestants *of* Mirandel *and* Cabriers *to the Fire and Sword; of which though he repented, and charged his Son to do Justice on the Mur-derers, yet was not that unseasonable Care accept-ed of by God; who cut off his Four Sons with-out Issue to succeed. And notwithstanding all their* Subtilty *and* Breach of Faith, *with all their* Massacres *upon those of the* Religion, *the* Crown *was set on his Head, whom they all endeavoured to ruin; and the* Protestants *are now in number and strength more than ever.*

Spain *has found God the same, as* Don Pe-dro *of* Castile *may witness, who as he became the most merciless of all Heathen or Christian Tyrants, (as the History of* Spain *records) so he perish'd by the Hands of his Younger Brother, who dispossessed all his Children of their Inheritance.*

John

John *D.* of Burgoign *may parallel this* King, *if any can; who after a Trayterous Murder of the D.* of Orleance, *caused the* Chancellor, Constable, *divers* Bishops, Officers *of* Justice, *of the* Treasury, Requests, Chamber *of* Accompts, *with Sixteen Hundred others, suddenly to be slain; which kind of Death eased the World of* himself.

Ferdinand *holding* Arragon *by Usurpation of his Ancestors, added* Castile *and* Leon, *which he held by force of Arms from the Daughter of the last* Henry, *and expell'd his* Neece *from the Kingdom* of Navarr: *He betrayed* Ferdinand *and* Frederick *King of* Naples (*his Kinsman*) *to the* French, *with the Army sent to their succour.* The Politick King, *who sold Heaven and his own Honour, to make his Son the greatest* Monarch, *saw his Death with his Wives, and her untimely* Birth *buried together; the like End he saw of his own Eldest Daughter; his Second dyed Mad; his Third was cast off by our* King Henry VIII. *and the Mother of a Daughter, whose unhappy Zeal shed a Deluge of Innocent Blood, and had all his Kingdoms possest by strange Masters.*

Charles V. *Son to Arch. D.* Philip, *who had Married* Ferdinand's *Mad Daughter, after the Death of many Multitudes of* Christian *Souldiers and renowned Captains, in his vain Enterprizes upon* France, Germany, *and other States, while the* Turk *took the City of* Rhodes; *was, in conclusion, chased out of* France, *and in some sort out of* Germany, *being persued by D.* Maurice *over the* Alps, *which he passed by Torch-Light, and crept*

crept into a Cloifter, *and became his Son's Prifoner, who paid him very flowly.*

Philip II. *his Son, not content to hold* Holland
and Zealand *(wrefted by his Anceftors from* Ja-
queline *their lawful Prince) and to poffefs many o-
ther parts of the* Netherland Provinces *in Peace,
by perfuafion of that mifchievous* Cardinal *of* Granvil *and other Tyrants; forgetting the remarkable
Services done to his* Father; *and the Forty* Millions *of* Florens *prefented him at his Entrance; and
his folemn* Oaths *twice taken to maintain their Privileges, which they had enjoyed under Thirty five
Earls, conditional Princes, began to Tyrannize o-
ver them by the* Spanifh Inquifition *and other intolerable Impofitions; and laftly, by Force of Arms
fought to make himfelf, not* Monarch *only, like the*
Kings *of* England, France, *&c. but* Turk-like,
to overturn all their National Fundamental Laws,
Privileges *and* Cuftoms. *To effect this, he eafily obtained a Difpenfation of his* Oaths *from the*
Pope, *and then divided the Nobility, under the
Government of his bafe Sifter* Margaret *of* Auftria,
and Cardinal Granvil: *Then he employ'd that
Mercilefs* Spaniard Ferdinand Alvarez D. *of* Al-
va, *who in fix Years cut off Eighteen Thoufand fix
Hundred* Gentlemen *and others, by the Hand of the
Hang-man. Failing of his purpofe by Force, he
tryeth Policy, and fent* Don John *of* Auftria, *his
Baftard Brother; who upon the Papal advantage,
made no fcruple to fwear; and having received Six
Hundred Thoufand Pounds of the Provinces to eafe
them of the Garrifons, he fuddenly furprized the
Citadel of* Antwerp, Namure, *&c. yet after fo*

many

many Thousands slain ; Thirty six Millions of Trea-
sure spent in six Years, he left the Countrey ; and
the King spent above One Hundred Millions, with
the Death of Four Hundred Thousand Christians,
to lose the richest Country he had.

Oh by what Plots ! by what Oaths, treacherous Pra-
ctices, Oppressions, Imprisonments, Tortures, Poy-
sonings ; and under what Reasons of State and Po-
lity, have these Kings pulled the Vengeance of God
upon themselves, upon Theirs, and upon prudent
Ministers? and at last have brought these things to
pass for their Enemies Advantage ; and found an
effect so directly contrary to all their own Counsels,
and Cruelties ; that the one could never have ho-
ped for it, and the other never have succeeded, had
no such Opposition been made : God hath said it,
and performed it ever ; I will destroy the Wisdom of the Wise.

But to what end do we lay before the Eyes *of*
the Living, *the* Fate *and* Fortunes *of the* Dead,
seeing the World is the same it hath been, and the
Children will obey their Parents? It is in the pre-
sent that all the Wits of the World are exercised ;
and to enjoy the Times we have, we hold all things
lawful ; and either hope to hold them for ever, or
hope there is nothing after them to be hoped for.
For as we are content to forget our own Experi-
ence, and counterfeit Ignorance of our Knowledge
in things that concern our selves ; or perswade our
selves, that God hath given us Letters Patents

b   *to*

to perfue all our *irreligious Affections with a* Non obftante; *So we neither look* behind *us what has been, nor* before *us what fhall be.* It *is true, the quantity we have is of the* Body; *we are by it joined to the* Earth, *we are compounded of the* Earth, *and inhabit the* Earth. *The* Heavens *are high, a-far off, and unexplorable: We have a fenfe of corpo-real things, but of eternal Grace only by Revelation: No wonder then, that our Thoughts are fo* Earthly; *and a lefs wonder that the Words of worthlefs Men cannot cleanfe us; feeing their Inftructions and Do-Etrine, whofe Underftanding the* Holy Ghoft *vouch-fafed to inhabit, have not performed it. For the Prophet* Ifaiah *cryed out long ago,* Lord, who hath believed our Reports? *And doubtlefs as he com-plained of his time; fo are they lefs believed every day, though Religion be ftill in Mens Mouths; we profefs to know, but by works deny him; which ar-gueth an univerfal Diffimulation. For Happinefs confifteth in a Divine Life, not in knowledge of Divine Things, wherein Devils excel us. Conten-tions about Religion have bred lamentable effetts; and the Difcourfe thereof hath near upon driven the Practice out of the* World. *He which obtaineth Knowledge only by Mens Difputations of* Religion, *would judge that* Heaven *were chiefly to be defired; but look upon many Difputers Lives, and nothing is found in the* Soul *but* Hypocrifie. *We are all* (in effect) *become* Comedians in Religion; *we act in Voice and Gefture Divine Virtues; but in courfe of Life we renounce the part we play; and* Charity, Ju-ftice *and* Truth *have their Being but in Terms, as the Philofophers* Materia prima.

That

That Wisdom which teacheth us the Knowledge of God, hath great Esteem enough in that we give it our good Word; but the Wisdom which is altogether exercised in gathering Riches, by which we purchase Honour in the World, These are the Marks we Shoot at; the Care *whereof is our own in this Life, and the* Peril *our own in the future; Though in our greatest Abundance we have but one Man's Portion, as the Man of the greatest Wisdom and Ability hath told us. As for those which devour the rest, and follow us in fair Weather, they again forsake us in the first Storm of our Misfortune, and fly away before Sea and Wind, leaving us to the Malice of our Destinies. Among a Thousand Examples take that of Mr.* Dannet : Charles V. *at* Vlushing, *in his return to* Spain, *conferring with* Seldius, *his Brother* Ferdinand's *Embassador, till the dead of Night, when they should part, called some of his Servants; and when none answered (being either gone or asleep) himself took the Candle to light down* Seldius, *notwithstanding his importunity to the contrary: But at the stairs foot, he desir'd him to remember when he was dead,* That whom he had known in his time environ'd with mighty Armies, he hath seen forsaken of his own Domesticks.*

But you will say Men more regard the Honour done to great Men than the former: It is true indeed, provided that an inward Love from their Justice and Piety, accompanying the outward Worship given to

their

their Places and Power ; without which, the applause of the Multitude is as the Out cry of a Herd of Animals, who without knowledge of any true Cause, please themselves with the Noise they make. Impious *Men in* Prosperity *have ever been* applauded, *and the most* Virtuous *(if unprosperous) have ever been* despised, *and Virtue and Fortune are rarely distinguish'd. For as* Fortune's Man *rides the Horse, so* Fortune *her self rides the* Man ; *who when he is descended on foot, the* Man *is taken from his* Beast, *and* Fortune *from the* Man ; *a base Groom beats the* one, *and bitter Contempt spurns at the* other, *with equal liberty.*

The Second thing which Men more respect, is raising of Posterity. *If these Men conceive that Souls departed take any Comfort therein, they are Wise in a foolish thing, as* Lactantius *speaketh.* De sal. sap. li. 3. c. 28. *For when our Mortal Spirits are departed, and dispos'd of by* God, *they are pleased no more in* Posterity, *than Stones are proud which sleep in the Walls of a* King's *Palace; neither have they more Sorrow in their Poverty, than there is Shame in the Prop of a* Beggar's *Cottage. The* Dead, *tho'* Holy, *know nothing, no not of their own Children :* For the Souls departed are not Conversant with the Affairs of the Living, said *Augustin, de Cura pro Mort. Job also, of whom we cannot doubt, tells us,* we shall neither understand of our Childrens Honour, or low Degree. Man walketh in a Shadow, disquieting himself in vain ; he heapeth up Riches, and cannot tell who shall gather them. The living, *saith Eccles.* know they shall die, but the Dead

know

know nothing at all; for who shall shew to Man, what shall be after him under the Sun? *And when he consider'd all his Labours, and could not tell whether a Fool or a Wise Man should enjoy the Fruit thereof, himself hated his own Labours.* What can other Men hope to know after Death, When Isaiah confesseth, Abraham *himself is ignorant of us?* Death's dark Night *shall cover us, till he return that hath Triumph'd over it; when we shall again receive Organs glorified and Immortal, the Seats of Evangelical Affections; and the Souls of the Blessed shall be exercised in so great Admiration, as that they can admit no mixture of less Joy, nor any return of Mortal Affections towards Friends, Children,* &c. *Whether we shall retain any particular Knowledge of them, or in any sort distinguish them; no Man can assure us, and the Wisest Men doubt.* But on the contrary, *if a Divine Life retain any of those Faculties which the Soul exercised in a Mortal Body; we shall not then so divide the Joys of Heaven, as to cast any part thereof on the memory of their Felicities which remain in the World: Whose Estates, be they greater than ever the World gave, we shall from the difference then known to us, even detest the Consideration thereof. And whatsoever shall remain of all that's past, the same will consist in the Charity which we exercised when living; and in the Piety, Justice, and firm Faith, for which it pleased the infinite Mercy of God to accept of us and receive us. Shall we then value Honour and Riches at nothing, and neglect them as unnecessary and vain?* cer-

b 3   *tainly*

tainly no. For that infinite Wisdom of God, which hath distinguished his Angels, the Light and Beauty of Heavenly Bodies; differenced Beasts and Birds; Created the Eagle and the Fly, the Cedar and the Shrub; given the fairest tinture to the Ruby, and quickest Light to the Diamond; hath also Ordained Kings, Dukes, Magistrates and Judges amongst his People. And as Honour is left to Posterity, as an Ensign of the Vertue and Understanding of their Ancestors; so being Titles with proportionable Estates, fall under the miserable Succours of other Mens Pity, I account it Foolishness to condemn such Care: Provided that Worldly Goods be well gotten, and that we raise not our Building out of other Mens Ruins, which God accurseth, by Jeremiah and Isaiah, and True Wisdom forbids, Prov. i. 10, to 18, 19.

And if we could afford our selves so much Leisure, as to consider, That he who has most in the World, hath in respect of the World nothing; and he who has the longest time to live in it, hath no Proportion at all therein, comparing it with the Time past, when we were not, or with the Time to come, in which we shall abide for ever: I say if our Portion in the World, and our Time in the World, be thus considered, they differ little from nothing: It is not out of any Excellency of Understanding, that we so much prize the one, which hath (in Effect) no being; and so much neglect the other, which hath no ending; Coveting the Mortal Things of the World, *as if our Souls*
were

were there Immortal ; *and neglect the things* Immortal, *as if our selves, after the World, were but* Mortal.

Let every Man value his own Wisdom as he pleases, the Rich Man *think all Fools that cannot equal his Abundance ; The* Revengeful *esteem them negligent, which have not trampled upon their Opposites : The* Politician *think them Blockheads, that cannot merchandize their* Faith : *Yet when we come within Sight of the Port of Death, to which all Winds drive us ; and when, by letting fall the fatal Anchor, which can never be weighed again, the Navigation of this Life takes End : Then it is (I say) that our own* Cogitations, *those sad and severe ones (formerly thrown off by Health and Felicity) return again, and pay us to the uttermost for all the pleasing Passages of our Lives past. Then it is we cry for* God's Mercy, *when we can no longer exercise* Cruelty ; *then this terrible Sentence,* God will not be mocked, *striketh through our Souls. For if* the righteous shall scarcely be saved, and that God spared not the Angels ; *where shall those appear, who having served their Appetites all their Lives, presum'd that the severe Commands of the dreadful God were given in Sport, and that the last faint Breath is forced to sound* Lord have Mercy, *without any kind of Satisfaction to Men, or Amendment ? Oh how many (saith a Reverend Father) descend to Eternal Torments and Sorrows with this Hope !*

It is indeed a Comfort to our Friends to have it said, we died well; *for all desire to die the Death of the Righteous, as* Balaam *did.* But what shall we call (indeed) a Mocking of God, *if that those Men mock him not, that think it enough for God, to ask him Mercy at Leisure, with the last Remains of a Malicious Breath?* This well-dying Prayer amounts to as much as this, We beseech thee, O God, that all the Falshoods, Forswearing, and Treacheries of our Lives past, may be well pleasing to thee; that thou wilt for our Sakes, (that have had no Leisure to do any thing for thine) change thy Nature, (though impossible) and forget to be a just God; that thou wilt love Injuries and Oppressions, call Ambition Wisdom, and Charity Foolishness. For I shall prejudice my Son (which I am resolved not to do) if I make Restitution, and confess my self to have been unjust, (which I am too proud to do) if I deliver the Oppressed. *These wise Worldlings have either found, or made them a* Leaden God, *like that which* Lewis *the Eleventh wore in his Cap, and used to kiss it, and ask it Pardon, when he had caused any to be murdered, promising it should be the last*; *as when by the Practice of a Cardinal, and falsified Sacrament, he caused the* Earl of Armagnack *to be stabbed at Prayers.* Of this Composition are all devout Lovers of the World, *that they fear all that is*

worthless

worthless and *frivolous*; they fear the Plots and Practices, *yea the very* Whisperings *of their Opposites*; they fear the Opinions *of* Men, *which beat but upon* Shadows: *They flatter and forsake the prosperous or unprosperous,* Friends *or* Kings: *Yea, they dive under* Water, *like* Ducks, *at every* Peble Stone *thrown at them by a powerful* Hand. *On the contrary, they shew an obstinate and* Gigantick Valour *against the terrible* Judgments of the All-powerful *God; yea, they shew themselves* Gods against *God, and* Slaves towards Men, *whose* Bodies *and* Consciences *are alike rotten.*

Now for the rest, if we examine the Difference *between the* Rich *and* Mighty, *whom we call* Fortunate, *and the* Poor *and* Oppressed, *whom we account* Wretched; *we shall find the* Unhappiness *of the one, and the* Misery *of the other so tyed by God to the very* Instant, *and so subject to* enterchange, *(witness the sudden* Downfall *of the* greatest, *and the speedy* Rise *of the meanest) that the one hath nothing certain whereof to* boast, *nor the other to* lament. *For no Man is so assured of* Honour, Riches, Health, *or* Life, *but may be deprived of either, or all, the very next hour; for what an* Evening *will bring with it is uncertain; and none can tell what shall be to morrow, saith St.* James: To Day *he is set up, to* Morrow *he shall not be found; for he is turned into* Dust, *and his* Purpose *perisheth.* And *though the* Air of Adversity *be very obscure, yet*
therein

therein we better discern God, than in the shining
Light of Worldly Glory, *through whose Clear-*
ness no Vanity whatsoever can escape our Sight.
And though Adversity seem ridiculous to the Hap-
py and Fortunate, who delight themselves at others
Misfortunes; though it seem grievous to those
which were in it: Yet this is true, that of all
that's past, to the very Instant, what remains is
equal to either. For though we have lived many
Years, and in them have rejoyced (according to
Solomon) *or have we sorrowed as long; yet look-*
ing back, we find both Joy and Sorrow sailed out of
Sight, and Death which hath held us in Chase
from the Womb, hath put an end to both. Let
him therefore, whom Fortune *hath served, and*
Time *befriended, take an Accompt of his Memo-*
ry, (the only Keeper of Pleasures past) and truly
examine what it hath reserved of Beauty, Youth,
or past Delights; or of his dearest Affections, or
whatsoever Contentment the amorous Spring time
gave his Thoughts, and he shall find, that all
the Art which his Elder Years had, can draw no
other Vapour out of these Dissolutions, than hea-
vy, *secret, and sad Sighs. He shall find nothing*
remaining, but those Sorrows which grow up after
our fast Springing Youth; overtook it, when it
was at a Stand; and overtopping it utterly, when
it began to wither. Looking back therefore from
the Instant of our present Being, and the poor
diseased Captive hath as little Sense of all former
Miseries and Pains, as the Man so blessed in com-
mon Opinion hath of fore-past Pleasures and De-
lights.

*tights. For whatsoever is cast behind us, is just
nothing; and what is to come depends upon de-
ceitful Hope. Only I must except those few* black
Swans, *who having had the* Grace *to value
worldly* Vanities *at no more than their worth,
do, by retaining the comfortable Memory of a
well-acted Life, behold* Death *without* Dread,
the Grave *without* Fear, *and imbrace both, as necessary Guides to* Endless Glory.

*For my self, this is my Comfort, and all
that I can offer to others, That the Sorrows of
this Life either respect* God, *when we complain to
him against our selves for our Offences; and confess,* Thou Lord *art* just in all that hath be-
fallen us : *Or respect the* World, *when we complain to our selves against* God, *as doing us wrong
either in not giving what we* desire ; *or taking
away what we* enjoyed : *Forgetting that humble
and just Acknowledgment of* Job, The Lord hath
given, and the Lord hath taken. *And out of
doubt he is either a Fool, or ungrateful to* God,
*or both, that doth not acknowledge, that how mean
soever his Estate be, it is far greater than* God
owes him : Or how sharp *soever his Afflictions
be, the same are yet far less, than those that are
due to him. If an Heathen called Adversities the*
Tributes of living; *a wise Christian ought to
know them, and bear them as the Tributes of offending. For seeing* God, *who is Author of all
our* Tragedies, *hath written out and appointed
what every Man must* play, *using no Partiality*
to

to the *mightieſt* Princes; *Why ſhould other Men who are but as the leaſt Worms, complain of Wrongs?* Did *not the* Lord *ſet* Darius *to play the part of the greateſt* Emperor, *and the part of the moſt miſerable* Beggar, *that begged Water of an Enemy to quench the Drought of Death?* Bajazet, *the* Grand Seignior *of the* Turks *in the Morning, the ſame Day became the Footſtool of* Tamberlane; *both which parts* Valerian *the* Emperor *had played, being taken by* Sapores. Belliſarius *had performed the part of a moſt Victorious* Captain, *and after became a Blind* Beggar; *with a Thouſand like Examples. Certainly there is no other Accompt to be made of this* ridiculous World, *than to reſolve, That the change of* Fortune *on this* great Theatre, *is but as the change of* Garments *on the* leſſer: *For when every Man weareth but his own Skin, the* Players *are all alike. If any Man out of Weakneſs judge otherwiſe, (for it is a Point of great Wit, to call the Mind from the Senſes) it is by reaſon of that unhappy Fancy of ours, which forgeth in Men's Brains all the Miſeries to which he is ſubject (the Corporal excepted) therein it is that Misfortune and Adverſity effect what they do. For ſeeing Death is the end of the Play, and takes from all, whatſoever* Fortune *or* Force *takes from any one; It were fooliſh Madneſs in the Shipwrack of Worldly Things, (where all ſinks but the Sorrow for the Loſs of them) to ſink under* Fortune, *which (according to* Seneca *) is of all other the moſt miſerable Deſtiny.*

Now

Now to the Picture of Time, (which we call History) *let my good Intent excuse my drawing it in so large a Table. The Examples of Divine Providence every where to be found,* (the first Divine Histories *being nothing else but a Continuation of such Examples) have perswaded me to fetch my Beginning from all Beginnings, the* Creation. *For these two glorious Actions of the Almighty are so linked together, that the one necessarily implieth the other: Creation inferring Providence, and Providence presuming Creation; though many seeming wise have gone about to separate them;* Epicurus *denies both, yet allows a Beginning: The* Aristotelians *grant* Providence, *but deny all* Beginning, *whose verbal Doctrine grounded upon a rotten Ground, was not able to stand against the Doctrine of Faith, touching the Creation in time,* Heb. 1. *though natural Reason might have inform'd him better. And though* Aristotle *failed herein, and taught little other than Terms in the rest, yet many do absolutely subject themselves to him, as not to indure any other search of Truth. The Law of their* Philosophical Principles *doth not so bind, but that where* Natural Reason *is in Force against them, it ought to stand in all Questions of* Nature *and* Finite Power, *as a Fundamental Law of Human Knowledge. For every* Human Proposition *hath equal Authority, if Reason make no difference. But where Reason is not admitted, and Inventions of Ancestors approved without*

Judg-

Judgment, Men suffer themselves to be led after the manner of Beasts.

This Sloath and Dulness *has made* Ignorance *a powerful* Tyrant, *and has set true* Philosophy, Phisick *and* Divinity *on the* Pillory, *and written over the First,* Contra Principia negantem, *over the Second,* Virtus specifica, *and the Third,* Ecclesia Romana.

But I will never believe that all natural Knowledge *was shut up in* Aristotle's *Brain, or that the Heathen only invaded* Nature, *and found out her Strength. We know that* Time *and not* Reason, *Experience and not Art both taught the Causes of such Effects, as that* Sowerness *doth Coagulate* Milk; *but ask the Reason why and how it does it, and* Vulgar Philosophy *cannot satisfie you; nor in many Things of the like Nature, as why* Grass *is green rather than red. Man hardly discerns the Things on Earth; his Time is but short to learn, and begins no sooner to learn than to dye: Whose Memory has but a borrowed* Knowledge; *understanding nothing truly, and is ignorant of the Essence of his own* Soul; *which* Aristotle *could never define, but by effects, which all Men know as well as he. Man, I say, who is an* Idiot *in the next cause of his own* Life, *and actions thereof, will notwithstanding examin the Art of* God *in Creating the* World; *and will disable him from making a* World without Matter; *and rather ascribe it to Atoms in the* Air, *or to* Fate,

Fate, Fortune, Nature, *or to two* Powers, *of which one was Author of* Matter, *the other of* Form : *And lastly, for want of a Work-man,* Aristotle *brought in that New Doctrin of the* Worlds Eternity, *contrary to these Ancients,* Hermes, Zoroaster, Musæus, Orpheus, Linus, Anaximenes, Anaxagoras, Empedocles, Melissus, Pherecydes, Thales, Cleanthus, Pythagoras, Plato, *and many others; who found in the necessity of invincible Reason, one Eternal Infinite Being, to be the Parent of the Universe.* Whose Opinions, tho' uncertain, (*saith* Lactantius) shew that they agree upon one Lord, Providence, whether Nature, Light, Reason, Understanding, Destiny, or Divine Ordination, which is the same we call God. *For as all Rivers in the World, tho' rising and running diversly, fall at last in the Ocean: So after all searches made by Human* Capacity, *all Man's Reason dissolves it self in the Necessity of this* Infinite Power.

Those who held the Matter of the World Eternal, hardly deserve an Answer, as giving part of the Work to God, *part to* Fortune, *by which* God *found this Matter. And were it Eternal, it either fitted it self to* God, *or he accommodated himself to it ; both which are* foul *Absurdities. But suppose this* Chaos *or Matter had been* too *little for the Work,* God *then Created out of nothing so much* New Matter *as was wanting; or if the* Matter *were too much, he* must *annihilate what was superfluous; both which are alike*
proper

proper to God only: It could not therefore be caused by a less than an All-sufficient Power; *for to say it was the Cause of it self, were the greatest* tism.

Again, if Matter *were* eternal, *of necessity it must be* infinite, *and so left no place for* infinite Form; *but the* finite Form *proves the* Matter *finite, and so not eternal.* He *who will believe the* contrary, eternal Death *be his Reward; for what Reason of Man (not stupify'd by pre-sumption) hath doubted, that That* infinite Power *(of which we comprehend but the Shadow) can want either* Matter *or* Form, *for as many Worlds as there are Sands in the Sea, if it were his* Will, *which is the only limitation of his Works?*

Can a finite *Man, a Fool and meer* Dust, *change the Form of* Matter *made to his Hand, and* infinite Power *cannot make a finite World without pre-existing* Matter? *The universal World has not shew'd us all his Wisdom and Power, which* cannot *be bounded.*

But others who hold the Worlds Eternity upon the ground of nothing, nothing *is made, (which is true where the Agent is finite) may consider their Master* Aristotle, *confessing, That all the Ancients Decree a kind of Beginning, and the same infinite; and he farther saith, There is no beginning of it; but it is found the beginning of all things, and embraceth and governs all things. If we compare the universal World, that Infinite it*

self,

felf, we may fay of the moft unmeafurable Orbs of Heaven, that they are neither quid, quale, *nor* quantum; *and therefore to bring Finite out of Infinite is no wonder in* God's Power. *Therefore* A-naximander, Meliffus, *and* Empedocles, *call the* World *not Univerfal, but a* part of the Univerfality and Infinite: Plato *calls it a* Shadow of God. *God's being a fufficient effectual caufe of the World, proves it not Eternal as he is: For as his Sufficiency is free, fo is his Will; no difficulty can hinder, nor neceffity force his Will in choice of* Time. *Again, tho' natural Agents which can work, do it not 'till they are moved, which argueth* Change *in them; yet it followeth not, that becaufe God cannot be moved, therefore he caufed the World from Eternity. For the fame* action of his Will *which intended the World for ever, from Eternity, did alfo fet down the time to effect it, 'till which time he* withheld it. *Others anfwer, That the* Pattern of the World *was Eternally with* God, *which the* Platonifts *call the* fpiritual World; *but the Material World was not eternal, but fhall continue for ever; which Chriftians underftood of a* new Heaven and Earth, *yet without new* Creation *of* Matter.

They who deny the World *fhall have any* End, *Reafon from the Heavens, which are neither* Corrupted, *nor have any fhew of* Age. *The little Change may argue* Newnefs, *but not* Perpeuity: *Yet to Anfwer Conjectures with Conjectures, many of old held the* Torrid Zone *not habitable by reafon of the* Suns Heat;

nor the Sea Navigable *under the Equinoctial Line ; but now we know the contrary, which argueth that the* Suns Heat *is* decayed *: And if little Change did prove* perpetuity, *then also many* Stone-walls, *which have stood two or three Thousand Years, and many things digged out of the Earth, might seem to remain* unchanged *ever since the* Flood *; and* Gold *probably held* Created *from the* Beginning, *&c. If Elementary Bodies shew so* little Change, *no marvel if* Celestial *shew* none. *And seeing inferiour Creatures are* generated *by* help *of* Celestial, *and receive* Virtue *from the* Sun, *their* general decay *argueth its* decay *also.*

But *if the World were* eternal, *why not all things in it ; especially* Man, *who is more Rational, why did he not* provide *for his Eternity ? Again, if there were no* common order *of the divers Natures, how came that Difference, who set the* Earth *in the* Center, *the* Sun *and* Celestial Bodies *in their* Courses, *&c. If those keep their* Course *of their own accord, to do good to the inferior Bodies, they are then* eternal Love; *yea, so many* Gods, *&c. And if they be limited to their* Course, *there is an efficient Cause which hath bounded them.*

New *as to* Nature : *As* Aristottle *hath by the Ambiguity of the Name recommended Errors, and* obscured God's *glory in the Creation and Government of the* World *; so his best* Definition *of it is but* Nominal *; only differencing natural Motion from artificial, which yet the* Academicks
explain

explain better, calling it Seminary strength, infufed into Matter by the Soul of the World;
and why give they the first place to Providence, the
second to Fate, and third to Nature. But be Nature what it will, it cannot be the Cause of
all things, if it hath not both Will and Know
ledge, said Lactantius. Nature cannot but
work, if Matter be present, and then also it
can but produce the same things, except she
have divers Matters to work upon, said Ficinus. But Nature could not chuse diversity of
Matters without Understanding and Will, Reafon and Power; why then is such a Cause called
Nature rather than God?

All Men assign the highest place among all their
Gods, to One, by Aristotle's confession, de Coelo;
and Reason teacheth us to Acknowledge and Adore
the most Sublime Power. I account it therefore monstrous Impiety to confound God, who
disposes all things according to his own Will, with
Nature, which disposes of nothing but as the Matter wherein it worketh will permit. Nature ex-
isteth not of her self, but as a Faculty infused into things existing, by the supreamest Power; who
therefore is to be Worshipped for creating such a
Nature in all things, as without understanding
what or how it worketh, yet bringeth all things
to perfection. If therefore Men will rest upon that
ground which all Antiquity held, That there is
a Power infinite and eternal; all things deliver'd in Holy Scripture do as easily flow to the
Proof of it, as the Waters to that of a running River. Reason teaching us, That Wis-

dom

dom *or* Knowledge *goes* before Religion, *for* God *is* first to be known, *and* then to be Worshipped. Wisdom, *said* Plato, is the Knowledge of the absolute Good. Faith is not extorted by Violence, but perswaded by Reason and Example, *said* Isidore.

To *inquire farther into God's Essence, Power, and Skill, is to grow mad with Reason: What is beyond the reach of true Reason, is no shame to be ignorant of; neither is our Faith weakened by our being Ignorant how God Created the World, which Reason perswades he did.*

I *cannot stand to excuse divers Passages in the following History, the whole being exceeding weak; especially the Division of the Books, I being directed to inlarge the Building after the Foundation was laid.*

Generally, *as to the Order, I took Counsel from the Argument:* After Babel's Fall, *the* Assyrians *are first, of whose Actions we find but little Recorded, and more in* Fame *than* Faith: *Other Kings Actions are also related by Digressions, with some other things belonging to those Ages: These Digressions, the whole Course of our Lives (which is but Digression) may excuse: Yet I am not wholly ignorant of the Law of History.*

The

The Perfian *Empire was by Order next to be attended, and the Nations which had reference thereto; then followed the* Grecians *and the* Romans*: Other Nations which* refifted *their Beginnings, are not neglected. The weak Phrafe fhews the Parent: In* Hebrew *words, I made ufe of learned Friends and Expofitors; though in Eleven Years I might have learn'd any Language at leifure. Many will fay, a Story of my own time would have pleafed better: But I fay, He which in a* Modern *Story fhall follow Truth too near the Heels, it may chance to ftrike out his Teeth; and no Miftrefs hath led her Followers into greater Miferies. He which follows her too far off, lofeth her and himfelf; He which keeps at a middle diftance, I know not which to call it, Temper or Bafenefs.*

I never labour'd for Mens Opinions, when I might have made the beft ufe of them; and now my Days are too few Ambitioufly *or* Cowardly *to flatter between the Bed and the Grave, even when Death has me on his Shoulders.*

If it be faid, I Tax the Living in the Perfons of the Dead, I cannot help it, tho' Innocent. If any, finding themfelves fpotted like the Tygers of old times, fhall find fault with me for Painting them over a-new; they fhall therein Accufe themfelves juftly, and me falfely: For I Proteft before the Majefty of G O D, *I*

have

have no Malice against any Man under the
Sun.

I know it is impoffible to pleafe all; *fee-*
ing few or none are fo pleafed with themfelves,
by reafon of their fubjection to private Paffions,
but that they feem divers Perfons in one and the
fame Day. Seneca *faid it, and fo do I:* One
is to me inftead of All: *Tea (as it hath de-*
plorably fallen out) as an Ancient Philofopher
faid, One is enough, None is enough. *For it*
was for the fervice of that ineftimable Prince Henry*,*
the fucceffive Hope, *and one of the greateft*
of the Chriftian World, *that I undertook this*
Work: And it pleafed him to perufe part
thereof, and to pardon what was amifs. It is
now left to the World without a Mafter; *from*
which, all that is prefented to it, receiveth both
Blows *and* Thanks: *For we approve and re-*
prehend the fame things. And this is the End *of*
every Judgment, *when the Controverfie is com-*
mitted to many: The Charitable *will judge cha-*
ritably; And againft the Malicious, *my prefent*
Adverfity hath difarm'd me. I am on the Ground
already; and therefore have not far too fall:
And for rifing again, as in the Natural Priva-
tion there is no receffion to Habit; *fo is it*
feldom feen in the Politick Privation. *I do*
therefore forbear to ftile my Readers, Gentle,
Courteous, *and* Friendly, *fo to beg their good*
Opinions: *Or promife a Second and Third Vo-*
lume,

lume (which I intended) if the First receive a good Acceptance. For that which is already done, may be thought enough and too much: And let us daw the Reader with never so many Courteous Phrases; yet we shall ever be thought Fools that Write Foolishly.

C 4   THE

THE
CONTENTS
OF THE
Chapters, Paragraphs, and Sections,
OF THE
First Book of the History of the *WORLD*.

CHAP. I.

Of the First Ages from the Creation to *Abraham*.

CHAP. II.

Man

The Contents.

The Contents.

The Contents.

The Contents.

Of

The Contents.

C H A P.

The Contents.

The Contents.

BOOK

The Contents.

THE

THE

HISTORY

OF THE

WORLD.

PART I.

OF THE

First Ages, from the Creation to *Abraham*.

CHAP. I.
Of the Creation and Preservation of the World.

§. **G**OD *Invisible is seen in his Creatures.* God *From the* acknowledged by the wisest men to be a *Creation to* Power *uneffable,* a *Virtue infinite,* a *Light* by the *Abraham,* abundant Clarity *invisible,* an Understanding which it *2009Years* self can only *comprehend,* an Essence eternal and spiritual, of absolute Pureness and Simplicity, *was,* and *is*

B   pleased

pleafed to make himfelf known by the Works of the
World : In the wonderful magnitude whereof, we
behold the Image of that Glory which cannot be mea-
fured, and that one Univerfal Nature which cannot
be defined. In the glorious Lights of Heaven, we
perceive a fhadow of his Divine Countenance; in his
Provifion for all that live, his manifold *Goodnefs* ;
and in creating, by the abfolute power of his own
Word, his *All-fufficiency* ; which *All-fufficiency* in Power
and Wifdom, which *Light*, *Virtue* and *Goodnefs* being
but Attributes of one fimple Effence, and one God ;
we in all admire, and in part difcern by the Glafs of
his Creatures, in the difpofition, order, and variety
of Bodies, Celeftial and Terreftrial : Terreftrial in
~~ftrange manifold Diverfities, Celeftial in their Beauty,~~
Magnitude, and continual contrary motions, yet neither repugned, intermixed, nor confounded. By
thefe potent Effects we approach to the knowledge of
the Omnipotent Caufe, and by thefe motions, their
Almighty wife Mover. In thefe more than wonderful Works God fpeaketh to Men, who by their Reafon may know their Maker to be God ; who with Corporal Eyes can no otherways be feen, but by his *Word*
and this vifible *World* : Of all which Works there
was no other Caufe preceding but his *Will*, no Matter
but his *Power*, no Workman but his *Word*, no other
Confideration but his own *Goodnefs*.

§ 2. *The Worlds Creation acknowledged by ancient
Philofophers. Mercurius Trifmegiftus* called God *the
Original of the Univerfe,*and that God made it only by
his Word. Jupiter *having hidden all things in himfelf,
did after fend forth into the grateful Light, the admirable
Works he had fore-thought.* Pindar calls him *the one
God, Father and Creator of all :* And *Original, of all,*
faith *Plato.* Though Scripture have no need of Foreign Teftimonies, yet St. *Paul* defpifed not the Ufe
of Philofophers, *&c.* Truth by whomfoever uttered,
is of the Holy Ghoft, faid *Ambrofe.*

*In Po-
wandro.
Orpheus
de fummo
Jove.*

§. 3. All

§. 3. All things began to be in the Creation, before which was neither *Matter* nor *Form* of any thing, but the Eternal : For had there been a former Matter, the Creation had not been first; and if any thing were before Created, there must be a double Creation ; if any thing had been uncreated but God, *Gen.* 1. 1. there must have been a Beginning and two infinite Eternals.

§. 4. *Heaven* and *Earth* first Created, was not Matter without all Form, without which nothing can exist ; but it was that solid Substance and Matter, as well of the Heavens and Orbs, as of the Globe of the Earth, and Waters which cover'd it; *the Seed of that Universal*, saith *Calvin*.

§. 5. As *Moses*, by Heaven, meant the Matter of all Heavenly Bodies, and Natures ; so by Earth comprehending the Waters, he meant the Matter of all things under the Moon : Waters in the plural, signifying a double Liquor of divers natures, mixed with Earth 'till God separated them.

§. 6. *Spirit of God moved*, &c.] Seeing that God is every way above Reason, though the Effects which follow his wonderful ways of working, may in some measure be perceived by Man's Understanding, yet that manner and first operation of his divine Power Ver. 2 cannot be conceived by any Mind or Spirit united with a mortal Body: And St. *Paul* saith, *they are past finding out.* Therefore whether that motion, vitality and operation were by Incubation, or any other way, that's only known to God. The English word *Moved*, is most proper and significant ; for of motion proceeds all production, and whatsoever is effected. This moving Spirit can be no other, but that infinite Power of God, which then formed and distinguished, and which now sustains the Universe. This motion of the Spirit upon the Waters, produced their Spiritual and Natural motion, which brought forth Heat, whereof came rarefaction of Parts ; thus

was

was Air begotten, an Element lighter and ſuperiour to the Waters.

Gen. 1.3. §. 7. *The Light is next,* which for Excellency is
firſt called *good*; but, as I conceive, did not yet di-
ſtinguiſh Day from Night, but with reference to the
Sun's Creation, in which this diſperſed Light was u-
nited, *v.* 1 4. 'till when, there was no Motion to be
meaſur'd by Time: So that the Day named, *v.* 5.
was but ſuch a ſpace as after by the Sun's motion made
a natural Day. As then the Earth and the Waters
were the Matter of the Air, Firmament, upper and
lower Waters, and of the Creatures therein; ſo may
the Light be called the Material Subſtance of the Sun,
and other Lights of Heaven. Howbeit, neither the
Sun nor other Heavenly Bodies are that Light, but
the Sun is enlightned by it *moſt of all other*; and
by it the Moon, and ſo the next Region, which the
Greeks call *Æther,* (the ſuppoſed Element of Fire) is
affeſted, and by it all Bodies living in this our Air.
And though the nature of Light be not yet underſtood, yet I ſuppoſe the Light Created the Firſt
Day, was the ſubſtance of the Sun, though it had
not formal Perfeſtion, Beauty, Circle, and bounded
Magnitude 'till the Fourth Day, when diſperſed Light
was united and fixed to a certain place; after which
it had Life and Motion, and from that time ſeparated
Day from Night: So that what is ſaid of the Day
before, was by Anticipation; for 'till the Creatures
were produced, God's Wiſdom found no Cauſe why
Light ſhould move, or give heat or operation.

Gen. 1. 6. §. 8. *Firmament between the Waters,* is the extended diſtance between the Sea and Waters in the Earth,
and thoſe in the Clouds, ingendred in the ſuperiour
Air: This Firmament in which the Birds flye, is alſo
called Heaven in *Scripture, Gen.* 49. 25. *Pſal.* 104. 18.
Mat. 8. 26. The Cryſtalline Heaven *Baſil* calls Chil-
diſh.

§. 9. God having Created the Matter of all things,
and

and diftinguifhed every general Nature, and given their proper Form, as *Levity* to what fhould afcend, and *Gravity* to what fhould defcend, and fet each in his place in the three firft Days ; in the three laft he beautified and furnifh'd them with their proper kinds ; as the Sun, Moon, and Stars in the higher Firmament of Heaven ; Fowls in the *Air*, Fifhes in the Waters, Beafts on the *Earth* ; giving generative power for continuation of their Kinds, to fuch as in the Individuals fhould be fubjeft to decay, or needed increafe.

§. 10. Nature is an operating Power infufed by God into every Creature ; not any felf-ability to be the Original of any thing of it felf, no more than the Helm can guide theShip without an Hand, or an Hand without Judgment. All Agents work by virtue of the firft Aft ; *and as the Eye feeth, Ear heareth,* &c. yet it is the Soul which giveth *Power, Life* and *Motions* to thefe Organs : So it is God which worketh by Angels, Men, Nature, Stars, or infus'd Properties, as by his Inftruments ; all fecond Caufes being but Conduits to convey and difperfe what they have received from the Fountain of the Univerfal. It is God's infinite Power and Omnipotence that giveth Power to the Sun and all fecond Caufes, and to Nature her felf to perform their Offices ; which operative Power from God being once ftopp'd, Nature is without Virtue. *Things flourifh by God,* faid *Orpheus.* I endeavour not to deftroy thofe various Virtues given by God to his Creatures, for all his Works in their Virtues praife him ; but how he works in, or by them, no Man could ever conceive ; as *Laftantius* confounding the Wifdom of Philofophers, denyed that all their ftudy had found it ; for could the precife Knowledge of any thing be had, then of neceffity all other things might be known.

§. 11. *Deftiny* might fafely be admitted, but for the inevitable neceffity even over Mens Minds and Wills, held by *Stoicks, Chaldeans, Pharifees, Prifci-*

lianifts, &c. *Hermes* and *Apuleius* conceived well
That *Fate is an obedience of second Causes to the First.*
Plotinus calls it *a disposing, from the Acts of the Celestial*
Orbs, working unchangeably in inferiour Bodies; which
is true in things not ordered by a rational Mind. *Fate*
is that which God hath spoken concerning us, say
the Stoicks, *Seneca, Ptolemy.* And no doubt Stars are of
a greater use, than to give an obscure Light; neither are the Seasons of Winter and Summer so certain in Heat and Cold, by the motions of Sun and
Moon, which are so certain, but the working of the
Stars with them. God hath given Virtues to Springs,
Plants, Stones, &c. yea, to Excrements of base Creatures: Why then should we rob the Beautiful
Stars of working power, being so many in Number,
and so eminent in Beauty and Magnitude?

The Treasure of His Wisdom, who is so Infinite,
could not be short in giving them their peculiar Virtues and Operations, as he gave to Herbs, Plants, &c,
which adorn the *Earth.* As therefore these Ornaments of the *Earth* have their Virtue to feed and cure;
so no doubt those *Heavenly* Ornaments want not
their further use, wherein to serve his Divine Providence, as his just Will shall please to determine. But
in this question of *Fate,* let us neither bind God to
his Creatures, nor rob them of the Office he hath given them: If second Causes restrain God, or God by
them inforce Man's Mind or Will, then wicked Men
might lay the fault on God.

§. 12. *Prescience,* or Fore-knowledge (if we may
speak of God after the manner of Men) goeth before
his *Providence*; for God infallibly foreknew all things
before they had any Being to be cared for; yet was
it not the Cause of things following, nor did it im-
pose a Necessity.

§. 13. *Providence* is an intellectual Knowledg, Fore-
seeing, Caring for, and Ordering all things: Beholding things past, present, and to come, and is the
Cause

Cause of their so being ; and such we call *Provident*, who considering things Past, and comparing them with the Present, can thereby with Judgment provide for the Future.

§. 14. *Predestination* we distinguish from *Prescience* and *Providence*; these belong to all Creatures, from the highest Angel to the basest Worm; but this only concerns Mens Salvation (in the common use of Divines) or Perdition, according to some. *Augustine* sets it out by two Cities, one predestinated eternally to reign with God, the other to everlasting Torments ; *Calvin, Beza, Buchanus,* and the like, are of the same Opinion. Why it pleased God to create *some Vessels to honour, some to dishonour,* though the Reason may be hid, unjust it cannot be.

§. 15. *Fortune,* the God of Fools so much Reverenced, and as much Reviled, falleth before *Fate* and *Providence,* and was little known before. *Homer* and *Hesiod* who taught the Birth of those humane Gods, have not a Word of this new Goddess ; which at length grew so potent, that she ordered all things, from Kings and Kingdoms to the Beggar and his Cottage: *She* made the *Wife* miserable, and prospered *Fools,* and Man's life was but her Pastime. This Image of Power was made by Ignorants, who ascribed that to *Fortune* of which they saw no manifest Cause. Yet *Plato* taught, That nothing ever came to pass under the Sun, of which there was not a just preceding Cause ; and the Scripture maketh it clear in things most casual, *Deut.* 19. 5. *Prov.* 16. 33. The best Philosophers held, that all things in Heaven and Earth were ordered by the Soul of the World, said *Cicero.* When Riches and Honour are given to empty Men, and Learned, Virtuous, and Valiant Men wear out their Lives in a dejected condition, the Cause is manifest to the *Wise,* tho' *Fools* ascribe it to blind *Fortune.* For either it is Affection in Men preferring others, or great Persons which endure no other Di-

B 4 scourse

scourse but that of *Flatterers*: So that Honest, Open-
hearted lovers of the *Truth*, which cannot *Form* themselves to it, must hang under the Wheel. Shall he who
tells a *Ruler* he is unjust, a *General* he is a Coward,
or a *Lady* that she is ugly, be made a *Counsellour*, a
Captain, or a *Courtier*? It is not sufficient to be Wise,
Just, and Valiant under such; but with the change of
the *Successor*, he must change, else the *base Observ-
vant* will out-go him in Honour and Riches, by that
only quality of Humouring Mens *Vices* as *Virtues*,
with which every Fool is won, said *Menander*: He
therefore that will live out of himself, and study o-
ther Mens Humours, shall never be Unfortunate; but
he who values *Truth* and *Virtue*, (except in a *Virtuous Age*) shall never prosper by the Possession, or
Profession of them. It is also the token of a Worldly Wise-man, not to contend in vain against the nature of the *Times*, but to give way to *Fury*. And he
which aims at the *Machivel*'s two marks, *Glory* and
Riches, must have a *Steel Back* to a *Wooden Bow*, to fit
both *weak* and *strong*; or as Men at Sea, must either
Hoise or Strike Sails, as Calms or Storms do require,
or use Sails of small extention, and content himself
to travel slowly; so must Men which esteem *Virtue*
for it self.

CHAP. II.

Of Mans Estate in the Creation, and of God's Rest.

§. 1. **M**AN was the last and most admirable of
God's Works: *The greatest wonder*, said
Plato, out of *Mercurius*, meaning of the internal
Form, whose Nature is an immortal Spirit, Essence,
and in quality, by God's Creation, Holy and Righteous in Truth, and Lord of the World. This Image
of God in Man, *Chrysostom* makes chiefly to consist in
Dominion; so *Ambrose* and others; but he denyeth
it

it to Women, contrary to the Text, *let them rule*, not excluding the Woman. Others conceive this *Image* to be in Man's immortal Soul; which is one, and *Incorporeal*, governing the Body, being in every part of it totally, as God is totally in every part of the World; but the Soul's being totally in every part more than potentially, is doubted of. School-men make the Resemblance especially to be in Man's *Mind*, whose Memory, Understanding, and Will, really differ, and yet are but one *Mind*, resembling the *Trinity*. They also, with *Victorinus*, made a difference of the *Image*, which they refer to the Substance of the Soul not lost, and the *Similitude*, which is in Holiness and Righteousness of quality. But as *Augustin* defended, that Man lost the Perfection of God's Image; so St. *Paul* makes it the same with *similitude*, 1 *Cor.*15. 39. *Ja.*3.9. *Col.*3. 10. *Rom.* 1. 23. *Zanchius* held this *Image* to be both in Body and Mind, because it was referr'd to the Hypostasis or whole Man. Yet he confesses, it may be answered *De op.r.* *Moses* used a Synecdoche. But *Augustine* anathematiz'd *Dei.* him who compar'd the Deity to Man's Body. *In general, Humane Virtue is, liker God, than his Figure,* said *Cicero.* Neither Dominion nor the Immortal Soul, indued with Memory, Understanding and Will, is this *Image*; seeing that Man has these common with Devils. *Sybill* called right Reason the Image of God, that is, rightly to know, confess, serve, love, and obey God.

§. 2. *Of the intellectual Mind of Man, and God's Image in it.* This *Mens*, or Mind, is not taken for the *Soul*, which is the Form of the Nature of Man; but for the principal Power of the *Soul*, whose Act is perpetual Contemplation of *Truth*; and is therefore called Divine Understanding, and a Contemplative Mind : *Cusan* calls it, a *Power compounded of all Powers of comprehending.* *Mercurius* held it the *Essence of* De Ment. *God, no other way separated from him, than the Light* Idiot.

from

from the Sun ; which Error the *Manichees* also held.
But as the Sun is not of the Essence of the Divine
Light, but a Body enlighten'd with a created Light ;
so this *Mind* or Understanding in Man, is not of the
Essence of God's Understanding, but the purest of
the Soul's Faculties, or the light of the reasonable Soul;
called the Soul of the Soul, or Eye of the Soul, by
Augustine, or Receptacle of Wisdom. Between this
Mens or understanding power and Reason, between it
and *Anima*, and *Animus*, is this difference, that by
the *Soul* we live, by Reason we judge and discourse,
by the Mind or *Animus*, we will and chuse ; but this
Mind called *Mens*, is a pure substantial Act of the
Soul, not depending on Matter, but hath relation to
that which is intelligible, as its first Object. *Mer-
curus* saith, the Soul is the Image of the Mind, which
is the Image of God, *&c*. *Ficinus* labours to prove
the Mind hath no need of Organs : *Zanchius* says, the
Mind needs no Means to understand by, yet confesseth that the Representations which come from the
Sense to the Phantasie, are the Objects of the Understanding ; which Resemblances are to the *Mind* as
Colours are to the *Sight*. Thus he makes the Phantasie an Organ to the *Mind*, as the Eye to the Sight,
contrary to his first Assertion. However these be determined, we may resemble our selves to God in Mind,
in respect of that pure Faculty which is never separated from Contemplation and love of God. *The
Mind, said Bernard, is not the Image of God, because
it understands, remembers, and loveth it self; but because it understands, remembers, and loveth God, who
Created it.* So that Immortality, Reason, and Dominion, do not make us God's shadow, *but the Habit of
Righteousness, most perfectly infused into the Soul and
Mind in the Creation.* It is not by Nature that we are
printed with the Seal of God's Image (though Reason be part of the essential Constitution of our proper Species or Kind) but this is from the Bounty of

God's

God's Goodneſs, which breathing Life into Earth, contrived therein the Inimitable Ability of his own Juſtice, Piety, and Righteouſneſs. So long therefore as Men walk in God's ways, which is called walking with God, and do fear, love, and ſerve him truly, *for the love of God only,* ſo long they retain this *Image.* But it cannot be in Unjuſt, Cruel, Falſe and Ambitious *Souls, &c.* And though Nature (according to common underſtanding) do make us capable, and apt enough to receive this *Image,* yet if God's exceeding Wiſdom and liberal Mercy framed not Eyes to our Souls, we could not come by it. For not only the Perfection, but the Image of it ſelf, to wit, the ſupernatural Gift of Grace and Glory, is wholly blotted out by Sin.

§. 3. *Adam*'s Body was made of *Adamah,* red fat Earth, of which God produced not an *Image,* but a *Body* of Fleſh, Blood, and Bones, in the Form it now has. And *though Nature and Experience aſſure our Mortality, and that our Bodies are but Anviles of Pains and Diſeaſes ; and our Minds but Hives of innumerable Cares, Sorrows, and Paſſions ; and that our greateſt Glories are but painted Poſts for Envy to caſt her Darts at ;* yet our unhappy Condition and darkneſs of Underſtanding is ſuch, that we only eſteem this Slave of Death ; and only at idle Hours remember the immortal impriſon'd Soul, the everlaſting Subject of Reward or Puniſhment. This we never think on while one *Vanity* is left us: We plead for *Titles* till our *Breath* fails us; *Dig* for *Riches* 'till *Strength* be ſpent ; and exerciſe *Malice* while we are able to *Revenge*: And then when time has depriv'd us both of Youth, Pleaſure, and Health, and *Nature* her ſelf hates the Houſe of her old Age, we remember with *Job,* we muſt go whence we ſhall not return, and that our Bed is made ready for us in the Dark. Then we look too late into the bottom of our Conſcience, and behold the fearful Image of *paſt Actions,*

with

with this terrible Inſcription, *God will bring every work to Judgment.* Let us therefore not flatter our ſelves, wilfully to offend God in hope eaſily to make our peace at the laſt, which is a Rebellious Preſumption, and Deriding the dreadful God that can ruin us eternally.

§. 4. To this corruptible Body, God gave a Soul ſpiritual and incorruptible, which ſhall again return to him, as the body to the Earth. The Soul's Immortality is manifeſt, comparing the manner of the Creation of other things with it, *Gen.* 1. 20, 24. with *v.* 26. & *cap.* 2. 7.

Man thus Compounded, became a Model of the Univerſe, having a *Rational* Soul, with ability fit for the Government of the World ; an *Intellectual* Soul common with Angels, and *Senſitive* with Beaſts ; thus he became a little World in the Great, in whom all Natures were bound up together; our *Fleſh* is heavy like *Earth,* our *Bones* hard as *Stones*, our *Veins* as the *Rivers, Breath* as the *Air,* Natural *Heat* like the *warmth* incloſed in the *Earth,* which the Sun ſtirreth up in procreation ; *Radical moiſture,* which feeds that Natural *Heat,* is as the fatneſs in the Earth; our *Hairs* as *Graſs,* our *Generative Power* is as *Nature* which produceth ; our *Determinations* like wandring *Clouds,* our *Eyes* like the *Lights* in Heaven ; our *Youth* like the *Spring,* our *ſetled Age* like the *Summer, declining* like *Autumn,* and *old Age* like *Winter* ; our *Thoughts* are the *motions of Angels,* our pure *Underſtanding* like the *Intellectual* Natures always preſent with God ; and the habitual Holineſs and Righteouſneſs of our Immortal Soul was the *Image* of God, as a ſhadow may be like the ſubſtance. Man's Four *Complexions* like the Four *Elements,* and his Seven *Ages* like the Seven *Planets.* Our *Infancy* is like the *Moon,* in which it ſeemeth only to grow, as Planets ; in our next Age we are inſtructed as under *Mercury,* always near the Sun : Our *Youth* is

wanton,

wanton and given to pleasures, as *Venus* ; our Fourth
Age Strong, Vigorous, and Flourishing, is like the
Sun : Our Fifth Age like *Mars*, striving for Honour ; our Sixth like *Jupiter*, Wise, and stayed ;
our Seventh like *Saturn*, slow and heavy, when by
irrecoverable loss we see that of all our vain Passions
and Affections the Sorrow only remains, and our At-
tendants are various Infirmities and Diseases, of
which, many are the remainders of former *Follies*
and *Excesses* ; and if Riches yet continue with us,
the more our Plenty is, the more greedily is our
End wish'd for ; we being now of no other use but
to detain our *Riches* from our *Successors*, and being
made unsociable to others, we become a burthen to
our selves. Now, and never before, we think upon
our Eternal Habitation, to which place we pass with
many sighs, groans, and doleful thoughts ; and in
the end, by *Death* we finish the sorrowful Business
of a wretched *Life*, toward which we have been always travelling, sleeping, and waking ; and by what
crooked Paths soever we have walked, yet it led us
the straight way to the gate of Death. Neither can
beloved Companions, or rather our Gods, *Riches* or
Honour, stay us one hour from entring that all-de-
vouring Dungeon of Death, which is not yet satisfy'd
with all those past Generations, but still cries *all
Flesh is grass*, 'till it have consumed all. Thus the
Tyde of Man's Life once declining, makes a perpetual *Ebb*, never to return hither, and his Leaf
fallen, shall never spring again.

§. 6. Our Parents having one Prohibition for
trial of Obedience, would need extend their freedom of Will to that, and so brought all Mankind into
endless Misery.

§. 7. God on the Seventh Day ceased to Create
more Kinds, having perfected those he intended, and
endued with Generative Power such as should continue by Generation.

C H A P.

CHAP. III.

Of Paradise, and many Opinions about it.

§. 1. PAradise, the firſt Habitation of *Adam*, Eaſtward in *Eden*, about which Mens Opinions are as various as the Perſons that Diſputed it; and many imbibe groſs Errors, led by the Authority of great Men, wherein many Fathers were far wide, as it is the Fate of all Men to err, neither has any Man knowledge of all things.

§. 2. Many held Paradiſe in *Moſes* Allegorical only; as *Origen*, *Philo*, and *Ambroſe* lean'd to that Opinion; ſo did *Strabus*, *Rabanus*, *Beda*, *Commeſtor*. *Chryſamenſis*; and *Luther* thought it not extant, though it was formerly. *Vadianus Noviomagus* held it the whole Earth. *Tertul. Bonaventure* and *Durand* place it under the Equinoctial; *Poſtellus* under the *N. Pole*.

§. 3. Paradiſe by *Moſes*'s deſcription, was a Place on Earth, in *Eden*, a Country Eaſtward, ſo called, for the Pleaſantneſs thereof; as in *America* a Country is called *Florida*. Here the vulgar Tranſlation is miſtaken in interpreting it a Paradiſe of Pleaſure from the beginning. This ſituation of Paradiſe in the Eaſt, occaſion'd the praying, and ſetting Churches to the Eaſt, contrary to the ſtanding of *Solomon*'s Temple, and the Prieſt turning to the Weſt; yet God is every where; neither is any Myſtery in the word Eaſtward, but the place ſtood ſo from *Canaan*. *Moſes*'s whole deſcription proves it an Earthly place, and *Ezechiel* witneſſeth *Eden* was a Country near *Charan*: So *Adam*'s actions, and end of placing in it, prove no leſs againſt thoſe vain Allegories of Scripture ſtories, confuted by *Jews*, as *Epiphanius*: Yet I exclude not an Allegorical ſenſe of ſome ſtories, beſides

the

the Literal, as *Augustine* and *Suidas* held Paradise had
both. *Homer*'s *Alcinous* Garden, and *Elizian* Fields,
were Poetical Fictions stoln out of the Divine Treasury, and profaned by them.

§. 4. It is no Curiosity to enquire after the Place;
seeing nothing is in Scripture, but for instruction;
and if the truth of the story be necessary, the place
set out for the proof of it, is not to be neglected,
and Mens fancies therein overthrow the Story. For
what is more ridiculous, than to seek *Adam*'s Paradise as high as the Moon, or beyond the Ocean
which he waded through to come to *Judea*; or that
it is a separated ground hanging in the Air under the
Moon, from whence the four Rivers fall with violence, and force through the Sea, and rise again in
our habitable World; as *Commestor* dreamed, and
others. That therefore the Truth might receive no
prejudice, God's Wisdom hath so carefully described
the place for our easie finding, as the choisest part
of the Earth. And if it be a generous mind to desire to know the Original of our Ancestors, this
search cannot be discommended.

§. 5. Paradise is not so defaced by the Flood that
it cannot be found, as *Augustinus Chrysaniensis* judged; for though the Beauty of it be lost, and Time has
made it as a common Field in *Eden*, yet eight hundred and seventy years after would not so particu-
lary have described it, nor the Prophets have mention'd *Eden* so often, if the same could not be found,
or if the Rivers which in his time bear the Names,
were not the same, of which *Euphrates* and *Tigris*
were never doubted, as the Country of *Eden* is yet
well known. As for the alteration made by the
Flood, changing the current of Rivers, and raising
of Mountains, as some judge, it is improbable; for
the Waters covered the Earth spherically, and did
not fall violently from higher places, or come in
with Storms ebbing and flowing, which makes such

choakings

choakings up of the mouths of Rivers. The Waters then were raiſed by univerſal erruptions, and
by down right falls of Rain, which uſe to ſcatter the
ſtrongeſt Winds. *Seth's* Pillar erected 1426 year
before, as Antiquitiy reports, and ſtanding in *Joſe-*
phus's days, and the City under *Libanus*, whoſe Ruins remained to *Annius's* days, and by *Beroſus*
forged Fragments call'd *Enochia*, built by *Cain*,
and the City *Joppa* remaining after the Flood,
argue the Flood had no ſuch effect to work
ſuch alteration, when even Bay-Trees outſtood it.
Antiquity alſo ſpeaks of *Baris*, and *Sion*, on which
the Fable is that Giants were ſaved, which argueth
their Judgment touching the Antiquity of Mountains. See *Pſal.* 90. 1, 2.

§. 6. Paradiſe was not the whole Earth, as *Ma-*
nichus, *Vadianus*, *Noviomagus*, and *Goropius Becanus*
judged, ſeeing the Text ſaith it was Eaſtward in
Eden, and the Angel was plac'd on the eaſt ſide of
Paradiſe, and *Adam* was caſt out of it, not out of all
the Earth. Yet the Error of *Ephrem*, *Athanaſius*,
and *Cyrill*, was greater, that Paradiſe was beyond
the Ocean, through which *Adam* walked when he
was caſt out, to return to the Earth of his Creation,
and was buried on *Calvery*.

§. 7. Paradiſe by *Bar-Cephas*, *Beda*, *Strabus*, and
Rabanus, was placed on a Mountain almoſt as high
as the Moon ; neither did *Rupertus* differ much. It
ſeemeth they took it out of *Plato*, and *Socrates* who
miſ-underſtood it, no doubt took this Place for
Heaven, the Habitation of Bleſſed Souls after Death,
though for fear of the *Areopagites*, they durſt not
ſet down in plain terms what they believed of that
Matter. And though in the end *Socrates* was put to
death for acknowledging one only ſufficient God,
yet the Devil himſelf did him that right, to pronounce him the wiſeſt Man. As for the place in
queſtion, *Tertullian* and *Euſebius* conceive, that by it
the

he meant the Celeſtial Paradiſe : ˙ *Solinus* indeed *reports* of a place called *Acrothonos*, upon Mount *Atho*, pleaſant and healthful, whoſe Inhabitants are called *Macrobioi*, long lived : Upon the aforeſaid *Lunary Hill*, they ſay *Enoch* was preſerved ; which *Iſidore* and *Lumbard* approve ; and *Tertullian*, *Ireneus*, *Juſtin Martyr* believed the Souls of bleſſed Men lived there ; which Fancies *Hopkins* and *Pererius* have Confuted. As for the Bodies of *Enoch* and *Elias*, they may be changed, as others ſhall be at the laſt Day. The School-men in this and their other Queſtions, were exceeding ſubtle, but yet taught their Followers to ſhift better than to reſolve by their Diſtinctions. The Fables of *Olympus*, *Atlas*, and *Atho*, higher than any Clouds, *Pliny* himſelf diſproveth.

§. 8. *Tertullian*, *Bonaventure* and *Durand* place *Paradiſe* under the *Equinoctial* ; to which *Aquinas* oppoſeth the Diſtemper of *Heat* there. But this is *Non cauſa* for *cauſa* ; the true Cauſe is, *Eden* and the Rivers are not there ; elſe the Clime hath as pleaſant fertile places as any other ; neither was any Region Created but for Habitation, and thoſe hot Countries are tempered by *Eaſt* Winds, and long cool Nights as I well know ; only where Mountains hinder the Wind, and in ſandy Grounds void of Trees, the Country is not ſo well Inhabited, as the other parts, which are ſo Fertile, that the Inhabitants Idleneſs maketh them Vitious, and the Countries to be *Terræ Vitioſæ*.

§. 9. *Paradiſe* not being in the former places, we are certain it was in *Eden*, not hard to have been found out, had not Names been changed ſince *Moſes*'s days ; and that other Nations have ſought to extinguiſh both the Name and Monuments of the *Jews*. For our help we have *Euphrates* and *Tigris* agreed upon, and that it was *Eaſtward* from *Canaan*; which latter might agree with *Arabia*, Stony and Deſart ; but the former cannot, neither has it the property of being

exceeding

exceeding *Fertile.* As for bordering Countries,
though *Moses* name none, yet *Esaiab* and *Ezekiel* do;
and though that *Amos* name *Eden,* which is *Cœlosyria,*
and *Beroaldus* findeth a City there called *Paradise,* yet
can it not be the *Eden* we seek, seeing *Cœlosyria* and
Cyprian Damascena is full *North* from *Canaan,* and
wants our known Rivers. Come then to the *Edo-
mits* in *Thelassar,* and the rest named by *Esaiab: Thelassar* was a strong City in an Island upon the Border
of *Chaldea* on the River *Euphrates,* towards the *North,*
which after *Senaebarib*'s death, *Merodach Balladan* in-
joyning *Babilonia,* fortified against *Esar Haddon,* which
City *Marcellinus* calls *Thelatha*; *Pliny, Teridata,* which
Julian durst not assault. The other places in *Esaiah* are
either in *Mesopotamia* as *Charan* and *Reseph,* or in
Media, as *Gosan*; so *Ezekiel* setting out the Countries which traded with *Tyrus,* joineth *Charan* with
Eden, as also *Calne,* which *Jerom* calls *Seleuiza,* standing upon *Euphrates* towards *Tigris,* called also *Canneh,*
and the Inhabitants *Schenits* by *Pliny*; who Inhabited
from *Seleucia* on both sides *Euphrates,* Westward to
Cœlosyria, as far as *Tapsachus,* where the River is
Fordable. *Charan* therefore cannot be *Channeh,* the
one standing on *Euphrates,* the other on *Chaboras,*
which falleth into *Euphrates,* far off in *Mesopotamia*:
Or *Aran* between the Floods. Besides *Channeh* or
Chalne, is by *Moses* named in *Shinar,* one of *Nimrod's*
Cities. Lastly, *Sheba* and *Rhaama* upon the *Persian*
Gulf, traded with *Tyrus* by *Tigris,* and so to *Seleu-
cia,* and so to *Syria* by *Euphrates,* 'till they came to
Aleppo or *Hierapolis,* from whence they went by
Land to *Tyre,* and after decay to *Tripoly,* and now to
Alexandretta in the Bay of *Issicus* or *Lajazzo. Chalmad*
is also joined with *Eden* by *Ezekiel,* a Region of high-
er *Media,* N.E. of *Eden* called *Coronitana* by Geographers. Thus *Eden* is bounded on the E. and N. E.
by *Elanah* and *Chalmad*: On the *W.* and N. W. by
Charan and *Chanah*: On the *S.* by *Sheb*; between
which

which *Chalds* (properly fo called) is contained, which is the *Eden* we feek.

§. 10. *Eden* hath not yet wholly loft the Name and notice of the old Country, as is to be feen in two Epiftles written by the Chriftians of *Mesopotamia*, to the *Pope, An.* 1552. Publifhed by *Mafius*, mentioning the Ifland of *Eden* in the River *Tigris*, which is commonly called *Gozoria* or *Gezer*. So that we may perceive, that *Eden* before the Flood, comprehended, befides the Land of *Babylonia* in the *S.* all *Affyria*, *Armenia*, and *Mesopotamia*, bounded by Mount *Taurus* in the *North*. In this Ifle, which is ten Miles compafs, is the Metropolitan City and Patriarchy of all the *Neftorian* Chriftians in *Affyria*, *Mesopotamia*, *Chaldea*, and *Perfia*, and is Twelve Miles above *Mofell*.

§. 11. An Objeftion is made out of the Text, That a River, in the fingular number, divideth it felf into Four Heads. *Anfwer*, *Kimchi* and *Vatablus* fay, the Singular here is put for the Plural, as is ufed with the *Hebrews*. But take it fingular for *Euphrates*, and we find it divided into Four Branches in the Country of *Chaldea*. And what alteration foever Time hath bred, clear it is, that *Parah* in *Mofes* is *Euphrates*, and *Hiddekel* is *Tigris*, which runneth through *Affyria*, whofe chief City is *Nineve*.

§. 12. An Objeftion touching the Fertility of *Paradife* no where found, is Anfwered; That no place after the Flood was the fame as it was in the Creation; yet *Herodotus* commends that Country about *Euphrates* near the which *Tigris* runs, beyond all he had feen; yielding Two Hundred for One; with plenty of Palm-Trees, of which they make Meat, Wine and Honey : *Strabo* and *Niger* added Bread, and *Antony* the *Hermite*, addeth Flax. They mow the Blade twice, and after feed it down with Cattel to prevent the Exuberance of overmuch Ranknefs : And it is free from Weeds. See *Pliny*, lib. 18. ca. 17.

C. 2   who

who faith the *Babylonians* reap a Crop the fecond
time without Sowing; and yet cut their Corn twice
in the Year they fow it, faith *Niger* : And left their
Cattel fhould perifh by too great a fatiety, they drive
them out of the Paftures, faith *Q. Curtius.*

§. 13. *Pifon* and *Gehon,* the other two Rivers of
Paradife, muft be found to branch out of the River,
or Rivers of *Eden* ; and therefore the Fancy was
ftrange to fearch out for *Ganges* in *India,* and *Nilus*
in *Egypt.* The Errour about *Pifon* was occafion'd by
miftaking *Havila* in *India,* whofe Founder was a
Son of *Jocktan,* for that *Havila* upon *Tigris,* afterwards called *Sufiana,* Planted by a Son of *Cufh.* If
Largenefs were refpected in choife of *Ganges,*
Indus is not inferiour; having *Hydafpis,* famous in
Great *Alexander's* Story, and many like Rivers falling into it, as *Coas, Suaftus, Acefinies, Adries, Hif-*
palis, Smnoch : Indus is alfo nearer *Tigris* by almoft
40 Degrees, between which and *Ganges,* is the great
Kingdom of *Magor.* As for *Nilus* it can no way be
a Branch of a River which runneth through *Eden* with
the reft, feeing it runneth contrary to them, fpring-
ing from the *South* Coaft, and falleth *North,* whereas
they fpring *North* and fall into the *South* Sea. *Pifon*
therefore will rather be found a River branching out
of *Euphrates* into *Tigris* at *Appanico,* called *Pifo-tigris,*
running through *Havila* or *Sufiana,* from *Hercelus's*
Altar, into the *Perfian Gulph,* and hath Gold, and
Bdelium and Onix-ftones. Time hath made greater
Change of other Names than this, as to call *Babylon*
Bandas, Baldady Bagded, Boughedor and *Bagdet* at
this Day. *Pifon* is called *Bafilius* or *Regius*; and *Ge-*
hon is *Mahar-fares, Marfias, Baar faris* in *Ptolomy* and
others. *Euphrates* at her Fountain was called *Pixirats*
and *Puckperah: Plutarch* calls it *Medus & Zaranda* ; o-
thers call it *Cobar,* which is a Branch of it : The *Affyri-*
ans name it *Armalchar* and *Nahor Malcha* ; now it is
called *Phrat-Tigris,* in Hebrew *Hiddekel*; others call it
Dighto,

Dighto, Diglath, Seilax, Sollax, now *Tegil. Mereer* conceived well the *Euphrates* and *Tigris* stream into Branches, and that *Euphrates* falling into *Gebon,* loft the Name, and is swallowed up in *Caldee Lakes* near *Ur :* But *Pison* breaking into *Tigris,* falls into the Sea, and produc'd a Name compounded of both, *Pysotygris,* running through *Havilah,* so named of the Son of *Chush,* inhabits both sides, and mistaken for *Ethiop.* 1 *Sam.* 15. 7.

§. 14. *Gebon* by mistaking *Ethiop* for *Chush,* drew them to *Nilus ;* which Error *Pererius* would evade by an *E. Ethiopia* in *Arabia-Petræa,* and part of *Felix,* which being granted, *Gebon* is not *Nilus ;* no, the 1000000 which *Zerab* brought against *Asa,* came beyond *Egypt,* but were *Chushits, Midianits, Amalekits, Ishmaelits,* inhabiting that Land of *Chush,* over which *Zera* in *Gerar* near *Juda* Commanded. But to *Pererius, Pliny* tells, the *E. Ethiopia* was about *Nilus, S.* of *Egypt ;* the *W.* was about the River *Niger.* So that all that take *Chush* for *Ethiopia, Numb.* 12. 1. do fail, as also 2 *Chron.* 21. 16. *Beroaldus* seeking *Gebon* at *Gaza* lost himself in the *Desart* by finding a River scarce Twenty Miles long for *Gebon,* which watered all the Land of *Chush,* Westward from *Tigris,* and went towards *Arabia* through the *South of Chaldea,* where was *Chusca,* after called *Chuduca ;* from whence either Increase or Force of *Nimrod*'s Posterity made them disperse themselves more towards the *West,* out of that part of *Shinar,* where *Nimrod* out of Wit and Strength had seated himself : As did his Father upon *Gebon,* and a Brother of his called *Havila,* on both sides of *Tigris,* and along the Sea towards *Arabia.*

§. 15. To Conclude ; it appeareth to me by Scripture, *Paradise* was a Created place in our Habitable World, in the lower parts of a Country called *Eden,* from the Pleasantness thereof, containing part of *Armenia,* all *Mesopotamia* and *Shinar.* This Region in

Thirty

Thirty five Degrees is moſt temperate, abounding with whatſoever Life needeth, without Labour ; exceeding both *Indies*, with their perpetual Spring and Summer, which are accompanied with fearful Thundring, Lightning, Earth-quakes, Venomous Creatures and deſperate Diſeaſes, from which *Eden* is free: I deſire no other Reward for my Labour in this Deſcription, but ſuſpence of judgment 'till it be confuted by a more probable Opinion.

CHAP. IV.

Of the two Chief Trees in Paradiſe.

§. 1. THAT the two Trees of *Life* and *Knowlegde*, were material Trees, the moſt Learned and Religious Writers doubt not of ; though they were Figures of the Law and Goſpel, yet ſome would have them only Allegorical, becauſe of *Salomon*'s Words, *Prov.* 3. 18, *Apoc.* 2. 7. But *Auguſtine* anſwers, the one excludeth not the other ; as *Paradiſe* was Terreſtrial, and yet ſignified a Celeſtial, as *Sara* and *Hagar* were Women, though Figures of the Old and New Teſtament : The words alſo of the Text join theſe Trees with the reſt that God produced. Touching the Tree of *Life* it is hard to think, that Bodies nouriſhed by *Corruptible means* ſhould be immortal ; yet if *Adam* had not diſobeyed God's Commandment, he and his Poſterity might have lived an healthful, unalterable Life, Four times longer than the firſt Fathers, and then been tranſlated as *Enoch* was. For God's infinite Wiſdom fore-ſaw that the Earth could not have contain'd a perpetual Increaſe, or. Millions of Souls muſt have been ungenerated. The Immortality of Man, if he had not fallen, muſt be underſtood of Bodies, Tranſlated and Glorified.　　　　§. 2. Touch-

§. 2. Touching the Tree of *Knowledge*, *Goropius Becanus* will have the honour to have found it to be the *Indian* Fig-tree; but however that Opinion be efteem'd, and that never Man thought better of his own, than he, yet herein he ufurped upon *Mofes Bar-cephas*, who hit on this Conjecture 600 Years before, and cited *Philaxinus* and others long before. *Becanus* upon a Conceit this Tree is only found upon the Banks of *Acefines*, which runneth into *Indus*, will therefore find *Paradife* there; but my felf have feen 20000 of them in a Valley of *America*, not far from *Paria*, as alfo in *Trinidado*. The magnitude of this Tree in *Pliny* and others, I am afham'd to report; the Stemm as ftreight as may be, without Branch for Twenty or Thirty Foot, where they fpread abroad their Boughs; and from the Head branches a Gumm that hangeth downward, and by increafing in a few Months, as a Cord, reacheth the Ground, taketh Root and becometh a Tree; which alfo by the like Gum maketh others, and in a fhort time, fuch a Grove arifeth, like which there is no Tree. And if a Branch hang over the Water, the Gum will pierce the Water and take root, fo that falling fometimes into a Bed of Oyfters, they are fo intangled, that plucking up one of thefe Cords, I have feen 500 Oifters hanging about it : The Leaves largenefs, and Fruits pleafantnefs I find not according to Report, yet have I travelled 12 Miles under them. In conclufion, though *Becanus* count it impudent Obftinacy to dare to think this not the Tree, yet *Philo* believes that the Earth never brought forth the Tree fince.

§. 3. *Becanus*'s witty Allegory of the *Indian* Figtree, believes it not worthy the Commendation given it.

§. 4. Touching the name of the Tree, *Bar-cephas* tranflated by *Mafius*, faith, it was fo called of the Event; for that after eating thereof, they fhould know by experience the Happinefs they had loft, and the Mifery their Difobedience would bring them into. *Junius* followeth this Expofition. *Adam* by excellency of Creation could not be ignorant of the Good and Evil of Obedience, and Difobedience ; yet as Men in ficknefs better know the good of health, and evil of ficknefs than they conceived before, fo was it with *Adam*. For looking into the Glafs of his guilty Confcience, which Evil he never knew, he faw the horrour of Gods Judgment, and fenfibly knew the lofs of the Good which could not be valu'd ; and purchas'd Evil not to be expreffed : And then he faw himfelf Naked both in Body and Mind, that is, deprived of Gods Grace and former Felicity ; hereupon was it called the *Tree of Knowledge*, and not of any Operation it had by a peculiar quality. For the fame Phrafe is ufed in Scripture ; and names are given to Signs and Sacraments, as to things performed and done. But *Adam* being betray'd and overrul'd by his own Affection, and ambitious of further Knowledge, and of the glory would attend it, and flightly looking on what the Lord had threatned, was tranfported with the gentle winds of pleafing perfwafion, whereupon Satan ftrengthened his progreffion, poifoning the roots of mankind, which he moiftened with the Liquor of the fame ambition, by which himfelf perifhed for ever. The means the Devil us'd, was his Wife, given to have been a Comforter, not a Counfeller. She defiring to know what was unfit for her, as doth all that Sex ever fince, and He unwilling to grieve or difcontent her, as all his Sex are to this day, yielded to her Charms. If this befell him in his perfection, not yet acquainted with bewitching Imbracements, and if *Solomon* the wifeft could not efcape the fnare of Female Allurements, it is not fo wonderful, as lamentable, that other Men perifh at that Rock.

CHAP.

CHAP. V.

Of memorable things between Adam *and* Noah.

§. 1. **C**AIN inheriting his Fathers Pride, and diſ-
daining his Brother, who was more acceptable than himſelf, became the firſt Murderer,
and made his Brother the firſt Martyr. And tho' God
mitigated his Revenge of this Sin upon *Cain*'s complaint, yet for the Sins of Cruelty and Injuſtice he
deſtroyed the World.

§.2. *Cain*'s dwelling in the Land of *Nod*, or agitati-
on, as *Junius* expounds it, is not as *Jerom* and others
held, that he ſetled in no certain Country ; but of
his diſtracted Thought and unquiet Conſcience the
Country was ſo called. This Country in which he
ſetled, and in which for fear of wandering he built
a City, *Junius* ſuppoſeth to be *Arabia* the *Deſart* ;
but the Text boundeth it on the Eaſt of *Eden*, whereas
Arabia is Weſt. As for the *Nomades* which liv'd upon
Paſturage, without Tillage, they were not any particular Nation, but it was a common Name for all that ſo
lived, as the *NorthernTartars*, *Getulians*, *Numidians*, Ancient *Britains*, and *Northern Iriſh*. Beſides, the World being unpeopled, and *Adam*'s Family ſmall, and that alſo
on the Eaſt ſide of *Eden*, in that part of *Aſſyria* which
Ptolomy calls *Calena*, it is unlike *Cain* would go ſo
far Weſt to *Arabia*. Touching the City *Enoch* built,
either for ſecurity, or to oppreſs others, as *Joſephus*
judged, probably it was of great Repute in the days
of *Noah*, when mighty Oppreſſors carried all the Fame.
It may be alſo, ſome Monuments of it remained, as
they ſay, of *Joppa*, after the Flood, which might induce ſome of *Noah*'s Poſterity, being of like violent
diſpoſition either to reedifie the ſame, or ſome other
of that Name. Hence it might be, that in time Colonies ſcatter'd from thence their Captives ; the
name

name of *Henochians* from *Bactria* and *Sogdiana*, *East*
from *Eden* (where *Pliny* and *Stephanus* find the Name
South from *Oxus*) unto *Iberia*, *Albania* and *Colchis*
near *Pontus*.

§.3. *Moses* has been very brief in the Story of *Cain*'s
Iſſue, it being utterly to be deſtroy'd : Yet the long
lives of that Age and the liberty his Children took in
Marrying, may well argue he might in one quarter of
his Life, people a large City, which his Iſſue were,
more ingenious to ſupply with the Inventions aſcribed to them, while *Seth*'s Poſterity is commended for
care of Religion and Heavenly things.

§.4. The Patriarchs Ages, when they began to gene-
rate, is not found in them that are named : For *Moses*'s
purpoſe was not to record a Genealogy of the firſt
begotten, but of the Anceſtors of *Noah* before the
Flood, and of *Abraham* after ; ſo that having the
Age of theſe that ſucceed one another in that Line,
it was ſufficient, whether they were younger or elder
Brethren. *Cain* was the Eldeſt of *Adam*'s Sons,
yet *Adam*'s Age when he begat him is not expreſſed, as it is of *Seth* : Neither can any one ſay directly,
Adam had but *Cain* and *Abel* before, nor that *Enoch*
was *Seth*'s Eldeſt Son. *Mehalaleel* begat *Jared* at 65.
who begat *Chanoch* at 162 ; the like or greater difference in the reſt, which cannot be aſcribed to the
long abſtinence from Marriage upon Religious reſpect,
as we ſee in holy *Enoch*. *Noah*'s Brethren periſhed
in the Flood, and ſo might ſome unnamed Children,
begotten before the three named, being 500 Years

* *See* Aug. old before *.
de Civ. D.

§.5. The Patriarchs Years have been queſtioned,
ſome holding them Lunary or *Egyptian*; but that cannot be ; for then ſome ſhould beget Children at 6, 7,
or 8 Years old, and the Eldeſt ſhould live not 100
Years, which is ſhort of many after the Flood ; yea
long ſince, *Pliny* witneſſeth under *Vespaſian*, in a ſearch,
many were found above 120, and ſome 140 Years
                               Old.

Old.   Simple Diet and temperate Life, made the
Essæans, Egyptian Priests, *Persian* Magicians, *Indian
Brachmans* live long, saith *Josephus. Pliny* reports
Nestor's 3 Ages. *Tyresia's* 6 *Sybils* 300 Years, *Endy-
mion's* little less. *Ant. Fumea* a good Historian, reports of an *Indian* above 300 Years Old, and my
self knew the old Countess of *Desmond, An.* 1589,
who lived many Years after, who had been married
in the Reign of King *Edw.* 4. To conclude, there are
three things (not to speak of Constellations) which
are natural *Causes of long and healthful Life* : Strong
Parents, pure Air, and temperate use of Dyet, Pleasure and Rest, all which excelled in the First Ages.
And though the Flood infused an impure quality into the Earth to hurt the means of Man's Life, yet
Time hath more consumed Natures Vigour, as that
which hath made the Heavens wax old like a Garment. Hereto add, our strange Education of Children, upon unnatural Curiosity nourished by a strange
Dugg : Hasty Marriage, before Natures Seed be ripe,
or Stock well rooted to yield a Branch fit to replant.
But above all, the Luxury of latter Ages, which wilfully oppresseth Nature, and then thinks to relieve
her with strong Waters, hot Spices, Sauces, &c.

§. 6. The Patriarchs knowledge of the Creation
might well come by Tradition from *Adam* to *Moses,* seeing *Methusalem* lived with *Adam* 243 Years,
and with *Noah* 500 Years, and he with *Abraham* 58
Years, from whom it was not hard to pass by *Isaac,*
Jacob and his Posterity to *Moses :* Yet for the more
certainty of the Truth, it was undoubtedly delivered to *Moses* by immediate Inspiration of the Holy
Ghost, as his many Miracles do prove. Questionless
also, Letters were from the Infancy of the World,
as *Enoch's* Pillars and his Prophecy witness, of which
part was found in *Saba,* saith *Origen,* and *Tertullian*
read some Pages ; neither can it be denyed there was
such, saith *Augustine.*

§ 7. The

§. 7. The Patriarchs Lives were lightly passed over 'till *Enoch*, whose Piety is commended, and his leaving the World not by Death : Whether his Change were such as shall be at the last day, let Divines judge. *Lamech*'s Prophecy of his Son *Noah* is touch'd upon, but *Noah*'s Life is handled more amply. The Wisdom, Policy and Wars of that World, were no doubt, great, as may be gathered, *Gen.* 5. 4. but the Universal Impiety which brought the Universal Destruction, deserved that the Memory of their Actions should be drowned with their Bodies. It were madness to imagine the Sons of God spoken of, *Gen.* 5. 24. were good Angels, which begat Giants on Women, as *Josephus* dreamt, and deceived *Lactantius*, Confuted by *Augustine* and *Chrysostom.*

§. 8. The Giants spoken of *Gen.* 5. *Becanus* strains his Wit to prove, they were not such properly, but so called for their Oppression : But *Moses* calling them Mighty, which argueth extraordinary Strength, and Men of Renown and great undertaking, there is more Reason to hold them *Giants* in a proper sense, especially considering what Scripture Reporteth of such in the Days of *Abraham, Moses,* and *Joshua, David, &c.* yea of whole Kindreds and Countries. If such were found in the Third and Fourth Ages of the Worlds decay, there is no Reason to doubt thereof in the First and Second flourishing Ages. From this Story grew the Conceit, That Giants were the Sons of Heaven and Earth : And from *Nimrod* grew the Tale of Giants casting up Mountains to the top of Heaven.

C H A P.

CHAP. VI.

The Original of Idolatry, and Reliques of Antiquity in Fables.

§. 1 THE *Greeks* and others, corrupting the Story of the Creation, and mingling their Fables with them, suppos'd that After-Ages would take those Discourses of God and Nature for Inventions of Philosophers and Poets. But as skilful Chymists can extract healthful Medicines out of Poison, and Poison out of wholsome Herbs, &c. so may much Truth be found out of those Fables.

§. 2. The Antiquity of Corruption was even from *Noah's* Family. For the liberal Grace of God being withdrawn after Man's Fall, such a perpetual Eclipse of spiritual things follow'd, and produc'd such effects as the general Deluge could not cleanse them, even in the selected Family of *Noah,* wherein were found those that renewed the Defection from God, for which they had seen the Worlds destruction. Hence the *Caldeans, Egyptians,* and *Phænicians* soon after became Idolaters, and the *Greeks* received their 12 Gods from *Egypt,* and erected to them Altars, Images and Temples, saith *Herodotus.*

§. 3. As Men, departed out of the way of Truth, stray on in unknown Vices to Eternal Perdition ; so these blind Idolaters being fallen from the God of Heaven, to seek God's on Earth to Worship, beginning with Men, they proceed to Beasts, Fouls, Fishes, Tr Herbs, the Four Elements, Winds, Morning, Evening Stars ; Yea, Affections, Passions, Sorrow, Sickness, besides Spirits infernal ; and among Terrestrials even the basest wanted not divine Honour, as Dogs, Cats, Swine, Leeks, Onions, &c. which barbarous Blasphemy, *Juvenal* thus derided,

> *O happy Nations, which of their own fowing,*
> *Have store of Gods in every Garden growing.*

§. 4. Of *Jupiter* and other Gods. That *Egypt* had knowledge of the First Age, by *Misraim* the Son of *Cham*, who had lived 100 Years in it, we doubt not. Having therefore learned that *Cain* did first build Cities, they made him ancient *Jupiter*, whom the *Athenians* also called *Pollyeus* and *Herceios*, Founder and Fortifier of Cities. This *Jupiter* married his Sister, as did *Cain* : His Father *Adam* they made *Saturn*, and his Sons *Jubal*. *Tubal*, and *Tubal-Cain* were made *Mercury*, *Vulcan* and *Apollo*, Inventers of Pastorage, Smiths-craft and Musick. *Naome*, *Augustine* expounds *Venusta*, which was *Venus Vulcan's* Wife, and *Eva* was *Rhea*; the Dragon which kept the Golden Apple, was the Serpent that beguiled *Eva*. *Paradise* was the Garden of *Hesperides* : So *Saturn's* dividing the World between Three Sons, came of *Noah* and his Sons ; and *Nimrod's* Tower was the attempt of Giants against Heaven. The *Egyptians* also Worshipped *Seth* as their most Ancient Parent, from whom they called their chief Province *Setheitica* ; and in *Bithinia* we find the City *Cethia* *.

* Strabo lib. 17.

§. 5. Of the Three Chief *Jupiters*; the First was Son of *Æther* & *Dies*; the Second of *Cælum* an *Arcadian*, and King of *Athens*; the Third Famous in the *Greek* Fables, was of *Creet* or *Candia*, as some say ; but there is no certainty, &c.

§. 6. *Jupiter Chammon*, more Ancient than all the *Grecian Jupiters*, was *Cham*, Father of *Misraim* in *Egypt* ; and before *Jupiter Belus*, Son of *Saturnus Babilonicus* or *Nimrod* : As for the latter *Grecian Jupiter*, he was a little before the Wars of *Troy*.

§. 7. The Philosophers opinion of God, *Pythagoras*, *Plato*, *Orpheus*, &c. believed not the Fooleries of their Times, though they mingled their Inventions
with

with Scripture: *Pythagoras* hung *Homer* and *Hesiod* in *Hell*, forever to be stung with Serpents, for their Fictions; yet *Homer* had seen *Moses*, as *Justine Martyr* sheweth in a Treatise converted by *Mirandula*. *Plato* dissembled his Knowledge for fear of the *Areopagits* Inquisition; yet *Augustin* excused him. He delighted much in the Doctrine of one God, though he durst not be known of it, or of *Moses* the Author of it, as may be gathered out of *Justin Martyr*, *Origen*, *Eusebius*, and *Cyril*, though he had from *Moses* what he writ of God, and of Divinity; as *Ambrose* also judged of *Pythagoras*. *Justine Martyr* observed, that *Moses* described God to be, *I am he who is.* *It is as hard to find out this Creator of the World, as it is impossible, if he were found, to speak of him worthily,* said *Plato*; who also said, *God is absolutely good, and so the Cause of all that is Good; but no Cause at all of any thing that is Evil.* *The Love of God is the cause of the Worlds Creation, and Original of all things.* *Apuleius* saith, *The most high God is also Infinite, not only by exclusion of Place, but also by dignity of Nature; neither is any thing more like or more acceptable to God, than a Man of a perfect Heart.* *Thales* said, *God comprehended all things, because he never had a Beginning: And he beholdeth all the thoughts of Men,* said *Zeno*; therefore said *Athenodorus, All men ought to be careful of their Actions, because God was every where present, and beholding all things.*

Orpheus calling Men to behold the King of the World, describes him to be one *begotten of himself, from whom all things spring, who is in all, beholds all, but is beheld of none,* &c, *Who is the First and Last; Head and Middle; from whom all things be: Foundation of Earth and Skye, Male and Female, which never dyeth: He is the Spirit of all, of Sun, Moon,* &c. *The Original and End of all; in whom all things were hidden 'till he produced them to Light.* *Cleanthes* calls God *Good, Just, Holy, possessing himself, alway doing good, and Charity*
it

it ſelf. Pindarus *ſaith, he is one God and Father, moſt high Creator and beſt Artificer, who giveth to all things divers proceedings,* &c. Antiſthenes *ſaith, God cannot be likened to any thing, and therefore not elſewhere to be known, but only in the everlaſting Country, of whom thou haſt no Image.* God, *ſaid* Xenophon, *ſhaketh and ſetteth all things at reſt : Is great and mighty, as is manifeſt to all ; but of what Form he is, none knoweth but himſelf, who illuminateth all things with his Light.* God, *ſaith* Plato, *is the Cauſe, Ground, and Original of the whole nature of things, the moſt high Father of the Soul, the eternal preſerver of living Creatures, and continual framer of the World ; a Begetter without propagation, comprehended neither in place nor time ; whom few conceive, none can expreſs him.* Thus, as Jerom ſaid, *We find among the Heathen, part of the Veſſels of God : But of them all, none have with more Reverence acknowledged, or more learnedly expreſſed One True God, and everlaſting Being, all ever-cauſing and ſuſtaining, than* Hermes the Egyptian. But of all theſe, ſee Juſtin Martyr, Clemens Alexandrinus, Lactantius, Euſebius, Du Pleſs. Danæus.

§. 8. *Hethaniſm and Judaiſm, when confounded.* Touching the Religions of the Heathen, they being the Inventions of Mortal Men, they are no leſs Mortal than themſelves. The *Caldean* Fire is quenched ; and as the Bodies of *Jupiter* and the reſt, were by Death devoured, ſo were their Images and laſting Marble Temples by Time. The Trade of Riddles for Oracles, and Predictions by *Apollo's* Prieſts, is now taken up by Counterfeit *Egyptians* and Cozening *Aſtrologers* ; yet was it long before the Devil gave way. For after Six ſeveral ſpoilings and ſackings of his Temple at *Delphos,* and as many repairings thereof, at laſt when *Julian* ſought unto it, God from Heaven, conſum'd all with Fire. So when the ſame Apoſtate incourag'd the *Jews* to re-build a Temple, God, by Earth-quake over-threw all, and ſlew many Thouſands of them. §. 9. *Sa-*

§. 9. *Satan*'s last Refuge to uphold his Kingdom; who being driven off the open Stage of the World, crept into the Minds of Men, and there set up the high and shining *Idol* of *Glory*, and all commanding *Image* of *Gold*. He tells men, that *Truth* is the Goddess of Danger and Oppression : *Chastity* is an Enemy to Nature, and all *Virtue* is without Taste ; but *Pleasure* delighteth every Sense, and *true Wisdom* gets Power and Riches to fulfil all our Desires. And if this Arch-politician find Remorse in any of his People, or any fear of future Judgment, he persuadeth them that God hath such need of Souls to re-plenish Heaven, that he will accept them at any time, and upon any Condition : And to interrupt their return to God, he layeth those great Blocks of *rugged Poverty* and *Contempt* in the narrow way which leadeth to his Divine Presence : Neither was he ever more industrious and diligent than now, when the long Day of Man-kind draweth fast to the Evening, and the World's *Tragedy* and *Time* near to an end.

C H A P. VII.

Noah's Flood, the Universality of it, and Noah's *memory of Antiquity.*

§. 1. **M**Oses's Divine Testimony of *Noah*'s Flood, natural Men regard no farther than Reason can reach, and therefore may have disputed the *Universality* of it ; and *Josephus* citeth *Nic. Damascen,* who reports, that many were saved on the *Mount Baris* in *Armenia* ; and the *Talmudists* held the same, saith *Annius.*

§. 2. *Ogyges*'s Flood, the *Greeks*, (the Corrupters of all Truth, saith *Lactantius*) make the most ancient, when yet *Ogyges*'s Flood was sixty seven Years after

Jacob, and fhort of *Noah*'s Flood by 500 Years ; neither do any Authors report, that it over-flowed any part of *Syria*, as *Mela*, *Pliny* and *Solinus* do of *Noah*'s, fpeaking of *Joppa*'s Ruins, &c. As for this Flood, as it exceeded not *Peloponefus*, fo was it forefeen by a concurrence of Caufes, which *Noah*'s was not. Touching *Varro*'s Report out of *Caftor*, of the ftrange Colour, quantity and fhape of *Venus* ; the Fogs which then rife, might caufe fuch Apperances : For *Galilæus*, a Modern Worthy Aftronomer, by Perfpective Glaffes, obferved many undifcover'd things in Stars, unknown to former Ages.

§. 3. *Deucalion*'s Flood, more certain for Time, being in the Reign of *Cranaus* King of *Athens*, according to *Varro*, cited by *Auguftin*, or under *Cecrop*'s, (after *Eufebius* and *Jerom*) in whofe latter times, *Ifrael* came out of *Egypt*, which, after *Functius*, was 753, or 739 Years, according to *Mercator*, after *Noah*'s Flood. But following the better Account, which giveth *Abraham* 60 Years more after the Flood, I reckon the Flood thus : The general Flood *Anno Mundi* 1656 ; *Jacob*'s Birth 2169, which is 519 Years after the Flood of *Ogyges* ; 100 after *Jacob*'s. Now *Deucalion* was born *Anno* 2356 ; and his Flood when he was 89 Years old, which is *Anno* 2438 ; after *Noah*'s 782 ; to which agrees *Xenophon* in *Annius*. This Flood over-ran moft of *Italy*, when *Egypt* alfo was afflicted with Water ; and the *Italians* which efcaped it, were called *Umbri*.

§. 4. *Noah*'s Flood, as *Berofus* reports, was heard of amongft the *Caldeaus* : *N. Damafcen* maketh particular mention of it. *Eufebius* alfo Records out of an Ancient Hiftory of *Abidenus*, that one *Siffithus*, fore-warned by *Saturn* of a Flood, fled to the *Armenian* Hills in a Ship, who after the Fall of the Waters, fent Birds three times to difcover, &c. *Cyril* cites *Polyhiftor* mentioning a general Flood : *Plato* alfo produceth an *Egyptian* Prieft, reporting to *Solon*

out

out of their Holy Books, of an univerfal Flood, long before *Ogyges*, in *Attica* ; and calls *Noah* Old *Ogyges*. He alfo fpeaks of a Flood of *Nilus* before that in *Attica*, which afflicted the lower *Egypt* under King *Prometheus*, 'till by *Hercules*'s direction, *Nilus*, was reduced within her Banks ; whereof grew the Tale of an Eagle, which feeding on *Prometheus*'s Liver, was flain by *Hercules*. *Xenophon*, cited by *Annius*, fpeaks of the Univerfal Flood under the firft *Ogyges*, of Nine Months continuance ; a fecond of *Nilus* under *Prometheus*, of one Month ; a third under *Ogyges Atticus*, of two Months ; a fourth under *Deucalion*, of three Months ; a fifth under *Proteus* of *Egypt* in *Helene*'s Rape. *Diod. Siculus* remembers another in leffer *Afia*, before *Deucalion*'s. There was one in the *Venetian* Territories, *Anno* 590. In *Friefland*, a Flood drouned 100000, *Anno* 1238. In *Dort* in *Holland*, 10000 perifhed *Anno* 1446. Others are mentioned by *Strozius*.

§. 5. *Noah*'s Flood was extraordinary, not upon natural Caufes, as the other ; but by God's fpecial Power ftrengthening the influence of Stars to fill all the Cifterns of Waters in Fountains and Clouds : And though *H.* of *Machline*, Scholar of *Albertus*, obferved a conjunction of *Saturn* and *Jupiter* in the laft, and of a watery Sign and Houfe of *Luna*, over againft the Ship, by which the Flood might have been forefeen ; and was alfo by *Noah*, as *P. de Aliaco* judgeth ; yet however God ufed fecond Caufes, he added fupernatural force to the Clouds and Fountains, to empty their whole Treafuries of Waters.

§. 6. There needed not new Created Waters in this *Flood* ; not to difpute whether God hath reftrained himfelf from Creating. For when he brake up the *Fountains* of the Deep, and opened the *Windows* or *Sluices* of Heaven, he fhewed no new Creation, but ufed his old Store, contained in the vaft Concavities of the Earth, and in the Clouds, wherewith he compaffed the Earth after an extraordinary manner ;

befides

besides his Condensation of the Air to convert it
into Rain, which is so ordinary; and thus might
the Waters grow to exceed the Mountains 15 Cubits. As for the Constellation they speak of, *L. Vi-*
ves reports from a great Astrologer, that the like
Gen. 6.11. was observed *Anno* 1524, after which it was exceeding Fair. To conclude, I find no other Myste-
ry in the word *Cataract*, signifying the Windows or
Flood-gates of Heaven, but the violent casting down
Waters, not diffusively, after the natural manner,
but as when it is emptied out of a Vessel in a whole
body, as it is sometimes in *India,* which are called
Spouts of Water. Thus God loosed the retentive
Power in the upper Air, and the Clouds, in which,
at other times, he shutteth up the Waters to carry
them to a place appointed.

§. 7. *Noah's* Memory among the Heathen, who,
for divers respects, gave him divers Names, as *Ogy-*
ges the first, because his Flood was before the *Grecian*
Ogyges ; *Saturn,* because he was Father of Nations ;
Prometheus, for his fore-sight; *Janus Bifrons,* for his
seeing what went before, and came after the Flood;
Chaos, and Seed of the World *Cœlum* ; *Sun, Virtumnus*
Bacchus, Liber Pater before him of *Greece*; but of old,
the word was *Boachus* of *Noachus*: He was also called *Nisius,* of Mount *Nisa* in *India,* joining to *Paro-*
panisus and other *Easterly* Mountains, where the Ark
rested, and where the *Grecian Bacchus* never came.
His Posterity also named Cities, Mountains and Ri-
Strabo. vers by his Name, as a City by the Red Sea ; the
River *Noachus* in *Thracia.*

§. 8. *Noah's Ark,* touching the Name, *Epiphanius* in
Ancyrius calls it *Arou,* which properly signifyeth the *Ark*
in the Sanctuary, as *Thebell* a Vessel which swimmeth,
called *Larnenx* in Greek. Certain places where it was
framed cannot be defined; yet *Becanus* conceives it
was neer *Caucasus,* where grow the noblest Ce-
dars, not far from the *Nisaans,* with whom *Alex-*
ander

ander made War. By all Probability, the place was
not far from where it landed, being fo large, heavy
laden, wanting Sails, of Form not apt to move, and
in a Calm, as it is in all Rains, down-right. It was
thought to have a flat Bottom, and a crefted Roof;
and the Wood *Gopher*, of which it was made, by all
probability was *Cedar*, being light, eafy to cut, fweet
and lafting; abounding in the EafternMountains; the
Pitch was like to a Bitume, which melteth only
by Fire, as is that by the dead Sea and *Babylon*.

§. 9. Of the *Ark's Capacity*; whofe Meafures, as
God prefcribed, fo the proportion, ᶜ faith *Auguftin*,
anfwered the fhape of a Man's Body, whofe Length
contained the Bredth fix times, and the Depth ten;
being a Figure of God's *City* or *Church* in this World,
&c. In the Meafure, the *Cubit* is queftioned; whether it were the common, which is from the Elbow
to the top of the Middle Finger, a Foot and a half;
or the plain *Cubit*, which is an handful more; or
the *Kings* and *Perfians* which is three Inches more
than the common; or the *facred*, which is double the
common, wanting a quarter; or the *Geometrical*, which
is fix common Cubits, and was embraced by *Origen*,
as alfo by *Auguftin*, who yet changed his Mind, becaufe Fifhes were not Curfed. Though Man's *De Civ.*
mifchievous Ignorance feeketh many Impoffibilities in
this work, yet no Monftrous thing is found in it;
for the number of Kinds to be ftored in it, was not
fo great, (excluding fuch as fprung from unnatural
Copulations, and diverfity of Soils) but that the common Cubit of thofe times may ferve; for add half
a Foot to the common Cubit of our times, which
is a Foot and half, and the length rifeth to be fix Hundred Foot, the Bredth one Hundred, the Depth
Sixty: As for the *Geometrical* Cubit, it was not in
ufe then, as we fee in the Meafure of Giants, and
height of the Altar, which might have no Steps,
Exod. 20, 26. *Buteo* hate prov'd that the Number

of

of Creatures might well be placed in the *Ark,* which contained 450000 Cubical Cubits, which is ſufficient for a Hundred kind of Beaſts, and their Meat in the lower and ſecond Story, and 280 Fouls, with *Noah* and his in the third.

§. 10. Of the *Arks reſting on part of Mount* Taurus *or* Caucaſus, *between* Eaſt-India *and* Scythia, paſſing by many needleſs Diſputes, I will endeavour to ſatisfie my ſelf and others in the place of the Arks reſting for the ſecond Plantation of the World, as I have done in the place of the Terreſtrial *Paradiſe* for Man's firſt Plantation. 2. The common Opinion is, The *Ark* reſted on *Ararat* in Great *Armenia;* the *Caldee* calls it *Kardu,* meaning the Hills *Gordei,* in Great *Armenia,* which *N. Damaſcen* calls *Baris.* *Beroſus* calls the Armenian Mountains, *Gordias.* *Strabo* found ſuch a Promontory in *Arabia Felix;* *Pliny,* a Mart-Town, which *Ptolomy* calls *Ociles;* Pintus *Acyla,* Niger *Zidon,* Toy E. *Gordei;* *Damaſcen* adjoins *Mimmynd,*perhaps for *Minni,* which word is uſed for *Armenia,* and ſeemeth compounded of *Minni* and *Aram,* that is, *Minni* of *Syria;* for *Armenia* was part of *Syria.* Theſe Mountains ſtand apart from all others on the North ſide of that Ridge of Mountains called *Taurus,* or *Niphates,* in the Plain of *Armenia* the *Greater,* near the Lake *Thoſpitis,* whence *Tigris* floweth in 75 Degrees Longitude, and 41 42 Latitude. One of theſe *Gordei Epiphanius* calls *Lubar,* which in the *Armenian* Tongue, ſignifieth Deſcent, of *Noah's* coming down, ſaith *Junius;* but any Hill of eaſy deſcent may be ſo called, as himſelf confeſſeth, correcting the Word *Kubaris* in *Joſephus;* from hence came *Lubra,* a Synagogue, being commonly on Hills, and the Latin *Delubra.*

My firſt Argument againſt the common Opinion is, from the time of 130 Years, which moſt, who follow *Beroſus,* give *Nimrod's* coming to *Shinar,* which by eaſy Journeys, might be travailed in 20 days from
the

Pliny.

the *Gordei* in *Armenia,* having only *Mesopotamia* between, and *Tigris* to help them.   This maketh it improbable, they should be so many Years before they Planted such a Country so near them ; which could not be to them so long unknown, being Encreased to a great Multitude long before those 130 Years.

My 2d. Argument is from the Civility and Multitude of the Eastern Nations, who had used *Artillery* and *Printing* long before the *West.*   It was thought a Fable in *Philostratus,* that the Wise Men inhabiting between *Hyphasis,* and *Ganges,* drive away their Enemies with Thunder and Lightning, whereby they defeated *Hercules* and *Bacchus,* and made *Hercules* cast away his Golden Shield.   *Jo. Cuthenberge* brought Printing from the *East*: *Conrade,* from him, brought it to *Rome*; and *Gerson* bettered it ; all about a 100 Years past. *Alexander Macedon* found more Cities and Magnificence in the little Kingdom of *Porus,* which lay close to *India,* than in all his Travels ; esteeming *Italy* barbarous, and *Rome* a Village : But *Babylon* was in his Eye, and the Fame of the *East* pierced his Ears. *Joppan,* now *Zippingari,* was exceeding Religious and addicted to Letters, Philosophy, Prayers, and Worshipping but one God.

5. My Third Argument is from the resistance which *Semiramis* found in *Est-India,* though her Army exceeded Three Millions, as *Diod. Siculus,* out of *Ctesias,* reports; besides 500000 Horse, and 100000 Waggons; of all which, admit but a third part true. *Nimrod's* Greatness is not doubted, nor that his People grew into such Multitudes by *Semiramis*'s time, Wife of *Ninus,* Son of *Belus,* Son of *Nimrod* : But that a Colony sent from *Babel* into the *East,* should so increase in so short a time, is incredible ; yet these Authors Report, that *Staurobathez,* King of *East-India,* exceeded her in numbers, which could not be, if the *East* were replenished by a Colony from *Babylon.*

6. My

6. My Fourth Argument is 1st. from *Noah*'s person, who being at *Babel*'s Confusion, and the 731st Year of his Age, was not like to be unsetled, and to seek a Seat. 2. The Text saith, he became a Husband-man; which argueth his setled Course of Life; not a Wanderer from *Armenia* to *Babylon*, then to *Arabia Felix*, then to *Africa*, so to *Spain*, *Italy*, &c. as they report; not considering his Years, the difficulty of Travel-ing in an over-grown wild World, which had lyen waste 140 Years. 3. Besides the place of his Landing, being *East* from *Babylon*, Rich and Pleasant, the Wise Father would not neglect the planting of it, and seek out less pleasing Parts with such difficulties. 4. Neither is it to be thought, the Reverend Father was at that presumptuous Work of *Babel*, and re-strained it not. 5. We find *Joktan*, *Havila* and *O-pher* Planted in *India*, which were not like to have turned back from *Shinar*. Lastly, The Scriptures si-lence of *Noah*, after his departure from the *East* to *Shinar*, argueth him left there; and so out of all oc-casions, which might touch the History of the *Jews*, which *Moses* was to prosecute.

7. *Annius* on *Berosus* lands the Ark on the *Caspian* Mountain of *Armenia*; to which purpose he con-founds the *Caspian* and *Gordian* Hills, which *Pto-lomy* sets far asunder, and *Mercator* sets 5 Degrees, and *Villanovanus*, much more Ancient, sets 7 De-grees, or 420 Miles one from the other. And tho' I grant, that Mankind was renewed in *Scythia*, 250 Years before *Ninus* (as *Porcius Cato* records) yet was not this *Scythia* in *Armenia*, but under the Mountains of *Paropanisus* in 130 Degrees of Longi-tude, according to *Ptolomy*; whereas the supposed *Armenia Araxea* is in 87. neither hath he any Scy-thia nearer *Armenia Araxea*; though he sets out 100 several Nations of *Scythians*, such as *Imaus* by the *Asian Sarmatia* on the *West*; *Imaus* on the *East*; the *Sacces*, *Sogdians* and *Margians* on the *South*; and the

the Mouth of *Oxus* and unknown *Countries* on the *North.* He also maketh the *Asian Sarmatia* to comprehend many Nations, and a great part between *Armenia* and *Scythia*, besides *Colchis*, *Iberia* and *Albania.* Neither *Prenetus*, *John Plancrapio*, *Haytonus* the *Armenian*, writing of *Scythia* or *Tartaria*, speak one word of *Armenia* ; nor *Matheus a Micon*, a *Sarmasian* Cannon of *Cracovia*, who travelled a great part of *Sarmatia Asiatica*; yet he observed that *Tanais*, or *Don*, and *Volga* or *Edel*, spring but of *Lakes* and *Marishes*, and not out of *Ripbian* or *Hyperborean* Mountains in *Scythia.* He also sheweth that the *European Sarmatia* contains *Russia*, *Lithuania* and *Moscho*, and is bounded on the *West* by *Vissa* or *Vistula*, parting it from *Germany* ; That the *Scythians* in *Asian Sarmatia*, came thither above 300 Years past out of the *East*, where the *Ark* rested ; and that the *Sacæ-Scythians* were North of *Taurus* or *Ararat* ; As for the *Ariacan Scythians*, between *Jaxartus* and *Jadtus* on the *East* of the *Caspian*, they are no *Armenians.*

9. My fifth Argument is from the place where *Noah* Planted a Vine, which could not be in *Armenia*, much colder than *Italy* and *France*, where yet Vines grow not naturally, as they did where *Noah* Planted, as his Husbandry witnesseth.

9. *Objection* 1. The Text saith, *from thence God scattered them*, &c. *Answer*, That is, the Builders of the Tower, which were not all, but certain of them, which were increased after the Flood.

Sybilla.

10. *Objection* 2. *Ararat* signifieth *Armenia*, which the *Caldean Paraph.* calls *Kardu.* 2. *Answer.* Writers agree not about *Ararat*: The *Sybill's* Books place it in *Phrygia*, near where *Cælenes* was built ; whereabout the River *Marsyas* joineth with *Meander* ; but this is far from the *Gordiean* Mountains. *Josephus*, out of *Berosus*, placeth *Ararat* between *Armenia* and *Parthia*, toward *Adibene* ; where they vent pieces of
the

Eaſt and *Weſt* from *Cilicia* to *Caucaſus,* as the *Alps, Pireneans, Andes* in *America,* which run Three Thouſand Miles, *&c.* So the *Mediterranean* Sea is a common Name, which yet upon divers Coaſts beareth proper Names, as do other Seas. Let us then appeal to the Word of Truth, and take it literally, ſeeing the plain Senſe carrieth no inconvenience, and let us fancy no ſtrange Expoſition from it. The Reverend Reſpect we owe the Holy Scripture, every Word having its full weight in Gods Book, ſhews that it is not to be taken otherwiſe than as we Read; as *Auguſtin* ſaid of the Goſpel. *Moſes* words are, *And as they went from the Eaſt they found a plain,* &c. Which prove without Controverſie the Ark reſted *Eaſtward* from *Shinar.* For *Moſes* is every where preciſe in ſetting out Coaſts, and Quarters of Countries, as *Nod Eaſtward* from *Eden, Sepher* in the *Eaſt, Gen.* 4. 16. and 10. 30. *and* 12. 18. *Ezek.* 38. 6. So *Mat.* 21. *and* 12. 42. Now *Armenia* is ſo far from the *Eaſt* of *Babylon,* that it is *Weſt* of the *North.* The *Gordian* Hills for Latitude are Forty One : *Babylon* Thirty Five for Longitude, (which makes the difference of *Eaſt* and *Weſt*) the *Gordian* are Seventy Five, and *Babylon* Seventy Nine, and Eighty, which makes Five Degrees from the *North* to the *Weſt* ; beſides a Quarter of the Compaſs from *Eaſt.* But in Scripture the leaſt difference may not be omitted, every Point and Accent being full of Senſe. The *Eaſtern* Parts then from *Shinar* were firſt Civiliz'd, having *Noah* himſelf for their Inſtructor, whoſe numerous Armies overmatched the Millions of *Semiramis,* and whoſe Fruitfulneſs made it fit for *Noab's* Husbandry, as *Iſh-Adamah,* a Man exerciſed in Earth, ſaith *Ar. Montanus.*

C H A P.

CHAP. VIII.

The Planting of Nations: Noah's Sons, *and which was Eldest.*

§. 1. SHEM, in *Augustin's* Judgment was Eldest; but the *Septuagint, Junius, &c.* prefer *Japhet,* from *Gen.* 10. 21. The *Hebrews* putting the word *Elder* after *Japhet,* which the *Latin* sets before. Gods Blessings are not tyed to Elder in Blood, but Piety: Otherwise *Japhet* was 2 Years older than *Shem,* being begotten in *Noah's* 500th Year; when *Shem* in *Noahs* 600th Year was but 98. Compare *Gen.* 5. 32. with 10. 10. & 9. 24. Namely *Cham* the Youngest.

§. 2. In this Plantation it is to be presumed. 1. So far as the Scriptures Treat of the Story of Nations, Profane Authors want Authority in point of Antiquity, whose Records have been borrowed from thence only. For *Moses* is found more Ancient than, *Homer, Hesiod,* or any *Greek,* saith *Eusebius, Proœm.* in *Chron.* 2. We are to consider, that *Noah* who knew the World so long before, sent not his Sons at Adventure, as Discoverers, but allotted them the Quarters of their Habitation. This could not be suddenly, Considering what Woods, Thickets, Pools, Lakes, Marishes, Fenns, and Boggs, 130 Years Desolation had bred in those fruitful parts. This made difficult, and slow Journeys and Marches, both from the *East,* and *Shinar,* till Increase of Issue forced them on further.

§. 3. *Japhet,* with whom *Moses* beginneth, Planted the Isles of the *Gentiles, Europe* and the Isles about it, besides a Portion in *Asia. Gomer,* his Eldest Son is without Reason, placed in *Italy* by *Berosus, Funci-*
us,

us, &c. in the Tenth Year of *Nimrod,* and when *Tubal*
was in *Austria,* or *Biscai,* in *Spain,* the Twelfth Year
of *Nimrod, Ann.* 142 after the Flood : For before
Babels Confusion the Company were not dispers'd ;
consider then the time of Building such a City, and a
Tower, to equalize Mountains, said *Berosus,* or reach
to Heaven, said *Nimrod,* which took an exceeding
compass, and whose Foundation in Marish Ground
was full of Labours : As for Materials the want was
great, and the Workmen unexperienced, and the
Work almost finished.

This time *Glicas* judged to be about 40 Years: So
that *Gomer* and *Tubal* could not Plant so soon : Besides the tedious conveying of Wives, Children, Cattel from *Shinar,* to *Italy,* and *Spain,* 4140 Miles,
through Countries, now of much more difficult Paffage. *Nimrod* spent many Years in a short and more
easy Journey to *Shinar* ; and why did *Tubal* leave
many rich Countries to Plant in *Biscay,* the most barren Country of the World ? To say they had the
Convenience of Navigation; shews Men know not
what it is to carry Multitudes by Sea, with Cattel, on
which they lived. Whether Navigation was then in
Use, is doubted, considering how long it was before
Men durst cross the Seas, and that the Invention was
ascribed to the *Tyrians* long after by *Tibullus.*

§. 4. *Gog* and *Magog, Tubal* and *Mesech,* settled
first about lesser *Afia,* where *Beroaldus* (whom I
find most judicious in this Plantation out of *Ezekiel*
38. and 39.) findeth the *Gomerians, Tubalines,* and
Togarminans. Josephus in this Plantation led *Eusebius,*
Epiphanius, and *Ar. Montanus* into many errours ;
and *Gog* and *Magog* have troubled many: But this *Gog*
the Prince of *Magogians,* or *Cælo-Syrians,* must needs
be the Successor of *Seleucius Nicanor,* who sought to
extinguish the *Jews* Religion, and force them to *Ido-*
latry. Hermolaus Barborus maketh the *Turks* come
from the *Scythians* : *Junius* makes it a National Name
from

from *Gyges*, who flew *Candaulus* King of *Lydia*, where *Strabo* finds the *Gygian* Lake ; and in the *South* Borders *Junius* finds *Gygarta*, or *Gogkarta* in *Syriak*, *Gogs* City in *Cælo-Syria*, where *Pliny* placeth *Bambice*, or *Hierapolis*, which the *Syrians* call *Magog* : Though *Strabo* make both to be *Edeſſa* in *Meſopotamia* ; but *Ortelius* doubts whether there be a miſtake; yet may the Name be common, but certainly both were *North* of *Iſrael*. *Magog* might be Father of the *Scythians*, who waſted much of leſſer *Aſia*, Poſſeſſed the *Cælo-Syria*, and built *Scythopolis*, and *Hierapolis*, which themſelves of *Syrians* call *Magog*, being *North* from *Judea*; which *Bellonius* makes *Aleppo*, where the *Mermaid* was Worſhip'd, called *Atergatis*, and by the *Greeks* *Derceto*. Thus we ſee the Ancient *Gomerians*, and *Tubalins* were no *Italians*, or *Spaniards* : Though long after they might ſend *Colonies* thither.

The *Iberians* of Old were called *Thobelos*, of *Tubal*, who from thence paſſed to *Spain* to ſearch Mines, ſaith *Juſtine* ; but 'tis more probable it was Peopled out of *Africa*. *Meſech* alſo is Neighbour to *Tubal*, of whom ſprung the *Miſeans* from Mount *Adeffas*, to *Pontus*, afterwards called *Cappadocia*, which is the *Mazoca*, and is *Magog*'s chief Country : *Gomer* was Neighbour to *Togarma*, Bordering on *Syria* and *Cilicia*, whoſe Poſterity Peopled *Germany* and the Borders of the Earth, as *Gomer* ſignifieth. But wanting Room forward to Exonerate their ſwelling Multitude, they returned back upon their Neighbours : Whereof they were called *Cimbri*, which ſignifies *Robbers*, in *Camden*'s Judgment. And though in Ancient times the *Gauls* uſed to beat them, as *Cæſar* Reports ; yet after they grew Warlike they purſued rich Conqueſts, even into leſſer *Aſia*, the Seat of their *Progenitors*. *Samothes* is by *Annius* made Brother of *Gomer*, and ſurnamed *Dis* ; but *Functius*, and *Vignier* do juſtly diſclaim him ; ſeeing *Moſes* knew him not.

§. 5. *Noah*

§. 5. *Noah* alfo by *Annius* is brought out of the *Eaft* into *Italy,* to build *Genoa,* and there to live Ninety-two Years ; but *Mofes* filence is to me a fufficient Argument to difprove this Report, feeing he did fo carefully Record *Nimrod's* Cities. As for *Berofus* and others, whom he quotes for it, their Fragments are manifeftly proved Spurious ; neither could *Noah* be that *Italian Janus* their Firft King, who Dyed but 150 Years before *Æneas,* according to *Eufebius,* and Lived in the days of *Ruth,* 704 Years after *Noah.* Let the *Italians* content themfelves with a *Janus* from the *Greeks,* who Planted them 150 Years before the Deftruction of *Troy* ; from whom they had their Idolatry, as their *Veftal Virgins,* and Holy Fire from *Vefta* his Wife, which no man will believe to proceed from *Noah.* There fucceeded him *Saturnus, Picus, Faunus, Latinus,* before *Æneas,* in the Days of *Sampfon.*

§. 6. *Nimrod* Seating himfelf in *Babylon,* Reafon and Neceffity taught the reft to remove, to take the Benefit of thofe far extended Rivers which ran along *Shinar,* as well for convenience in their Journeys, as to provide for mutual entercourfe for time to come. Thus *Chufh* the Father fettled near his Son *Nimrod* in the *South* of *Chaldea* along *Gehon,* which Tract *Mofes* calls the Land of *Chufh, Gen.* 2. 13. *Havila-ab,* the other Son of *Chufh* took down *Tigris* on both fides, efpecially the *Eaft,* which alfo is called the Land of *Havila, Gen.* 2. 11. afterwards *Sufiana. Chufh* in length of time fpread into *Arabia* the Defart, and *Stony,* where was the City of *Chufca* afterwards called *Chufidia* by *Ptolomy.* So *Seba* and the reft Planted *Arabia* the Happy towards the *Perfian* Gulf, from whence after the ftoppage of *Euphrates,* they Traded to *Babylon* by *Tigris. Gomer, Magog,* and the other Sons of *Japhet* took the leffer *Afia,* the better to fpread themfelves *Weft* and *North: Tubalin* afcended into *Iberia* . The *Magogians* to *Sarmatia.*
                                                      The

The *Gomerians* in *Asia* were called *Cymerians*, saith *Herodotus*; and their Country was afterwas called *Galatia* by the *Gallogreeks*; whom the *Scythians* drove into *Albania*, and some into *Phrygia*, both called *Cymerians*, as was *Bosphorus*, and a City by it.

Togarma, *Gomers* Son, dwelt near *Sidon*, and overspread the lesser *Armenia*, whose Kings were called *Tigranes*. *Meshach*, *Japhet's* Son, setled in *Syracena*, in *Armenia*, between the Mountains *Moschici* and *Periards*; out of whose *North-East* springs *Araxis*; and *Euphrates* out of the *South* : Of whom came the *Moscovites*, in the Judgment of *Melancton*. *Madai*, the Third Son of *Japhet*, Planted *Media*.

§. 7. *Javan*, the Fourth Son of *Japhet* (from the *West* of lesser *Asia*) sent *Colonies* into *Greece*, whose Inhabitants were called *Iones*, that is, *Athenians*. *Strabo*, out of *Hecasius*, says the *Iones* came out of *Asia*, where the Name also remain'd. *Meshech*, the Sixth Son of *Japhet*, of whom before. See §. 4. which Name differs little from *Aram's* Sons, *Gen.* 10. 23. which, 1 *Chron.* 1. 17. is the very same. They dwelt *North* from *Jury*, and were Enemies to the *Jews*; and it may be they were under one Prince : but this *Meshech* commonly joined with *Tubal*. If therefore he Planted first near *Jury*; yet his Issue might pass into *Cappadocia*, and so into *Hircania*. Those which came of *Aram*, nearer the *Jews*, might be those to whom *David* fled in his Persecution, *Psal.* 120. 5. *Tiras* is Father of the *Thracians*, as is generally held, and was *Japhet's* Seventh Son.

§. 8. *Ascanez*, Son of *Gomer*, *Eusebius* makes Father of the *Gothians*: *Pliny* finds *Ascania*, and the River of *Ascanius*, and the Lake of *Ascanez*, between *Prusia* and *Nice* in *Phrygia*: *Junius* takes them for Inhabitants of *Pontus* and *Bythinia*, in which *Ptolomy* hath such a Lake : *Strabo* finds a City, River, and Lake in *Mesia* near *Gio*, as *Pliny*. But *Jer.* 51. 27. determins it *North* of *Asia* near *Ararat*, and *Minni*,

Moun-

Mountains of *Armenia*. *Riphat*, *Gomer*'s Son, Father of *Riphcior Paphlagone*, Famous in the *North* of *Sarmatia*, after called *Henites* ; of whom *Polonia*, *Ruffia*, and *Lithuania* were Peopled: *Melancton* thinks they spread from the *Baltick* to the *Adriatick* Sea, and findeth a *Venetian* Gulf in *Ruffia*, called *Heneti*, the same with *Veneti*.

§. 9. *Elifa*, eldest Son of *Javan*, was Father of the *Nicolians*, from whence the *Grecians* were called *Helens*, saith *Montanus*; and *Ezek.* 27. 7. mentions the Isles of *Elefa*, that is, of *Grece*.

Tharfis, his Second Son, Planted *Cilicia*, where is the City *Tharfis*. This word is often put for the Sea, becaufe the greateft Ships were there, and they were called Seamen, and the firft *Iones*. *Montanus* and *Cal.* Paraphrafe miftake it for *Cartbage*.

Cittim, his Third Son, Father of the *Macedonians*, not *Italians*, *Efa.* 23. with 1 *Mac.* 1. Yet it may be, he firft Planted *Cyprus*, where *Jofephus* found the City, which remained in *Jerom*'s days, faith *Pintus*; but this Ifle proving too narrow, they fent out and Peopled *Macedon*, whofe Plantation *Melancton* afcribes to him.

Dodanim, his Fourth Son, fettled at *Rhodes* ; *Dodanim* and *Rhodanim* being eafily confounded : He alfo fent *Colonies* to *Epirus*, where was the City *Bodana*.

§. 10. *Chufh*, Eldeft Son of *Cham*, with his Affociates, Peopled *Babylonia*, *Chaldea*, and all the *Arabias*. *Ethiopia* was not his, as *Jofephus*, the *Septuagint*, and others mifled by them, judged. *Firft*, From *Numb.* 12. 2. *Mofes*'s Wife was a *Chufhite*, not an *Ethiopian*, as *Jofephus* Reports ; who tells us, that *Mofes* leading an *Egyptian* Army againft the *Ethiopians*, the Kings Daughter fell in Love with, and betrayed the City *Sheba* to him, after called *Meros*. On the contrary, *Strabo*, and all *Geographers*, place *Sheba* in *Arabia*, whence the Queen came to vifit *Solomon*. *Damianus*, and *Goes*, tell us, that the *Prefter Johns* of the

Abif-

Aybſſinians came of that Queen by *Solomon.* But without Scripture or Probability, ſeeing her ſuppoſed
Baſtard aſſiſted not his Brother *Reboboam* againſt *Shi-
ſhack* King of *Egypt.* But *Moſes* cleareth his Wives
Kindred againſt *Joſephus,* making her a *Midian,* not
far from *Horeb.* So *Jethro's* coming to *Moſes, &c.*
Chriſamenſis alſo proveth *Midia* cannot be *Ethiopia.* Thirdly, So *Ezek.* 29. 10. *Nebuchadonoſor's* Conqueſt
of *Egypt* is ſet out by the Bounds *Seveneth,* which is
next *Ethiopia* and the *Chuſhits,* ill Tranſlated Black
Moors, for *Arabians,* the other next Neighbours; whereas the *Moors* were beyond *Seveneth,* or *Syene,* as *Scotland* is beyond *Barwick.* Fourthly, So *Ezek.* 30. 9. *Chuſh*
cannot be *Ethiopia,* but *Arabia:* Whereto *Nebuchadonoſor* (having Conquered *Egypt,* even the Tower
Syene in *Thebaida* bordering on *Ethiopia*) ſent Ships o-
ver the *Red-Sea*; which to the *Ethiopians* joyning to
Syene, he needed not to have done, neither would
the fall of *Nilus* ſuffer; nor was his invading that
part of *Arabia* ſo fit by Land, all the length of *Egypt*
being between, and all the tedious Deſarts of *Paran.*
Laſtly, This placing a Family of *Chuſh,* from all the
reſt to go and come through *Miſraim,* would make
a confuſion in the Plantation: Beſides, there was never any thing between *Jews* and *Ethiopians,* as
between them and *Chuſhits.* Fourthly, So *Eſa.* 18. 1.
turning *Chuſh,* to *Ethiopia* for *Arabia,* puts one Kingdom for another, confounding the Story: For what
Kingdom beyond the River of *Ethiopia* can be found,
which *Aſſur* was to waſte as an Enemy to the *Jews,*
who were never injured by the *Ethiopians,* much
leſs by any beyond them? But I acknowledge, that
here *Egypt,* which threatned *Iſráel,* is threatned, and *A-
rabia* with it, *Eſa.* 19. 20. The like Errour is committed in 1 *Kings* 19. 9. Making *Tirhaka* an *Ethiopian,* for
a *Chuſhite,* or *Arabian,* as in *Zerah,* 2 *Chron.* 14. 9.
For how ſhould he bring ſuch an Army through ſuch
a Kingdom as *Egypt?*

E 2 §. 11. *Mi-*

§. 11. *Mizarim,Cham*'s Second Son,took into *Egypt* along *Nilus* unto *Syene*, bordering on *Ethiopia* to the *South* from the *Mediterranean* Sea; which was his *North* Border. *Phut*, the Third Son travell'd to the *Weſt* beyond him along the Sea, Inhabiting *Mauritania*. *Egypt* was known to *Moſes* and the Prophets by the Name of *Mizraim*, but was called *Egypt* by a King of that Name, otherwiſe called *Rameſes*, the Son of *Belus*, who chaſed his Brother *Danæus* into *Greece*, where he ſetled in *Morea* after the Flood, 877. Many are the Fancies of the *Egyptian* Antiquity of Three Hundred and Thirty Kings before *Amaſis*, Contemporary with *Cyrus*; and of their Story of 13000 Years, *&c.* And *Mercator* pleads their Antiquity from their *Dynaſties*, of which the Sixteenth began with the Flood, ſo that the firſt muſt reach the Creation. But *Euſebius* begins the Sixteenth with *Abraham* 292 Years after the Flood. *Annius* begins the firſt *Dynaſty* 131 Years after the Flood, forgetting that he had ſaid, that *Nimrod* came but that Year to *Shinar*, ſo that the *Dynaſty* could not begin till after the Confuſion. But where *Pererius* holds it impoſſible that *Egypt* could be Peopled 200 Years after *Adam*, and ſuppoſing it not repleniſhed at all before the Flood, I find no force in the aſſertion. For we have no reaſon to give leſs Increaſe to the Sons of *Adam*, than *Noah*, the Age of the one being double, and after a while treble to the other, which Argueth ſtrength to beget many a long time. This appeared in *Cham*, who repleniſhed Five Cities with his own Iſſue. *Nimrod*'s Troops at *Shinar* were great, no doubt ; yet it is probable all came not thither, as may be gathered by the Multitudes, which Encountered *Semiramis* in the *Eaſt Indian* Wars. As for *Egypt* being an Eſtabliſhed Kingdom in the Days of *Abraham*, it argues 'twas Inhabited long before : And contrary to *Pererius*, we may rather wonder how the World could contain the Iſſue of thoſe long living

ving heathful Fathers, than doubt the Peopling of it. For if our short Lives, wherein scarce one in Ten Liveth to 50 Years, the World wants no People: And if Wars and Pestilence did not cut them off by Thousands, the World could not contain them: What would it do if none dyed before 50 or 100 Years? Then Conceive the Millions, when Men Lived 8 or 900 Years &c. *Pererius* is likewise deceived in the occasion of their dispersing at *Babel*: For had not that occasion happened, their Increase would in short time have forc'd them to seek new Habitations, &c. That therefore the World was all over Peopled with offenders, it appeareth by the Universality of the Flood. As for *Egypt's* Antiquity, it is probable that *Mizaraim's* Sons found some Monuments in Pillars, Altars, or other Stones, or Metals, touching former Government there, which the *Egyptians* added to the Lives of the Kings after the *Flood*, which succeeding Times through Vain-Glory amplified. So *Berosus*, and *Ephigenes*, tell us of the like Antiquities of *Chaldea* where the *Babylonians* knew Letters and Astronomy 3634 Years befor *Alexander* the Great. *Egypt* was divided in the Upper, called *Thebaida*, from *Syene* to *Memphis*, and in the lower, from *Memphis* to the *Mediterranean* Sea, making the Form of a Δ by *Memphis*, *Pelusin* and *Alexandria*. *Thebes* had 100 Gates, called *Diospolis* by the *Greeks*; *No-hamon* in Scripture, from the incredible number of Inhabitants. *Phut*, the Third Son of *Cham*, Planted *Lybia*, whose Ancient People were called *Phuts*, said *Josephus*; and *Pliny* found the River of *Phut* in *Mauritania*, running from Mount *Athos* Two Hundred Miles: *Phut* and *Lud* Associated *Egypt*, *Ezek.* 30.

§. 12. *Canaan*, Fourth Son of *Cham*, Possessed *Palestine*, from *Sidon* to *Gerar* in length, *Gen.* 10. *Sidon*, his Eldest Son built a City of his Name in *Phœnicia*. See ca. 7. 6. 3. *Heth*, his Second Son, Father of the *Hittites*, in the *South* about *Beersheba*, near *Pharan*.

E 3   Je-

Jebusen, the Third Son, Father of the *Jebusites,* about *Jebus,* or *Hierusalem,* Conquered by *David. Amoreus,* the Fourth, *East* of *Jordan* from *Arnon,* past the Sea of *Galilee,* containing two Kingdoms. His Posterity also Inhabited the Mountains of *Juda,* part of *Idumæa* near *Libania. Gergeseus,* the Fifth, *East* from the *Galiloan* Sea; where was *Gerasa;* he also Built *Geris,* after called *Beritus,* Three Miles from the River *Adonis* in *Phœnicia. Hevius,* the Sixth, under *Libanus,* near *Emath :* The *Caphtorims* expelled many of them. *Archius,* the Seventh, between *Libanus* and the Sea over against *Tripolis :* He Built *Archas. Sinius,* the Eighth, *Junius* placeth him *South* of *Jebus;* more probably he Built *Sin,* which the *Jews* call *Sein,* or *Symira* by *Ptolomy,* or *Synochis* by *Arcas,* after *Brocardus. Aradeus,* the Ninth, Built *Arados* in the Isle against *Phœnice,* opposite to *Antarados* in the main Ocean. *Zemari,* the Tenth Son, 'tis uncertain whether he Inhabited *Cœlosyria,* or was Father of the *Perizzites,* or the *Emisani ;* or of *Samaria,* which latter the Scripture seemeth to disprove, *1 Kings* 16.28. *Hamath,* the Eleventh Son, Founder of *Emath* in *Iturea, East* of *Hermon,* joining to *Libanan ;* not *Emath,* which *Josepus* and *Jerom* confound with *Antioch,* or *Epiphania, &c.*

§. 13. *Seba,* or *Saba,* Eldest Son *Chush,* setled in the *West* of *Arabia* the Happy , *East* of the *Red Sea. Regama,* or *Raama,* the Fourth Brother, and *Sheba* his Son took the *West* side by the *Persian* Gulf. *Pliny* saith, the *Sabeans* dwelt along the *Persian* and *Arabian* Seas, where *Ptolomy* places the City *Saba* toward the *Red Sea,* and *Regma* toward the *Persian;* where also *Sabta,* another Brother, is found by *Montanus* out of *Ptolomy. Beroaldus* thinks it strange, that any of these *Sabeans* should go One Thousand Two Hundred Miles to Rob *Job* in *Traconitis,* between *Palestine* and *Cœlosyria :* But *Guilandinus Melchior* findeth *Sabeans* nearer in *Arabia* the Desart,

whom

whom *Ptolomy* calls *Save*, now *Semiscasac*, from whence the *Magi* came to Worship Christ, as he judgeth. The Queen of *Saba*, which came to *Solomon*, *Bero-aldus* and *Pererius* bring from East *Arabia*; I rather think the West next *Midian* and *Ezion Gaber*, then under the command of *Solomon*. *Sabeta* hath there left his Name in the City *Sabbatha* or *Sabota*. *Plin.* L.14. 12.

Josephus's fancy is, that *Saba* was Father of the *E-thiopians* about *Meros*, and *Sabta* of the *Aabanies*, is Confuted by the Names. For in *Arabia Desert*, are the Cities of *Saba*, or *Save*, and *Ragana* for *Regma*, and People called *Raabeni*, of *Raamah*. In *Arabia* the *Happy*, are *Rhegama* and *Rabana*, and the Cities *Sapta*; in the South of *Arabia*, is *Sabatta* the Metropolis, and the great City *Saba* toward the Red Sea, and the Region *Sabe* more Southern.

Didan the second Son of *Raamah*, whom *Josephus* and *Jerom* carry to *West-Ethiopia*, but *Ezechiel* joyned with Father and Brother, in Trade to *Tyre*, with precious Cloaths, which Naked *Black-Moors* never knew 'till the *Portugals* Traded with them. But *Je-remy* and *Ezechiel* will shew us *Dedan* near *Idumea*, which will remove all Scruples.

§. 14. *Ludim*, Eldest Son of *Mizraim*, Father of the *Lybians* in *Africa*, where the *Lydians* are also adjoined, as a Nation of *Africa*: For 2 *Chron.* 12. *Lubim*, or *Lubæi* is the same with *Ludim* in *Hebrew*, saith *Montanus*, with some difference in writing from the *Lybies*. *Mistraim*'s other Sons are assigned no certain place in Holy Scripture; only the Philistins are said to come of *Caslubim* and *Caphtorim*, in the Entrance into *Egypt* by the Lake *Serbonis*, and the Hill *Cassius*. *Caphtorim*, between that and *Pelusium*, is a Tract called *Sithroitis*, where *Pliny* and *Stephanus* place the City *Sethron*, which *Ortelius* takes to be *Hercules parva* in *Ptolomy*. The *Philistins* Inhabited the South of *Canaan*, driving out the *Avims*, or *He-vites*, saith *Junius* on *Gen.* 10. 14. *Deut.* 2. 23. *Jos.*

13.*3. where their Bounds are set forth, and their five Principalities.

§. 15. *Sem's* Posterity *Moses* reckoneth up last, that he might proceed with the Genealogy of the *Hebrews* to *Abraham,* for which *Arphaxad's* Age only is expressed, and his Children, and of *Aram.* The common Opinion possessed him of what was beyond *Tygris* to the *Indian-*Sea, saith *Jerom,* saving *India,* which I believe *Noah* held ; to whom, after *Joctan,* came *Ophir* and *Havilah,* and planted there ; of whom hereafter.

Elam, Father of the *Elamites,* the Princes of *Persia,* whose Seat was *Susan,* by the River *Ulai,* which *Ptolomy* calls *Eulæus,* which runneth into *Hiddekel.* *Asher,* the Second Son of *Sem,* Father of the *Assyrians,* disdaining *Nimrod's* Pride, left *Babel,* and built *Ninivy,* according to the common Opinion, and contended for the Empire. *Arphaxad* was Father of those *Chaldæans* which were about *Ur* ; the rest were possessed by the Sons of *Cham.* *Lud,* *Sem's* Fourth Son *Josephus* and *Jerom* place in lesser *Asia,* but I question it. *Aram,* his Fifth Son, Father of the *Syrians,* as well about *Mesopotamia* as *Damascus.* *Padan Aram,* or *Aram Neharaim,* that is, *Syria* between two Rivers, which were *Tygris* and *Euphrates*: *Strabo* reports it was antiently called *Aramenia,* or *Aramia*; and the Name *Aram* was changed into *Syria* by *Syrus,* before *Moses,* saith *Eusebius.* Part of it is called *Ancobaritis,* by *Ptolomy,* being divided by the River *Chaboras,* saith *Junius.*

Uz or *Hus,* *Aram's* Eldest Son, built *Damascus,* saith *Josephus, Jerom,* and *Lyra.* It hath *Jordan* West, Mount *Seir* East, *Edrai* South, and *Damascus* North, in the East part of *Traconitis,* and adjoining to *Basan,* where *Job* the Son of *Hus,* the Son of *Nahor* dwelt ; full of petty Kings in the days of *Jeremy,* 25. 20.

Hal, Aram's Second Son, Father of the *Armenians,* saith *Jerom* ; but *Junius* placeth him in the *Palmerian* Desarts,

Sect. 1.
Sect. 3.

Defarts, by *Euphrates*; where *Ptolomy* places the City *Cholle.* *Gether,* the Third Son fet down in *Caffiotis* and *Seleucis,* and is feated where *Ptolomy* places the City *Gindarus.*

Mefech, the Fourth Son fet down North of *Syria,* tween *Silicia* and *Mefopotamia,* near the Mount *Mafius.* Thefe Plantations can no other ways be known, than by this probability: The Fathers having large Regions, planted their own Children in them for mutual Comfort, 'till Ambition bred expulfion of Natives; and that every Man began to defire a diftinct place, and difliked to live in Common.

Phaleg, Son of *Heber,* in whofe time fell the divifion of Tongues, which the *Hebrews* refer to his Death, *Anno* 340 after the Flood; for at his Birth, *Anno* 101, there could be no multitude to divide. They fay farther, that *Heber* gave *Phaleg* his name by Prophefy, forefeeing the divifion to come. But *Heber* might, without Prophecy, forefee the divifion of Families would grow upon the encreafe of the World; befides, *Phaleg* might change his Name upon that occafion, as *Jacob* into *Ifrael,* long before he died. For his death fell in *Ninus's* days, but 12 Years before *Abraham,* whereas the divifion had been long before, and the Multitudes were infinite in *Ninus's* days.

Joctan, Heber's other Son, had thirteen Sons, all inhabiting from *Copux* or *Coas,* a Branch of *Indus,* into the Eaft, faith *Jerom*; but their particular places are uncertain.

Sheba, or *Seba,* one of them may be he of whom *Dionyfius Apher,* writing of Eaft *India,* faith, The *Sabæi* and *Taxili* do dwell in the midft of them. As for the *Sabeans* which fprang of *Chufh,* we found them in *Arabia*; and many will place *Shaba, Abraham's* Grand-Child there, in *Arabia Deferta,* where *Ptolomy* places a City of his Name, whofe Inhabitants pillag'd *Job. Job* 1. 15.

Ophcr, another of *Joctan's* Sons, *Jerom* placeth in

an

an Island of East-*India*; and indeed *Opher* is found a-
mong the *Molucks*. *Ar. Montanus* and *Dieffis* feek
it in *Peru* of *America*; and *Junius* taketh *Barbatia* in
Characene, a Province in *Sufiana* to be it, corrupted
from *Parvaim* to *Barbatia*, As for *Peru*, *Jucatau, &c.*
in *America*, they are late miftaken Names.

Havilah, another of *Joctan*'s Sons, is thought to
Inhabit the Continent of *East-India*, watred by the
River *Ganges*; as the Country of *Havilah* the Son of
Chufh, was watred by *Pifon*, Weft of *Tygris*, or rather to *Shur*. But if the common Opinion of *Jerom*
be true, *Joctan* and his Pofterity fetled about *Mefech*,
or the Hill *Mafius*; between *Cilicia* and *Mefopotamia* : And that thefe Three Sons, or their Iffue, went
afterwards into *East-India*.

As for *Sepher*, a Mountain of the Eaft, as *Jerom*
looks for it in *East-India*, fo *Montanus* in the Weft,
maketh it *Andes* in *America*: But for *Mofes Sepher*,
we find *Sipphora*, placed by *Ptolomy*, on the Eaft
fide of *Mafius*; neither is it ftrange to fay, *Mefopotamia* is in the Eaft, *Numb.* 23. 7. This Order of
Plantation which I have followed, doth beft agree
with the Scripture, Reafon, and Probalities; which
Guides I follow, little efteeming Mens private O-
pinions.

C H A P. IX.

Of the Beginning and Eftablifhment of Go-
verument.

§. 1. GOvernment hitherto in the World, was only Paternity and Elderfhip, from which
the word *Elder* was ufed, as well for Governours as
the Aged ; to fhew that the Wifdom of Years fhould
be in Governours; the firft Government being from
the

the Father to the Elder Son. Hence grew *Segnour* and *Segnourie*, for Lordship and Dominion, which is Puissance in Property and Power; Power having command of Subjects, as Property hath Mastership of Servants. *Cæsar* hath Power to Command whatever a Man possesseth, but Property only in his own. When *Paternal* persuasion grew too weak to resist Inclination to *Evil*, and to Correct it when it grew Habitual ; Necessity, which bindeth all Mortals, made both the Wise and Foolish at once, to perceive, that the Estate of Men would prove more miserable than that of Beasts, if a general Obedience to Order and Dominion did not prevent it; and that licentious Disorder promising *Liberty*, upon Tryal, would prove no less dangerous to all, than an intolerable Bondage. *Necessity* propounds, and *Reason* confirms this Argument : All Nations were persuaded to submit to a *Master* or *Magistrate* in some degree ; which Change was pleasing when compared with former Mischiefs in want of Government. Yet Time brought out therein some Inconveniences, which Necessity also sought to avoid, and thereupon thought upon some equal Rules, to limit *Dominion*, which before was *lawless*. *Laws* being then set for Government, acquired the Title of *Regal* Power or Government ; and want thereof was known to be *Tyrannical* ; the one Ordained by God for his People's good, the other permitted to afflict them. In this Infancy of *Regal* Authority, Princes, *Just* and *Religious*, were esteemed Gods, said *Fabius Pictor*. And though Necessity and Reason seem Authors of Government, yet God kindled this Light in the Minds of Men, and set them a Pattern in the Law of Nature, wherein they see *Bees, Cranes, Deer*, &c. to follow a Leader ; and God, in his Word, taketh it upon him to appoint Government, *Prov.* 8. 15. *Dan.* 2. 21. and 5. 21. *John* 19. 21.

§. 2. What was the Government before the Flood

more than *Paternal*, is uncertain; or from what better kind of publick Government, the Tyranny of that Age did grow. After the Flood, Three forts of Government are found approved. 1ft. The Government by one Ruling by Juft Laws, called *Monarchy*, oppofed to *Tyranny*. 2*dly.* The Government by divers principal Perfons, Eftablifhed by Order, and Ruling by Laws, call'd *Ariftocracy*, oppofed by *Oligarchy*, in Ufurpation of a few. 3. The Government of the People, called *Democracy*, oppofed to *Ochlocracy*, which is a *tumultuous Will* of a confufed Multitude without Law.

　　The Eldeft of every Family at the firft, fet Order to his Iffue, and upon increafe, planted them about him in one Field, of which grew *Villages*; then followed *Society*, by divers Villages, called *Pagus*, Πηγὴ, which is a *Fountain*; for that all thefe *Villages* drank of the fame *Fountain*, like our *Hundreds*. And when Malice, Pride, and Emulation fet one Race againft another, Men joined divers Villages, which had Banks and Ditches for defence, calling it *Oppidum*, as oppofed to their Enemies : *Urbs, ab Orbe*, a Circuit firft made with a Plough, faid *Varro* ; which word was firft ufed for the Walls and Buildings, as *Civitas* for the Inhabitants, but were after confounded; yet every Inhabitant is not properly a *Citizen*, but he which hath the Freedom and Priviledges of it, and is capable of bearing Rule in it. And as *Cities* grew by Affociation of *Villages*, fo did Common-Weals by Affociation of *Cities*.

Pagus.

　　§.3. The Firft Age after the *Flood*, was called *Golden*, while Ambition and Avarice, *&c.* were in the Blade, Men being more plain, fimple, and contented; yet in refpect of Government, they were as the following Ages, in which as good Kings made *Golden times*, fo the contrary; yea, Princes Beginnings are commonly *Golden*, in which their Game is commonly fmoothly plaid, but Time fhrinks their Hearts, and

　　　　　　　　　　　　　　　　　fmall

ſmall Errors at firſt, breed greater; as it is alſo in e-
very Man's Life, his Youth is *Golden,* which when
Time hath eaten up, and bred ſuch alteration, we
praiſe what is paſt. It is the Vice of our Malignity
to extol the paſt, and loath the preſent; ſuch inquire
not wiſely, ſaid *Eccleſiaſticus.* Our Anceſtors have, we
and our Children will make the ſame Complaints;
and what is *new* ſhall be *old,* ſaith *Arnobius.* The
Virtue of Kings (next after God) produc'd their
Crowns, and the Peoples Love ſo purchas'd, kept
them on their Heads.

§. 4. From this beginning of *Regality* grew *Nobi-*
lity; Princes chuſing by the ſame Rule of *Virtue,*
Men to aſſiſt them; which Honour ſucceeded not
by *Blood,* but *Virtue,* which is true *Nobility,* the
note of one Excelling another in Virtue; and ſhould
bind *Nobility* not to degenerate. As for Riches,
Power, Glory, &c. they do no more define *Nobi-*
lity, than bare Life defines a Man. *Honour* is the
Witneſs of Virtue and well-doing; and true *Nobi-*
lity is the continuance of it in a Family; ſo that
where Virtue is extinguiſhed, they are like painted
Images, worſhipped by the Ignorant, for Chriſt, our
Lady, and other Saints. Flowers not manured,
turn to *Weeds,* and the pureſt Fountain running
through a filthy Soil, is ſoon Corrupted. Race
and Linage is but the *Matter,* Virtue and well de-
ſerving of a Common-wealth, is the *Form* of true
Nobility, which being found in Poſterity, over-weigh-
eth our proper Honour acquired by our own Virtue;
but if Virtue be wanting to *Nobility* by diſcent, then
Perſonal acquired Nobility is to be preferred without compariſon, for that by Deſcent may be in a very Villain. There is a third *Nobility,* which is in
Parchment, purchaſed by Silver, or Favour, being
Badges of Affection, which when Princes change,
they could wiſh they were blotted out. But if we
had as much Senſe in our denegeration in Worthi-
neſs,

ness, as we have of Vanity in deriving our selves from such Parents, we shou'd perceive such Nobility to be our Shame.

CHAP. X.

Of Nimrod, Belus, *and* Ninus.

§. 1. NIMROD, the Sovereign after the Flood, was generally held a *Tyrant :* But *Melancton,* and *Onomasticum Theologicum* judge otherwise. And it seemeth, that his leading this Troop to *Shinar,* was rather given him, than Usurped, seeing it is not Recorded that *Noah,* or any of the Sons of his Body came with him, or were in that presumptuous Action. Some Ancients conceive *Suphne* and *Joctan* were also Leaders ; but joyned not in that unbelieving Attempt, and therefore lost not their Language.

§. 2. *Nimrod, Belus* and *Ninus,* were different Persons, though *Eusebius* and *Jerom* confound the two first ; and *Augustine* makes *Belus* King of *Babylon,* which Argueth him to be *Nimrod. Mercator,* with less probability confounds *Nimrod* and *Ninus,* out of *Clemens. Diodorus Siculus* Reports that *Ninus* subdued *Babylon,* which perhaps had Rebelled upon setling the Empire at *Ninive,* which was also in *Shinar.*

§. 3. *Nimrod,* not *Assur,* Built *Ninive,* as *Junius* hath rendered *Moses*'s Text agreeable to Reason and Sense, though Writers differ. That *Assur* Built it, greeth not with *Moses*'s Order, who especially intending the Story of the *Hebrews,* first handleth the Birth of *Noah*'s other Sons, beginning with *Japhet,* proceeding with *Cham,* and lastly with *Shem,* not intermingling one with the other, till he had set down a brief of all Three. In the Narration of *Cham* he makes a distinct Discourse of *Nimrod* and his Brethren, being to speak after at large of *Babels* Confusion by it self,

to

to shew us the Founder of the place, and of the Empire, which first over-ruled all the rest. As for the *Assyrian* Kingdom, it arose from the *Babylonian*, according to *Junius*: So *Calvin* before followeth *Epiphanius. Jerom, Cyril, Methodius* and *P. Comestor*, with *Cedrenus*, took *Assur, Gen.* 10. 11. to be *Nimrod's* Son, as doth *Torniellus* of late: But *Rab. Maurus* understood it as *Junius*. Yet *Calvin* contrary to *Junius* and himself, objecting *Esay* 23. 13. (than which no place more difficult) to prove *Assur* founded the *Chaldean*, much more the *Assyrian* Empire. But the City of the *Chaldeans* founded, and after destroyed by the *Assyrians*, may with good probability be understood of *Ur*, called *Urcha* by *Ptolomy*, *Chaldeopolis* by the *Greeks*, and *Cameria* by *Hecateus*. This *Ur* stood upon the chief stream of *Euphrates*; by which it passed into the *Persian* Gulf, though now it is stopped and runneth into *Tigris*, of which stoppage *Niger* and *Pliny* speak. This City then had Trade with *Tyrus*, and was a Port Town: By which the *Sabeans* sent Commodities to *Babylon*, and so to *Tyre*. This *Ur* founded by *Shem's* Son *Assur*, was afterwards destroyed by the *Assyrians*, which God fore-seeing, sent away *Abraham* from thence. That the Founder differs from *Assur* the destroyer, is agreeable to the Truth and circumstances. For thus *Seth's* Posterity which followed *Assur*, being Planted at *Ur*, were separated from the Idolatrous *Chushits*. And if *Sem's* Son *Assur* founded *Ninive*; how left he it to *Ninus* Son of *Belus*, and Husband of *Semiramis?*

§. 4. *Nimrod*, called *Saturn* by *Julian Africanus*, established the *Babylonian* Monarchy, which he inlarged into *Assyria*: Where he Founded *Ninive* and other Cities, which his Son *Belus* finished, who after *Nimrods* 114 Years Reign succeeded, and spent much time in draining the Marshes of *Babel*, and began

with

with *Sabbatius* in *Armenia*, and *Scythia Saga*, which *Ninus* finished.

§. 5. *Ninus's* days might well afford many Kingdoms, if we confider the order of their departing from *Babel* according to their Kindred, every Family following the chief thereof, whom Nature and Neceffity taught the reft to fubmit unto; and who took opportunity from Time and *Nimrod's* examples to exercife Regal Authority. *Belus*, who fucceeded *Nimrod*, found *Sabatius* King of *Armenia* and *Scythia*, able to refift him, whom I take to be *Tanais* in *Ju-ftine.* As for his *Vexoris*, *Reineccius* hath judicioufly taken to be *Sefoftris* the Great, fome Ages after *Ni-nus.* *Belus* in common accompt Reigned 65 Years.

§. 6. *Belus*, I judge to be a Name, rather given by *Ninus*, for Honour to his Father, than taken by him. *Cyrill* calls him *Arbelus*; and faith he was the firft that would be called God. *Bel*, fay the Learned, fignifying the Sun in *Chalde*, and there Worfhipped for God : And many words in Scripture grew from it, *Bel*, *Baal*, *Belzebub*, *Baalim*, which Name was given to God, till upon abufe he forbad it. The firft *Idolatry* grew from hence, &c. The Old, the moft Ancient of every Family, and Kings which Founded Cities, were called *Saturns*, their Sons *Jupiters*, and Valiant Nephews *Hercules*.

§. 7. Image-Worfhip began from *Belus* in *Babel,&c.* Schoolmen fhift off this fearful Cuftom ftrangely. For feeing the very Workman-fhip is forbidden, how can the heart of a wife Chriftian satisfie it felf with the diftinction of *Douleia*, and *Latrua*, and *Hyperdou-leia*, which can imply but a difference of Worfhip; and it is moft ftrange, that Learned Men do ftrain their Wits to defend what Scripture oftentimes ex-prefly forbids, and Curfes the practicers. And where they fay, the Prophets condemn Heathen Idols only, it is manifeft *Mofes* fpake of the Living God, faying, *You faw no Image when the Lord fpake to you in* Horeb.

Bafil

Basil forbids us to imagine any Form of God, left we limit him in our Minds; what Presumption then is it, to put him under the Greasy Pensil of a *Painter*, or the rusty Tool of a *Carver?* *Rome* for 170 Years by *Numa's* Law, held it impiety, till *Tarquin*, *Priscus*, and *Varro*, condemned it, as *Augustin* shews: So *Seneca, Sybil, Sophocles*. And though *Papists* say, that Heathen Images are instead of Letters; yet as Heathen Pictures proved notorious Idols, so those Stocks, Stones, *&c.* called Pictures of Christ, our Lady, *&c.* were by the Ignorant, not only Worshipped, but thought to live. It is safest then for Christians to believe Gods Commandments directly against Images, and that which the Prophets and St. *Paul* speak plainly and convincingly.

§. 8. *Ninus* the first Idolater, an Invader of others, and publick Adulterer: Of whom nothing is certain which is written; for *Berosus* who chiefly followed him in the *Assyrian* Succession from *Nimrod* to *Ascalodius*, in the days of *Joshua*, is disproved by many. *Ctesias*, who lived with *Cyrus* the Younger, a gross flatterer of Princes, speaks of incredible numbers in *Ninus* and *Semiramis's* Wars. He, with the help of *Aricus* King of *Arabia*, subdued *Syria*, *Barzanes* of *Armenia*, and *Zoroaster* of *Bactria*, at his second Expedition, by the Valour of *Semiramis*, whom he took from *Menon* her Husband, who for Grief drowned himself.

CHAP. XI.

Of Ninus, Semiramis, *and* Belus.

§. 1. N I N U S finished *Ninive*, as *Semiramis* did *Babel*, begun by *Nimrod*: *Ninive*, Four Hundred Forty Furlongs in Circuit; the Wall an Hundred

dred Foot high, and had One Thousand Five Hundred Towers; yet *Semiramis* exceeded him in *Babylon.*

§. 2. *Ninus* Dyed after 52 Years Reign, *Anno Mundi* 2019. *Plutarch* Reports he gave *Semiramis* one days absolute Rule, as she desired; in which she commanded his Death. She, saith *Justin,* was so like *Ninias* her Son, as that she took upon her to Personate him; but it is highly improbable, considering she Reigned 42 Years, and used her own Name.

§. 3. *Semiramis,* as to her Parentage and Education is variously Reported, but not determined by any Author.

§. 4. Her *Indian* Expedition, if *Ctesias* were worthy of Credit, would yet burthen any Mans faith to believe she had Three Millions of Foot, One of Horse, Two Hundred Thousand Charets and Camels Mounted. All which Power perished with her, by the hand of *Stenobates.*

§. 5. *Belus*'s Temple Built by her Four Square, a Mile high by Eight Ascents, each a Furlong high, and of lesser Circuits, on whose top the *Chaldean* Priests observed the Stars. Many take the Ruins of it, made by *Xerxes,* for *Nimrod*'s Tower, *&c.* See *Pyramids* of *Egypt.*

THE

THE
HISTORY
OF THE
WORLD.

BOOK II. Part I.

FROM

Abraham's Birth, to the Destruction of *Solomon*'s Temple, which was, 1525 Years.

CHAP. I.

Of the time of Abraham's *Birth, and Order of the* Assyrian *Empire.*

NINEAS, or *Zameis*, succeeded *Semiramis* in the Empire; altogether Effeminate and unlike to Conquer *Bactria*, as *Berosus* reports, contrary to *Diodorus*, *Justinus*, *Orosius*, and all others. He changed Governours Yearly out of Jealousie of them.

F 2 *Arrius*

Arrius succeeded, whom *Suidas* calls *Thuras*: He only reduced the Revolted *Bactrians*. *Aralius* succeeded, sumptuous in Jewels, and the Inventer of some Warlike Engines. *Baleus Xerxes* succeeded. The Date and Term of these *Assyrian* Kings Reigns, are best found out by the times of *Abraham*, and his Posterity, set down by Scriptures, which are only void of Errors, whereto all other Writings are subject : No marvel then, if in the Ancient Affairs, History want assurance, said *Plutarch*.

Abraham's Birth Year is therefore forc't to be ascertained ; all agree it was in the 43*d* of *Ninus* ; but the Disagreement between *Chronologers* is about the Year after the Flood, in which he was Born. *Archilochus de Temporibus* in *Annius*, maketh but 250 Years from the Flood to *Ninus*, whereto add 43, which make 293 Years at *Abraham's* Birth : Others do accompt 352 from the Flood to *Abraham*. In this Labyrinth and unresolved Question, I chuse rather the scandal of Novelty, than sluggishly to proceed in that easie way of Ancient mistaking, seeing to be Learned in many Errours, or to be ignorant in all things, hath little advantage of each other.

§. 2. *Arguments for the First Date of* 293. §. *First*, they Argue from Scripture. *Secondly*, from Authority of *Josephus*, *Augustine*, *Beda*, *Isidore*, and others. *First*, The Scripture is *Gen.*11.26. when *Abraham* is first Named the Worthiest, and Son of the Promise ; therefore First-born. *Secondly*, *Moses* respected, the History of *Abraham*, not *Nahor*. *Thirdly*, If *Abraham* were not the First-born, his Birth is uncertain. *Fourthly*, Unprobable ; *Terah* had a Child at 130 Years of Age.

§. 3. *Answer to the Objections.* §. Leaving what Divines have Answered ; to scan this Question, we are to consider, whether *Abraham* made two Journies from *Charran* unto *Canaan* ; the former before ; the latter after his Fathers Death, as some conceive
upon

upon what is said, *Heb.* 11. 3. Againſt this fancy, *Martyr Stephen* Witneſſeth, that God brought him into the Land after his Father was Dead. This can be no other than that of which *Moſes* writ, *Gen.* 12. as *Beza* proveth on *Act.* 7. 2. *&c.* For as *Stephen* had none of whom to Learn the Story of *Abraham's* Life, but *Moſes*; ſo he would not give ſo great a ſcandal to the *Jews*, therein to diſagree with *Moſes.*

Secondly, Conſider the Journey from *Charran* to *Canaan,* diſtant Three Hundred *Engliſh* Miles, unknown to him, and tedious, over Mountains and Deſarts, which he muſt paſs three times in two Journies, and ſo make Nine Hundred Miles ; beſides his Travel from *Ur* to *Charran,* as much more. And conſider the Train *Abraham* had with him, *Gen.* 12. 5. which ſhew no inclinations of returning to Dwell at *Charran,* till his Fathers Death, as 'tis plain, *Act.* 7. 4. when alſo by their account, *Abraham* muſt be about 135 Years Old, and *Iſaac* alſo muſt be about 35: When he might well have Married him, and not ſend 5 Years after thereabout on ſuch a Journey : Neither can this Opinion agree with that which *Abraham's* Servant Reported to *Laban,* touching his Maſter, which he could not be ignorant of, if he had been ſo lately there ; *Moſes* hath carefully ſet down all *Abraham's* Journies, moſt of them of leſs importance than this ; neither can any reaſon be given, why *Abraham* did return this ſecond time to *Charran,* but only to ſupport their Opinions.

§. 4. To the Objection of *Terah's* Age unfit for a Child, as *Abraham* was at One Hundred, *Gen.* 18. 11. it is hardly worth anſwering ; but if they conſider *Sarah's,* the wonder was in her own diſability, not *Abraham's,* who had divers Sons 37 Years after ; yea many Ages after, that *Boaz, Obed,* and *Jeſſe,* Begat Sons at 200 Years, or there about.

§. 5. To the Objection of making *Abraham's* Age uncertain, and ſo the ſucceeding Times : I Anſwer, *A-*

braham's

braham's Age is as certain as any other from his Father's death, as if his Birth had been dated. For as St. *Stephen* tells us, his departure followed his Father's death, so *Moses* recordeth his Age to be 75 Years, and his Father's 205 at his Death. To the Objection, that *Moses* respected not *Nahor* and *Haran*, to set out their Age, as he did *Abraham*'s; I Answer, There were great Reasons to respect them also, considering the Church of God was to spring out of them by *Abraham, Isaac,* and *Jacob*'s Marrying with them. And though they had Worshipped strange God's, as *Terah* himself, *Jos.* 24. Yet after *Abraham*'s being called, their willing departure with him from their Country and ordinary reverend Speeches of *Jehova,* prove they were no *Infidels,* and without Faith, *Gen.* 24. 31, 50. I dare not therefore pronounce them out of the Church, who, I am sure were in the Faith.

§. 6. Abraham's *being first named, proveth him not the Eldest :* §. If in Scripture it appear not that God made especial choice of the First-born, as it is in *Seth, Isaac, Jacob, Juda, David,* &c. the being first named can prove no Birth-right. *Shem* is first named among the Sons of *Noah,* whereof, said *Augustine,* Order of Nativity is not here respected, but signification of future Dignities, in *Gen.* 25. And he rather judged *Abraham* the Youngest of the Three. *Piety,* saith he, *or rather Divine Election, which draweth with it Piety and the Fear of God, gave precedence to* Shem *among the Sons of* Noah, *and to* Abraham *among the Sons of* Terah.

Again, *Moses* testifies *Abraham* was 75 Years old when he left *Charran* : *Stephen* saith it was after *Terah*'s death; at 83, he rescued *Lot* ; at 86, *Ismael* was born; and *Isaac* at 100, and all in *Canaan.* But if he begat *Abraham* at 70, *Abraham* must be 135 Years old when he entred *Canaan, &c.* Moreover, by this Accompt, *Isaac* must be 35 years Old, and

Ismael

Ismael 49. at *Terah*'s death, and Born in *Mesopotamia*, contrary to Scripture. Thirdly, by this reckoning, *Terah* should be but 145 Years Old at his Death, when *Abraham* was 75. Fourthly, *Sarah* being within Ten Years of *Abraham* her Unkle, *Haran* her Father being his younger Brother, must beget her at Nine Years Old, which Reason *Lyra* useth. The like Reason is taken from the Age of *Lot*, the Son of *Haran*, called an Old Man at *Abrahams*'s Eighty third year.

§. 7. *The Conclusion, noting the Authors on both sides.* §. It agreeth with Scripture, Nature, Time, and Reason, that *Haran* was *Terah*'s Eldest Son. *Augustin* was herein uncertain, and what he saith in his *City of God*, lib. 16. 15. is answered in his 52d Question on *Gen*. And as he follow'd *Josephus*, so *Isidore* and *Beda* follow him. The *Hebrews*, and generally the *Romanists* following the first Opinion, allow but 292 Years from the Flood to *Abraham*. But *Theodoret* and divers later, *Beroald, Codornan, Beucer, Calvin, Beza, Junius*, &c. hold *Abraham* begotten in the 130th Year of *Terah*. *Scaliger, Seth, Calvisius*, &c. to the contrary, call it *Heresy* in Chronology; *Bucholcreus, Chitreus, Functius*, and others, follow them; yet *Torniellus* in his Annals confutes them. But if we advisedly consider the state of the World in *Abraham*'s days, we shall rather increase the time from the Flood to *Abraham*, as the *Septuagint* did to 1072; than shorten it to 292: For such paring of Time to the quick, draws the Blood of the Story, if Scripture's Testimony were not supreme. Seeing then we know the World was so peopled, and Kingdoms so furnished with Cities of State and Strength, more time is required for it than many imagine, &c.

§. 8. *The* Assyrians *Times order'd by* Abraham's *History.* §. Thus *Abraham*'s Birth being 352 Years after the Flood, and so the 2009th Year of the

World, bringeth *Ninus*'s 43 to the fame date of
the 352 Years, we muft confider what probably
was fpent before the coming to *Shinar*, admitting
Chus were born the Year after the Flood.   His
youngeft Son *Nimrod*, Founder of the Empire,
born after *Dedan* Son of *Raamah*, the fourth Son of
Chus, could not, according to the ordinary courfe
of thofe Times, be efteemed Born, 'till 65 Years
after *Chus*, allowing 30 Years to *Chus*, before his
firft Son, and 30 Years to *Raama*, Father of *Dedan*,
born before *Nimrod*, and 5 Years for his five Elder
Brethren.   Allow 60 Years after for two Generations before their fetting forth before *Shinar*, and fix
Years for their Travail with Wives, Children, and
Cattel out of the Eaft, through over-grown Countries and Mountains.   Thus 131 Years are fpent before *Babel* is taken in hand; the 221 Years which remain of 352, are divided, to *Ninus* 42 before *Abraham*'s Birth, 65 to *Belus*, and 114 to *Nimrod*, yet
this maketh *Nimrod* in all, not above 180 Years old,
which was not much for that Generation, *Gen.* 11.
3. in which they lived; yea, 400 Years.   *Ninus* lived 9 Years after, and *Semiramis* fucceeded 42 Years,
when *Abraham* was 52 Years old.   *Ninias*, or *Zameis* fucceeded 38; in whofe 23d Year, *Abraham* at
75 years old, came to *Canaan*; and 10 years after,
Abraham over-threw *Amraphel* King of *Shinar*, which
may feem to have been *Ninias*, in whofe 33d year it
happen'd; though the Reafons to the contrary are
not eafily anfwer'd.

   §. 9. Amraphel, *King of* Shinar, *probably, was* Ninias.   §. *Ninias* was King of *Babylon* at that time,
in the 85th year of *Abraham*.   It is objected, that
Chedorlaomer was greater now than *Amraphel*, who
therefore was not like to be *Ninias*.   To this it may
be anfwered, under *Ninias*, the *Babylonian* Command
was fallen, and the *Perfian* his Neighbour King of
Elam was enlarged.

                              §. 10. Arioh

§. 10. Arioch *King of* Ellaſſar. §. This Country can neither be *Pontus* nor *Helleſpontus*, as ſome think; being ſo far out of the way to be drawn by the *Perſian*; who little needed to ſeek ſuch aid againſt ſuch petty Kings, which had not in all, ſo much ground as *Middleſex*; of which ſort *Canaan* had 33 deſtroyed by *Joſhua*. And the whole Country theſe four Kings ſubdued, was no more than the two little Provinces of *Traconitis* or *Baſan*; and the Region of the *Moabites*. *Stephanus*, a *Grecian* Coſmographer *de Vrbibus*, findeth *Ellas* in the Border of *Cœloſyria*; and *Hierom* calls it the City of *Arioch*. This City was alſo in the Borders of *Arabia*, of which *Arioch* indeed was King, and Confederate with the *Aſſyrian* Kings, as in *Ninus*'s Life, &c.

§. 11. *Tidal* King of *Nations*. §. There were divers petty Kingdoms adjoining to *Phœnicia* and *Paleſtine*, as *Palmirenia*, *Batanea*, *Laodicene*, *Apamena*, *Chalcidice*, *Caſſiotis*, *Chalibonitis*, having *Meſopotamia* on the *North*, and *Arabia* on the *Eaſt*. It is probable theſe were joined together under *Tidal*.

§. 12. *Chedorlaomer* the chief of the Four. §. He was not King of *Aſſur*, and the other three Vice-Roys, as *Pererius* judgeth; for *Moſes* never uſeth *Elam* for *Aſſyria* or *Babylon*. Neither do I believe the *Aſſyrian* or *Babylonian* Kingdoms were very large at this time. 1. From Example; Things haſtily ſet up with violence, laſt not, as *Alexander*'s Conqueſts, and *Tamberlain*'s, whoſe Empires dyed with them; neither had they time to review what they had done, God adjoining ſhort life to aſſwage Fury; and Nature cares leaſt for what ſhe doth in haſt. *Ninus* perſued boundleſs Dominion with Violence; *Semiramis* exceeded him, &c. 2. *Ninias* having changed Nature and Condition with his Mother, preferring Pleaſure and Eaſe before Honour and Greatneſs; as he indured his Mother's Reign, ſo wanted he Spirit to maintain what ſhe left him, a-

gainſt

gainſt Neighbouring Princes, whoſe Wounds and Wrongs from his Parents, put them in mind to cure the one, and revenge the other. 2. And it was God's will, when he would impoſe that long and tedious Journey upon *Abraham*, that the Countreys ſhould be in Peace, through which he waudred ; to which end thoſe Millions of Warriours and Engins periſhed with *Semiramis*, to make the Recovery of loſt Liberty the more eaſy. Laſtly, Hiſtories report, that *Arrius*, who ſucceeded *Ninias*, recovered *Baɑria*, and *Caſpia*, and *Baleus* or *Xerxes* reduced the reſt, even to *Egypt* ; which argueth their former Revolt.

§. 13. Conſent of Writers almoſt forceth us to think as I have delivered, touching the Four Kings; yet if we take them rather for Four petty Kings, which in that ſluggiſh Reign of *Ninias* had gathered Colonies out of thoſe Four Countries, and Planted themſelves elſewhere, we ſhall remove ſome difficulties. For if *Chedorlaomer* were King of *Perſia* it ſelf beyond *Babylon*, what a Journey were it to come ſo far and gather ſuch Forces which muſt paſs ſo great Countries as *Aſſyria*, *Chaldea*, *Meſopotamia*, *Syria*, and part of *Arabia*, to Conquer five ſmall Cities, and leave all the reſt of *Canaan*; yea, to come in Perſon, and that the ſecond time. But the Scripture maketh this Invaſion no great matter, but as matching four Kings to five, as if the five were not ſo unequally matched, though petty Kings, as of neceſſity they had been, if theſe four had been abſolute Kings of the Kingdoms, whoſe Names they bear. If then the former Conjectures cannot agree to the Text, to the Authority whereof, all Human Reaſon muſt ſubſcribe, let the received Opinion ſtand, that *Amraphel* was *Ninias*, who was become inferiour to *Chedorlaomer* of *Perſia*. From the *Aſſyrian*, the Hiſtory of *Abraham*, leadeth us to the *Egyptian* Kingdom, then alſo flouriſhing.

CHAP.

C H A P. II.

, Of the Kings of Egypt, from Cham to the
Delivery of the Iſraelites.

T H E *Kings of* Egypt, *'till* Iſrael's *Deliverance*;
and the cauſes of the uncertainty of the Hiſtory.
§. *Cham,* after *Babel's* Confuſion, having known
Egypt's Fertility, Planted it *Anno* 191 after the Flood.
Oſiris ſucceeded *Anno* 352. *Typhon,* or *Hercules,*
Anno 603. *Orus,* 620. *Seſoſtris* the Great, 735. *Se-*
ſoſtris the Blind, 786. *Buſiris,* or *Oris* 2d. *Anno* 782.
Acencbere, or *Thermutis,* or *Meris,* 820. *Ratboris*
832. *Chencbreſe* 841, drowned. *Auguſtin,* a diligent ſearcher of Antiquities, omitted the Succeſſion of *Egyptian* Kings, finding no certainty of them,
through the Ambition of their Prieſts, who, to mag-
nify the Antiquities, which they only kept, filled the
Records with Romances and Names of Kings, which
never Reigned.   Other good Authors were over-
credulous of what they found ſo Recorded, Publiſhed the ſame in their own Names.   Of theſe, *An-*
nius finding ſome Fragments, and adding what he
would, is no farther to be Credited, than where
approved Writers Confirm his Aſſertion.   Herein
the Old Chriſtian Writers follow *Euſebius* ; but the
Modern, *Annius* and Prophane Authors; follow
Diodorus, *Herodotus,* &c.
  §. 2. *Cham began his Reign in* Egypt, *after the*
Flood, *Anno* 191. §. This is gathered from the
Dyanaſties of *Egypt,* whoſe 16th began in the 43d.
year of *Ninus*: The 12 firſt under their 12 great
Gods, laſted 84 Years, ſeven a-piece; the 13 indured 14 years ; the 14 laſted 26 ; the fifteen was 37,
which three laſt were under three younger Gods :
All the 75 added together, make 161 years ; which
being

being deducted out of 352, the remainder is 191, the beginning of Government there, after *Cham*'s arrival. The same also is probable from their coming to *Babel*, which being after the Flood, *Anno* 131, and Forty years, according to *Glicas*, spent in Building, we can allow no less than Twenty years, for the slow passing such a Company through such a difficult long way; which Sums being added, make up 191 years, when the first *Dynasty* began; for to begin them sooner, were either to plant *Egypt* as soon as *Babel*, or with *Mercator*, to make them before the Flood; which their number, exceeding the number of those long-liv'd Fathers, will not admit.

§. 3. *The Dynasties of Egypt were not absolute Kings, but Vice-Roys under Kings.* §. The probability of this will appear by the custom of Kings governing by Great Men, as of old, the Kings of *France*, by the Master of the Palace; the *Turk* by a Grand *Visier*; the *Philistin* Kings which came out of *Egypt*, had a Captain, as *Abimelek* had *Phicol*; the Kings of Israel, as *Saul* had *Abner*; *David* had *Joab*. And *Cham*'s lewd disposition to follow Pleasure, might breed the Custom, which continued even to the days of *Joseph*, advanced to the place by *Pharaoh*; from which Example, *William* Arch Bishop of *Tyre* affirms the same Form of Government continued in *Egypt* in his days, when the Sultans govern'd under the *Calif*, as Lieutenants under a King. How these Dynasties succeeded, and how long they continued, is uncertain.

§. 4. *Cham. and Mizraim or Oris.* §. Of *Cham* the Scripture calls that Country the Land of *Ham*, not for being Peopled by his Sons, for so were other Countries, which yet are never so called, but for that himself planted it. *Osiris* called himself the Eldest Son of *Saturn*, as in *Diodorus*, lib. 1. which *Saturn* of *Egypt*, was Grand-father of *Ninus*; as in his Monument. Of *Cham* came the Temple of *Hammon* near *Egypt*: And in *Jerom*'s days the *Egyptians* called their

their Country *Ham*; so *Ortelius* saith out of *Plu-tarch*, that *Egypt* was called *Chemia.* That *Cham* reigned 161 years, is not improbable, considering *Sem* his Brother lived 600 years. *Mizraim* or *Osiris*, according to *Diodor*, succeeded, of whom the Land also took its Name, and by the Natives, is yet called *Mezre*, as *Reineccius* sheweth. How long he Reigned, is hard to determine; but that he began at *Abraham's* Birth is probable, when the *Dynastie* of the *Thebæi*, began according to *Eusebius.*

§. 5. *Osiris* Reign is guessed at by his Son *Lehabim*, or *Hercules Lybeus* his Warring with *Typhon*, and the *Giants*, his Associates in Revenging his Fathers Death. His *Egyptian* Wars he ended, and begun his *Italian*, in the 41 Year of *Baleus* King of *Assyria*, according to *Berosus*, when he left the Kingdom to his Brother *Orus*. To this *Egyptian*, and many other Wars before his *Italian*, *Krentzhemius* alloweth but 6 Years, which draweth *Osiris* Death to the 34th Year of *Belus*, and so makes him Reign 297 Years, and so should end 7 Years after *Israel* came into *Egypt*. This cannot be, for the King under whom *Israel* came, out-lived *Jacob*, and had Reigned from before *Joseph's* standing before *Pharaoh*; yea, we may give 13 Years more of *Joseph's* Bondage to him. This King then could not be *Osiris*, who lived not so long as *Jacob*; nor *Typhon*, nor *Hercules*; but *Orus*, Son of *Osiris*, advanced by *Hercules.*

§. 6. *Typhon*, and *Hercules*, their Reigns are not distinctly defined; only *Orus*, is placed 7 Years after *Osiris* by *Krentzhemius*, and whose Reign seemeth to last 115 Years, and from whose Death, to the *Israelites* Departure are 122 Years.

Sesostris, or *Sesonchosis*, succeeded according to *Scholiast. Apollonii* : He was a great Conquerour in *Asia*, even into *India*, and *Europe* : Whom *Justin* erroniously maketh *Vexoris*, saith *Reineccius*, some Ages after *Ninus.* This *Sesostris*, some think is *Besak*, but

but it is not so, as divers differences in setting out
their Wars do manifest. Whereas after *Orus, Menas*
is Reported by *Herodotus* and *Diodorus. Reineccius* noteth that *Osiris* was so called by way of Dignity.
Krentzhemius probably gathers that *Menas* was *Mercurius, Ter-maximus,* Conquerour, Philosopher, and
Benefactor to Mankind, giving good Laws, and teaching profitable Arts to his Conquered People. After
33 Years he fell Blind, as did *Pherones* his Son,
whom 14 Years after *Orus,* the Second, or *Busiris*
succeeded 75 Years before *Israel's* Departure out of
Egypt.

§. 7. *Busiris,* or *Orus* the Second, whom *Reineccius*
judgeth to have been a new Family, (though according to all Mens computation) he began 5 Years after *Moses's* Birth; yet might he be first Author of
the *Israelites* Misery, Ruling as *Vice-Roy* under the
blind King, whom he might easily draw to that Oppression of Strangers, so to ease the Subjects, and to
win their Favour, to promote his Off-spring to the
Crown which he attained, and held 30 Years, according to *Eusebius.* After him *Thermutis, Pharaoh's*
Daughter, which took *Moses* out of the Water, succeeded. *Eusebius* calls her *Acencris,* but placeth *Ameno-
phis* next before *Busiris. Herodotus,* and *Diodorus,* call
Sesostris Son *Pheron*; so it may be she was his Daughter, who Marrying *Busiris,* Reigned after him 12
Years.

§. 8. *Rathoris,* or *Athoris,* succeeded his Sister 9
Years; and after him, *Chencris,* who perished in the
Red Sea; and *Achencris* succeeded 8 Years, and *Cher-
res* 15, in whose 15 Years, *Epaphus,* Son of *Teligonus,*
Rathoris Brother Reigneth, in the lower *Egypt,* and
Built *Memphis. Epaphus* had *Lybia,* which had *Age-
nor, Belus,* and *Busiris. Belus* had *Amœus,* or *Danæ-
us,* who Reigned 4 Years after *Cherres,* and then by
Egyptus, or *Ramesses,* his Brother expelled, who
Reign

Reigning 68 Years; he had Fifty Sons; *Danæus* had Fifty Daughters: He began the Kingdom of *Argos* in *Greece*.

C H A P. III.

Of Israels *Delivery out of* Egypt.

§. 1. **O**F *Israel's Captivty, and* Moses *Birth.* §. *L. Vives,* on *Augustin,* cites divers Opinions of *Moses* Birth; but to me it is most Probable, that he was Born while *Saphrus,* called *Spherus,* and *Ipherus* Govern'd *Assyria, Orthopolis Cicyonia,* and *Criasus* the *Argives,* and *Sesostris* 2d. the *Egyptians.* For according to *Augustin,* he led *Israel* out of *Egypt* about the end of *Cecrops,* King of the *Athenians*; which falls about the 9th Year of *Ascatades* of *Assyria,* who Ruled 41. *Sparetus,* his Predecessor, 40. *Mamelus,* before him, 30. And *Saphrus,* 20 before: So that from the 19th of *Saphrus,* to the 9th of *Ascatades,* which was the 46th of *Cecrops,* are 80 Years, which was *Moses* Age when he brought *Israel* out of *Egypt.* There being then 64 Years between *Josephs'* Death and *Moses's* Birth, the *Israelites* Oppression seemeth to begin some 8 or 9 Years before *Joseph* Dyed, *Anno Mundi* 2370. *Moses* 80th Year of Age was 2514.

§. 2. *Of the Cities of* Egypt *mentioned in Scripture.* §. *Zoan, Num.* 13. 23. called *Taphnus, Jer.* 2. 43. *&c: Ezek.* 30. The *Septuagint* calls it *Tanis, &c.* This was near *Gosen,* and chief City of the lower *Egypt. On,* or *Heliopolis,* in the South of the lower *Egypt, Gen.* 41. 45: after *Junius:* Here *Onias* Built a Temple for the Jews under *Ptolomy Philopater,* which stood till *Vespasian's* time. *Noph* the City, *Esa.* 19. 13. *Hos.* 9. 6. is called *Moph,* or *Memphis*; by the *Septuagint, Pelusium,* which the

Sep-

Septuagint calls *Sois. Montanus Lebna, Junius Sin. Belbeis* after, now the *Septuagint* calls *Diospolis,* and was afterwards called *Alexandrina,* by *Jerom.*

Moses's Preservation and Education. Pharaoh having by Oppreſſion diſcontented the *Iſraelites,* and then doubting what a Poor Oppreſſed Multitude might be provoked to, by ſuggeſtion of the Devil, reſolved the Slaughter of the Male Children in their Birth, giving Order to all their Midwives, by Two of the Chief of them. But being by their Piety diſappointed, he Commanded all his People to perform his Bloody Decree, which yet his Beloved Daughter finding *Moſes* in an Ark of Reeds in *Nilus,* was ſo far from Executing, that ſhe took him out of the Water, and gave him Princely Education, as her own: Whoſe Excellent Learning teſtified by *Philo* and *Joſephus, Martyr Stephen* Confirmeth.

Leaving *Joſephus's* Fancy of *Moſes* Beſieging *Saba* of *Ethiopia,* which he won by the means of the Kings Daughter, whom he Married, &c. *Moſes* in Reſcuing an *Iſraelite,* having ſlain an *Egyptian,* fled into *Arabia Petrea,* in whoſe Mountainous Deſarts, apart from the Glory of the World, the Glory of God covered him over, being from an Honourable, Adopted Son of a Kings Daughter, turned into the Condition of an humbe Shepherd. In this Country, lying between *Judea* and *Egypt,* he lived 40 Years skilful in the ways of the Wilderneſs, through which he was to lead *Iſrael*; and by exerciſe in a Paſtoral Life, he was prepared to Principality, and perfected his Learning gotten in *Egypt,* by Meditation in the Wilderneſs. From Government of gentle Cattel, Kings are called Shepherds, to teach them to rule Men. *Moſes* being called back into *Egypt,* is Taught a Name, by which he Deſcribes God to the *Hebrews,* ſetting out his ever only *Being:* there being nothing, that hath being of it ſelf

but

but that Eternal One, of whofe *being* all other things are but fhadows. Of all the Ten Plagues, the laft only brought that Tyrant *Pharaob*, to an abfolute fubmiffion, when he began to fear his own Life. The *Pafcbal Lamb* was a Sacrament of our fpotlefs Saviour.

§. 3. *Pharaob* feeing the *Ifraelites* departure, with the Spoil alfo of the *Egyptians*, bethought himfelf, and purfuing them with all his Power, *Exod.* 14. 7. over-took them after Three Days March. And though *Mofes* knew he went out with the mighty Hand of God, yet he neglected nothing, becoming a Wife Man and a Valiant Conductor. So he removed from *Ramafes* in *Gofhen*, whither the difperfed *Hebrews* were gathered as to their Rendezvous, and Marched Eaftward toward *Etham*, and Encamped at *Succotb*, the Fifteenth Day of *Abib*, which thenceforth was accounted the firft Month of their Year, for Religious Occafions, leaving another for Politick, which they diftinguifh from Sacred, in Recording things Tranfacted.

§. 4. *Ifrael* paffing from *Succotb*, kept Mountainous, rough Ground on his left-hand to *Etham*, that *Pharaob*'s Chariots fhould not compafs him. From *Etham*, the next day he Marched *Soutb* Eight Miles, and on the Third day he came to *Pibacboroth*, between the Mountains of *Etham*, on the *Nortb*, and *Baalzepbon* on the *South*, and Encamped upon the wafh of the Sea.

§. 5. *Mofes*, who feared nothing but God himfelf, comforting the fearful Multitude, *Exod.* 14. 13. called on God; and putting in practice his Direction, fafely paffed over the Foord which the Lord had made, and left their ftupified Enemies to the mercilefs Waves, which returned upon them. This Sea, called *Chencrefe*, in which *Pharaob* Perifhed the 16tb Year of his Reign, is commonly called the Red Sea, though of the Colour of other Waters. It

G   feemeth

seemeth to me, that Name grew from the Clifts, Sands, Islands, and much of the Bordering Continent, which being Red, by reflection makes the Water seem Red also. The *Greeks* call it the *Erythrean* Sea, of King *Erythreus*; and for that *Erythros* signifies Red, some think it was so called. The *Portugals* Report that store of red Stones are found in it, on which, store of Red Coral groweth. At *Pibacheroth*, which is from *Ramases*, not above Thirty Miles, the Sea is about Four Miles broad to *Arabia*, where *Moses* passed over, and not at *Elana*: For that part of *Egypt* which is opposite to *Elana*, is from *Ramases* Eighty Miles, which *Moses* with his Multitude, unfit for such Marches, could not pass in three days.

§. 6. This Passage proved Miraculous; and not an Ebb, as the *Egyptians*, and other *Heathens* object; for had it been an Ebb, all that part from *Sues* at the end of the Sea, unto the place of *Moses*'s passage, and further, which exceeded Ten Miles, must have been dry, and so have served *Pharaoh*, and his Men to have fled from the flowing of the Water. Neither could an *East* Wind make an extraordinary Ebb, seeing that Sea lyeth *North*, and *South*. And why should *Moses*, whom they Honoured as a great Captain against the *Ethiopians*; leave this passage over the Mountains, and venture a Foord upon an Ebb, which he knew not whether *Pharoah* would prevent him of? And who will think, that the *Egyptians* were so ignorant of their own Sea and Havens, as to be overtaken in the Ebbing and flowing thereof? *Lastly*, If the ordinary flowing had drowned the *Egyptians*, their Carcases had been carried up to *Sues*, and cast upon the *Arabian* Shore, where the *Hebrews* then lay.

CHAP.

CHAP. IV.

The Israelites *Journey from the* Red Sea *to* Sinai.

§. 1. MOSES having recovered the *Arabian* Banks, proceeded to the Desart of *Arabia Petræa*, called *Sur* : And from thence for want of Water came to *Merah* in *Etham* Desart, which is also called *Sur*, *Exod.* 15. 22. from the Sea Twenty Five Miles ; where he made the bitter Waters sweet, by casting Branches of a Tree therein : A plain Type of our Saviour, who upon the Cross changed the Bitterness of everlasting Death, into the sweetness of Eternal Life. From thence he removed to *Elim* ; which by all probability, was a City, it being so well watered ; of whose Ruins *William Tyre* Reports, *In Bello Sacro*. From thence he returned to the Sea, and so to the Desart of *Zin* ; then to *Daphca*, and next to *Alus*, and so to *Raphidim*.

§. 2. *Of the* Amalekites, Midianites, *and* Kenites, *and of* Jethro. §. The *Amalekites* at *Raphidim*, setting upon the *Israelites*, were overthrown by the Efficacy of *Moses*'s Prayers, which were more prevalent than all the resistance of the Bodies of Men. Here *Jethro*, *Moses* Father in Law, came to him, with his Wife, and Sons. He was a *Kenite*, *Judg.* 4. 11, 17. which was a Nation of the *Midianites*, which came of *Midian*, a Son of *Abraham*, by *Keturah*, 1 *Sam.* 15. with *Gen.* 25. There were others also which bare the same Names, like to spring from *Chus*. *Gen.* 15. 19. As for the *Midianites* which came from *Midian*, the Son of *Abraham*, they were divided into Five Families, *Gen.* 25. 4. of which some were Planted near the Red Sea, with whom *Moses* matched himself, as not corrupted with Idolatry : Others corrupted with the Idolatry of the *Canaanites*, joined

G 2   with

with them, and lived near the River *Zered*, tributary to the *Amorites*, and after their overthrow joyned with *Moab*, and were destroyed by *Moses* for their Practices against *Israel*, *Num.* 22. 31. *Jos.* 13. 21.

§. 3. *When the Law was given.* §. The Twelve Tribes of *Israel* were in the Wilderness of *Sinai*, near the Mountain of *Sinai*, or *Horeb*, which are the same, *Exod.* 3. 1. and 24. 16. though parted in the top in two, of which *Sinai* is highest; but *Horeb* sendeth a fair Spring into the Valley, where now stand two Monasteries, furnished with pleasant Gardens of Fruits and Wine. It was like to be so in *Moses*'s days, who continued thereabout almost a Year, where he had Water, *Exod.* 32. 20. Hither being arrived about the Forty Fifth Day, the First Year, he received the *Law* the Fifthieth Day, and removed the Twentieth Day of the Second Month of the Second Year.

P. Belonius.

CHAP. V.

The Story from Receiving the Law, *to the Death of* Moses.

§ 1. MOSES having Received and Published the Law, and finished the Tabernacle of the Ark, he Mustered the Tribes, to see what number of Men were therein, from 20 Years Old and upward ; over whom, by the Lords direction, he placed Leaders, the most Eminent Men in every Tribe. The whole Army was 603550 able Men for War, *&c.* and was divided into 4 Battalions, of which each contained Three Tribes. The first containing 186400, consisted of Three Regiments. *Juda*, 74600, *Issachar*, 54400, *Zabulon*, 57440, all under the Standard of *Juda*,

who

who held the Vaungard, Marched first, and Quartered at the general Incamping on the *East* side of the Army, as in the chief place. The Second, containing 151450, consisted of *Reuben* the Leader, and *Simeon* and *Gad*. The Third, containing 108100 under *Ephriam*, whom *Manasse* and *Benjamin* followed. The Fourth containing 157600, Led by *Dan*, and followed by *Naphtali*, and *Asher*.

Besides the Twelve Princes of the Twelve Tribes, they had Captains over Thousands, over Hundreds, over Fifties, and over Tens, as appears by the Insurrection against *Moses*.

In the midst of these Four Armies, was the Tabernacle, or Portable Temple, carried, surrounded by the *Levites*; to the service whereof Twenty Two Thousand Persons were Dedicated, of which Eight Thousand Five Hundred and Eighty had peculiar Charge. All these Incamped within the general Armies, next the Tabernacle in Four Quarters. *Moses* Reverend care about the least part of the Tabernacle, did Witness his inward humble Zeal to God. The industry in Framing, curiosity in Working, charge in Provision, observance in Preserving, Solemnity in removing, *&c.* all Ages have in some sort imitated; yet our Age hath bred up many Familists, Anabaptists, Brownists, and other Sectaries, which esteem all Cost bestowed upon the Church wherein God is Worshipped, to be a kind of Popery, *&c.*

§. 2. *The Offering of the Twelve Princes, the Passover, and* Jethro's *Departure*. §. The Twelve Princes Offered Six covered Chariots, and Twelve Oxen for carrying the Tabernacle, which were delivered to the Sons of *Gershom*, and *Merari*: As for the Sanctuary, the *Koathites* bare it on their Shoulders, when it was taken down: Each of the Princes also offered a a Charger, and a Bowl of Silver, and an Incense Cup of Gold; the weight was after the Shekel of the

Sanctuary

Sanctuary, which contained Twenty *Gerahs*, every *Gerah* worth Three-half-pence, Sterling ; after which rate all the Plate came to Four Hundred and Twenty Pound Sterling. The common Shekel was but Ten *Gerahs.* This done, the Passover was Celebrated the Fourteenth of the Second Year, and upon the Twentieth, the Host removed from *Sinai* to *Paran*, Marching in their prescribed Order. At this time, *Jethro* the Father in Law to *Moses*, called also *Hobab*, left *Moses* and returned to *Midian* ; but it seemeth either he, after setting his Country in Order, or his Children, returned and became incorporate with *Israel.*

§. 3. Israel's *Journey from* Horeb *to* Kades. §. In this Journey they murmured for Flesh, and were fed with Quails, even to a Surfeit, of which great numbers Dyed. Then after the First Month, they came to *Hazaroth*, where *Miriam* was smitten with Leprosie ; and so to *Rithma*, near *Kades Barnea*, whence the Spies were sent ; upon whose Return they mutined the Tenth time, which being more Rebellious than all the rest, God punished it accordingly, extinguishing every one of those Seditions, even the whole Multitude that came out of *Egypt*, Two only Excepted. And though the mildest of all Men was earnest with God for their Pardon, yet not one escaped. He spared them Forty Years, till their Children were grown up and Multiplyed ; that in them he might perform his Promise, which was never frustrated.

§. 4. *Of their Return, and unwillingness thereto,* &c. §. *Moses* having related the Commandment of God, touching their Return back toward the Red Sea, they bewailed their Folly too late ; and as it is with Men whom God leaveth to themselves, they wou'd needs amend their former Passionate Murmuring, with a second desperate Contempt. For now, when God forbids with Threats, they will desperately venture their own Destruction, and were repelled, and with Slaughter forced to take their way back to the Sea, as as God Commanded, and came to *Remmoparez*, &c. Their Twenty Fourth Manſion was at *Pharez*, where began the dangerous Inſurrection of *Korah*; for which Offence, and Contempt of God, and his Miniſters, as 14700 Periſhed ſuddenly by Peſtilence, and 250 by Fire ; ſo thoſe Lay-Men, who would Uſurp Eccleſiaſtical Authority, were ſuddenly ſwallowed up alive of the Earth. Form thence the 30th Manſion was at *Jetabata*, where *Adrichomius* maketh a River which runneth into the Sea, between *Midian* and *Aziongaber*. Now though it be Probable there was ſtore of Freſh-water at *Aziongaber*, where *Solomon* furniſhed his Fleets for *Eaſt-India* : And though *Herodotus* mention a great River in *Arabia* the Stony, which he calls *Corys*; yet is *Adrichom* deceived in this, as in many other things. For it was at *Punon* that thoſe Springs are ſpoken of, which in *Deut.* 10.7. is alſo called *Jetabata*, a Land of running Waters, which by probability falls into the River *Zared*, next adjoyning ; whereas that way is very long to *Aziongaber*. Beſides, *Belonius* reports of divers Torrents of Freſh-waters, in thoſe Sandy parts of *Arabia*, which running a few Miles, are drunk up in the Sands. From *Jetabata*, they came to *Hebrona*, and after *Aziongaber*, called *Beronice* by *Joſephus*, and *Eſſia* by *Jerom*, which as yet, was not in the command of *Edom*, as after in *Solomon's* days.

§. 5. From *Aziongaber* they removed to *Zin*, *Kades* or *Beeroth*, where *Miriam* dyed. Then they came to Mount *Hor*, where they murmured for Water, and where *Aaron* dyed, and *Eleazer* his Son ſucceeded.

§. 6. *Iſrael* leaving the way by *Edom*, after they had compaſſed the *South*, they turned to the *North*, toward the Wilderneſs of *Moab*, leaving *Edom* on the *Weſt*. When *Arad*, King of the *South-Canaanites*, thinking they would come by him while they lay at *Hor* ; having had his Forces ready upon his Borders,

Borders, made out into the Defart, before *Israel* was
removed, and fet upon fuch part of the Army as
lay for his Advantage, and took fome Prifoners. It
is probable, that either this *Arad*, or his Predeceffor,
had joined before with *Amalek*, and worfting
thofe Mutineers, were thereupon incouraged to
this Attempt. As for the Overthrow which is reported, *Num.* 21. to be given them by *Israel*, it is
rather to be underftood of what was done after by
Josua, than now by *Moses*. For had *Moses* given
them this Overthrow and deftroyed their Cities, he
would never have left the *South* of *Canaan*, once entred by him, to wander about *Edom* and *Moab*, and
to feek a new Paffage: Neither could *Israel* have
caufe to Murmur the next day for Bread: Or been
weary of the Way, if they had fo lately taken the
Spoil of *Arad*'s Cities. Yea, they would rather have
mutined againft *Moses*, for leaving fuch an Entrance
into the intended Conqueft; and to lead them back
into the Defarts, which had confumed them. They
murmured prefently upon their leaving *Hor*, when
they came to *Phunon*, croffing the way to *Aziongaber*
through *Moab* to *Cœlosyria*; and here the Brazen
Serpent was erected. From thence they proceeded,
as in the Holy Story, and fo came to *Diblathaim*;
Whence *Moses* fent to *Sehon* King of the *Amorites*,
to defire a Paffage through his Country, which he
denyed.

§. 7. *Of the Book of the Lord's Battels, and other loft
Books.* §. *Junius* underftanding thereby, no fpecial
Book; and *Vatablus* doubts. *Siracides* refers it to *Joshua*,
who fought the Lord's Battles, *cap.* 46. But it feemeth probable there was fuch a Book loft, as many others,
whereto reference is often made, as *Jof.* 10. 13. and
2 *Sam.* 1. 18. and 2 *Chron.* 33. 18. and 2 *Chron.* 9.
29. and 12. 15. and 20. 34. 1 *Kings* 4. 32, 33. *E-*
noch's Books, *&c.*

§. 8. *Of* Mofes *fparing* Lot's *Iffue.* §. *Moab* at
this

this time inhabited the *South* of *Arnon*, having loft the better fide, which the *Amorites* won from *Vatablus* the Predeceffor of *Balac.* What therefore *Moſes* found in the Poffeffion of *Moab*, as alſo of *Ammon*, he might not attempt ; but what the *Amorites* had taken from them. The *Emims* and *Zamzummims*, Giantly Nations, had formerly dwelt there, as the *Anakims* in *Canaan* ; but *Moab* and *Ammon* deſtroyed them. *Sibon* proud of his Conqueſt againſt *Moab*, preſumed againſt *Iſrael*, and loſt All. *Og* King of *Baſan*, or *Traconitis*, an *Amorite*, was alſo deſtroyed, and his Sixty Walled Towns taken by *Jaer*, a Son of *Manaſſes*.

§. 9. The *Midianites* with the *Moabites* practiſe againſt *Iſrael*, and draw them to *Idolatry* ; for which God deſtroyed 24000 with the *Peſtilence.* The third time of numbring of the People, who are found to be 601730, of which 12000 are ſent againſt the *Midianites*, who ſlew there Five petty Kings, and deſtroyed their Cities ; after this, *Moſes* having divided his Conqueſt, and bleſſed the Twelve Tribes, dyed.

§. 10. Obſervations out of *Moſes*'s Story, touching God's Providence, working his own purpoſes ordinarily by Mens affections. *Pharaoh*'s Fears bred his ungodly Policies and ſalvage Cruelties ; by this *Moſes* is caſt upon the Compaſſion of *Pharaoh*'s Daughter, and ſo provided of Princely Education. Mens Affections caſt him into Exile, procured him a Wife, and ſo a long ſtay to know the Wilderneſs, to wean him from Ambition, and ſo fit him to know God, and to Govern. Thus what Men think moſt caſual, God ordereth to the Effecting his own purpoſes many Years after.

CHAP.

CHAP. VI.

Of the Bordering Nations: Of other Renowned Men; and of Joshua's *Acts.*

§. 1. *HOW the Bordering Nations were prepared to be Enemies to* Israel. §. Though the *Ismaelites, Moabites, Ammonites,* and *Edomites,* descended from *Abraham* and *Isaac,* as did the *Israelites,* and were not molested by them, and therefore they should not have hinder'd their Conquest of *Canaan*; yet God's all-disposing Providence, had order'd to the contrary, by ordinary means. For first, these Nations having setled there from the beginning, and matched with *Canaanites,* and fallen to their Idolatry; and having had neighbourly Commerce with them, it could not be, but they should affect them, being also the ancient Inhabitants. Secondly, the *Israelites* by long abode in *Egypt,* were become strangers to them, and the less affected for differences in Religion, and feared, for being a Potent, United People; whereas the *Canaanites* were divided, and therefore not feared of them so much. Thirdly, both *Ismalites* and *Edomites* being Carnal People, might resent the Actions of *Israel* for their old Quarrels between their first Parents; yet none of these directly opposed them in defence of the *Canaanites.* Only the *Amalekites* (which are commonly taken to be a Tribe of *Edom*) offered them violence, which was never forgiven.

See cap. 8. Sect. 3.

§. 2. *Of the Kings of the* Canaanites *and* Moabites. §. Speaking of the *Canaanites,* we understand the seven Nations descended from *Cham* by *Canaan*; whose proper Habitation was bounded by *Jordan* on the *East,* the *Mediterranean* Sea on the *West.* Of these, the first we read of, is *Hamor* the Hittitish Lord in

Jacob's

Jacob's days, of the *Hittites*. *Arad* is the Second, who is named King of the *Canaanites*, in the *South* of *Canaan*, bordering on *Edom* and the Red Sea. *Sibon* King of *Heshon*, and *Og* King of *Bashan* were next; who had driven out the *Moabites*, and *Ammonites* out of all the Valley *East* of *Jordan*. *Adonizedek* is the Fifth, with whom *Joshua* nameth Four other Kings, all *Amorites*. *Jabin* King of *Hazor*, or which afore-time was head of those Kingdoms, and *Jobab* King of *Madon*; then *Adonibezek*, that Tyrant of *Bezek*, and *Jabin* the Second, King of *Hazor*, *Judg.* 4. overthrown by *Baras*.

The *Midianites* descended from *Abraham*, by *Midian* the Son of *Ketura* : Some of them dwelt by the *Red Sea*, where *Ragvell*, or *Revell*, called also *Jethro* and *Kenis*, was King and Priest; others of them were mixed with the *Moabites*, and dwelt in *Nabothea*, on the *South-East* of the Dead Sea, whose Five Princes are named. There are four others named, slain by the *Ephramites* and *Gideon* : *Oreb* and *Zeb*, *Zeba* and *Salmunna*.

§. 3. *Of the* Amalekites *and* Ismaelites. *Of Amalek's Original.* §. Of them and of the *Israelites* few Kings *See* cap. 8. Sect. 3. are named, and though the *Ismaelites* were more in number, yet in *Moses*'s days, *Amalek* was more renowned than the rest of the *Ismaeliets*, as after in the days of *Saul*, when they were increased so far, that he pursued them from *Sur* to *Havila*. It seemeth the *Israelites* had left the barren Desarts of *Arabia Petræa*, called *Sur*, *Paran*, and *Sin*, to the Posterity of *Ketura*, which joined with them, and planted themselves in the better parts thereabout. *Nabaioth* the Eldest of the Twelve Princes, enjoy'd that fruitful part of *Arabia Petræa*, which borders on *Judæa* on the *East*; they also peopled a Province of *Arabia Felix*. *Kedar* the Second, gave name to the East part of *Basan*, or *Batanea*, called *Kedarens*, or *Cedrens*. *Abbiel* the Third,

gave

gave Name to *Adubenes,* near the Mountains, and divideth *Arabia Felix* from the Deſart. The *Raabens* were of
Moſhma; which joyns to the *Orchen* near the *Arabian*
Gulf; by *Zagmais Duma,* of whom came the *Dumeans*
between the two former, where was the City *Dumeth.*
Maſſa bred the *Maſſams.* *Hadar,* or *Chadar* the
Athrites in *Arabia Felix* by the *Napatheans. Thema* begat the *Theminians* among the Mountains, where is
the City *Thema.* *Jetur,* Father of *Itureans,* or *Cha-*
mathens, whoſe King was *Tobu,* in *Davids* days.
Naphiſh bred the *Nubeans* in *Syria Zoba,* under
King *Adadezer* in *David's* Days. *Cadma,* of whom
came the *Cadmonæans,* or *Aſitæ,* Worſhipping the Fire,
as did the *Babylonians.* The *Amalekites* oppoſed *Iſ-*
rael from their coming out of *Egypt,* joyning with all
their Enemies, as with the *Canaanites, Moabites, Mi-*
dianites, and *Edumæans.*

§. 4. Prometheus, Atlas, *and* Pelaſgus, *flouriſhed in*
Moſes *Days.* § *Pelaſgus* was now choſen King of
Arcadia, for teaching the Inhabitants to Erect Cottages, and to make Food and Bread of Acorns, who
before lived on Roots and Herbs. So long was it
before Agriculture and Civilty came into *Europe,*
out of *Egypt,* and the *Eaſt. Prometheus,* alſo flouriſhed in this Age of the World : Of whom it was
Reported, he formed Men out of Clay, for his fram-
Auguſtine. ing Men unto Wiſdom. His ſtealing Fire
from *Jupiter,* was his skill in the Stars, which with
great Study, he got on *Caucaſus,* which occaſion'd
the Fable of his being bound there, *&c. Africanus*
makes him within 44 Years of *Ogyges* ; *Porphyry* puts
him with *Inachus. Atlas,* his Brother now flouriſhed, both Sons of *Japetus,* who according to *Æſcu-*
lus had two others, *Oceanus,* and *Heſperus,* Famous in
the *Weſt.* There were others of the ſame Name, but
Mount *Atlas, South* of *Marocco,* came from him ;
and both theſe, of *Cepheus,* and his Wife. *Cicero*
ſaith, their Divine Knowledge occaſioned thoſe Fables.

bles. *Atlas* skill in Astronomy, produced the *Plei-*
ades, and *Hyades*, from his Daughters. Some
ascribe the finding out the Course of the Moon
to him, but others to *Archas*, of whom *Arcadia* took
Name, who boast they are more Ancient than the
Moon, that is, before her Motion and Influence
was observed. But *Isacius Tzetzes*, a curious
searcher of Antiquity, ascribes it to *Atlas* of
Lybia, of Incomparable Gifts and Strength, of whom
Thalis Mirtius had his first Rudiments.

Ducalion, King of *Thessaly*, was the Son of *Prome-*
theus, says *Herodotus Apollonius*, *Hesiod*, and *Strabo*.
In his time fell that great Inundation of *Thessaly*, in
which, so few escaped the Vengeance which their
exceeding Wickedness had drawn upon them: Only
Ducalion and *Pyrrha* excelling in Virtue, escaped upon his Fathers fore-warning. *Phaetons* Conflagration
happened in *Ethiopia*, and in *Istria*, and the Mountain
Vesuvius.

§. 6. *Mercurius Ter-Mximus*, called *Hermes* of the
Greeks, now flourished, excelling all the Heathens in
Wisdom. *Plato* ascribes all invention of Letters to
him, whom *Philo Biblius* calls *Tauntus*, *Egyptians*
Tooyth, *Alexandrians Thot*. As for the Conjecture,
that a *Grecian Mercury* carried Letters into *Egypt*, is
improbable, seeing all profane Antiquity acknowledge that *Greece* had Learning out of *Egypt*, and
Phœnicia: And that *Cadmus* brought Letters out of
Egypt into *Greece*, which was while *Minos* was King
of *Crete*. *Lyncius*, the King of the *Argives*, who succeeded *Danaus*, who had Reigned 50 Years, and
Stenelus, 10 Years before him, and *Crotopus* before
him, in whose 10 Years *Moses* Dyed: So much difference of time is between *Hermes* and *Cadmus*, his
coming into *Boetia*. Neither did the Two *Mercu-*
ries of *Egypt*, mentioned by *Augustine*, come out of
Greece; but *Epolemus*, and *Artapances*, ascribe that
invention to *Moses*, who taught it the *Hebrews*, of
whom

whom the *Phœnicians* had it, and *Cadmus* from them.
Ficinus is deceived, thinking that *Mercury*, upon
whose Book he Commenteth, was Four Descents after *Moses* : So *Ludovicus Vives* thinks the Author
of those Books, was Grand-child to *Mercury Ter-
Maximus.* His long life of 300 Years, might give oc-
sion to , some, to find him at one time, to others
at another ; and they which Collected the grounds
of *Egyptian* Philosophy, make him more Ancient
than *Moses*, being Author of the *Egyptian* Wisdom,
wherein *Moses* was Learned.   True it is, that *Hermes* Divinity is contrary to *Moses*, in many things ;
especially, in approving Images : But the advised,
rather may perceive those Books have been corrupted by the *Egyptian* Priests ; and were they in all
things like themselves, it were not unsafe with *Eupolemus* to say, *Hermes* was *Moses* ;   And that the *E-
gyptian* Theology was devised by the more Ancient
Hermes, which others judge to be *Joseph.*   But these
are over-curious Opinions : Whoever he was, God
knoweth ; and *Lactantius* testifieth this of him.   He
Writ many Books of Divine things, touching the
Majesty of the most High, and one God, calling him
by the Name of one God, and Father, as we do, *&c.*
And his acknowledgments of God, are so contrary
to *Egyptian* and *Grecian* Fictions, that what is found
in his Book inclining thereto, was by corruption in-
serted ; For thus he speaketh, *God is the Lord and
Father of all things ; the Fountain, Life, Power, Light,
Mind and Spirit, and all things are in, and under him.
For his Word which out of himself proceedeth, being most
Perfect, Generative, and Operative, made Nature Fruit-
ful and producing.*   And saith *Suidas*, he was called
Ter-Maximus, for affirming there was one God in
Trinity.   He fore-saw, saith *Ficinus*, the Ruin of the
Old (or superstitious) Religion, the Birth of the
New Faith, the coming of Christ, future Judgment,
Resurrection, Glory of the Blessed, and the Punish-
                                                    ment

ment of finners. *Lastly*, *Calcidius* the *Platonist*, and *Suidas* cited by *Volaterius*, Report this his Speech, *Hitherto*, *O my Son, being driven out of my Country, I have lived a Stranger and Banished Man; but now I am repairing homeward again in safety: And when after a while being loofed from the Bonds of the Body, I shall depart from you, fee you do not bewail me as Dead: For I I do return to that best and Blessed City, whereto all her Citizens by the Condition of Death are come.* For there is *the only God, the most High and Chief Prince, who replenishing his Citizens with wonderful Sweetness, in regard whereof this, which many call Life, is rather to be called Death. I therefore adjure thee, O Heaven! Thou Wise work of the great God, and thee, O Voice of the Father, which he first uttered when he framed the whole World; I adjure by his only begotten Word and Spirit, comprehending all things, have Mercy upon me.*

§. 7. *Æfculapius* alfo flourifhed in this Age, and became the God of *Physitians*; he was Brother of *Hermes*, as *Vives* on *Augustin* Judged. *Jamnes*, and *Jambres*, thofe notorious Sorcerers that oppofed *Mofes*, now lived and made fuch a Figure, as if *Mofes* and they had ufed the fame Art, as the beholders of common Capacity judged. Though *Mofes* charge them not with familiarity with the Devil, and the *Greeks* call them Φυσιαxυς, Workers by Drugs; yet did they excel in the impious Art, as in dazling Eyes, whom we call Preftigiators in natural Magicks, which is a knowledge to ufe the Creatures qualities beyond common Judgment, which difcern not the beft Virtues, that God hath indued them with: This the *Cabalift* calls the Wifdom of Nature, ufed by *Jacob* in the Pied Lambs, as *Mofes* did; that which they call the Wifdom of Divinity in his Miracles. Hereby God made him excell all that ever were; when he fhewed himfelf fo often to him, and imployed him in fuch Services. *Mofes*, is remembred by Profane Authors, *Clearchus*, *Magaftenes*,

and

and *Numenius.* The Patriarchs long lives are remembred by *Eftius, Hyeronimus, Egyptius, Heafteus, Elanicus, Acufilaus, Ephorus* and *Alexander,* the Hiftorian. The deluge by *Berofus, Nicen, Damafcenus.* The Confufion at *Babel,* by *Abidemus, Eftieus, Sybil. Abraham* was Honoured by *Berofus*; written of by *Hecolæus*; and his Journey into *Canaan* by *Damafcen: Eupolemon* writ of him, beginning from *Babel's* Building, to his calling out of *Canaan,* or *Ur* in *Chaldea. Eufebius* collects many which confirm the Books of *Mofes.* *Lastly,* Worthy is the Teftimony of *Strabo,* faying, Mofes *taught the* Egyptians *were miftaken in Attributing to God, the Image of Beafts*; *and the* Africans, *and* Greeks, *Erred greatly, giving their Gods the fhape of Men*; *whereas, that only is God indeed which contains both us, Earth, Sea, the Heaven, the World, and the Nature of all things*; *whofe Image doubtlefs, no Man will dare to Form to the likenefs of any thing. Their rejecting all Images, that worthy Temple and Place of Prayer was to be Erected to him for his Worfhip without Images.*

§. 8. Of Jofua, *and fo to Othoniel, and his Contemporary.* § *Jofua* entred upon the Government in the Firft Month, *Nifan,* or *March,* the 14th Year of their Egreffion, in the Reign of *Aminias,* the Eighteenth King of *Affyria. Corax,* the Sixteenth. *Siciona, Danus* of *Argives,* and *Erichthonius* of *Athens,* faith *Auguftin, de civ. Jofua* appointeth *Reuben, Gad,* and the half Tribe of *Manaffes* unto the Vanguard, to lead the Hoft till the Land was Conquered, as *Juda* had in the Wildernefs: So upon the Tenth Day he led them over *Jordan,* which gave way to them, and Incamped in *Gilgal,* and Circumcifed them; and on the Fourteenth, they Celebrated the Paffover the Third time, when the *Manna* ceafed. The Wars and Victories of *Jofua,* the Miraculous affiftance of God, and the Divifion of the Land are particularly at large fet down in God's Book. In the whole
Story

Story I obferved in thofe Petty Kings, *Firft*, want of
Wifdom (as it is with Governours forfaken of God)
to Unite themfelves againft a ftrong and common
Enemy, before he had broken divers of them. *Secondly, Jofua,* though fure of Divine affiftance, yet ufed
the uttermoft skill of a Wife Leader ; As, fometime
by Ambufcades, Stratagems, and fhew of flying ;
So by Surprize, and Night-Marches, and by purfuing his Victory. *Thirdly,* In the Paffage between
Jofua and the *Gibeonites*, the Doctrine of keeping
Faith, is excellently taught, taking away all perfidious
cunning of Equivocating, or crafty diftinctions. It
is not poffible to have a Cafe affording better Pretence to go off ; they were *Hivites*, of whofe Deftruction God had given Exprefs Commandment ;
they Counterfeited in Word and Deed deliberately,
to deceive, and lye in the very Point, touching the
Perfons to be Covenanted with ; they were detefta-
ble Idolaters ; and as long as they lived, were the
Memory of *Ifraels* Errour, and *Jofua*'s overfight to
be fo overtaken, and to be a fcandal to *Ifrael. Jofua* might fay, he Covenanted not with the *Gibeonites,*
but with Strangers, and had no Commiffion, but a
former Exprefs Law to the contrary ; yea, and the
People Mutined about it, *&c.* All notwithftanding,
Jofua durft ufe no Evafion to ftart from the Oath of
the Lord, wherein he was bound, not to Man fo
much as to God. It were a great fin to call God to Witnefs a Lye, and fo make him a Deceiver ; but we
call him to be our Surety : Yea, we call him to Judge,
and fo make him falfe in Witneffing, in undertaking
our Faith, and corrupt in Judgment, the leaft of
which Offences were heinous to a King ; how odious
then is it to God, to make him break Promifes, to
Deceive, to pervert Judgment ? Four Hundred
Years after, *Saul's* breaking this Oath of his Fore-Fathers, brought evil on all *Ifrael*, which manifefted
that God had not forgotten, that his Name had fe-

cured

secured that Poor People, and he did them Justice on *Saul*'s House. And certainly if Equivocating may delude another, the strength of the Objection is broken, and Truth in all Tryals is driven away, and honest Men are Inthralled to Villanies : No League between Kings, nor Truce between Armies, but the Sword must still be held unsheathed. Yet can it not do oftentimes, what the Powerful Name of God in an Oath can do, in making of Peace, and procuring Passage ; for Men held no security like an Oath, no Witness, Surety, or Judge like God ; neither durst Men which feared him, call him forth to their occasions, but with Religious Truth. *Almarick*, the Fifth King of the Christians in *Palestine*, breaks Faith with *Elhadech*, *Caliph* of *Egypt*, who thereupon called the *Turk* to aid ; who after he had made War, beat the Christians out of *Palestine*; neither could the Wooden Cross, brought into the Field, as the last Refuge, Save them, having for-sworn by him which was Crucified on it. So when *Eugemenes* Commanded the King of *Hungary*, after a great Victory, to break the Oath with *Amurath*, he lost himself, and Thirty Thousand Christians. *Lastly*, Observe how it pleased God, that the unconquered Cities became Thorns in their Eyes, &c. See *Josh.* 1. & 2. & 11. & 13. *Joshua* Governed 18 Years ; others hold more, or less ; but the Necessity of 480 Years, from their Delivering, to *Solomon*'s Temple, admits no more, nor any space between him and *Othoniel*. *Erichthonius* King of *Athens*, *Lynceus* of *Argive*, *Phœnix*, and *Cadmus* flourished now.

CHAP.

C H A P. VII.

Of the Phœnician *Kingdom, and of the Invention
of Letters.*

§. 1. I Have gathered a Brief of thofe Kings, of
whom Time hath left any Record to Pofterity: The Limits of this Kingdom of *Phœnicia* in
the *South,* are uncertain : *Strabo* extends it to *Pelufium*
the firft Port of *Egypt* : *Corvinus,* and *Budæus,* to
Gaza : *Pliny* takes but *Joppa.* *Ptolomy,* who feldom
failed in his Art, ftayeth at *Chorfeus,* which feemeth
to be the River at *Megiddo* : He alfo begins it in the
North at *Elutherius,* which falls into the Sea at *A-
radus,* *North* of *Orthofia.* Thus it comprehends thefe
Maritime Cities, *Aradus, Orthofia, Tripolis, Botris,
Biblus, Beritus, Sidon, Tyrus, Acon, Dora,* and *Cæfarea*
of *Paleftine* ; fo that it Commanded the Trade of the
Mediterranean for all the Eaft. *Zidon* was the Regal Seat, and fo continued till *Jofhua* ; and all the
People were called *Zidonians,* as *Procopius* confirmeth in his *Vandal* Wars. That *Zidon,* the Firft Son
of *Canaan* was the Founder, we doubt not, and yet
it was in his Pofterities command in *Mofes* Days : As
for *Agenor,* whether he was an *Egyptian* of *Thebes,* or a
Native of this Country bred up there, it may be that
in *Jofhua's* days, he and his Four Sons, *Cadmus,
Phœnix, Cyrus,* and *Cilix,* might come out of *E-
gypt,* with fuch Force as the *Egyptians* could fpare,
to the fuccour of the Coaft, and fo to Fortifie the
Sea Towns, having the benefit of fuch Ships as were
then in ufe. And when *Cadmus* his Eldeft, purfuing *Taurus* King of *Crete,* who had ftoln away his
Sifter *Europe* in the Surprize of *Tyre,* was drawn into *Greece,* he feated himfelf there. *Agenor* commit-
ing this Country to his Two Sons, called it by his

H 2   Name,

Name ; when alfo *North Tyrus* was Built, and *Zidon* Fortified, whereof it was that *Agenor* was reputed the Founder , from whofe time *Phœnicia* became more Famous. *Belus*, whether Grandfather, or Father to *Agenor*, as fome judge, it is no matter ; but it feemeth he was Ancienter to the *Phœnicians*, who Honoured that Name ; great was the ftrength of thefe *Phœnicians* Cities, which held out againft the *Jews*, but put *Nebuchadonofor*, and *Alexander*, to great difficulties.

Touching the mention of Letters, the *Ethiopians* claim it ; and that *Atlas, Orion, Orpheus, Linus, Hercules, Prometheus, Cadmus*, had the firft light from them, and that *Pythagoras* was inftructed by the *Lybians*. The *Phœnicians* boaft of it, and indeed they were very Ancient, and had Famous Records ufed by *Jofephus*. *Laftly*, Some afcribe it to *Mofes*, without all probability, feeing Learning then flouriſhed in *Egypt*, and *Affyria* ; but true it is, the Excellent Spirits of the Firft Age found it, either *Seth, Enos,* &c. And God every where prefent, hath given this Invention to Nations, which never had Commerce with others. As in *Mexico*, were found Books like *Egyptian* Hieroglyphicks : The *Americans* have an Heraldry.

§. 2. *Of the* Phœnician *Kings, efpecially of* Tyrus. §. *Agenor* living with *Joſhua*, *Phœnix* fucceeded, after whom, till the Siege of *Troy*, when *Phafis* Governed, we find not who fucceeded. In *Jeremy*'s time we find *Zidon* and *Tyre* had petty Kings ; and in *Xerxes* time, *Tetranneftus* Ruled that part of *Phœnicia* at the *Perſians* Command, and afterwards fubdued by *Nebuchadonofor*. *Alexander* alſo, caft out *Strabo* King of *Zidon*, and put in *Balonimus*, a Poor Gardner, of the decayed Royal Blood, preferred by another Citizen, to whom *Hepheſtion* offered it by *Alexander*'s gift ; more we find not of *Zidon*.

Tyrus, fometime a Daughter of *Zidon*, outlived her Mother, and had her own Kings, of which
                                                Twenty

Twenty in Defcent are found in *Jofephus*, and *Theophilus Antiochius*, though they differ in the time of their Reigns, and other particulars. *Abibalus* the Firft, whom *Suron* fucceeded, and paid Tribute to *David* and *Solomon*. Others, Named by *Jofephus*, and *Theophilus*, Fellow to *Ithabalus*, called in Scripture *Ethbaal*, Father to *Jezabel*, who is there called King of the *Zidonians*, and by *Jofephus* King alfo of the *Tyrians*. The Third from him, they Name *Pigmalion*, whofe Sifter *Elifa* Married *Sycheus*, whom *Pigmalion* flew for his Wealth, but was prevented by *Elifa*, who Conveyed it to a Ship, and fled into *Africa*, where fhe Built *Carthage* 143 Years, 8 after *Solomon*'s Temple, and as long before *Rome*, and 289 after *Troy*'s Deftruction. *Eluleus* fucceeded, who overthrew *Salmanaffers* Fleet in the Port of *Tyrus*. *Ethobales* fucceeded, in whofe time *Nebuchodonofer*, after 13 Years Siege, won *Tyrus*. *Baal* fucceeded *Ethobales*, and after *Baal* 'twas govern'd by *Judges* fucceffively.

§.3. *Bozius* believes that the *Tyrians* proceeded from the *Edumæans*, &c. But is confuted by Scripture, by which it appears, that *Eliphas*, which came from *Theman* to *Job*, was no *Edomite*, nor was that *Theman* in *Edumæa*, but in *Arabia*, *Eaft* from *Job*, whereas *Edom* was *South*. *Ifmael* had a Son called *Theman*, who by all likelihood gave Name to *Theman* in the *Eaft*. From whom *Eliphaz*, *Jobs* Friend defcended. *Suhe* alfo a Son of *Kethura*, and *Midian* his Brother, of whom came *Bildad*, the *Shuite*; and the *Midianites*, at their firft fetling were fent by *Abraham* into the *Eaft*, which from *Canaan*, was *Arabia* the Defart, not *Seer* which was *South*. So in the Hiftory of the Judges, the *Midianites* and *Amalekites* are faid to be of the *Eaft*: Yet were there of them Dwelling in the *South*; they were grown fo many, that the *Eaft* could not hold them.

§. 4. *Kings of the Ten Tribes from* Jeroboam *to A-chab*. §. *Jeroboam* flying from *Salomon* into *Ægypt*, to

H 3　　　　　　　　　　*Shifhak*

Shishak (whom *Eusebius* calls *Osochores*) whose Daughter he Marryed, as *Adad* the *Edumenian*, had his predecessor's Wive's Sister, and were prepar'd by *Shishak*, to shake the Kingdom of *Judea*, that he might pillage it, as he accordingly did in the fifth year of *Reboboam*. This Man was exalted to be King of the Ten Tribes, preferring the Policies of the World before God's Service and Honour. To prevent the Peoples falling from him by resorting to *Jerusalem*, he erected the two Calves, *&c. Jeroboam* reigned at *Sichem* Twenty two years. *Nadab* his Son succeeded two years, and was slain by *Baasha*, who rooted out all *Jeroboam*'s Seed, and reigned twenty four Years at *Therfa*, and *Ela* his Son succeeded two years, and was slain in his Cups by *Zimri*, who succeeded seven days; but *Homri*, in revenge of *Ela*, besieged him, and made him burn himself, and succeeded; transferring the Regal Seat to *Samaria*, and reigned twelve years.

§. 5. *Abab* succeeded his Father, married the Daughter of the King of *Zidon*, and embraced her Religion, as *Jeroboam* had his *Egyptian* Wives: *Abab* was slain after twenty two years. *Ochazius* succeeded his Father, and dyed of a Fall, in his second year, and his Brother *Joram* succeeded 12 years; who, with Aid of *Juda* and *Edom*, could not subdue *Moab*, who sacrificed *Edom*'s Son taken in an Eruption which he made out of the City; whereupon the Siege was broken up through *Edom*'s displeasure against *Israel*, for refusing to make Peace with *Moab*, to save his Son, *Amos* 2. 1. *Jehu* slew *Joram*, and succeeded twenty eight Years; whose Son *Jehuahaz* succeeded seventeen years, and was molested by *Aza*. *Joas* succeeded his Father sixteen years; recover'd from *Aram* what his Father lost, and sacked *Jerusalem*.

Jeroboam succeeded his Father forty one years; recover'd all from *Hamath* to the dead Sea, and
Zacharias

Zacharias his Son succeeded Six Months, and was slain by *Shallum*, who succeeded two Months, and *Menahen* slew him, and succeeded ten years, with much Cruelty. *Pekahia* his Son succeeded two years, and *Peka* slew him, and succeeded twenty years. In his time *Tyglath Pileser*, King of *Assyria*, Invaded *Israel*, and carried many Captives into *Assyria*: He was drawn in by *Achas* King of *Juda*, whom *Peka* of *Israel*, and *Rezin* of *Damascus* wasted; and first he surprized the Monarchs of *Syria* and *Damascus*, and then *Israel* prepared the way to *Juda*. *Hosea* slew *Peka*, and succeeded nine years, in whose time *Tiglath Pileser* carried the rest of the Ten Tribes Captives, and re-peopled the Country with *Cuthites* out of *Arabia Deserta*; the *Persians* with *Calaneans*, bordering on *Syria*, and *Sepharims* out of *Mesopotamia*, with the *Avims*, of old inhabited the Philistins Land, but now Inhabited *Deserta*, and called *Havæi*.

C H A P. VIII.

The History of the Syrians *bordering their Tribes on the* East *of* Jordan.

DAmascus in this Border, most famous for Antiquity, Beauty, Riches, is called the City of Joy, and House of Pleasure. The *Hebrews* think it built by *Hus* Son of *Abraham*; others, as *Jerom* ascribe it to *Damascus*, Son of *Eleasar*, *Abraham*'s Steward; but was before *Eleasar*; *David* subdued it in the overthrow of *Adadezar*; but *Rezin*, Servant to *Adadezer*, escaped with the broken Forces, recovered it, and was made King. *Adadezer* returned out of *Egypt*, and forced out *Rezin*, and became King of *Syria* for Nine Descents.

H 4 §. 2. *Of*

§. 2. *Of the first Kings of* Damascus, *and their growing up.* §. That *Damascus* was of Note in *Abraham's* days, his Steward is an Argument; what the Government was then, and long after, the Reason of *Moses's* Story led him not to handle. The first occasion was in *David's* Reign, who seeking to Establish the command of *Israel* unto *Euphrates*, as God had promised, Invaded *Adadezer*, who was then of the greatest Force in *Syria*, strictly taken; containing *Damascus*, *Saba*, *Camath* or *Ituræa*, and *Geshur*. *Adadezer* King of *Saba*, called to his assistance the *Damascenes*, who are not ranked under a King, but after the overthrow. *Rezon* a Commander under *Hadadesar*, gathered the broken Forces, surprised *Damascus*, where *David* had put a Garrison, and was made King there, as it seemeth after *David's* death. So that as *Rehob* and his Son *Adadezer* are the first Kings of *Syria*; *Saba* and *Toi* the first Kings of *Camath*; so *Rezon* is the first King of *Damascus*, which before was commanded by the Kings of *Saba*, whose Power became formidable to the King of *Camath*. The next King is *Adad* of *Edom*, who coming out of *Egypt*, whether he fled from *David*, and finding his Forces too weak to recover *Edom*, it seemeth he surprised *Damascus*, and became King of *Aram*. The next King of *Aram* was *Hezion*, whom his Sons *Tabremmon* succeeded, the Father of *Benhadad*, who assisted *Asa* King of *Juda* against *Baasha* King of *Israel*. Almost Fifty years after *Benhadad* was taken Prisoner by *Achab*, and promised to restore what his Father had taken from *Israel*: This was a Second *Benhadad*, who slew *Achab*, and Besieged *Samaria* the second time, and was smothered by *Hazael*; who succeeded him, and did much mischief to *Iud*, but brought *Israel* to a low Ebb, 2 *Kings* 13. 7.

§. 3. Of the later Kings was *Benhadad*, two or rather

1 *Judg.*

rather three, who loſt what *Hazael* had gotten; three other ſucceeded of the ſame Name, in one of whoſe times *Jeroboam* 2d. recovered *Damaſcus* it ſelf, and *Chamath* to *Iſrael*, which by *David*'s Conqueſt had belonged to *Juda.* *Rezin* the 10th, after *Adad* 1ſt, moleſting *Achas*, and was taking *Elath*, is, by *Achas*'s Procurement, taken, and Slain by *Tiglath Pileſer*, and the Kingdom of *Damaſcus* diſſolved.

§. 4. Of leſſer Kingdoms in *Syria*, *Geſſur*, where *Talmat* reigned after *Ammibur*, *Sophena*, or *Syria Saba*, or *Cœloſyria*, had *Rebob* and *Adadezer* after him; whoſe Kingdom tranſlated to *Damaſcus* by *Rezin*, ended with the Kingdom of *Iſrael*, not long after *Ninus*'s Race in *Sardanapalus* had been ended by *Phul-Belochus*, Father of this *Tiglath*, whoſe Son *Salmanaſſar* led *Iſrael* Captive, as his Father had *Damaſcus*; *Senacharib*, Son of *Salmanaſſer*, attempted *Jeruſalem* in vain; but 132 years after *Iſrael*'s Captivity, it alſo went to *Babylon.*

N. Daſcenus Numb. 12. in ſucceſſ.

§. 5. *Hieruſalem*, in *Joſhua*'s days, had *Adonizedek* for King, and was not inferiour to *Hozar* the chief of all *Canaanites.* This City of old, called *Jebus*, Inhabited of by *Jebuſites*, and therefore likelieſt to be Builded by *Jebuſæus*, the Son of *Canaan*, and not by *Melchiſedek*; for it could not be in *Abraham*'s way returning from his Victories; but rather that *Salem* by *Jordan*, of which we ſpake in *Manaſſes.* Though *Joſhua* ſlew their King, yet they held out 400 Years till *David* won it. *Solomon* ſo perfected the Strength, Beauty, and Riches of it, (beſides the renowned Temple) that the World had not the like: That Ditch hewn out of the Rock, Sixty Foot deep, and Two Hundred and Fifty broad, with Walls, Gates, and Pallaces, defended One Hundred Fifty Thouſand Men, beſides Women and Children. It endured many changes: *Shiſhak* of *Egypt* Sackt it; ſo did *Joas* of *Iſrael*; but *Nebuchadonozor* fulfilled all Gods Judgments, threatned,

ned, and made way to SeventyYears Defolation, and
Captivity of City and People. After the reftoring
by *Cyrus*, *Bagofes Lieutenant*, and *Artaxerxes* fpoiled
it; and after *Alexanders* Empire was divided, *Ptolomy* the Firft, pretending to Offer Sacrifice; then
Antiochus Epiphanes, and *Apollonius* his *Lietuenant*
after him fpoiled it; and *Pompey* long after took it.
But after all Repairs, that wicked *Herod* did fo Reedifie, and Adorn both Temples, and Cities, that it
far exceeded what *Solomon* did; continuing in this,
ftate, about Forty Years after our Saviour's Death.
Titus invefted it till it was taken, and Demolifhed it,
in which by Famine, Peftilence, Sedition, and Enemies Sword, 1100000 were confumed, 65 Years
after being in part repaired. *Elius Adrian*, for a
new Revolt Overthrew all, and Built another, which
he called *Elia Capitolia*; and Decreed that never *Jew*
fhould dare after to enter, or from high place look to
behold it. Yet after the Chriftian Religion flourifhed
in *Paleftine*, it was Inhabited after by Chriftians 500
Years; and then it was taken by *Egyptian Sarazens*, and
held 400 Years; and then regained by *Godfrey Bouil-
lon*, and fo continued 88 Years, when the *Souldan*
of *Egypt* won it; but laftly, *Selim* the *Turk* took it,
and called it *Cufunbaris*.

§. 6. Malicious Reports of the Heathen, as *Quin-
tilian*, *Diodor*, *Strabo*, *Juftin*, *Tacitus* touching the
Jews Original, anfwered by *Jofephus*, againft *Appion*,
and *Tertullian*, in his *Apologet*.

CHAP.

C H A P. IX.

Memorable things from Joshua, *to* Jeptha, *and the Destruction of* Troy.

§. 1. **I**$U D A$, by Gods Directions took the Management of the War, after *Joshua* was Dead. *Caleb* with *Phineas*, and the affistance of Seventy Elders were in *Joshua's* time, Commanding in Chief. Their Achievements we read, *Judg.* 1. as alfo of the other Tribes, which fought to eftablish their own Territories. What befel them after, upon their making Peace with the *Canaanites*, and their affliction 8 Years, and how *Othniel*, the Son of *Cenas*, Younger Brother to *Caleb*, delivered them from *Chushan* a King of *Mesopotamia*, who Oppreffed them, we read in Scripture. How long it was between the Death of *Joshua* and *Othniel*, is uncertain ; though it could not be a short time, confidering what Wars followed; and the Surprize of *Laish* by the *Danites*, and their Warring with *Benjamin* are thought to be in this interim ; which War fo weakened them, that they could not fo ftrongly refift their Bordering Enemies.

§. 2. *Othniel* Governed 40 Years, in whofe 20th year *Pandarus*, Fifth King of *Athens* entred, and Reigned 40 Years, Father of *Erictheus*, and *Progne* and *Philomela* in the Fables. *Cadmus*, about this time obtained *Thebes*, which *Amphion*, and *Zethus* Governed after. *Triptolemus* is placed firft by *Augustine*; of whom, and the reft, Authors fo difagree, that I defire to be excufed, if I Err with better Judgments, whereto I fubmit. For if the firft Authors had but a borrowed uncertain light from other Conjectures, all our labour in Example to uncover the Sun, is for ought I fee a more over-fhading.

§. 3. *Ehud*

§. 3. *Ebud* was next, who Delivered *Israel* from *Eglon*, King of *Moab*, after 18 Years Misery. *Samgar* his Successor, freed them from the *Philistins*; so from *Othoniel's* Death 8 Years expired : *Elimelek*, went to *Moab* in *Ebud's* days, and *Ruth's* Story is referred hither. *Adoius*, King of the *Molosseans* in *Epirus*, had by *Ceres* his Wife, a Fair Daughter called *Proserpina* (a common Name of such) whom *Peritheus* intending to steal, drew *Theseus* into the attempt, which being discovered, *Aidonius* surprized them, cast *Peritheus* to *Cesarus* his Mastive, and kept *Theseus* Prisoner, till *Hercules* delivered him by a strong hand. *Pindus's* Mountains in *Epirus*, of which *Oeta* is Chief, whence *Acheron* springeth. *Erictheus*, was King of *Athens*, whose Daughter *Orythia*, *Boreas* King of *Thrace* Forced. *Tereus*, King of *Phocis* in *Greece*, Inhabited by *Thracians*, Married *Progne*, the Daughter of *Pandarius*, and Ravished her Sister *Philomela*, and cut out her Tongue, for which *Progne* killed his Son *Itys*, and made Meat of him for *Tyrus*, and fled to *Athens*. *Tros* began to Reign in *Dardania*, the 47th Year of *Ebud*, about which time *Tantalus* was King of *Lydia*, not *Phrygia*; whose study of Wisdom made him neglect the Pleasure of Riches, of which he had great Plenty : Others said his covetous Mind made him miserable, whereof grew that Fable, &c. Here the Author is out, Taxing the unfolding of Secrets to Vulgars, perverting *Mat.* 4. 11. *Cecrops* 2d. & 7th. King of *Athens*, and *Arrisius*, Thirteenth King of the *Argives* now Reigned the first 40 Years; the other 31, toward the end of the 8 Years *Pelops* lived, of whom *Peloponesus* took Name. *Titius* Tyrant of *Panopea*, in *Phocis*, slain by *Apollo*; *Admetus*, King of *Thessaly*, *Perseus* of *Peloponesus*, and *Medusa* slain by *Perseus* Souldiers, of whose Blood sprang *Pegasus*, *Belerophon's* Horse, with which he slew *Chimera*, a Pyrat of of the *Lycians*. *Ion*, of whom the *Athenians* are called *Iones*, or rather of *Iavan*, &c.

§. 4. The

§. 4. The former 80 Years of Peace and Plenty, having bred security, it brought forth neglect of Gods Commandments, and their ripe Sins called for God's Judgment, who raised *Jabin* King of *Hazor*, who laid an heavy yoke on *Israel* 20 Years, keeping his chief holds, even in *Naphtalim*, and reduced them to such a weakness, as among Forty Thousand a Weapon was not seen. But as Volumes may be gathered of Examples, proving all Power is the Lords, how impotent soever his means be; so now the Lord set it out in delivering *Israel*; two Women, *Deborah* and *Jael*, striking the chief stroke. Thus Forty Years were expired under *Jabin, Deborah,* and *Barac.*

Argos's Kingdom, which had continued 544 Years, was Translated to *Micenæ,* Built by *Perseus* Son of *Danae,* Daughter of *Acrisius* King of *Argos.* The King of *Argos.* The King of *Argives,* we find *Inachus,* whose Daughter *Io,* was the *Egyptian Isis, Phoronius, Apis, Argus, Pirasus, Phorbas, Triops, Crotopus, Sthelenus, Donaus, Lynieus, Abas, Acrosius, Pelops.* After the Translation to *Micenæ, Perseus, Sthenelus, Eurystheus, Atreus,* Son of *Pelops, Agamemnon. Egypthus, Orestes, Tisamenus, Penthilus,* and *Cometes. Midas,* now King of *Phrygia,* and *Ilus* who Built *Ilium,* Contemporaries with *Debora.*

§. 5. *Barac* was no sooner dead, but *Israel* returned to their impious Idolatry, and God raised up the *Midianites,* assisted with the *Amalekites* to infest them; yet his Compassions, which never fail, raised them up a Deliverer, *Gideon* the Son of *Joash,* whose story is largely set down in Holy Scripture. His severities in the revenge upon *Succoth* and *Penuel,* his own Sons found shortly after his death: For the debts of Cruelty and Mercy, were left unsatisfied. And because he Converted the Gold into an Ephod, a Garment proper to the High-Priest, and set it up in his City *Ophra*; as it drew *Israel* to Idolatry, so

was

was it the deſtruction of his own Houſe. *Ægeus*
Son of *Pandeon* now reigned in *Athens*: *Euriſtheus*
in *Micenæ*, whom *Atreus* ſucceeded, who killed *Thyeſtes* his Brother's Children, and feaſted their Father
therewith, which Cruelty was revenged on him, and
Agamemnon his Son, and all his Linage, by a natural
Son of *Thyeſtes*. *Minos* was now King of *Crete*, whoſe
Wife *Paſiphae* inamoured of *Taurus* her Husband's
Secretary, *Dedalus* being her Pander, had a Child by
him, and another at the ſame Birth by *Minos*, of
which grew the Tale of the *Minotaurs*. *Dedalus* upon diſcovery, fled with *Icarus* in two Boats with
Sails, unto *Cocalus* King of *Sicily*: In the flight, *Icarus* was drowned, and *Minos* was ſlain in perſuing
Dedalus, whom *Cocalus* defended. *Sphinx* a Woman Robber by Sea and Land, upon the Borders of
Corinth, was overcome by *Oedipus*, Commander of
the *Corinthian* Forces; her Swiftneſs and Cruelty
bred the Tale of her Wings, and Body of a Lyon.
Anteus the ſtrong and cunning Wreſtler near *He-
ſpendes* in *Mauritania*, lived about this time.

§. 6. The *Argonauts* Expedition fell out about *Gideon*'s Eleventh Year. Many Fabulous Diſcourſes have
been hereof written, and myſtical Expoſitions made,
but *Dercilus*'s Opinion is moſt probable. That *Jaſon*
with the Harveſt-men of *Greece*, went by Ship to
rob *Colchos*, enriched by certain ſteep falling Torrents, not far from *Caucaſus*, which waſh down
many Grains of Gold, which the Inhabitants get by
ſetting many Fleeces of Wool in thoſe Water-falls.
The many Rocks, Straights, Sands, and other difficulties in the Paſſage between *Greece* and *Pontus*,
are Poetically converted into fierce Bulls, Armed
Men riſing out of the Ground, *Syrens*, a Dragon
caſt aſleep, &c. by *Orpheus*, one of them.

§. 7. *Abimelech*, *Gideon*'s natural Son, Ambiti-
ouſly Fought, and got what his Father had refuſed
as unlawful, without ſpecial direction, a Ruler over
God's

God's peculiar People; and for his Establishment in his Usurped Power, he slew Seventy Brethren upon one Stone; *Jotham* the youngest, only escaped this unheard of Inhumanity. Such is Human Ambition; a Monster which neither feareth God, nor respecteth Nature, and forgetteth the All-powerful Hand, whose Revenge is without date. All other Passions and Affections which torment the Souls of Men, are by Contraries oft-times qualified; but this darling of *Sathan*, and first-born Sin that ever the World knew; more Antient than Human Nature, looketh only toward the end, which it self sets down; forgetting nothing how Inhuman soever, that may conduce thereto, and remembers nothing that Pity or Religion can offer to the contrary. As for the deplorable effects that such attempts have had, it ascribes to the Errors or weakness of the Undertakers, and rather praiseth the Adventure, than fears the like Success. The *Sechemits* in a vain Glory to have a King of their own, readily condescended to his Ambitious motion, imbrue themselves, with him, in the Blood of Innocents, and fit themselves to partake with him in the Vengeance fore-told by *Jotham.*

The *Tapithæ* and *Centaurus* made War about this time against the *Thebanes*; these were the first in those parts which learned to ride on Horses; so that coming from the Mountains of *Pindus* on Horseback, they were thought compounded Creatures.

Thola, of *Issachar*, govern'd after *Abimelek* 23 Years, and *Jair* 22 years after him. *Priamus*, after that sacking of *Ilium* by *Hercules*, being Ransomed, began to Reign, having rebuilt *Troy*, and inlarged the Dominion almost over all the lesser *Asia*. Of Fifty Sons, he had Seventeen by *Cuba*, Daughter of *Gisseus* King of *Thrace*: *Paris*, one of them, attempting to recover his Aunt *Hesione*, carried into *Greece* by *Hercules*, took *Helena* the Wife of *Menelaus*, &c.

See cap. 1. 4. Sect. 2.

Theseus

Theſeus, the Tenth King of *Athens,* in his Father *Æ-geus's* Reign he put himſelf among the Seven young Men, which the *Athenians* ſent for Tribute yearly to *Minos* King of *Crete,* who gaining *Ariadne* the King's Daughter's Affection, received of her a Bottom of Thread, by which to conduct himſelf out of the *Labyrinth* after he had ſlain the *Minotaur,* that is, the Son of *Taurus,* begotten of *Paſiphae,* to whom thoſe Youths were committed, *&c.* He took *Hip-polita* the *Amazon* Queen, Priſoner, and by her had a Son *Hyppolitus,* whom he after ſought to kill upon his Step-mother *Phædra's* falſe Accuſation, whoſe In-ceſtuous Careſſes he had rejected : In his Eſcape, he had received many dangerous Wounds, of which be-ing Cured, the Tale of *Eſculapius* grew, *&c.* After much good done to the ungrateful multitude, they baniſh'd him. They ſay he ſtole *Helen* from *Aphid-na,* in the Firſt Year of *Jair,* according to *Euſebius,* which is not probable, ſeeing ſhe ſhould prove Fifty Years old at the fall of *Troy.*

Under the two former Judges in *Aſſyria,* reigned *Mitreus* and *Tautanes* after, and in *Egypt, Ameno-phis* Son of *Ramſes,* and *Anemenes* after him. In *Sicyo-nia* reigned *Thyæſtus* the Twenty ſecond King, Eight years ; *Adraſtus* ſucceeded Four years ; then *Polyphi-des* the Thirteenth. *Mutſchea* ſucceeded *Theſeus* King of *Athens.*

§. 8. The *Theban* War, the moſt antient that ever the *Grecian* Writers handled, happed in this Age, wherein *Greece* continued but ſalvage, holding and getting all by ſtrong hand, Robbing by Sea and Land, little uſing Merchandiſe, and not acquainted with Money ; and having few walled, and but ſmall Towns. As ſome latter idle Chroniclers wanting good Matter, fill their Books with Reports of Feaſts, dry Summers, *&c.* So they which write of *Greece* then, tell us of great Floods ; Metamorpho-ſes of Men-killing Monſters ; Adulteries of their

Gods,

Gods begetting Mighty Men, &c. This *Theban* War, (the first *Grecian* Story of Note,) arose upon the disagreement between *Eteocles*, and *Polynices*, Sons of *Oedipus*, Son of *Laius* King of *Thebes*. These Brethren having Covenanted to Rule by Course ; *Eteocles* beginning, was unwilling to lay down a Scepter once taken into hand, which forced *Polynices* to fly to *Adrastus* King of the *Argives*, who gave him a Wife, and raised Forces to re-establish him in *Thebes*. *Eteocles* withstands the Force, and both Armies, after great loss, desire the Brethren to end the Quarrel by a single Combat, in which both lost the day, with their Lives; and yet another Battel was fought, in which the *Argives* were discomfited and fled, and of the Commanders, only *Adrastus* came to *Athens*. At his request, the *Argives* sent Forces under *Theseus* against *Creon*, Governour of *Thebes*, for denying Burial to the slain *Argives*, who took the City and buried the slain. But this contented not the Sons of the Noble *Argives*, who Ten years after, levied new Forces, and forc'd *Laodamas*, Son of *Eteocles*, to fly, and some says he was slain ; the Town was destroyed, but repaired by *Thirsander*, Son of *Polynices*, who reigned after, and led the *Thebans* to the War of *Troy* shortly after.

§. 9. *Jephtha* judged *Israel* Six years, and relieved them from the Oppression of the *Ammonites*, which lay heavy upon the Tribes on the East of *Jordan*, along *Gilead*. He defended the *Israelites* Right against the *Ammonites* Claim, both by Reason and the force of Arms; and drove them, not only out of all those Plains, but also over the Mountains of *Arabia*, to *Minneth*, and *Abel* of the Vine-yard : As for his Vow, the Opinion that he did not Sacrifice his Daughter, is more probable. The *Ephramites* quarrell'd with *Jephtha*, who slew in that Encounter 42000, which so weakened the Land, that way was thereby made to their future Calamities, and most grievous

I   slavery

flavery under the *Philiftins*, that ever they indured. *Ibzan* fucceeded, and judged Seven years. *Elon* after him, Ten. The Seventy, and *Eufebius* hath him not.

CHAP. X.

Of the War of Troy.

§. 1. **H**Abdon Succeeded and Judged *Ifrael* 8 Years. The *Philiftines* 40 Years Tyranny cannot be from the 9th of *Jair*, to the end of *Abdon*, as fome would have it; for then *Ephraim's* ftrength had been fo diminifh'd, as not to have quarrel'd with *Jephtha*; or being able to bring 24000 Men into the Field, they would not have neglected a common Oppreffor, to fight againft a Brother; thofe 40 Years muft therefore be fupplied elfewhere, as from the death of *Abdon*, 'till after *Sampfon*. *Troys* Deftruction feemeth to fall upon the 3d Year of *Abdon*, after 10 Years Siege, began about the 3d of *Elon*. The Original and Continuance of the Ancient Kings are uncertain; but it is commonly held that *Teucer* and *Dardanus* were the firft Founders of that Kingdom, of which, *Teucer* the firft, according to *Virgil*, Reigned before *Dardanus* built *Troy*, and came out of *Crete*; though *Reineccius* following *Diodorus*, think him a *Phrygian*, and Son of *Scamander*. *Dardanus*, Son of *Electra*, Daughter of *Atlas*, and Wife of *Jupiter*, had for his fecond Wife *Boetia*, Daughter or Niece of *Teucer*. As for this *Atlas*, I take him rather for an *Italian*, than *African*, and *Jupiter* to be more ancient than he, whofe Children liv'd about the *Trojan* War. Touching

ing the Deſtruction of *Troy,* *Diodorus* maketh it to
be 780 Years before the 94*th* Olympiad, which is
408 before the firſt. *Dionyſius Halicarnaſſus* agrees
hereto, placing *Rome*'s Foundation in the firſt of
the ſeventh Olympiad, which is 432 after the fall
of *Troy.* *Solinus* alſo makes the Inſtitution of the
Olympiads by *Iphitus,* 480 years later than *Troy*'s
Deſtruction; the Deſtruction then being 408 Years
before the Olympiads. *Euſebius* leadeth us from
Dardanus, through 4 Kings Reigns, by the ſpace of
225 Years. For *Laomedon*'s time he takes it upon
truſt, from *Annius,* out of *Menetho.*

§. 2. *Helen*'s Rape by *Paris* Son of *Priamus,* all
agree to be the Cauſe of the *Greeks* taking Arms;
but what mov'd him to that Undertaking is doubted.
Herodotus's far-fetched Cauſe hath no probability,
as have they which ſay he enterpris'd this Rape to
procure the Re-delivery of *Heſione,* King *Priamus*'s
Siſter, taken away by *Hercules,* and given to *Tela-
mon*; yet I do not think this was the ground of *Paris*'s attempt, but rather his Luſt, which was an
uſual incitement in thoſe days, as *Thucydides* ſheweth;
whereupon none durſt dwell near the Sea-Coaſt.
Tyndarus alſo, the Father of *Helen,* remembring
that *Theſeus* had Raviſhed her, cauſed all her Wooers,
which were moſt of the principal *Greeks,* to Swear,
that when ſhe had choſen an Husband, they ſhould
joyn in ſeeking her recovery, if ſhe were taken a-
way; which Oath taken, ſhe choſe *Menelaus.* Thus
the *Grecian* Princes, partly upon the Oath, and upon the Reputation of *Agamemnon* and *Menelaus,*
were drawn into this buſineſs of the *Trojan* War.
The Fleet was 1200 Sail of ſmall Ships, meet for
Robbing, the greateſt carrying but 120 Men; ſo
that the Army might be 100000. which argueth the
Trojan Power able to hold out againſt ſuch Forces ſo
many Years. But their aids out of *Phrygia, Lycia,
Miſia, Amazonia, Thrace,* yea *Aſſyria,* were great.

§. 3. The *Greeks* being prepared, ſent *Menelaus* and *Ulyſſes* Embaſſadors to *Troy*, to demand *Helen*; and as *Herodotus*, from report of an *Egyptian* Prieſt makes it probable, were anſwer'd, that *Paris* in return being driven by ſtorm into *Egypt*, *Helen* was taken from him; which Report, *Herodotus* ſeeketh by Reaſon to confirm. But whatſoever the Anſwer was, the *Greeks* incenſed, ſet forward to *Troy*, notwithſtanding *Chalchas* the Soothſayer objected great difficulties, &c. Their Names under the Command of *Agamemnon*, were *Menelaus*, *Achilles*, *Patroclus*, &c.

§. 4. After their Landing, in the firſt encounter, *Patroclus* was ſlain by *Hector*, and others; but want of Victuals ſoon diſtreſſed the *Greeks*, who were forced to imploy a great part of their Men to and fro in ſeeking relief for the Camp, by Sea and Land. And *Herodotus* Report is credible, that after the firſt Year, 'till the tenth, the *Greeks* lay little before *Troy*, but rowed up and down by Sea and Land for Booties and Victuals, waſting the Country round about. But being all returned to the Camp, the tenth Year a Peſtilence fell among them, and a Diſſention about dividing their Captive Virgins, which made *Achilles* refuſe to Fight, becauſe *Agamemnon* had taken away his Concubine. But after his Friend *Patroclus*, to whom he had lent his Armour, was ſlain by *Hector*, and pillag'd of his Armour, as the manner was, *Achilles* deſirous of Revenge, was content to be reconcil'd, upon *Agamemnon*'s ſeeking to give ſatisfaction by Gifts and Reſtitution of his Concubine *Briſeis*. After this, in the next Battel, *Achilles* ſlew *Hector* (though *Homer*'s Narration of his flying about the City thrice be unprobable) and drew him at his Chariot about the Field, and then ſold his Body to *Priamus* at a great rate. Not long after, *Paris* reveng'd that Cruelty, and ſlew *Achilles*, though Authors differ in the manner.

§.

§. 5. *Troy* at length was taken, either by the Treachery of *Æneas* and *Antenor* opening the *Scæan Gate*, whereon was an Image of an Horse, or that the *Greeks* by an Artificial Engine, like to an Horse, batter'd the Walls as *Romans* did with a Ram, or scal'd the Walls at that Gate suddenly, while the *Trojans* slept securely, upon the departure of the *Greek's* Fleet to *Tenedos* the day before, &c. The Wooden-Horse fill'd with Armed Captains is unprobable. The numbers slain on both sides, 600000 *Trojans*, and 800000 *Greeks* is Fabulous; so is the report of many Nations in those parts, striving for a descent from the remainders of *Trojan* Princes; though it be probable the *Albans*, and from them the *Romans* came from *Æneas*, and first *Padanus* from *Antenor*.

§. 6. The *Greeks* after their Victories, tasted no less Miseries than the *Trojans*, by division of Princes, separating in return; Invasion of Borderers, and Usurpation of Domesticks in their absence; and Tempests at Sea; so that few returned home; and of them, few joyned their own. The rest driven on strange Coasts, gladly planted where they could, some in *Africk*, some in *Italy*, *Apulia*, *Cyprus*, &c.

CHAP. XI.

Of Sampson, Eli, *and* Samuel.

§. 1. OF *Sampson*, read *Judges* 13, 14, 15, and 16. In whose Story observe, 1. His Mother is forbidden all strong Drink, and unclean Meat, as that which weakneth the Child conceived. 2. The Angel refused Divine Worship, which proveth, the Diviners Angels which accept Sacrifices, are Devils. 3. Whom no Force could overthrow,

Volup-

Voluptuousness did.   4. Though he often revenged
Israel, yet he delivered them not, *Chap.* 15. 11.
Lastly, his Patience was more provok'd by Contu-
mely, than Pain, or Loss.

§. 2. Of *Eli,* see the First Book of *Samuel.* He
was the first of the stock of *Ithamar,* that obtained
that High-Priesthood, which continued in his stock,
until *Solomon* cast out *Abiathar,* and put in *Zadok,*
descended from *Eleazer,* 1 *Kings* 2. 26, 35. In
his time, for the Sins of the Priests and People, the
Lord gave his Ark, the Sacrament of his Presence,
into the hands of the *Philistins,* as he did his Temple,
to be destroyed by the *Chaldeans,* and after by the
Romans, because they put more Confidence therein,
than in the Lord himself, whose Law they would
not observe. Whereas, after the Captivity, and in
the time of the *Machabees,* while they feared the
Lord, they were Victorious without an Ark, more
than they were when they guarded themselves with
the Sign, void of substance. *David* also knew the
Ark was not made for an Ensign in the Field. The
Trojans believed, that while the *Paladium,* or
Image of *Minerva* was in the City, it should never be overthrown. The Christians also carried
into the Field, in the last Fatal Battel against *Sala-
dine,* the very Cross (as they were made to believe)
whereon Christ died, and yet lost themselves, and
the Wood. But *Chrysostom* said well upon St.
Matthew, (if that be his work) of them which wore
part of St. *John*'s Gospel about their Necks, for an
Amulet, or Preservative, *If the words profit thee
not in thine Ears, how can they about thy Neck?*
For it was neither the Wood of the Ark, or of the
Cross, but the Reverence of the Father that gave
them, for a memory of his Covenant, and the
Faith of his Son, which shed his Blood on the other,
for Redemption, that could or can profit them, or

us,

us, either in this Life, or after it. The Holy ftory, telleth us how after this Victory of the *Philiftins*, the Ark of God was in Captivity ; yet they overthrew the *Philiftin's Dagon*, and brake off both Head and Hands, to fhew he had neither Wifdom nor Power in God's Prefence ; and that God and the Devil cannot inhabit in one Houfe, or one Heart. If this Idol then could not endure the reprefentation of the true God, what Marvel is it, that when it pleafed him to Cloath his only Begotten with Flefh, and fent him into the World, that all the Oracles wherein the Devil derided and betray'd Mortal Men, loft Power, Speech, and Operation at that inftant ? For when the true Light, which never had any beginning of Brightnefs, brake through the Clouds of a Virgins Womb, fhining upon the Earth, long obfcured by Idolatry, all thefe ftinking Vapours vanifhed. *Plutarch* rehearfeth, a Memorable Hiftory of that Age, of the death of their great God *Pan*, but could not find the true caufe thereof, *&c.* God alfo plagued the *Philiftims*, as well as their God, and forced them to return his Ark, and to give him Glory, after they had tried all their wit to the contrary. *See the Story.* Thus God is acknowledged of his Enemies, as he had been of *Pharaoh*, and was after of *Nebuchodonezer*, *Darius*, &c.

§. 3, Of *Samuel's* Government, 1 *Sam.* 7. He defcended of *Korah*, 1 *Chron.* 6. 22. for his Father *Elcana*, a Levite of Mount *Ephraim*, came of *Korah*, the Son of *Izaar*, Son of *Cheath*, Son of *Levi*. His Mother, after long Barrenefs, obtained him by earneft Prayer, to avoid the reproach of Barrennefs, as it was efteemed, confidering it was God's Promife, *Deut.* 7. and Bleffing to *Adam*, and *Abraham*, &c. Under his Government, the Lord freed *Ifrael* from the *Philiftins*, who at his Prayers,

were

were miraculously overthrown; as were the *Amalekites*, at the Prayer of *Moses*. He Miniftred Juftice at three fit places: Of which, fee *Cap.* 12.
§. I.

C H A P. XII.

Of Saul, *the Firft King of* Ifrael.

§. I.   THE deliberation to change the Government into a Kingdom, arofe upon *Samuel*'s being grown unable to fuftain the Burthen of fo careful a Government, which he put over his Sons; who failing of their Father's Care and Uprightnefs, and relifhing nothing but Gain, fold Law and Juftice to the beft Chap-men. The Elders obferving this, and that the Old Man, though a Prophet, yet as a natural Father, difcerned not his Sons Errors; and remembring the lamentable fuccefs of *Eli's* Sons Rule, faw no other way to put them off, than by defiring a King. This Motion difpleafed *Samuel*, who feeking Counfel from God, as in a Caufe of fo great confequence; he was order'd to hear the Voice of the People; yet fo as God accounted it a Wrong to himfelf, rather than to *Samuel*, and therefore commanded him to declare unto them, the Inconveniencies and Miferies which fhall befall them under that Government. All which are not intolerable, but as have been, and are ftill born by Subjects free Confent. But the Oppreffions threatned, *verfe* 14, *&c.* give an occafion to the Queftion, Whether a King fearing God, or
one

one which will Rule by his own diſcretion, and playeth the Tyrant, be here ſet out, as ſome judge; or that the Text only teacheth, what they ought, with patience, to bear at their Sovereigns hand, as others judge. The firſt ground themſelves upon *Deut.* 17.14. *&c.* and on the words of the Text, which do not ſay, he *may*, but he *will* do ſo and ſo, ſhewing, what Power, ſevered from Piety, will do, as in *Achab*'s Example, contrary to the Law, *Deut.* 16. 18. The Arguments on the other ſide are largely handled in that Diſcourſe of free Monarchies, which I ſhall not take upon me here to Inſert.

This change of Government God fore-told, *Gen.* 15. and 17. and 49. and provided for the direction of it by Laws, *Deut.* 17. But whether the Reaſons which move moſt Nations, moved them to chooſe a Monarch, or thereby to be cleared from the Sons of *Samuel*, doth not ſo plainly appear; for neither Perſwaſions nor Threats could draw them from their deſire of a King.

§. 2. Saul's *Election.* §. *Samuel* by God's direction, having yielded to the People, returned to his City *Rama*, expecting the Lord's direction, touching the King to be choſen, which the Lord accordinly performed, giving him warning the day before. *Samuel* hereupon, prepared to entertain whom God ſhould ſend; and *Saul* intending nothing leſs than a Kingdom, found it, and was Anointed, and Confirmed by ſigns given him by *Samuel*, and returned home. Thus God oft by meaneſt occaſions, ordereth the greateſt things, and in *Moſes* and *David's* Calling from feeding Sheep, *James* and *John* from Fiſhing, *&c.* Among the Signs given to *Saul*, one was of the Company of the Prophets; not ſuch as by divine Revelation fore-told things to come, as *Moſes*, *Joſhua*, *Samuel*, *&c.* but ſuch as were exerciſed in Expounding Scriptures, as were thoſe,

1 *Cor.*

1 *Cor.* 14. at which time God changed his Heart from a Vulgar condition to a Kingly. After this, another Assembly at *Mispezh, Saul* was Published, and designed King by God, and accepted of the People, and saluted King.

§. 3. *Saul's* Establishment after his Victory against the *Ammonites*, 1 *Sam.* 11. The *Ammonites* attending the Advantage of Times, for recovery of their Territories taken from them by the *Amorites,* having in vain attempted it in *Jephtha's* days, finding *Israel's* weakness by long oppression of the *Philistins,* who had disarmed them, had also slain 34000 of them, and that 50000 perished about *Bethshemes,* and their King was not yet so acceptable to all his Subjects, who were encouraged to begin with *Jabesh Gilead,* so near unto them. *Saul* to shew himself King, being pro-probably descended of one of the Four Hundred Virgins taken from the *Gileadits,* undertook the relief of *Jabesh,* assembling 330000 Men, and Defeated the *Ammonites.* Hence *Samuel* drew them all to *Gilgal,* where *Saul* was again Confirmed King; where also *Samuel* exhorted them to fear the Lord, and rehearsed his own Justice. After a Years Reign, *Saul* chose him a strong Guard of Three Thousand, 1 *Sam.* 13. 2.

§. 4. Saul's *Disobedience and Rejection.* §. *Jonathan* with his Regiment of 1000, surprised a Garrison of the *Philistins,* which some judge was in *Careatjearim,* where was the Ark; but *Junius* taketh it to be *Gebah* in *Benjamin,* near *Gibha,* where *Jonathan* stayed with his Thousand; so that though the *Philistins* were much broken under *Samuel,* yet they held some strong places in *Israel,* of which this was one, whose Surprise so enraged them, that they gathered together the greatest Forces, mention'd 1 *Sam.* 12. while *Saul* was at *Gilgal,* expecting *Samuel,* as he had been required, 1 *Sam.* 10. 8, But because *Samuel* came not so soon as *Saul* expected,

he

he haftened to Sacrifice, taking the Office of a Prieft on him, as fome think ; or, as others judge, he in diffidence, and diftraction upon the *Philiftins* Power, and his Peoples deferting him, attended not the Prophet's coming to direct him, and pray for him. For *Samuel* had fharply reproved and threatned him with great Indecency, had he not had extraordinary warrant from the Lord. So they departed each from other. *Saul* being come to *Gibeah*, his own City, being of ftrength; his Forces were but 600 between him and *Jonathan*, and of thefe not one had Sword or Spear, of which the Reafon is rendred in the Text. The like Policy *Nebuchadonozer* us'd in the Conqueft of *Judæa*, and *Dyonifius* in *Sicily*. It may be, the other *Ifraelits* had fome, though thefe Six hundred had not, for they might gain fome at the overthrow of the *Philiftins*, and *Ammonites*. As for the Weapons the *Ifraelites* ufed in thefe Wars, they were Clubs, Bows, and Slings, wherein they were expert, 1 *Chr.* 12. 2. and their Victories were rather extraordinary, as by Thunder or Aftonifhments fent from God, as in this next Overthrow by the hand of *Jonathan* and his Armourbearer, wherein God fet them at diffention, *cap.* 14. 10. So that the *Ifraelites* needed no Swords, when every *Philiftin*'s Sword fupplyed the want. After this Victory, *Saul* undertook by turns, all the bordering Enemies, and by fpecial Commandment, the *Amalekites* in *Arabia Petræa* and the Defart, ravaging from *Havila* to *Shur*. But for prefuming contrary to God's exprefs Charge, to fpare *Agag*, &c. he was utterly rejected of the Lord, for all his pretence of Sacrifice; and *Samuel* never after vifited *Saul*.

§. 5. *Samuel* fearing to Anoint another King, as God willed him, is directed how to do it fafely. So that by cautious care to avoid danger, he did no way derogate from God's Providence ; feeing the Lord
himfelf

himſelf, tho' All-ſufficient, inſtructed *Samuel* to a-
void *Saul*'s Fury, by the accuſtomed cautious ways
of the World ; and therefore Men neglecting of Prayer to God, and exerciſe of that Wiſdom he hath indued the Mind of Man with, for his preſervation,
are ſtupified with the Opinion of Fate, *&c.* *Jeſſe*
having preſented all his Sons, but *David*, to *Samuel*,
he only whom the Father neglected, is choſen of
God, and anointed by *Samuel.* The *Philiſtins* in
the mean time conſidering how *Saul*'s Power increaſed, while they ſat ſtill, and doubting leaſt *Iſrael*
might become able to revenge themſelves, if they
were ſuffer'd thus to encreaſe, thought it good to
offer a new Check, preſuming of their own Abilities and former Succeſſes ; as for late Diſaſters,
they might ſuppoſe the one was by a caſual Tem-
peſt, and the laſt by a miſtaken Alarum, which
wrought needleſs fear, and put the Army to Rout.
Having therefore taken the Field, Encamping near
Saul's Army, and both keeping their ground of advantage, they maintained ſome Skirmiſhes, not joining in groſs ; which the *Philiſtins* had cauſe to fear,
conſidering their late Succeſs, and thereupon perhaps, provoked to ſingle Combat with their Giant,
upon Condition of a general ſubjection of the vanquiſhed Nation, in their Champion.　This gave occaſion to *David*, now to make a famous entrance into the publick notice of the People, with the ſucceſs Recorded in Scripture.　By this Victory, *David*
fell under the heavy diſpleaſure of *Saul*, by reaſon of
his great Merits ; whereupon he became a Convert
Tyrant, faithleſs to Men, and irreligious to God,
as the Hiſtory ſheweth, which brought him to the
end we read of.

§. 6. *Of ſuch as lived with* Samuel *and* Saul. §. *Æ-
neas Sylvius* began to Reign over the *Latins* in *Alba*,
about the 11th year of *Samuel*, and Reigned Thirty
one years.　The ſame year *Dorcillus* began in *Aſſyria*,
being

being the Thirty first King, and Reigned Forty
years. The *Dores* which came with *Heraclides*, obtained *Peloponnefus* in this Age. Here follows the
Account of the First Planters of *Greece*, from *Jopetus*,
Father of *Prometheus*, Father of *Deucalion* and *Pyrrha*, King and Queen of *Theffaly*, of whom came
Helen. Father of *Xuthus*, *Dorus*, and *Æolus*. *Xuthus*
fled to *Erichtheus* of *Athens*, of whose Daughter came
Achæus and *Ion.* *Achæus* for a flaughter, fled to *Laconia* in *Peloponnefus*, and gave it his Name, and after,
recovered *Theffaly.* *Ion* was made Governour of
Attica, which he brought into a civil Courfe, and
Planted *Syciona*, then called *Ægiolio*, and Married *Helice* the Kings Daughter, of whom also
the Land took Name. *Dorus* fecond Son of *Helen*,
Planted about *Parnaffus* and *Lacedemon* ; but when
the *Heraclides*, Nephews of *Hercules*, Invaded *Peloponnefus*, the *Dores* affifting, they expelled the *Achæans*
in *Laconia*, who feeking Habitation, drove out the
Ionians, who failed into *Afia*, on whofe Weft Coaft
they Built Twelve Cities. *Hercules*, Anceftor of the
Heraclides, and his Twelve Labours of Fabulous
Poets rehearfed, Sure it is *Greece*, was oblig'd to him
for freeing it from many Tyrants and Thieves,
which oppreffed the Land in the Reign of *Euriftbe-
us*, who employed him therein, being Jealous of
him for his Virtue and Defcent from *Perfeus*. His
Children after his Death, fled to the *Athenians*, who
affifted them againft *Euriftheus*, whom they flew ;
but upon the death of *Hillus*, Son of *Hercules*, flain
in Combat by *Echenus* King of *Tegeates* in *Arcadia*,
who affifted *Atreus*, Succeffor of *Euriftheus*, they were
to leave the Country for one Hundred years, now
expired, when they returned under *Ariftodemus*,
when *Tifamenus* was King of *Achæa*.

§. 7. *Homer* the Poet feemed to live about this
time ; but the diverfity of Mens Opinions, and cu-
riofity about this Age is fo Ridiculous, that I would
not

not offend the Reader therewith : But to ſhew the uncertainty of Hiſtorians, as well in this, as other Queſtions of Time, *&c.* *Euſebius* in his *Evan. præpar.* out of *Tatian,* nameth many *Greek* Writers more Antient than *Homer.* *Heſiodus*'s Age is alſo queſtioned ; ſome hold him Elder, ſome Younger than he : But *Varro* leaves it uncertain, finding that both the Fathers lived ſome Years together. *Senyes,* or *Senemyres* ſeemed to have Ruled *Egypt* at this time : For *Teneferſobris,* his Succeſſor, preceded *Vaphres* Father-in-Law to *Solomon.* About the end of *Saul,* the *Amazons* and *Cymmerians* Invaded *Aſia.* After the Fall of *Troy,* Six Kingdoms grew up, as the *Latins* in *Italy*; *Lacedemon,* *Corinth,* and *Achaia* in *Greece*; *Syria, Soba,* and *Damaſcus,* under the *Adads* in *Arabia,* of which were Ten Kings, which began and ended, in effect, with the Kings of *Iſrael,* which now changed their form of Government into a Monarchy.

C H A P. XIII.

Of David; *Firſt of his Eſtate under* Saul.

§. 1. DAvid's hazards after he was deſigned King, were many ; firſt, with *Goliah,* which won him Fame with all; Love with *Jonathan,* like that he bare to his own Soul ; and a ground of deadly Hatred in *Saul,* though it brake not out 'till he had entertained him to play on his Harp, and had made him his Son-in-Law ; when in a raving Fit, he threw his Spear at him. *Cenſorinus* ſpeaketh of *Eſculapius* a Phyſician, and *Seneca* of *Pythagoras*'s Curing Frenzie by Muſick ; but *Saul*'s Madneſs aroſe from the Cauſe of Cauſes, and therefore incurable ; and the eaſe he had, God ordained for the

Muſi-

Musician's good, more than the King's. *Saul* after this, fearing to trust *David* about his Person, imploy'd him against the *Philiftins*, hoping of his Fall by them : And being difappointed therein, he moved *Jonathan* and his Servants to kill him; but in vain. From many other defperate Perils the Lord delivered him at home and abroad, yea in a Mutiny of his own, &c. as the Hiftory of this part of his Life witneffeth. *Saul* being flain, the *Philiftins* Victory was fuch, as fome Towns, even beyond *Jordan*, were abandon'd, and left to their Oppreffion, without refiftance. It is therefore to be wonder'd at, that they being Warlike and Ambitious, did not follow the Victory, to make the Conqueft entire. But it may be, that the Civil Wars between *David* and the Houfe of *Saul* immediately breaking out, gave them hope of an eafie Victory over both; whereas their farther Purfuit might inforce an Attonement againft a common Enemy.

§. 2. *David's* beginning of his Reign was oppofed by *Abner*, who fought to advance *Ifhbofheth* the Son of *Saul*, yet without right, while *Mephibofheth* the Son of *Jonathan* lived. The firft War was defenfive in *David*, when *Abner* fought it upon a Challenge of twelve Combatants on either fide, which flew each other; like the Combate between 300 *Lacedemonians*, and as many *Argives*, wherein three furvived; and between the *Horatii*, and the *Curatii*, for the *Romans*, and the *Latins*. The Text Chap. 3. 1. makes it probable. The Wars between *David* and *Ifhbofheth* lafted longer than two years; fo that thofe two Years mentioned, Chap. 2. 13. fome *Rabins* refer to the time when this was written.

§. 3. *Abner* being reconciled to *David*, was murthered by *Joab*, in revenge of *Afael*, and in jealoufie of his Place and Dignity, which admitted of no Companion, much lefs a Superiour, as he doubted *Abner* would prove, being General of Ten Tribes.

Tribes. Upon like jealouſie, he alſo murdered his own Kinſman *Amaſa.* The death of *Abner* might greatly have endanger'd *David's* Condition, if any thing could withſtandGod's Ordinance; therefore he wiſely bewailed it ſo openly, complaining of *Joab's* Greatneſs; ~~which makes Princes~~ oft put up Wrongs at their hands; yet he publickly Curſed him, &c.

§. 4. *David's* Reign over all *Iſrael* after *Iſhboſheth's* death being confirmed, his firſt Enterprize was a-gainſt *Jeruſalem,* the Center of the Kingdom, held by the *Jebuſites,* from *Joſhua* to that day; whoſe ſtrength was ſuch, that in deriſion they Manned the Wall with Blind and Lame Men, but loſt it. The *Philiſtins* hearing of *David's* Anointing, thought it good to try him before he was warm in his Seat; but were overthrown twice. *David* after this, brought the Ark to the City of *David*; after which he intended to Build a Temple, but was forbidden, becauſe he was a Man of War. The Wars which he had made were juſt, yet God refuſed to have the Foundation of his Temple to be layed by his hands; whereby the damnable Pride of Princes appeareth, who by terrours of Wars think to grow to Greatneſs like the Almighty; not caring to imi-tate his Mercy and Goodneſs, or to ſeek the bleſſed Promiſe by our Saviour to Peace-Makers; yet God ſo accepted his Religious intent, that his Kingdom was confirmed to him, and his; and a Promiſe is made of that Everlaſting Throne to be Eſtabliſhed in his Seed.

§. 5. *David* after this overthrew the *Philiſtins,* and demoliſhed their ſtrong City of *Gath,* which was their Frontier Town, at the entrance into *Ju-dah,* and *Ephraim*; from whence they made their incurſions, and thither retreated; and was there-fore called in the Text, the Bridle of *Amgar.* * After this he gave them 4 Overthrows; of which ſee 2 *Sam.* 21. 17. But the Conqueſt of *Moab,* and the

* *See* Ju-nius.

the *Arabian* Wars came between. Of *Moab* he slew two parts, and saved a third to till the ground; yet the occasion is uncertain; only *Moses* forbad them to seek their peace. From thence to *Syria Zoba*, against *Hadadezer*.

§. 6. *David* overthrew *Hadadezer*, going to inlarge his Borders to *Euphrates*; which purpose for *Euphrates* cannot be understood of *David*, who upon this Victory, and winning of *Damascus* upon it, had a fair way and help of Chariots and Horses now won, fit for such a Journey, if he had intended it; all which, notwithstanding he returned to *Jerusalem*: This purpose is better referred to *Hadadezer*. Next hereto, followed the Victory against the *Ammonites*, and their Confederates, with the severe Revenge *David* took for the Affront *Hanun* shewed his Ambassadors. But before *Rabba*, afterwards called *Philadelphia*, was Besieged, *David* gain'd another great Victory over the *Aramites*, brought to *Helam* by *Adadezer* out of *Mesopotamia*; from whence yet *David* proceeded not to *Euphrates*.

§. 7. *David's Troubles in his Reign.* §. As Victories beget Security, and Prosperity, Forgetfulness of former Misery, and many times of God himself, the giver of all Goodness; so it fell out with this good King. For being free from dangerous and apparent Enemies, he began to indulge Human Affections, as we see in his Carriage towards *Uriah* and his Wife; forgetting the zealous care which formerly he had to please God, in the precise keeping of his Commandments. After this he fell by degrees from the highest Happiness, and his Days were filled with inter-changeable Joys and Woes, and the Sword never departed from his House. Then followed the death of the Adulterous Child, Incestuous Rape of *Thamar*, Murder of *Amnon*, Insurrection, Usurpation, Incest, and Death of *Absalom*, the Treachery of *Ziba*, the Affront

K

front of *Shimei*, the Infolence of *Joab*, the Rebellion of *Sheba*, the Murder of *Amafa*, *&c.* The Land
also indured three Years Famine for *Saul*'s wrong to
the *Gibeonites*, which was relieved by the death of
Seven of *Saul*'s Iffue, of which Five were the Sons
of *Michol*'s Sifter, as by an Elipfis the Hebrew will
bear, as in the like, *ver.* 19. As the Lord by this
Execution fecured *David*'s Houfe from Competitors, fo was the Nation ftrengthened by the valour of many brave Commanders, of which, Six
Colonels under the General, had Thirty Captains
of Thoufands, among whom the difference of place
and Honour, grew by meer confideration of Virtue, as we fee *Abifhai*, Brother of *Joab*, and the
King's Kinfman, fhort in Honour of the firft Three.
David thus Eftablifhed, in oftentation of his Power, provoked the Lord to punifh his People with
Peftilence, for his numbring of them, and flew Seventy Thoufand.

§. 8. David's *laft Acts.* §. *Abifhag* in his impo-
tence, keepeth him Warm, *&c.* *Adonijah* afpireth,
which caufeth *David* publickly to declare *Solomon*
his Succeffor, and to fet him in his Throne; whereupon *Adonijah* and his Affociates were fcattered.
After this, *David* having two efpecial Cares remaining, of which he defired to difcharge his
Thoughts, one concerning *Solomon*'s peaceable holding his Crown, the other about building the Temple;
he called a Parliament of all the Princes, *&c.* In
this Affembly, he fignifieth his purpofe, and the ap-
probation of God ; chargeth all, and *Solomon* by
Name, *v.* 9. and produceth the pattern of the
Work, according to the Form which God himfelf
had appointed, laying down his own preparation;
whereto the Princes and others added their free-
will offering. This being done, *David* made a folemn Feaft, at which time *Solomon* was again anointed King, and received Fealty of the Princes, People,

ple, and the King's Sons. After all this, *David*, as upon his Death-Bed, again with powerful words, giveth *Solomon* the Charge of the Lord his God; and then adviseth him concerning *Joab*, who otherwise tho' of exceeding desert, yet for his intolerable Insolence, came to such an end by Justice, when time served, as many worthy Men had done for acts of the like presumption. *David*, after Forty Years Reign, died, being Seventy Years old, having been a Man of small Stature, exceeding Strength; and for internal Gifts and Graces, passing all others; and putting his Human Frailty apart, commended by God himself, to be according to his own Heart. Being a Prophet as well as a King, he fore-told Christ more ~~lightsomly~~ *plainly and lively than all the rest, and writ many Psalms; but whether all the Book, is disputed, though *Chrysostom* and *Augustin* hold it. Christ *De Civ. li.* 13. 14. and his Apostles cite him.

§. 9. David *and* Solomon's *Treasures.* §. *David*'s Treasure exceeded, as appeareth by what he gave toward the Temple, 1 *Chron.* 22. 14. which amounteth to 3333¼ Cart loads of Silver, or 6000 *l.* sterling to every Cart-load; and 23 Millions and 1000 *l.* in Gold; a matter incredible, but for Testimony of Scripture; where consider how such a Treasure could be raised by Parcimony. *Eusebius* cites *Eupolemus* for a Navy which he sent from *Melanis*, or *Achanis*, to the Isle *Upher*, or *Opher*, by *Ortelius*; then his Husbandry, which was great, his Presents, Tributes, Taxations, Capitations, his Spoils; the Riches of the Sanctuary long increasing by large Gifts, and the Portion out of all Prizes from Enemies, even from *Joshua*'s days. Of *Solomon*'s Treasure, see 1 *Kings* 9. 20. and 10. 14. 29. See *Josephus* of the Treasure he hid in *David*'s Sepulcher, out of which *Hircanus* took 3000 Talents, and *Ant. li.* 7. *Herod* more. 12.

§. 10. David's *Contemporaries.* §. *Achis* a Philistin

ſtin King of *Gath,* and another in *Solomon's* days, *Latinus Sylvius,* King of *Alba. Cedrus* the laſt King of *Athens,* after whom they changed the Government into a Principality for Life, without Regal Title. This change was made in honour of *Codrus,* voluntarily ſlain for their ſakes in a War with the *Dores,* to diſappoint the Oracle. *Eupalus* the Third King of *Aſſyria,* ſate 38 Years; *Ixion* the ſecond King of the *Heraclids* in *Corinth,* Son of *Eurythenes. Agis* the ſecond King of the *Heraclids* in *Lacedemon,* he reſtored the *Laconians,* and made the Citizens of *Helos* Slaves, for refuſing Tribute, as at length, all the *Meſſenians* were, and thereof called *Helons,* that is, Slaves: Slave came from *Sclavi,* which were *Samaritans,* now *Ruſſians,* which Conquering *Illyria,* would be called Slaves, which with them ſignifieth glorious; but when the warm Clime had thawed their Northern hardneſs, (but not ripened their Wits) the *Italians,* which made many of them Bond-men, uſed their Name in Reproach, calling all Bond-men Slaves. *Achetratus* ſucceeded *Agis,* in whoſe time *Androchus* the Third Son of *Codrus,* aſſiſted by the *Iones,* built *Epheſus* in *Caria,* and was ſlain of the *Carians.* He alſo held *Eritbræ,* famous for *Sybyls,* which writ Verſes of *Jeſus Chriſt,* Son of God, the Saviour, reported by *Auguſtine,* who ſaw them. *Vaphres* King of *Egypt* began to Reign, when *David* Beſieged *Rabba, Magneſia,* on *Meander* in *Aſia,* founded now, and *Capua Campania.*

C H A P.

C H A P. XIV.

Of Solomon, *Anno Mundi,* 2991.

§. 1. SOlomon began to Reign in the 2991*st* Year of the World ; and was firſt Congratulated by *Hiram* King of *Tyre,* according to the' Ancient Cuſtom of Princes. Though his Reign were peaceable, yet his beginning was with the blood of his Brother *Adonijah,* without warrant either from his Father, or the Law of God. The occaſion was his deſire of *Abyſhag* ; but being his Elder Brother, who alſo had ſought the Kingdom, it was enough, as a word is to the Wife ; and he which ſeeth the Claw, knows whether it be a Lyon or no. *Solomon* took the motion, as a demonſtration of a new Treaſon ; ſuch was the jealouſie of ſeeking a King's Widow, or Concubines ; as *Abſolom's* taking his Father's Concubines, was a taking poſſeſſion of a Royalty, ſo it was applied to *David* by *Nathan,*&c. 2 *Sam.* 12. 8. Birth-right pleaded by *Adonijah,* was according to God's Law, and of Nations ; but the Kings of the *Jews* were more Abſolute, and not without Example in *Jacob,* for private Inheritance. As for what we read of Peoples Elections, it was but an acknowledging him whom the Lord choſe, and not to fruſtrate the Elder's Right. *Solomon* alſo executed *Joab,* depoſed *Abiathar,* and put *Shemei* to death. He Married the Daughter of *Vaphres* (as *Euſebius* calls him) King of *Egypt* ; and according to his requeſt to God, obtained extraordinary Wiſdom, eſpecially for Government; as appeared in the Example purpoſely ſet down, of his judging the two Harlots ; yet did he excell in all other Knowledge.

§. 2. Solomon's *Building and Glory.* §. Renewing the League with *Hiram* of *Tyre,* he had much of his Materials for his Buildings from him. Of the Glorious Temple, and parts of it, many Learned Men have Written; as *Salmeron, Montanus, Bibera, Barradas, Azorius, Villalpandus, Pineda,* &c. The Letters which passed between *Solomon* and *Hiram, Eusebius* sets down out of *Eupolon,* which *Josephus* also Records in his Antiquities, *Lib.* 8. §. 2. Besides the matchless Temple, he made many other Magnificent Buildings, of which *Gerar* on the Border of *Ephraim,* taught the *Egyptians* to visit those parts in *Reboboam*'s days, before they were sent for. *Thadimor, Joseph* held to be *Palmyra,* in the Desart of *Syria,* to the North-East of *Libanus,* the utmost Border of *Solomon*'s Dominion, which *Jerom* calls *Thermeth*; and by *Adrian* Rebuilt, and called *Adrianopolis.* He also Repaired and Peopled the Towns *Hiram* refused, and made his first and only Journey in *Syria Zobah,* to establish his Tributes, and then visited all the Borders of his Dominions; from *Palmyrena* in the North, to *Eziongaber* and *Eloth* in the South, upon the *Red-Sea.*

§. 3. *Solomon* from *Eziongaber,* sent a Fleet to *Ophir,* an Island of the *Molucca*'s in *East-India,* from whence he received 430 Talents of Gold, all Charges defrayed. Of the word *Tharsis* see before, *lib.* 1. *c.* 8. §. 9. & 10. *Pineda* dreamt *Ophir* was in the *Cades,* or *Calis-Malis,* his Country in *Spain,* of old called *Tartessus,* whereto the next way by the Mediterranean was hindred by the great *Atlantick* Island, exceeding all *Africa,* swallowed up and choaking the Streights with Mud; like his Dream of *Jonas*'s Whale, which in 3 days swam about all *Africa,* into the *Red-Sea,* to cast him up, 12000 Miles in compass. *Solomon*'s Chariots, Horsemen, daily Provision, Wisdom, &c. See 1 *Kings* 4. 10, with 2 *Chron.* 9.

§. 4.

§. 4. Solomon's *Fall, and term of Life.* §. Solomon forgetting what the Lord Commanded; as he
had plenty of all other things, so of Wives, even of
Idolatrous Nations, 1 *Kings* 11. 1, 2. prohibited;
whereupon they turned his heart after other Gods;
for which, the Lord punish'd him with Enemies in,
his Age, and rent his Kingdom from his Son, as
he threatned, 1 *Kings* 11. Touching his Age, it is
conjectur'd by his Father's Actions, whose Conquests
were ended, before he wan *Rabba,* when *Solomon*
was not Born. So that half of *David*'s Reign being
spent at the time of vanquishing the *Ammonites,* Solomon's Birth must fall after *David*'s 20 Years; and
above a Year it could not be, seeing *Rehoboam*'s Age
at *Solomon*'s death, compared with the many heavy
things which befell *David* after; and that *David* in
his Charge to *Solomon,* speaketh as to a Man grown;
though *Solomon* at Nineteen Years old, speaking to
the Lord about his weighty Charge, might well call
himself a Charge. Some time after, *Ammon* forced
Thamar, and two Years after was slain by *Absolom,*
who fled to *Geshur,* where he abode three Years, yet
saw not his Father's face for two years. How long
after he brake into Rebellion is uncertain, which
seemeth to be the 30th Year of *David*'s Reign, but
the 40th Year after his Anointing; as those words
2 *Sam.* 15. 7. may well be taken. Which 40, *Josephus, Theodoret,* and the Latin Translation read
4 Years; to wit, from *Absolom*'s Return.

§. 5. *Solomon*'s Writings. In his *Proverbs* he
teacheth good Life, and correcting the contrary.
In *Ecclef.* the Vanity of Humane Nature. In the
Canticles he singeth the Epithalamion of Christ and
his Church. The *Book of Wisdom,* the best Learned
make us think it none of his; and *Kimchi* ascribeth
the 3 other to *Isaiah* the Prophet. *Josephus* also
tells us of his own Invention, rather than truly that
Solomon wrote Books of Enchantments. But certainly

K 4

tainly fo ftrange an Example of Human Frailty was never read of; that a Man endowed with Wifdom, by God himſelf; in honour of whom, and for his Service he built the firſt and moſt glorious Temple of the World; was made King, not by Law, but the Love of God, and became the Wifeſt, Richeſt, and Happieſt of all Kings, did in the end by perſwaſion of weak, wretched, Idolatrous Women, forget and forſake the Lord of all the World, and giver of all goodneſs, of which he was more liberal to him than to any that ever the World had.

See Siracides. 47. 13,14.&c.

§. 6. *Solomon's* Contemporaries, were *Agelaus* in *Corinth*; *Labotes* in *Lacedemonia*; *Silvius Alba* over the *Latins*; *Leoſthenes* in *Aſſyria*.; *Argaſtus*, and after *Archippus* in *Athens*; *Baliaſtrus* ſucceeded *Hiram* in *Tyre*; others put *Bozorius* between: *Seſac*, after *Vaphres* in *Egypt*, whom *Euſebius* calls *Smerides*; and others by other Names.

CHAP. XV.

Solomon's Succeſſors to Jehoram. *The Kingdom divided.*

R*Ehoboam* ſucceeded his Father, but was not fo Wife as to reſolve the People's Petition without Counſel; nor yet to diſcern of Councils, which is the very beſt of Wiſdom in Princes and all others; for though he conſulted with grave adviſed Men, yet he was Tranſported by his Favourites, who, ignorant of the nature of Severity, which without the Temper of Clemency, is Cruelty it ſelf, thruſt him on to threaten an Increaſe of what was unſupportable already; ignorant alſo, that Severity is to be uſed for the Help, and not for the Hurt of Subjects. Theſe fooliſh Paraſites could better judge of the

King's

King's difpofition, which Learning was fufficient for to enable them to the Places they held. This Anfwer of *Rehoboam*, fet forward *Jeroboam*'s defigns; and the Prophecie of *Abijah*, as the fequel fhewed; for the People at once chofe *Jeroboam*; and after the manner of all Rebels, forgetting Duty to God, and Bonds of Nature, renounced all intereft in *David*; the Honour of their Nation, and murder the Officers fent to appeafe them. After this, *Rehoboam* intended Wars upon them, but was ftayed by the Prophet from God. *Jeroboam* fortified himfelf, and to prevent re-uniting by communion in Religion, impioufly fet up a new Worfhip, learn'd in *Egypt*, expelling the Levites. Thus by irreligious Policy, he founded that Idolatry, which rooted *Ifrael* out of the Land at laft; neither could he be ftayed by the Prophet that foretold his Advancement, nor Miracle upon his own hand. This point of Policy muft be made good, though it caft off God, and the Religion of his Fathers. Whereunto an *Italian* Hiftorian compares the Policy of his Nation, in making good the State they have gotten, by what means foever, as if God would not oppofe it. Upon this ground, *Amos* muft not Prophecie at *Bethel*, it is the King's Court. *Jehu* will upon this ground maintain the Worfhip of Calves; and *Hen.* IV of *France* change Religion, *&c.* whom yet the Proteftants whom he forfook, never hurt, as the Papifts did whom he followed. But of the wretched end of fuch Policy, all thefe are notable Examples.

§. 2. Rehoboam's *Impiety, Punifhment, End, and Contemporaries.* §. *Rhehoboam* Fortified his Cities, as well againft *Egypt*, as *Jeroboam*; and then forfook the Lord, 1 *Kings* 14. and 1 *Chron.* 11. But in his Fifth Year, *Sefac* of *Egypt*, who favoured *Jeroboam*, taught him how weak Fortifications are, where God watcheth not the City. *Sefac* brought

with

with him the *Lybeans,* *Cufits* of *Arabia,* and *Succæans,* which were not the *Troglodits* fpoken of by
Pliny, and *Ptolomy,* as *Junius* judgeth. Thefe were
600 Miles from the beft of *Egypt,* and were in the
22d degree North from the Line, too far for fuch
an occafion. The *Succæans* were rather *Arabian
Egyptians,* as the *Ichthyophagy* in *Ptolomy,* between
the Mountains *Alabaftrine,* and the *Red-Sea,* when
this powerful *Sefac* wan *Jerufalem,* and other Cities
of *Juda,* and added to the Spoil of them the Temple, and the King's Houfe, and the Egyptian Kings
after claimed Sovereignty of *Juda.* After 17 Years
Reign, *Reboboam* died, and *Jeroboam* out-lived him
4 Year. *Terfippus* in *Athens, Doriftus* in *Sparta, Pri-
minas* in *Corinth, Sylvius Alys* over the *Latins, Pe-
riciades* in *Affyria,* and *Abdaftrartus* in *Tyre,* whom
his Fofter-Brother Murdered, and Ufurped 12 Year;
but *Aftartus* Son of *Baleafter,* recovered the Kingdom from them.

§. 3. *Abia* fucceeded *Reboboam* in his Kingdom
and Vices; yet God was pleafed to give him the
Victory over *Jeroboam,* of whofe Subjects he flew
500000, though he fuffered his Father to be vanquifhed by *Sefac* the *Egyptian*; not for want of
Strength, but Wifdom and Carriage, which God
giveth when and where it pleafeth him : Who by
the *Affinity* by which *Solomon* thought to affure his
Eftate, the Lord brake it in his next Succeffor. And
tho' then God ufed to fhew the Caufes of fuch Judgments by his Prophets, yet is he the fame juft God,
to raife and throw down Kings and Eftates for the
fame Offences. And thofe Afflictions of *Ifrael,* and
the Courfes thereof, are fet down for Prefidents to
fucceeding Ages. As the Famin for *Saul's* Cruelty,
David's Calamities for *Uriah, Solomon's* lofs of Ten
Tribes for Idolatry, *Reboboam* for Idolatry and Sodomy in the Land : *Jeroboam, Joram, Abab, Jefabel.*
The like Judgments are executed daily for the like
Offences

Offences, though Men, wiſe in the World, raiſe theſe effects no higher than to ſecond Cauſes.

§. 4. *Aſa*, after three years, ſucceeded *Abijab*, who reformed Religion, and proſpered. He overthrew *Zerab* and his 100000 Men, *&c.* That *Zerab* was an *Arabian*, not an *Æthiopian*, was proved before *. But after he fell to rely on Man, and hired *Ben-* *badad* againſt *Baaſha*, not relying upon the Aſſi-ſtance of God, he fell to perſecute the Prophet which reproved him, and to oppreſs the People, for which God plagued him. There lived at the ſame time, *Ageſilaus* and *Bacis* of *Corinth*, *Aſtartus* and *Aſtarlaius* Kings of *Tyre* ; *Alys* and *Capis*, Kings of the *Latins* ; *Ophrateus* in *Aſſyria*. *Terſippus*, and *Phorbas* in *Athens* ; *Chemmis* in *Egypt*, whom *Cheops* ſucceeded, and Reigned Fifty ſix years, to the ſixteenth of *Joas* ; *Baaſa* King of *Iſrael* began in the Third year of *Aſa*, and Reigned Twenty four years, which was about the Twenty ſixth Year of *Aſa* ; ſo that his Attempt againſt *Aſa*, 2 *Chron.* 16. 1. was the 26th of *Aſa*, but the 36th of the Kingdom of *Juda* called *Aſa*'s, becauſe he there Reigned in it. Conſider that *Rehoboam* Reigned ſeventeen years, *Abijab* three, and *Aſa* Forty one, in whoſe Third *Baaſan* began, ſo the Thirty ſixth year of *Juda*'s Kingdom, fell in the Sixteenth year of *Aſa*.

the margin note: * *Lib.* ſ. Sect. 3, 14. *and* c. 10.

§. 5. The Alterations in the Kingdom of *Iſrael* in the Reign of *Aſa*, might have reduced the Ten Tribes to the Houſe of *David*, if God had not determined the contrary. *Jeroboam* loſt 500000 : *Nadab* his Son, in two years, loſt his Life and Kingdom, ſo that of his Fathers Worldly Wiſdom, to Eſtabliſh a Kingdom in his Poſterity, nothing remained but the hateful Memory, that he made *Iſrael* to ſin. *Baaſa* rooting out *Jeroboam*'s Houſe, yet imbraced his Idolatry, which drew the ſame Sentence of God's Wrath upon him and his Family ; and tho' he thought it Wiſdom, to Fortify his Kingdom, which

which he found weakened by *Asa*, by making League
with *Benhadad*; yet God turned his Wisdom into
Foolishness, and by the same Hand destroyed *Nepht-
talim*. *Ela* Son of *Baasha* succeeded, and was slain
by *Zimri*; who wanting strength to defend himself
against *Omri*, had Courage enough to burn himself
in *Terza*. *Omri* by the People's Division was a while
opposed by *Tibni*, but prevailed.

§. 6. *Israel* thus afflicted under those unhappy
Princes, it is a wonder that the People returned
not to their ancient Kings, and reunited not to
those Two Mighty Tribes; but they still continued in grievous oppressions of the Factious Usurpers
and Competitors, and under the revenging hand of
God for their defection. To say God's secret Will
was such, was not reason either to the Ten Tribes
not to return, nor to *Abijah*, after he had so weak-
ned *Israel*, not to perfect his Conquest; for though
his Father was restrained expresly by the Lord, yet
was not he. We may then boldly look into two
Causes. *First*, Why the People bore so quietly the
slaughter of *Nadab*, and interpretation of *Jeroboam*
their own chosen King, and revenged the death of
Ela Son of *Baasa*, an Usurper. It is therefore
probable, that the People by defection from *Reboboam*, seeking ease of former Burthens, found *Jeroboam* and his Son to retain some Kingly Prerogatives, which had been grievous to them under *Solomon*, which *Baasa* had forborn, and reduced the
form of Civil Government to a more temperate Method, which much pleased them. *Secondly*, the same
may be the Reason they returned not to the House
of *David*, whose Scepter they found so heavy under
Solomon, and were threatned by his Son with more
burthen. They had seen *Joab* and *Shimei* slain
without all form of Judgment, *Adonijah* without
Cause, as *Jeroboam* should have been; which lawless
Power

Power grew more barbarous in *Jehoram, Manaf-es*, &c. As for the Kings of *Israel*, we find no such arbitrary proceeding; for even *Jezabel* kept the form judicial against *Naboth.* And well it may be, though *Jeroboam* had established a Law against the Prophets of God, which the Idolatrous People approved; by which Law *Jezabel* slew so many. This difference of Power, Arbitrary, and according to Law, made the People of *Judah* less affectionate to their Princes than the *Israelites*, who were accustomed not to kill their Kings as the *Judeans* did, but revenged when they were able, such as were slain by Usurpers. The like moderation of Kingly Prerogatives in the Government of *England*, gained such affection of the People, as never any perish'd by the Fury of the People, whose heat in greatest Insurrection was extinguished with the blood of some great Officers. Let not Monarchs fear straitning of their Absoluteness by mighty Subjects, as long as by their Wisdom they keep the hearts of the People, who will be sure to come in on their side: As *Briarius* with his hundred hands assisted *Jupiter*, when all the Gods conspired against him. For a good Form of Government is sufficient of it self, to retain the People, not only without assistance of a laborious Wit, but even against all devices of the shrewdest Politicians; every Sheriff and Constable being sooner able to arm the Multitude in the King's behalf, than any over-weening Rebel against him. Princes immediately assign'd by God, or getting Command by strong hand, have presumed of more Absolute Prerogatives than Kings Chosen; and the People which thought Obedience to Princes a part of Duty to God, will endure much more with patience, than others who have Kings of their own chusing.

§. 7. *Jehosaphat*, a Religious Happy Prince, succeeded *Asa*, whose Forces of Men of War were

were 1160000, by which he recovered his Tributes
from the *Arabians* and *Philiftins*, befides his own
Garifons; yet his Country did not exceed the Coun-
ty of *Kent* in largenefs.   This number may be
thought ftrange in fo fmall a Territory, being far
greater than any Mufter ever taken of that Country.
Joab had found 500000, *Reboboam* 180000, *Abia*
408000, *Afa* 580000, *Amazia* found 300000,
Uzziah 307000; and furely if *Jehofophat* had
1160000 Men, he would not have feared *Moab* and
Ammon, &c.   I am therefore of Opinion (fubmitting to better Judgments) that the numbers fpoken
of, 2 *Chron.* 17. were not all at one time, but that
the two firft numbers under *Adnah* and *Jehohanan,*
were after Muftred, and Commanded by *Amafia, Eli-
ada,* and *Jehofabad* ; yet this Mighty Prince made a
League with *Ahab,* and matched his Son *Joram* with
his Daughter, and affifted him at *Ramoth-Gilead,* for
which he was reproved by *Jehu* the Prophet ; as he
was a fecond time by the Prophet *Eliezer,* for joyning with *Ahab's* Son in preparing a Fleet.   So he
joyned with *Jehoram* againft *Moab,* and had perifhed
by Famine, if *Elifha* had not relieved them from
God, whofe Goodnefs was ever prone to fave the
Evil for the fake of the Good, but never deftroyed
the Good for the Evil.

    Ophratenes now Reigned in *Affyria,* *Capetus* and
Tiberinus at *Alba* in Italy, *Atazedes* in *Athens,* *Agefilaus* in *Corinth, Archilochus* in *Lacedemon,* *Badeforus*
in *Tyrus,* *Achab, Ochozias,* and *Jehoram* in *Ifrael.*

CHAP.

CHAP. XVI.

Of Jehoram, *and* Ahazia.

JEboram, the Son of *Jebosaphat,* being thirty two
Years old, began to Reign, and Reigned 8 Year,
of which, 4 was in his Father's Life; who at his
two Journeys with *Abab* and *Jeboram,* Kings of *Israel,* left him Viceroy 'till his return. The first was
in *Jebosaphat's* 17th Year, when also *Abazia* Son of
Abab began to Reign; whose Brother *Jeboram,* the 2d
year after, succeeded K. of *Israel* in the 2d year of *Jeboram,*King of *Juda*; that is,of hisReign when his Father *Jebosaphat* took the sole Government again upon
him, 'till the Fifth year after, when he reassumed
his Son *Joram* into the Government, 2 *Kings* 8.
two years before his death, in the fifth year
of *Jeboram* King of *Israel.* So that *Jebosaphat* Reigning Twenty five years, 2 *King.* 22. 42. it is evident,
his Son *Jeboram* could not be King of *Juda,* 'till the
Eighth year of *Jeboram* King of *Israel.* The like regard is to be had in accounting the Reigns of other
Kings of *Juda* and *Israel,* whose years are sometime
to be taken compleat, current, or confounded with
other Kings preceding, or succeeding, as the comparing of their Times together shall require. In this
History, consider that *Jebosaphat,* a Religious King,
is the first of *Reboboam's* Issue, that entred a League
both Offensive and Defensive with the Kings of *Israel,* with whom his Predecessors had tyred themselves in vain with continual Wars. This Confederacy with one which hated the Lord, could not long
prosper, not issuing from the true Root and Fountain of all Wisdom ; yet as a piece of sound Policy,
it wanted not fair Pretences of much common good,
as mutual Fortification of both Kingdoms against
Uncircumcised Ancient Enemies. For confirmation
of

of such an apparent Good unto Posterity therefore, the Bond of *Affinity* was knit by Marriage of *Jehoram* with *Athalia*, a Lady of a Masculine Spirit, who had learned so much of *Jezabel* her Brother's Wife, that she durst undertake more in *Jerusalem*, than the other in *Samaria*, as a Fire-brand ordained by God, to Consume many Nobles in *Juda*, and perhaps some, whose Worldly Wisdom, regardless of God's pleasure, had brought her in. The *Syrian* Wars at *Ramoth-Gilead*, were the first Fruits of this League, undertaken upon equal Adventure, but upon the hope of Benefit only to *Abab* : As godly Princes seldom thrive by matching with Idolaters, but rather serve the Turns of those false Friends, who being ill-affected towards God, cannot be well affected to his Servants. At this time also, as *Ahaziah* was designed King by *Abab* his Father, so was *Joram* by *Jehosaphat* after the others Example, without Example in any of their Predecessors,

§. 2. *Jehoram*'s Reign so diversly dated in Scripture, argueth, that *Jehosaphat* having taken him into the Government, as *Abab* had given Example, found cause after to recall that Power. Probable it is, that his Insolent Idolatrous Wife having corrupted him, was the cause that the Government, both for Religion and Justice, grew so far out of order, that *Jehosaphat* was forced to the Reformation we read of, and sequestred his Son from the Government, 'till it were setled again ; and so after five years called him to it the second time, which bred a new Date, as did his Father's death two years after, breed a third : Many things might move *Jehosaphat* to *Jehoram*'s second calling to Govern him, as to try what Wisdom his restraint had wrought, or to prevent his Brethrens Insolency against him, if *Jehosaphat* had at his Death, left him in disgrace, which might be the cause of great Tumults ; it may be also, *Jehoram*, by dissimulation, had won the good Opinion on of his Father and Brethren, formerly offended, it being usual in violent fierce Natures, to be as abject and servile in their Adversity, as insolent and bloody upon Advantage. Howsoever it was, this is manifest, that his Father at his death, doubting his Affection to his Brethren, for their better Security, besides great Riches, gave them the custody of strong Cities, and unusual means against unusual Perils.

§. 3. Jehoram's *Reign alone, in which* Edom *and* Libna *Rebel.* §. *Jehosaphat's* providence for his younger Sons availed nothing against the determination of an higher Providence; for these strong Cities were a weak defence for the young Princes against his Power, to whom the Citizens were obedient. If they came in upon the King's Summons, he had them without difficulty; if they refused, they were Traytors; yet could not hold out, when all would fail them, for fear of a Potent King. However it was, all were slain, and many great Men with them, who had any way offended the Tyrant, either formerly, or in behalf of his Brethren. *Jehoram,* after this, made innovation in Religion, not only incouraging the People prone to Idolatry (of all other sins detested of God) but using Compulsion also, and was the first we read of, that inforced Irreligion. *Edom,* in the mean time, revolted, and made themselves a King, having, from *David's* days, been Tributaries, and govern'd by Vice-Roys. Now *Isaac's* Prophecy began to take effect, that *Esau* should break the Yoke of *Jacob*; for after this, *Edom* was never subject to the Kings of *Juda*: Yea, in process of time, *Antipater* and *Herod*, *Elumeans,* Reigned as Kings in *Jerusalem.* *Lybna,* also a City of the *Levites* in *Juda,* rebelled against him, because he had forsaken the Lord God of his Fathers; In defence of whose Worship, these *Levites* thought themselves bound, especially against his inforcement to the contrary.

L   Wherein

Wherein alſo they might take. Incouragement for
Jehoſaphat's Charge, 2 *Chron.* 29. 8. But as *Jehoram*
had left *Edom* in their defection, ſo he attempted
nothing againſt *Libna*; which ſeemeth to proceed
from a doubtful Mind, whether to put Weapons into the Hands of his Subjects againſt their Fellows,
whoſe Cauſe might well be favour'd by many, who
yet durſt not diſcover themſelves, being unarmed,
as they might when Weapons were put into their
Hands. So deſperate is the Condition of Tyrants,
who think it a greater Happineſs to be Feared than
Loved; yet are oblig'd to fear thoſe whoſe Love
would make them dreadful to others.

§. 4. *Jehoram* taking no notice of God's diſpleaſure by theſe Afflictions, was threatned by a Pro-
phetical Writing ſent to him; being ſuch a Tyrant,
as the Prophets durſt not reprove him to his Face,
as they had done many of his Predeceſſors, bad as
well as good, but they writ to him, keeping themſelves from him; *Elias* being Tranſlated, might have
left this Writing, or, (as ſome conjecture) by mi-
ſtaking in Writing one Letter for another, *Elias* is
put for *Eliſha*, *&c.* The Accompliſhment of the
Prophecy, proved as terrible as the Sentence, when
the *Philiſtins*, which from *David*'s days durſt never
look out, brake in upon him, *&c.* with the *Arabians*, a naked People on Horſe-back, of no Force,
dwelling in a Barren Deſert. So that the one quarter of thoſe whom *Jehoſaphat* Muſtered, had been
able to repel greater Forces than both theſe Enemies
could raiſe, had the *Judean* People been Armed, as
by their Prince's Jealouſy, they were not, according to the Policy of the *Philiſtins* in the days of *Saul.*
The Houſe of *Jehoram*, which they ſurpriſed, ſeemeth rather a Country Houſe than in *Jeruſalem*, conſidering they made no further Ravages. It is probable, all *Jehoram*'s Children were not now ſlain,
conſidering the Slaughters made after by *Jehu* and
Athaliah,

Athaliah, within two years : Laftly himfelf, after two years Torment, voided his Guts, *&c.* And as the People had fmall caufe of comfort in his Life, fo they obferved not the decency of pretending Sorrow for his Death ; neither had he the Honour of his Anceftors Burial, though his Son Succeeded, and his Wife did all. *Athaliah* bufie in Plotting her own Greatnefs, and providing trufty Counfellors for her Son, thought it unfeafonable to offend the Eyes of the People with a magnificent Funeral of a Man by them detefted ; and chofe rather to let the Blame of paft Actions lie upon the Dead, than by doing him Honour, to procure an ill Opinion of her felf and Children, which it now concerned her to avoid. Such is the quality of Wicked Inftigators, to charge the Man whofe Evil Inclination they corrupted by finifter Counfel, not only with his own Vice, but with their Faults alfo, when once he is gone and can profit them no longer. Thus we may clearly fee, how the corrupted Affections of Men impugning the Revealed Will of God, accomplifh neverthelefs, his hidden Purpofe ; and without miraculous means, confound themfelves in the feeming Wife Devices of their own Folly. All Men may likewife learn to fubmit their Judgments to the Ordinance of God, rather than to follow Worldly Wifdom, contrary to his Commandments.

§. 5. *Ahaziah* fucceeded his Father in the Twelfth year of *Jehoram* King of *Ifrael*, and was guided by the fame Spirits that had been his Father's Evil Angels. Touching his Age, 2 *Chron.* 22. 2. a Point more difficult than important ; I fee not a more probable Conclufion than that of *Torniellus's* mentioning an Edition of the Seventy at *Rome*, *Anno.* 1588, which faith, he was Twenty years old when he fucceeded; and the Annotations thereon, which cite other Copies, which give him two years more, *&c.* He accompanied *Jehoram* King of *Ifrael* to *Ramoth Gilead*,

L 2 and

and returneth home after the Battle, and presently took a new Journey to visit *Jehoram*. It seems his speedy return to *Jerusalem* was not pleasing to *Athaliah*, as interrupting her in her Plots, who therefore sought to oblige him abroad, if it were but in a vain Complement, to visit one whom he had seen but yesterday. But however these things may seem accidental, yet all concurred, as disposed at this time, to fulfil the high pleasure of God; yea, *Athaliah's* secret Plots, which intended nothing less.

§. 6. Ahaziah *and that Family perished with the House of* Ahab. §. *Jehu* is anointed King, and made Executioner of the Sentence of God against the House of *Abab*, according to the Prophecy of *Elias*, and is proclaimed by all the other Captains. He having this Honour upon the sudden thrown upon him, was not slow in the heat of their Affections, to put himself in possession, and to set on foot the Business which so nearly concerned him, and not to be retarded, being no more his own than God's. *Abab's* House never so flourished, having Seventy Princes of the Blood, a valiant King, honoured with the Victory of *Ramoth Gilead*; so deeply Allied with *Judah*, and Courted by the King, and so many Princes of his Blood, that it might discourage all common Enemies, and make Rebellious Enterprises hopeless. In this Security and Joy of the Court for the King's Recovery and Entertainment of the Princes of *Judah*, the King, his Court, and Friends are suddainly surprized and slain; neither could *Jezebel's* Painted Majesty, nor Man-like Spirit, with untimely brave Apothegms, terrify her Adversary, who, of her Servant, became her Lord; at whose Command, her base Grooms feared not to violate her affected Majesty: *Ahaziah* is also wounded to Death.

C H A P.

CHAP. XVII

Of Athaliah, and Joash, that succeeded her.

§. 1. **A**Thaliah *Usurpeth, and upon what pretences,*
§. *Ahaziah* being dead, after one Years
Reign his House was not able to retain the Kingdom, 2 *Chron.* 22. 9. which Speech hath bred the
question of *Joash's* Pedigree. *Athaliah* having Reigned
under her Sons Name, had laid the Plot to play the
Queen under her own Title, if her Son fail'd; and
to that end, had furnished the King, Councel, and
Places of Chief Command, with Men fittest for her
purposes. And though Ambition be violent, yet
seldom is it so shameless as to neglect Beauty. It is
not therefore improbable to think that *Athaliah* seeing
the Royal Blood so wasted in her Husband and Son's
days, had by some means drawn her Husband or
Son to make her Heir if the King's Blood should be
extinct; considering, that without some such order
taken, when the King's Blood fail'd, the Kingdom
were like to be torn in sunder by Competitors, or
some Popular Seditious Man should be chosen, that
would subvert all regularity, and exercise his Cruelty on such as they loved most, and cast aspersions
on the Royal House. Pretence of Testaments to
thrust out true Heirs is no new thing: Yea, what is
new under the Sun? To prefer a younger before the
natural Heir, hath proof in *David*; and for State-
Policy to slay a Brother, by example of *Solomon*, &c.
And though these had ground of their doings, yet
they which follow Examples which please them,
will neglect the Reasons which please them not.
Solomon slew *Adonijah* which had Rebelled, and was
entred a new practice; *Jehoram* slew his Brethren
better than he; *David* purchased the Crown, yet he

gave

gave it by God's direction, when as *Abaziah* fought to cut off *David*'s Issue, which the Lord had appointed to Reign, 2 *Chron.* 23. 3.

§. 2. *Jehu* had so much business in establishing his own Kingdom, that he could not molest *Athaliah* as he desired, she being of *Ahab*'s House. Among other things about Religion, he destroyed *Baal*'s Priests; and though never King of *Israel* had such a way to overthrow *Jeroboam*'s Idolatry, seeing he needed not fear the Peoples return to *David*'s House (in appearance) quite rooted out, and had his Calling by an unexpected Favour of God; and for his Zeal against *Baal*, had a special promise for Four Generations; yet he wou'd needs piece out God's Providence with his own Circumspection. He had, no doubt, displeased many about *Baal*, and should offend more in taking away *Jeroboam*'s ancient Idolatry; yet all these never thought of making him King, if God had not done it; when more difficulties appeared in getting them now, than in keeping them, though with their offence whom he sought to retain by forsaking God. This Ingratitude of *Jehu*, drew terrible vengeance from God on *Israel*, executed by *Hazael*, according to *Elisha*'s Prophesie, 2 *Kings* 8. 12. with 10. 32. Thus *Israel* succeeded under *Jehu*, whose carriage and success was better in murthering his Master that trusted him, than in defending his People from Cruel Enemies. And thus it commonly falls out, that they which can find all difficulties in serving him, to whom nothing is difficult, instead of finding what they propound, by contrary Courses, overwhelm themselves with troubles they sought not; and are by God, whom they first forsook, left unto the miserable Labours of their own blind Understanding and Wisdom, wherein they reposed all their Confidence.

§. 3.

§. 3. *Athaliah*'s Government, by *Israel*'s Calamities, stood the safer, she having leisure to settle it. It is probable also she held Correspondence with *Hazael*, as King *Asa* had done, and had secured her self by Gifts, having robbed the House of God for *Baalim*, whose Idolatry she set out with Pomp, to recommend it to the People, as she sought by want of means to make the Service of the Sanctuary neglected.

§. 4. *Joash*'s preservation was by means of *Jehosbabeth*, *Abaziah*'s Sister, and Wife unto *Jehojada* the High-Priest, the upholder of God's Service in those unhappy times. By her Piety it seemeth she was not *Athaliah*'s Daughter, yet had she access to the Court, and conveyed the young Child with her Nurse into the Temple, where he was secretly brought up, that the Tyranness could not discover it; and thought it not fit to make much ado about him, but rather let it be thought he was dispatched with the rest; lest the People hearing of his escape, should hearken after Innovation.

§. 5. *Athaliah* had acted as Queen above 6 Year, without molestation, when suddenly the Period of her Glory and Reward of her Wickedness met together, and the young Prince's Age required no longer to be concealed, for his better Education, to fit him with Courage and Qualities proper for a King, and to prevent the over-deep rooting of Impiety by the longer Reign of that Cursed Woman. *Jehojada* wisely considered this, and combined with Five Captains, of whom he was best assured, by whom he drew over other great Men to *Jerusalem*. And because it was difficult to draw open Forces together, he gave order to the Levites, which waited by course in the Temple, that they should not return home 'till they knew his further pleasure. Thus admitting new Comers, and retaining the old, he secretly gathered together a competent number to

encounter

encounter the Queens Guard, and furnished them
out of the Armory of the Temple which King *Da-*
vid had made ; with which also he armed the Captains and their Followers, *&c.* All things being in
readiness, they proceed to the Execution, and the
young King is joyfully Crowned ; and the Tyranness Ufurper coming in defperately, without Forces,
ignorant of the bufinefs, ended her own Tragedy
with a fudden and fhameful death. *Jofephus's* Report of her coming with her Power, which were
repelled, *&c.* is not credible; though all the Forces fhe could bring, could not fruftrate the Council
of God, yet her Indifcretion made the effect more
eafie.

§. 6. *Athaliah* had no doubt confidered *Jehoram*
King of *Ifrael's* rafhnefs, cafting himfelf into the
gaping Gulf of danger ; yet her felf is by the like
Bait drawn into the fame Trap; and as fhe lived
like *Jezebel,* fo was fhe rewarded with her.

Thefe two Queens were in many things alike;
each Daughter, Wife, and Mother to a King;
each over-ruled her Husband, was an Idolater,
Ambitious, Murderous ; each flain by Confpiring
Subjects fuddenly, *&c.* We read not what became of *Athaliah's* Sons, her Sacrilegious Imps which
robbed the Temple, *&c.*

CHAP.

C H A P. XVIII.

Of Joash, Amaziah, *and their Contempora-*
ries.

§. 1. JOASH about Seven Year Old began to
Reign, under the protection of *Jehojada*
during his Minority. When he came to Age, he
took two Wives by *Jehojada's* Advice, repairing
David's Family, almost worn out. The first Act he
took in hand after he Ruled without a Protector,
was the reparation of the Temple, which had been
his Sanctuary, which he followed with much
Zeal.

§. 2. *Jehojada* the Priest being 130 Year Old,
died, before his Country could have spared him,
and was buried among the Kings, as he well deserved. This Honour seemeth to have come from the
People, for the King had soon forgot him, as one
eased of Debt, and was easily flattered by the Princes, so that he quickly forgot his old well-deserving
Counsellor, yea God himself, Author of all Goodness. He which had 30 Years shewed Zeal to restore true Religion, and root out Idolatry, which
had been growing some 16 Years, was easily drawn
to fall away, when he perceived his Princes Inclinations; and being once entred that course, he ran
headlong, as one who thought Liberty the only Token of a King, no longer to endure the sower Ad-
monitions of Devout Priests. Hereby it appears,
he which had been so long among the Devout, as
Saul among the Prophets, was not of them; but
like an Actor upon the Stage, had counterfeited, to
express more Zeal and lively Affection than they
could do, which were truly Religious.

Jehoahaz

Jehoahaz Son of *Jehu* King of *Israel*, Reign'd 17 Years, from the 25*d* of *Joash* King of *Judah*.

§. 3. *Joash* having broken loose from God, is given over to Men not so easily shaken off; for *Hazael* King of *Aram*, returning from *Gath*, set on toward *Jerusalem*, which forc'd *Joash* to buy his Peace with all the Treasure he could make, Holy, or Common; yet he never enjoyed Peace with *Hazael*, who sent a small Army after, and destroyed his Princes, and ravag'd his Country. Many might be the Motives to excite *Hazael* against *Judah*; he had an experienc'd Army; *Judah* had assisted *Israel* at *Ramoth*, and the Journey from *Gath* to *Jerusalem* short; yet it is probable that the Sons of *Athaliah* encouraged him, with hope of a great Party to be drawn by them, of such as favoured them; otherwise it is improbable that *Hazael* would have awaked a sleeping Enemy. However it were, it was of God, who knoweth how to prefer Motives to such as he will imploy, though they intend it not. Some confound the two Invasions of *Hazael*'s; but they are different; the first was a compleat Army, which frighted *Joash*, and had *Hazael*'s presence; the second was small, and was encounter'd by the *Judeans*, when the King of *Aram* was at *Damascus*. Some hold the Invasion was in *Jehojada*'s days; but it seemeth otherwise, seeing the Service of the Temple flourished all his Days. God sometimes prevents Men's Sins by affliction, before Men see cause, because it reforms them. As for the Wicked, usually their Sins get the start of their Punishment, which can do no good upon them, through hardness of heart by custom of Sin, as it was by this unhappy Man, whose villanous Pattern few Tyrants can endure to imitate.

§. 4. *Zecharias* the Son of *Jehojada*, after other Prophets, is moved by the Spirit of God to admonish them of their Wickedness; whom though many

personal

perfonal Reafons might move *Joafh* to refpect, be-fide the Reafon of Reafons, that he was a Reverend Prophet of God, yet at *Joafh's* Commandment they murdered him. Not unlike the Husbandmen, who killed the Heir, in whom all the hope to win any thing at their hands did reft. For it might well be expected, that this Man might be bolder, and pre-vail more than all the reft; yet of all the reft, he fucceeded leaft. It feems *Joafh* thought himfelf no free Prince, as long as any might be thought to have fuch intereft in him, as to dare to deal plainly with him.

§. 5. *Joafh* having committed this odious Murder, as the unthankful Snake upon the Man in whofe Bo-fom he had been foftered, as a wretched Tyrant be-came hateful to his own Times, and his Memory de-teftable. Neither did the deferved Curfe of the Mar-tyr ftay long; for within the Year, when the Ty-rant thought he was now abfolute King without Controul, the *Aramites* broke into his Country, ra-ther for Pillage, than to perform any great Action, being fo few. The King of *Judah* many ways dif-covered his Cowardife, as by drawing blood of Friends, bafely buying Peace with Enemies, when he was able to draw into the Field 300000. Men, as his Son did after; and now in levying a great Ar-my againft a few Foreigners, or Bands of Rovers. Againft thefe his Wifdom thought fit to advance a-mong his Princes, to fhew his Valour, when he pre-fumed through incomparable odds to be free from danger. But God, that laugheth at the Folly of Wife Men, and cafteth contempt upon vain-glorious Princes, intending to do more by the few *Aramites* than themfelves merit, whether by Folly of Leaders, amazement of Souldiers, &c. this great Army fell before them, and they had the flaughtering of thofe Princes, which had drawn their King to Rebel a-

gainſt the King of Kings, and the beating and ran-
zoming of *Joaſh* himſelf, who thereupon was forced
to take his Bed, in which two of his own Servants
ſlew him, for the blood of *Jehojada*'s Children.

§. 6. Contemporaries with *Joaſh*, were *Mezades*
and *Diognetus* in *Athens*; *Eudemus* and *Ariſtodemus*
in *Corinth*; *Agrippa*, *Sylvius* and *Syvius*. *Alladius* in
Italy; *Cephrenes* the 4th from *Seſac*, ſucceeded *Cheops*
in *Egypt*, the 16th of *Joaſh*, and Ruled Fifty Years;
Ocrazapes, or, *Anacynderaxes* ſucceeded *Ophratanes*
in *Aſſyria*, Forty two years; *Joas* 18th. *Pigmalion*
King of *Tyrus*, in whoſe Seven years *Dido* built *Carthage*, from the Building *Solomon*'s Temple 143
Years, as *Joſephus* found in the *Tyrian* Annals;
which was 143 years before the Birth of *Romulus*,
and 289 years after the deſtruction of *Troy*. Thus
all *Virgil*'s Tale of *Dido* and *Æneas*, is Confuted,
as *Auſonius* noteth in his Epigram upon her Statue.
The Hiſtory of *Carthage* is referred to the *Punick* Wars.

§. 7. *Amaziah*, Son of *Joaſh*, ſucceeded, being
Twenty five Years old, who having learned the Art
of Diſſimulation of his Father, finding the Princes
dead which favoured Idolatry, and ſeeing the Peoples diſlike of his Father's Courſes, by their Counte-
nancing his Murder; he framed himſelf to the neceſſity of the Times, forbore the Traytors, indured
his Father's diſgrace in his Burial, and Conformed
to Religion. But after the Peoples out-cry againſt
his Father, had tyred it ſelf, and that he ſaw the
Conſpirators had neither Might, Partakers, nor A-
bettors, he put them to Death, but ſpared their
Children; which gave Content to the People, as
a point of Juſtice; thus by long Peace and Con-
formation to Religion and Juſtice, he grew ſtrong.

Joaſh, alſo, King of *Iſrael*, grew in Power, following the War againſt the *Aramites*, and proſpered, tho' following the Idolatry of the Calves,
which

which had almost confumed the Ten Tribes by *Hazael* and *Benhadad.* Yet at the Prayer of this *Idolater,* God had Compaffion in giving him fuccefs, that he recover'd his Father's temporal Loffes; but God's Favour more worth than all, he neither fought nor got. This Man entred in the 37th year of *Joafh* King of *Judah,* and in the Fifteenth of *Jehoahaz,* his Father, who lived two or three after. He receiving his Father's poor Stock of ten Chariots, Fifty Horfemen, and One Thoufand Foot, his thriving with this Stock, he afcribed to the Prayers of the Holy Prophet *Elifha,* 2 *Kings* 13. 14. This Prophet dyed about the Third or Fourth year of *Joafh,* and for a Legacy, beftowed three Victories upon him, whereby he fet *Ifrael* in a good way to recover all their Loffes.

§. 8. *Amaziah,* inflamed with defire to undertake fome Expedition, by Example of *Joafh* King of *Ifrael,* tho' he could furnifh 300000, yet knowing they had lived without Exercife a long time, except that with the *Aramites,* which rather difcouraged them, he therefore thought good to hire 100000 Experienced Men out of *Ifrael,* with which he would recover *Edom,* which revolted under *Jehoram.* But upon a Prophet's Warning, he dimiffed the *Ifraelites,* not beloved of God, and went in confidence of God's Affiftance, and profpered; while his difcontented hired *Ifraelites* ravag'd in their return; yet he recover'd not *Edom.* He took fome of *Edom*'s Idols, which might have been led in Triumph, but the wretched King which took them, was befotted by them, and made them his Gods; neither would endure the Prophet's reproof from the true God. If the coftly Stuff, or the Workman-fhip ravifhed his Fancy, he might have difpofed them to Profit or Ornament; if the *Edomites* Devotion to them, it fhould rather have moved laughter at them and their Gods, who had failed their Old Clients.

Clients. I therefore think a proud Diſcontentment carried him from God, whom having Obeyed in ſending back his Mercenary *Iſraelites*, he looked that the Lord would have ſubdued *Edom* unto him, as well as give him a Victory ; forgetting that God had promiſed that *Eſau* ſhould break off the Yoke of *Jacob* at length ; and therefore ſhould have limited his deſire, and been contented with an honourable Victory. But as Men careful before the Battle, to pray to God, acknowledging him the giver of Victory ; and when the Field is won, vaunt of their own Exploits, as if God uſed their Fore-ſight and Courage therein ; ſo *Amaziah* finding God did nothing extraordinary, arrogated what was ordinary, to himſelf, and ſcorned to be checked by a Prophet, having before loſt One Hundred Talents by one of them, without any Benefit. From this proud Contempt of God, and Conceit of his own Sufficiency, little Inferior to *David*, he challenged *Joaſh* King of *Iſrael*, and upon occaſion of the late Wrongs done by his Subjects, perhaps required Subjection of the Ten Tribes, by Right from his Anceſtors *David* and *Solomon*. Had he only required Satisfaction, It may be, *Joaſh* would not have returned ſuch an Anſwer, as argueth an Inſolent proud Challenge. *Ajax*'s Father wiſhed him the Victory by the Gods aſſiſtance. He anſwered, that Cowards got Victory ſo, but he would have it without them ; after which proud Speech, and many valiant Acts, upon ſome diſgrace, he fell Mad and killed himſelf. *Amaziah*'s Thoughts were like Parents of like words, and he might as well have ſaid, he had the Victory without God ; which made him inſolently challenge *Joaſh*, as if he were able to encounter a valiant Leader, and People trained up in a long Victorious War, becauſe he had defeated the weak, broken *Edomites*. As his firſt Counſel among his Paraſites, to defy *Joaſh*, was fooliſh, ſo was his proceeding, which was careleſſ-
neſs

ness in providing and preventing; in both which, his Adversaries took the start, and prevented *Amaziah* with a brave Army in his own Country, to save him the labour of a long March. This sudden Invasion much discouraged *Judah*, who having devoured *Israel* in their greedy hopes, saw themselves disappointed, and their own Estates seized by the others : This Issue was, that *Amaziah* was taken, and was led in Triumph to *Jerusalem*, which, to save his Life, He basely procured to be opened to the Conqueror, who made a large breach in the Wall, at which he rid in, made what Spoil he thought fit, and departed.

§. 9. *Joash* King of *Israel*, being in Possession of *Jerusalem*, it may be marvelled why he seized not upon the whole Kingdom ; especially considering he might think the Kingdom was not tyed to the House of *David*, as appeared in *Athaliah* ; and that the *Judaeans* were liklier to endure his Government, being such a Conqueror, and descended of Kings, of which *Jehu* was Anointed from God. I need not add the Commodities growing by Union of these two Kingdoms ; neither read we of any special Prohibition to him ; but it appears, *Joash* minded not the Kingdom, for then he would not have aimed at such a Triumph and Entrance at a Breach, which is one of the greatest Affronts to Citizens, but would have entred at a Gate with fair Intreaty of a People, rather yielding than vanquished ; he would also have forborn the Spoil, especially of the Sanctuary, which the People prefer to their Lives ; and in forbearing whereof, he had won the Opinion of Piety, as the Sacrilege upon the House of their God and his, branded him with a Mark of extraordinary Prophaneness, who by execrable Church-Robbery, became odious, and lost the Inheritance of the whole Orchard, by stealing a few fair Apples. The Citizens provoked by these Indignities, after a few days, would gather Spirit,

to

to conceive the Enemy was of their Mould, and that themselves were not disarmed, were a great multitude, had Provision and such advance of Place as Armed Women and Children; and considering the Evils grown, and like to encrease by former Cowardize, would grow to a desperate Resolution to correct the first Errors. Upon these grounds, it is certain that great Towns entred by Capitulation, are not so easily held as entred, as *Charles* VIIIth of *France* found at *Florence*, which made him come to Terms, when he saw the Citizens Resolution, rather to hazard all, than to submit to his intollerable Conditions, being now entred the Town. Besides, *Joash* might consider how hardly he could make good his Possession against the Army of *Judah*, rather terrified than broken; and lastly, *Joash* having had the Three Victories against *Aram*, promised by the Prophet, he should not expect a perpetual Success against them; and therefore thought it best to return home with the best Security he could for conveying his rich cumbersom Booty, and to make head against the *Aramites*, who, in his Absence, had taken the Advantage, and given *Israel* such a Blow as he could never recover; taking therefore Hostages for his quiet Passage, he returned home.

§. 10. *Amaziah*, who threatned to work wonders, and raise again the Empire of *David*, was stript of his *Lions* Skin; and appeared nothing so terrible a Beast as he had been painted, and became an Argument of scoffing to many; as the Shame which falls on an Insolent Man, seldom fails of much Reproach. Governours are commonly blamed by the Multitude, for the Calamities which befall them, though by the Peoples default; but every Child could see the Root of all this Mischief in this Bastard, which having provoked a valiant Adversary, for Fear betrayed the City, opened unto him by this base intreaty, to save his Life (which his Brutal Father would not do)

which

which he redeemed at so dear a rate, as the Spoil
of City and Temple, which might easily have been
saved by a little delay, which would have forced *Joash* faster home than he came out, hearing of the *A-
ramites*; and a little Courage, in that space, recover'd,
would have perswaded him to leave his Baggage behind him, had not this good King given Hostages
for a Convoy. That this punishment and dishonour
brought him back to God, appeareth not, but the
contrary, by the Reason of the Conspiracy Related
by the Holy Ghost. He which tells a Man in Adversity, of his sins past, shall sooner be thought to
upbraid him with his present Fortune, than to seek
his Reformation; which might make the Priest and
Prophets little welcome to him. On the other side,
his Flatterers which sought to raise up his Heart, of
which themselves might always be Masters, wanted
no plausible Matter; and he was not the first Noble
Commander which hath been foiled, as *David* himself abandoned *Jerusalem* to *Absalom*. *Sesac* was sent
into the City as well as *Joash*; the Temples Pilla-
ging had been excused by Necessity of State; his
Captivity excuseth his Command to open the City,
but they which opened it were to blame, knowing
he was not his own Master, when he commanded
it; his Captivity was his Honour, who might have
escaped by Fight, as others did, which betrayed him
by running away while he fought to incourage them
by his Example; yet his Mischance saved Thousands, while the Enemy wisely preferred the surprize of a Lyon, before the Chase of an Army of
Stags which followed him. These, or the like Speeches might have satisfied Men, if the King had studied
to please God; but as he still neglected the Favour of God, so after this, he out-living his Honour Fifteen Years, recovered no Love of his Subjects by his Government, but increased their Hatred
to his Ruine. He which thinketh himself less Honoured

M   than

than he deferveth in his own Opinion, will force his
Authority, to be efteemed a fevere Man ; that by
affected Sowernefs, he may be thought a grave, wife
Man, and that by the Fear in which the Opprefled live,
he may be thought a Reverence to the Oppreffed;
at leaft it will dazel the Eyes of Underlings, keeping them from prying into the weaknefs of their Governours. Thus the time in which, by well ufing it,
Men might attain to be fuch as they ought, they
do ufually mifpend it in feeking to appear fuch as
they are not, fo procure more Indignation than was
feared, inftead of the Refpect that was hoped; which
is of dangerous Confequence in an unable Spirit in
high Authority, too paffionate in Execution of an
Office, and cannot be checked but by violence. If
Amaziah thought by extreme rigour to uphold his
Reputation; what did he but make the People think
he hated them, who eafily believed he did not love
them ? He had indeed provided for his own fecurity, by revenging on his Father ; but who fhall take
Vengeance (or on whom) of a Murther in which e-
very one hath a part ? Surely God himfelf, who
hath not given Leave to the People to fhed the blood
of his Anointed. Yet as he was carelefs of God,
and was carried head-long, with his own Affection;
fo his Subjects, by his Example, not enquiring what
was their Duty, rofe up againft him with a precipi-
tant Fury, which yet he could not avoid by flying to
Lachifh, as a choice Town for Strengh and Affection,
where yet he found no other Favour, but that they
would not kill him with their own Hands, but
abandon'd him to the Confpirators fent after him,
who difpatched him with little Oppofition.

§. 11. *Amaziah* being Slain, the Throne of *Judah*
was vacant Eleven Years ; for as he out-lived *Joafh*
King of *Ifrael* 15 Years, which *Jeroboam* held, and
muft dye the 15th of *Jeroboam*, fo it is exprefly
faid, *Uzziah* his Son began to Reign in the 27th of
Jeroboam

Jeroboam, being 16 Years old, and Reigned 52 Years; which argueth 11 Years Inter-regnum. Others (to avoid this Inter-regnum, have made divers Conjectures ; as *G. Mercator, &c.* But I know not why it may not be admitted in *Judah,* seeing the like necessity hath inforced it in the Kingdom of *Israel,* as between the death of *Jeroboam* 2. and his Son *Zecharias,* and between *Peka* and *Hosea.* Such suspence of the Crown of *Judah* is more probable, considering how things stood at the death of *Amaziah,* although the computation were not so apparent. For the Publick Fury which extended so far against the King's Person, was not like to be appeased, 'till order was taken to redress the Matters which caused that eruption. We need not then wonder that they who involv'd themselves in the former Treason against the Father, would stay the Crown 'till things were set in order, the Prince being so young, and to be under protection, *&c.* To make *Jeroboam's* Reign to begin the 11th with his Father, were the best, but only for swallowing up so much of *Joash's* Reign, extending the Years of the Kings of *Israel,* and contracting the Years of the Princes of other Nations.

§. 12. Contemporaries with *Amaziah,* and Eleven Years after, were *Joash and Jeroboam* in *Israel* ; *Cephreras* and *Mycerinus* in *Egypt* ; *Sylvius Alladius,* and *Sylvius Aventinus* in *Alba* ; *Agamemnon* in *Corinth* ; *Diognetus, Pheredus,* and *Ariphron,* in *Athens*; *Theleftus* in *Lacedemon,* when the *Spartans* won Towns from the *Achaians.*

Sardanapalus in the 21st Year of *Amaziah,* succeeded *Acrozapes* his Father in *Assyria* 21 Years, and was slain the Year before *Azariah* entred, and ended *Ninus's* Line after 1240 Years Empire. This unhappy voluptuous Prince was so base, he durst let no Man see him ; 'till at length *Arbaces* Governour of *Media,* got a sight of that beastly Spectacle of a Man in Woman's Attire counterfeiting an Harlot ;

which

which moved him to such indignation, that he brake with *Belosus* a *Chaldean,* about casting off the Yoke of so unworthy a Creature. *Belosus* pleased him too well, to tell him he should enjoy the Kingdom, who promised him thereupon the Kingdom of *Babylon.* Being thus agreed, the one stirr'd up the *Medes* and *Persians,* the other the *Babylonians* and *Arabians,* and so drew together 40000 Men against *Sardanapalus,* who, contrary to his former course of Life, became a Man, gathered his Forces, and encounter'd the Rebels, and foil'd them in three Battles ; and had not *Belosus* promised unexpected Succors, *Arbaces* had broken up the Camp. About that time an Army out of *Bactria* was coming to assist the King ; but *Arbaces* encountring it, upon promise of Liberty, drew them to joyn with him : In the mean time, the King supposing *Arbaces* to be fled, Feasted his Army, Triumphing before Victory. The Rebels strengthned with new Supplies, came upon him by Night, forced his Camp, unprepared for resistance, and made the King retire into the City *Ninive,* leaving *Salaminus,* his Wives Brother, to keep the Field 'till new Succours came. *Arbaces* overthrew the King's Army, slew *Salaminus,* and lay two whole Years before the City, in hope to win it by Famine; for force it he could not, the Wall being an hundred Foot high, and so thick, that three Chariots might pass in the Front upon the Rampire. But what he could not now do, the River *Tygris* did the third Year ; for in a swelling after a Rain, it cast down 20 Furlongs, and made a fair Breach for *Arbaces* to enter. *Sardanapalus* either terrified with accomplishment of the old Oracle, that *Ninive* should never be taken, 'till the River became an Enemy to it; or seeing no means of resistance, he at last consumed himself and Family with fire in his Palace. *

* *Diodorous Siculus* out of *Ctesias.*

C H A P.

C H A P. XIX

Of Uzziah, *and his Contemporaries in* Israel, *and elsewhere; of his two Successors.*

§. 1. UZziah, or *Aaria* being Sixteen Years of Age, succeeded his Father *Amaziah,* in the Twenty Seventh Year of *Jeroboam,* and Reigned Forty Two Years; he served the God of his Fathers, and prosper'd. His Victories and Atchievments were far beyond any since the time of *David,* and his Wealth exceeded any since *Solomon's* days. *Jeroboam* also King of *Israel* prospered in the North, and won *Damascus,* and *Hamath;* not for his Piety, being an Idolater: It was only the Lord's compassion on *Israel,* so extreamly afflicted by *Aram.* Yet as God's goodness to *Jehu* his Grandfather, could not win him from *Jeroboam's* politick Idolatry of the Calves, no more could it make *Jeroboam* his Son render the Honour due to the only giver of Victory; so that the Promise made to *Jehu* for Four Generations, grew to an accomplishment, to be a fair warning to his Son to expect a Change, except himself or his Son would change his Idolatry. But as *Jeroboam* ended his days in his Idolatry, so his Son *Zachary,* who should have succeeded presently, was held out many years without apparent reason, but only the two Calves at *Dan* and *Bethel;* yet Secondary Causes were like not to be wanting. Probable it is, that as *Jeroboam's* Reign had bred many brave Captains, so they saw so little in *Zechary* to respect him for, or perhaps found something which moved disdain, that they could not agree to submit unto him 'till some principal of them were dead; every Man of them in the mean time holding what he could, &c. This

Anarchy

Anarchy laſted about 23 Years, from the 11th Year of *Uzziah*, when *Jeroboam* died, unto the 38th of the ſame *Uzziah*, in the which *Zechariah* entred, and ſate 6 Months. And though ſome ſuppoſe *Jeroboam* to Reign 11 Years with his Father, and to cut off ſo much of this Inter-regnum, yet they leave 12 Years; but I prefer the former, as beſt agreeing with the Reign of other Princes, and not extend *Jeroboam*'s Reign and Life as this doth. *Zechariah* the Son of *Jeroboam*, the laſt of *Jehu*'s Line, after 6 Months Reign, was by *Sallum* ſlain, fulfilling the 4 Generations following to *Jehu*; yet not warranting *Sallum* to ſlay him, as *Jehu* had been againſt *Jeboram*. Thus *Jeroboam*'s Captains were grown ſo headſtrong, that they neither indured his Son, nor one another; ſo that in 14 Years their Reigned five Kings. *Sallum* after 1 Month's Reign in *Samaria*, was ſlain by *Menahem*. *Menahem* of *Tyrza* Reigned 10 Years, a Cruel Perſecutor of *Sallum*'s Friends. In his time came *Pull* the *Aſſyrian*, whom he pacified with a Thouſand Talents of Silver, and ſo was confirmed in his Kingdom, againſt ſuch as oppoſed him.

Pekahiah ſucceeded his Father 2 Years, in the Year of *Azariah* King of *Judah*. *Peka* the Son of *Remaliah* ſlew *Pekahia*, and Reigned 20 Years.

§. 2. *Uzziah*, whoſe Succeſſion had been endangered by the hatred to his Father, but by Holy Men brought up and advanced, as was *Joaſh*, and had his Holy *Zechariah*, under whoſe direction he proſpered, as *Joaſh* under good *Jehojada*. But as *Joaſh* after his Tutor's death, ſo *Uzziah* after his *Zechariah*, forgetting the Law of God, which had ſeparated the Prieſt's Office from the King's, would needs uſurp the ſame; for which preſumption, being reprov'd by *Azariah* the Prieſt, the Lord ſeconded the juſt reprehenſion, and ſtruck the King with Leproſie.

Thus

Thus he which presumed to draw near the Holiest, was cast from among common Men. *Josephus* enlargeth this History, and reports of an Earthquake, which some mistake for that in *Amos*, which was in *Jeroboam* the 2*ds* days, long before *Uzziah.*

§.2. Contemporaries with *Uzziah.* Among the small Prophets, *Hosea,* *Joel,* *Amos,* *Obadiah,* and *Jonas* lived with *Uzziah,* if *Hierom's* Rule hold, to range a Prophet whose time is not expressed, with the next before; then *Joel* and *Obadiah* are of this time. *Jonas* seems to me the first that foretelleth *Jeroboam's* Victory, and Prophecied of Christ, rather by Sufferings, than Writing now extant; whereas all the other Prophets have express Promises of the Messias. *Esaiah* also now prophecied, writ much, with excellency both of Stile and Argument; foretelleth the Birth, Miracles, and Passion of our Saviour, with calling of the *Gentiles*; more like an History of things past, than a Prophecy of things to come, as *Hierom* saith. *Bocboris* had Reigned in *Egypt* 10 Years when *Uzziah* entred; *Asychis* succeeded, then *Anysis,* whom *Sabacus* succeeded 50 Year; of which, the 10 first were with *Uzziah.*

Ariphron's 2 last Years of 20. *Thespeus* 27. *Aganeftor's* 20. and *Æschylus's* 3 first of his 23 in *Athens,* ended with *Uzziah,* so did the 7 last of *Sylvius Aventinus's* 37. with 23 of *Sylvius Procas,* and the first of *Sylvius Amulius.* 22 in *Alba.* In *Media,* *Arbaces* began his new Kingdom with *Uzziah,* and held it 28. and *Sofarmus* his Son 30 Year.

§. 4. *Arbaces* having taken *Ninive,* utterly ruined it, to transfer the Empire to the *Medes,* as he had promised; he also made his Partakers Rulers of Provinces, retaining only the Sovereignty; yet with such moderation, as neither offended the Princes his Assistants, nor the generality of the People. For calling *Belosus* into question for Embezling the Treasure, he referred his Condemnation to the

M 4 Captains,

Captains, and then pardoned him, and gave him the Province of *Babylon*, with the Treasure. He also freed the *Perfians* and *Baclrians* as he promised, and so weaken'd his Sovereignty; so that in time, the *Affyrian* incroached upon some Towns of the *Medes*, and extended it self to *Ifrael*; but when the *Affyrian* cast off the *Mede's* Yoak is uncertain: As also when *Babylon* and *Ninive* became subject to one. The Opinion current 'till of late, is according to *Metaftenus* in *Annius*; That *Belofus*, called also *Phut Belofus*, and in Scripture *Pul*, or *Phul*, Reigning 42 Years in *Babylon*, got part of *Affyria* into his hand, and left it to *Tiglah Pilefer* his Son, and his Pofterity, 'till *Merodach* prevailed. This Tradition, though *Annius's* Authors be suspected, is justified by Circumstances in other Authors; as *Belofus* enjoying *Babylon*, *Diodorus* relates, and no Authors speak of any special Governour of *Affyria*; neither stood it with Policy to set a particular King in *Affyria*; when to prevent the rising again thereof, *Ninive* was ruined, and the Inhabitants transplanted. Upon the like Considerations, *Rome* destroyed *Carthage*, and *Capua*, being Towns Capable of Empire, &c. It is not then to be thought that *Ninive* and the *Affyrians* could rise in three or four Years, by any other than *Belofus*, so near a Neighbour, and of so rich a Province; for *Herodotus* esteemed it, for Riches and Power, as the third part of the *Perfian* Empire; who also joyned the Treasure found in the Palace of *Ninive*.

§. 5. The *Olympian* Games were restored by *Iphylus* in the Fifty first of *Uzziah*. The first Founder of them was *Hercules*, and were so called of the City *Olympia* or *Pifa*, near *Elis* a City in *Peloponefus*, near the River *Alpheus*, where *Jupiter* had a Temple, reputed one of the Worlds Wonders. These Games were exercised after every Four years end; which were discontinued long, until the days of *Iphitus*, when

when *Lycurgus* lived ; and continued in *Greece* 'till
the Reign of *Theodosius*, faith *Cedrenus* ; or to *Con-
stantine*, after others. *Varro* held all *Grecian* Stories
Fabulous before these ; but *Pliny* esteemeth none true
before the Fifty fifth *Olympiad*, when *Cyrus* began to
Reign. Many seek to find the Years of the World
when they began, but can set down no certainty ;
others seek it from *Troy*'s Fall, more uncertain than
they. The certainty of things following the *Olympiads*, teacheth to find their beginning, to which use,
Eratosthenes hath set down the years ensuing unto
the death of *Alexander* from the *Olympian* Institu-
tion, Four Hundred fifty three years. So for placing their beginning the 51st of *Uzziah*, we have
Cyrus's Reign to prove it, being the first of the
Fifty fifth *Olympiad*. So *Alexander*'s death the First
year of the 144th *Olympiad*. So the Eclipse when *Xerxes*
mustered at *Sardis*, the last of the Sixty fourth *Olympiad*, or the Two Hundred Sixty Seventh year of
Nabonassar, which leads us back to *Xerxes*, and so to
Cyrus, whence we have Seventy Years to the destruction of *Jerusalem*, and so through the Reigns of the
Kings of *Judah* to *Uzziah*'s 51st. The Solemnity
was such by concourse from all the *Greeks* ; their Exercise was all bodily Feats ; and the Reward, a Garland of Palm or Olive; so that the choice Orators, Poets and Musicians resorted thither to shew their skill
in setting out his Praise that won the Garland, with
such Vanity (said *Tully*,) as if it had been a Conquest of a Province. The time of the year was the
Fifteenth of *Hecatobæon*, our *June*, whereto they
brought the Full Moon.

§. 6. *Jotham*, Twenty Five years old, succceeded
his Father *Uzziah* in his life time, and reigned 26
years ; happy in all things, as he was. Devout and
Virtuous, 2 *King.* 15. 33. Contemporaries, *Aucomo-
nus* succeeded *Pelesteus* in *Corinth*, whom *Annual
Magisteus* succeeded ; contrary to *Pausan.*

Æscu-

Strabo,Plu-
tarch.

Æsculus in *Athens*; *Accamenes* in *Sparta*. *Tig-lath Pileser* in *Assyria*, Twenty five years, and Two with his Son, Twenty Seven in all. *Nahum* the Prophet now fore-told the destruction of *Ninive*, One Hundred and Fifty years beforehand. *Sosarmus* and *Medidus* succeeded *Arbaces* in *Media*, the Second and Third Kings there.

§. 7. *Achas* succeeded in *Judah* one year, with *Jotham*, in the Seventeenth year of *Peka*; he was Twenty years old, and Reigned Sixteen years; an exceeding Idolater, Sacrificing his Sons to *Moloch*, or *Saturn*, after the manner of the Heathens used of old, *Levit.* 18. *Deut.* 12. by many Nations, and at this day by the *Americans*, as *Acosta* witnesseth, &c. God raised him Enemies on all sides, so that when he saw his dead Gods failed him, yet neglecting the living God, he sought Aid of *Tiglath Pileser*, who embraced the Advantage to go through with what his Father entred, but had no leisure to finish it. He therefore invaded *Syria*, and won *Damascus*, all *Israel*; made *Judah* Tributary, though *Achaz* had hired him.

Contemporaries, the *Ephori* in *Lacedemon*, 130 years after *Lycurgus*, opposed to Kings, as the Tribunes in *Rome* against Consuls. *Alcamenon* in *Athens*, the last Governour for Life; after which followed a Magistrate for Ten years. *Sylvii* of *Æneas*'s Race, ended after Three Hundred Years. *Romulus* now built *Rome*, the Eighth of *Achaz*, the First of the Seventh *Olympiad*.

C H A P.

C H A P. XX.

Of Italy, *and* Rome's *Foundation in* A-
haz's *time.*

§. 1. ITALY, before the Fall of *Troy*, was known
to the *Greeks*, by the names of *Hesperia*,
Ausonia, Oenotria, of a Colony of *Arcadians*; and *I-*
taly of *Italus*. *Reyneccius* derives the Name rather
from a Colony of *Ætolians*, which Inhabited *Brun-*
dusium, from whose Names, with small Change, that
part was called *Italia*, which in time grew the common name, saith *Pliny*. Such change in the *Æolic*
Dialect is Familiar, as to call an Island Peopled
by *Ætholians, Æthalia*. The Original of *Greeks*
and *Latins*, was from *Javan*, who sailing over the
Ionian Sea, between *Ætolia* and the Western Ocean, planted *Greece* and *Italy*. *Reyneccius* makes *At-*
lai Italus, one which *Berosus* calls *Cethim Italus*,
but is deceived, for *Atlas* is esteemed more Antient
than *Moses*; and if he were *Cethim* or *Kithim*,
Noah's Grand-Son, his Antiquity exceeds that of
Italy; which Name, *Virgil* confesseth later, and from
a Captain. But seeing *Hercules* a little before
Troy's Fall, left a Colony of *Eleans* or *Ætoleans*,
it may be under the command of one called *Ai-*
tolus, a Name famous among *Ætolians*: *Italy*
might take Name of him.

§. 2. *Aborigines*, that is, the Natives of the place
Inhabited *Latium*, whom *Halycarnassus, Varro*, and
Reyneccius, think to have been *Arcadians*, who
used to vaunt of their Antiquity, having more con-
stantly kept their Country in *Peloponesus*, than o-
ther *Greeks*; yet being fruitful, sent Colonies to
other Countries, as when *Evander* was sent into the
same parts of *Italy*.

Pelasgi

Pelasgi, an Antient Nation, after gave Name to all *Greece*, but such of them as came into *Italy*, lost the Name of their Tribe in a short time. *Sicani, Ausones, Aurunci, Rutili*, in after Ages, disturbed *Latium*, which *Saturn* had brought to some Civility, and taught to dung the Ground.

That *Latium* took the name of *Saturn's* lurking there from *Jupiter*, is far fetched, and question-less a Fable; yet many Fables were occasioned from some Antient Truths. It may be then that *Saturn* hiding himself, was some allusion to the old Opinion of the Wise Heathen, that the true God was an unknown God, to whom *Paul* found an Altar de-dicated. It cannot be in vain, that the word *Saturnus* should also signify hidden, coming of the *Hebrew Satar* to hide (as some think) &c. *Reyneccius* proceedeth in deriving *Latium* from the Poste-rity of *Javan*, Inhabiting a Territory in lesser *Asia*, called *Elaitia*, who after the *Trojan* War, went into *Italy*, whence might grow *Elaitinus*, and so *Latinus*, &c.

§. 3. The *Latin* Kings 'till *Æneas*, were *Saturnus, Picus, Faunus, Latinus*. Whether *Saturnus* were he whom the *Greeks* called *Cronos*, &c. the time of the *Aborigines* will admit; but his Names of *Stercus*, or *Sterculius*, do argue him another; so called of the Dungs he taught them to lay upon their ground. *Ezechiel* often cals Idols, *Deos Stercoreos*, as *Belzebul* is *Dominus Stercoreus*, &c.

§. 4. *Æneas*, a *Trojan* of the Blood-Royal, came to *Latium* with some 1200 *Trojans*, and Married *Laviana*, King *Latinus's* Daugher. He had a Son before, by his Wife *Creusa*, Daughter of *Priamus*, called *Ascanius*, and Sirnamed *Julus*. After *Æneas's* death, *Lavinia* was great with Child by him, and fearing *Ascanius*, fled into a Wood, where being Delivered, the Child was called *Sylvius Postbumus*. But upon the Peoples disapproving of *Lavinia's* flight,

flight, *Ascanius* called her home, used her like a Queen, and Educated her Son. *Ascanius*, to avoid dissention, left the City *Lavinium*, to *Laviana*; and Founded *Alba-Longa*; where he Reign'd about 30 Year, and left his Son *Julus*; who upon contention with *Sylvius*, whom the People favoured, left the Kingdom, and took the Priesthood, for him, and his Posterity. *Sylvius Posthumus* Reigned 29. *Sylvius Æneas*, 31. *Sylvius Latinus*, 10. *Sylvius Alba* 39. *Sylvius Atis* 36. *Sylvius Capijs* 28. *Sylvius Capelus* 13. *Sylvius Tiberinus* 8. *Sylvius Agrippa* 41. *Sylvius Alladyus* 19. *Sylvius Aventinus* 37. *Sylvius Procas* 23. *Sylvius Amulius* 44. He expelled his Elder Brother *Sylvius Numitor*, slew his Son *Ægestius*, and made his Daughter *Ilia* a Vestal-Virgin. *Numitor*, who yet, either by her Uncle, or some Warlike-Man, conceived 2 Sons, *Romulus*, and *Reineccius*, who in time slew *Amulius*, and all his Family, and restored *Numitor*, in whom the Kingdom of *Alba* ended, and received Magistrates. Yet it contended with *Rome*, 'till her Three *Curiatij* were vanquished by the Three *Horatij*, Champions for *Rome*. After this, *Metius* the *Alban* Dictator, following *Tullus Hostilius* in his War, upon *Tullus*'s disadvantage; withdrew his Companies to distress *Tullus*; for which he was torn in pieces at two Chariots, and *Alba* Reigned; but the Citizens were made free Denisons, and her Nobles, Patricians of *Rome*; among whom was a Family of *Julij*, which hath since risen in *Julius Cæsar*, &c.

§. 5. *Rome*, which devoured the *Alban* Kingdom, and brake all the *Kingdoms* from *Euphrates*, to the Western Ocean, as that *Alban* the IV*th*, a Beast with Iron-Teeth, forespoken of, cometh now to be handled, only touching her Original, which some seek to derive from *Janus*, others from the *Greeks*. *Plutarch* in the Life of *Romulus*, remembers many Founders of the City, but *Livie* will have it the Work of

of *Romulus*, &c. Of his Begetting, Birth, and E-
ducation, *Plutarch* ſaith, it is probable, that *Amulius*
came armed to *Rhea*, which occaſioned the Tale of
Marce ; as the Nurſing the Children by ſome Harlot, occaſioned the Tale of a Woolf; for Harlots
of old were called Wolves. *Halicarnaſſus* tells us
of the like Reports they have of *Cyrus*'s Nurſing by
a Bitch, and *Semiramis* by Birds. So of his End,
they ſay he was taken away in a ſtorm of Thunder, *&c.* Which was probably the fury of the Senators, remembred alſo by *Livie*. But as many Authors ſpeak of great Lightning and Thunder that
day, ſo it may be he was ſlain by it, as was *Ana-
ſtaſius* the Emperor, and Emperor *Carus*. *Halicarnaſſus* ſaith, they caus'd it to be remembred,
neareſt to Truth, which ſay his Citizens ſlew him, *&c.*
Plutarch reports of his Conqueſts of a few Miles about
him, not worth the ſpeaking of, if the following Greatneſs of *Rome* had not caus'd it to be remembred. He
Reign'd 37 Years ; firſt alone, then with *Tatius*,
and after his death ſingle, 'till he was ſlain. *Numa*
a Man unknown to *Romulus*, ſucceeded, more Prieſt-
like, *&c.* well reſembling *Rome*'s latter days ;
which falling from Emperors Command, into ſubjection of a Prelate ; ſwelling by degres, from a
Sheep-Hook, to a Sword ; wherewith Victorious,
to exceſſive Magnificence, it fell to Luxury ; and
being unfortunate in defenſive War, is driven again
to betake himſelf to the Croſier-Staff.

CHAP.

CHAP. XXI.

Of Hezechiah, *and his Contemporaries.*

§. 1. **H**Ezechiah at 25 Years old succeeded, about the end of *Achaz* 14 Years, in the 3d of *Hosea* King of *Israel,* and Reigned 29 Years. His first Work testified his Pious Zeal in opening the Temple, shut up by his ungracious Father, and reformed Religion, &c. Comp. 2 *Chron.* 29, and 30. with 2 *Kings* 18. It is uncertain whether he did this in his Father's time, or in his sole Government, as I rather think. He invited also the Ten Tribes to the Passover, which the Generality scorned. In the fourth Year of *Hezekiah,* the *Israelites* which scorned to Celebrate their Deliverance out of *Egypt,* fell into a new Servitude, wherein they continued to this day. For *Salmanasser,* Son of *Tyglath,* hearing that *Hosea* King of *Israel,* practised with *Soe* King of *Egypt,* against him; came, and after Three Years Siege, won *Samaria,* and carried the Ten Tribes into *Assyria,* and *Media,* and placed others in the Land.

These later *Assyrian* and *Persian* Kings following, are the first we find mentioned both in Profane and Sacred Books, and therefore must serve to joyn the times of the old World with that following, seeing none but Prophets have written otherwise than Fabulous of former Times. True it is, that *Cyrus* and some *Persian* Kings bear the same Name in Scripture, and Profane Stories; but of others the diversity of Names have bred question of the Persons, as whether *Salmanasser* in Scripture be *Nabonasser* in *Ptolomy,* and *Nebuchadnezzar* be *Nabopolassar,* both which points *Bucholcerus* out of good *Mathematick* Observations, hath well proved; for by them it appears, that from *Nabonasser* to *Christ,*

were

were Seven Hundred Forty fix years, which agrees alfo to *Salmanaffar*, which is proved ; for that the fpace between *Merdocenpadus* and *Nabonaffar* is found the fame between *Merodach* (who was *Mardocenpa-*
So   *dus*) and *Salmanaffar*.   * That as from the
Funétins. deftruction of *Samaria* to that of *Jerufalem* are 133 years, fo in *Ptolomy*, the fame time is found between *Nabonaffar* and *Nabopolaffar*, the Eighth year differing in *Ptolomy*,being before the winning of *Samaria*, fpent in his Reign.

§. 2. *Hezekiah* having denied the Tribute to *Senacherib*, which had been Covenanted with *Tiglath* his Grandfather, acknowledged his Fault, and laboured to purchafe his Peace by Three Thoufand Talents of Silver, and Thirty of Gold, by *Senacherib's* intending to fet down the Conditions with his Sword, fent from *Lachifh*, where he lay and invefted *Jerufalem*, &c. where Vengeance from Heaven deftroyed fo many Thoufands for their Mafter's Blafphemy ; who alfo drunk a Cup of the Wrath of God, from his own Sons.

§. 3. *Hezechiah* his Sicknefs, Prayer, Recovery and Sign thereof, 2 *Kings* 20. His Lamentation, faith *Jerom*, was for want of a Son, of whom the *Meffias* might fpring. His entertaining the *Babylonian* Embaffadors, and vain-glory therein, reproved. Yet, according to Humane Reafon, he thought fit to entertain them familiarly, coming to Congratulate his Recovery with Prefents, being one which had weakened the *Affyrian*, his greateft Enemy, by feizing upon the Kingdom of *Babylon*, of which he had been Lieutenant under *Senacherib*, whofe Son weak in Underftanding, and molefted by his Elder Brethren, gave him opportunity to Ufurp *Babylon*, as *Belochus* had dealt with *Sardanapalus*. Thus *Belochus* Forty Eight years, *Tiglath Pilefar* Twenty Seven, *Salmanaffar* Ten, *Senacherib* Seven, *Efarhaddon* Ten, the Three laft being Contemporaries with *Hezechiah*.

§. 4. *Heze-*

§. 4. *Hezechiah's* Contemporaries in *Media,* after *A-rabaces* and *Sofarmus,* according to *Eufebius,* are *Me-didus* Forty years, *Cordiceas* Fifteen Years. Then followed *Deioces* Fifty four, *Phraortes* Twenty four, *Cyaxares* Thirty two, *Aftyages* Thirty Eight, and *Cyaxares* Two, according to *Xenophon. Metafthenes* in *Anneus* and *Diodorus* out of *Ctefias,* differ much from *Eufebius,* whom *Mercator* would fain reconcile, but in vain. In *Athens,* Four of the Four Ten year Governours. In *Lidea Candaulus* flain by *Gyges,* who fucceeded.

C H A P. XXII.

Egyptian *Kings from* Mofes *to* Hezekiah.

§. 1. THE *Egyptians* at this time, contending with the *Affyrians* about Sovereignty, gi-veth the occafion to confider the ftate of the Coun-try which had flourifhed fo long. Of *Cham, Ofiris,* and *Orus,* and the reft with their *Dynafties,* 'till *If-rael* came out of *Egypt,* we have heard ; and are to proceed from thence, not regarding the idle Cata-logue of Names of *Kings,* fet out by *Herodotus* and *Dyodorus,* from the Mouths of the *Egyptian* Priefts, who, for the moft part, were but Vice-Rovs, or Stewards, like *Jofeph,* and fuch as were the *Soldans* in later Ages. For Firft, we may not believe that the number of Generations we fpeak of, were above Eighty from *Abraham* to the *Perfian* Empire ; where-as we know, there were but Forty two Generations to our Saviour *Chrift;* efpecially, confidering many of them were of about Forty years continuance; we muft therefore proportion the number to that of o-ther Countries, according to the time ; and efteem the reft but Regents, who yet Ruled as Kings ; of

N which

which sort there might be many, as may be well
conceived in Reading *W.* Arch-Bishop of *Tyre,*
who sheweth that there was the *Caleph Elhadech,* supream over *Egypt,* under whom the *Soldans* ruled
as Kings, making War and Peace ; yea, supplant-
ing one another without the *Calephs* privity, as fell
out under *Elhadech,* under whom *San.* was *Soldan,*
and yet chased away by *Dagon,* and upon his death
recovered again without the great *Caleph's* Hand,
who-in the mean time only attended his state, and
delights in his Pallace, which manner of Ruling by
Vice-Roys, the Author judgeth to have been from
the Ancient Kings of *Egypt.*

§. 2. It were vain to be curious about these Kings,
seeing *Diodorus* varies from *Herodotus,* and *Eusebius*
from both, neither do late Writers know whom to
follow. The Kings from *Chencres* or *Tuoris,* or *Proteus,* are agreed upon, of which according to *Eusebius, Acherres* was next, whom *Reyneccius* thinks to
be *Uchoreus* in *Diodore,* Founder of *Memphis* ; but
then *Timaus* cannot be the great *Osymandias* as he also
judgeth; for there were more than Eight Generations
between them, contrary to *Diodorus.* Touching *Osy-
mandais, Mercator,* makes him the Husband of *A-
cencheres, Daughter* to *Orus* Second, and finds *Uchoreus*
the Eighth from him : But I will pass over these in-
extricable doubts, *&c.*

§. 3. *Cherres* after Eight years of *Acherres* succeeded Fifteen years ; *Armeus* five years; *Rameſſes* Sixty
Eight years, which two last are the *Danaus* and *E-
gyptus* spoken of by the *Greeks,* who make *Danaus*
expelled *Egypt,* become King of *Argos* in *Greece* : But
Reyneccius believes not *Armeus* to be *Danaus,* though
their time agree ; but rather thinks he was *Meris,*
which made the great Lake *Myris,* 3600 Furlongs
compass, and Fifty Fadoms deep, to receive *Nilus*
over-flowing, for store, when Water was scarce.

§. 4. *Ameraphis* succeeded his Father Forty years; then
Sethosis Fifty years, to whom some ascribe improbably,
the

the famous Acts of Great *Sesostris.* In him began
the *Dynastie* of the *Zarths,* or Generals, which Title
Five only held, *Ramases* succeeded Sixty years, mistaken for *Sesostris* the 2d. *Amenophis* succeeded Forty
years. *Andemenes* Twenty six years; *Thuoris,* the last
Zarth, Seven years, whom some make *Proteus,*
whose Son *Remphes* succeeded, but I doubt neither
Father nor Son were Kings.

§. 5. Many other Names of the *Egyptian* Kings
are found scattered, as *Tonephersobis* ; *Senemues* or
Senepos ; *Banchistis Thulis* in *Suidas,* who asking *Se-
raps* the *Divel,* who was, or should be, so mighty as
he, was answered, *First God, and then the Word, and
then the Spirit, which Three be One, and join in One all!
Three, whose Power is endless. Get thee hence frail Wight,
the Man of Life unknown, excelling thee.* *Cedreus* hath
the same, and gives this King as great Antiquity as
the *Indies,* citing a Book called *Little Genesis,* which
word little, alone argues Impostor, besides the
Frierly stuff he cites out of it. His List of Old *Egyptian*
Kings here set down, are not worth writing out, neither the Kings named by others. *Vaphres* and *Sesac*
will lead us into a fair way a while ; the first was
Solomon's Father-in-Law, according to *Clemens A-
lexandrinus* and *Eusebius* ; the second, *Eusebius* calls
Smendis, with whom he begins the Twenty First
Dynastie, whose Entrance is found about the Twentieth of *Solomon,* reckoning from *Neco*'s death in the
Fourth of *Jehojakim,* King of *Judah* upward ; as
from the Fifth of *Rehoboam,* wherein he plunder'd
the *Sanctuary,* but injoyed that Sacriledge, as did
Joas and *Craseus,* not one Year. For the Kings,
from *Sesac* to *Necho,* I chose the *Greek* Historians,
for *Eusebius* is out, by failing to keep the reckoning
between the Kings of *Judah* and *Israel.*

§. 6. *Chemmis* or *Chembis* succeeded *Sesac* Fifty
years, and built the great Pyramid, whose Base was
Seven Acres square, and Six high; which *Diodore*
saw One Thousand Years after, in *Augustus*'s days.

Chabræus or *Cheops* succeeded Fifty years, and then *Cephrenes* Fifty six, both Builders of *Pyramids* for their *Sepulchers* : *Mycerinus* his Son Six years, as the Oracle had threatned for his opening the Idols Temple, which his Predeceffors had fhut. It may be *Chemmis* had learned their Vanity at *Jerufalem*, and thereupon fhut the Temple up. *Reynoccius* gives him Fifty years; *Bocboris*, or *Banchyris* by *Suidas*, fucceed Forty four years. Then *Sabacus* an *Æthiopian*. But *Herodotus* omits both, and hath *Afychis*, who decreed the Debtors dead Body, fhould be given to the will of the Creditor, 'till the Debt were payed. *Anyfis* fucceeded him, and both could be but Six years. Then came the former *Æthiopian*, who Reigned fifty years ; Scripture calls him *Zonaras*, *Sua*, with whom *Hofea*, King of *Ifrael*, made a Vain League againft *Salmanaffar*. They fay he left his Kingdom, and returned into *Æthiopia*, to avoid his God's Commandment to kill all the Priefts of *Egypt*; fuch was their Zeal to their Priefts.

§. 7. *Sethom* fucceeded in the Twelfth of *Hezekiah*, and Fifth of *Senacherib*, when *Affur* and *Egypt* contended which fhould Rule or ferve. *Hezekiah*, though fixing fpecial Confidence in God, held it fit to make a League with *Egypt* by his People, relying more on *Egypt* than on God. *Egypt* promifeth much, but only furnifhed him with fome Treafure, fent to hire *Arabians*, which was intercepted : *Herodotus* tells us a Tale of *Sethom's* Praying to *Vulcan* his God for Aid againft the *Affyrians*, who lay before *Pelufium*, and he fent *Mice* which gnawed their Bowftrings, and Straps of their Armour, which made them depart. His Reign *Funĉtius* refolves to be 33 years, giving no Reafon ; yet upon fearch I find it within One Year, by dividing the years from *Rehoboam's* 5th to *Jehojakims* 4th among the Kings of *Egypt*, giving each his fet time, and the Remainder to *Sethom*.

C H A P.

CHAP. XXIII.

Of Manaffes, *and his Contemporaries.*

§. 1. **M**Anaffes, Son of *Hezekiah* fucceeded, being Twelve Years Old, and Reigned Fifty
Five Years, of whofe Idolatry, and extraordinary
Wickednefs, fee 2 *Kings* 21. and 2 *Chron.* 33. Of his
putting the Reverend Prophet *Ifaiah* to death, with
a Wooden Saw, being Eighty years old, *Eufebius,*
Epiphanius, Ifidore, and others confirm. His Captivity in *Babel,* his Repenting, Prayer, Reformation,
and Death, fee 2 *Chron.* 33. *Merodach* having loved his Father, might more eafily be perfwaded to
reftore him.

§. 2. *Ægypt,* after *Sethom* was miferably diftra-
cted with Civil diffention two Years; then ill reform'd
by a Government of 12 Princes, of which 11 falling
out with the 12th. were. by him fubdued, and the
Kingdom Ufurped; which Anarchy *Diodore* put, after *Sabacus,* omitting *Sethom,* contrary to *Herodotus.*
Thefe Twelve, for a Monument of their Government,
made a Labyrinth near the Lake *Maris,* which *He-*
roclus prefers to the Chief Pyramid, which excelled
Diana's Temple. *Diodorus* reports it the work of
Marus, or *Menides,* five Generations before *Proteus,*
or the *Trojan* War; and *Reyneccius* takes him to
Annemenes, as he doth *Amenophis* to be *Amafis,* and
Sethom to be *Actifanes.* But he was deceived,
for the times we are now in, fhew us *Amafis*
was *Anifis, Actifanes Sebacus,* and *Marus* one of
the 12 Governours which made this Work. Whereto ferve the 12 great Halls in it, &c. *Pfammiticus*
one of the 12. caft out by the reft upon an Oracle
(as *Herodotus* tells the Tale, which *Diodore* believes

N 3   not)

not) hired Power out of *Caria*, and *Ionia*, with which he overthrew his Fellows, and Ruled alone 54 Years, faith *Hierom*; which *Mercator* divides; 44 alone, and 10 before, according to *Eufebius*. And to make the reckoning fall even with the years from the 5th of *Reboboam*, and the 4th of *Jebojakim*, we muft confound the laft of the 15, afcribed to the 12 Governours, with the firft of *Pfamnitius*. He firft entertained Amity with the *Greeks*, difpleafing his Souldiers, with preterring his Mercenaries to the right Wing, in an Expedition into *Syria*. So that 2000 deferted their Country, and went to dwell in *Æthiopia*. He won *Afotus* after 29 Years Siege, by reafon the *Babylonians* deferr'd it long. The Report of breeding up Two Infants for trial of the Original Language, is afcribed to him; and that the firft word they fpake was *Beccus*, which in the *Phrygian* Language is Bread. Hereof *Goxeus Becanus* is proud, becaufe in his low *Dutch*, *Becker* is a Baker, &c.

§. 3. *Manaffes's* time of Bondage and Enlargement is diverfly difputed; and were it certain, it is like we fhould find the *Egyptian* Troubles no fmall occafion of both. *Torniel* repeats 3 Opinions, 1. of *Bellarmine*, who thinks him taken in his 15th Year of his Reign. 2. Great Hebrew Chronologers hold it the 27th, 3. *Kimchi*, after 40 years of Idolatry. *Torniellus* rejects the two laft, and defends the firft; but in Affection rather than Judgment. It is more probable *Manaffes* lived longer in his Sin than 15 years, if not 40. by two places of Scripture, 2 *Kings* 21.17. and 2 *Kings* 24. 3, 4. utterly remits his Repentance. *Manaffes's* 15th Year was *Merodach's* 31. his 27th was the other's 43. and his 40th the 5 of *Nabolaffar*, Son of *Merodach*; now which of thefe, or what other, were the Year of his Captivity, I forbear to fhew my Opinion, &c. This was the firft Maftery the *Babylonians* had over *Judah*, greater than what *Salmanaffar*

naffar had of *Achaz*.; by which the *Babylonians* utterly alienated *Manaffes* and his Son from *Egypt*,
and made them joyn againft it.; as was feen in *Jofias*, againft *Necho*.

§. 4. Contemporary Actions were the firft and
fecond *Meffenian* Wars; one in the Reign of *Heze-
chias*, the other of *Manaffes*. The occafion was
flight, about private wrongs between a *Meffanean*,
and a *Spartan*; but fufficient to the ambitious *Spartans*,
tho' they were the Aggreffors; who could be drawn to
no fair Compofition, offered by the other, but the
Sword muft end it; fuch was their reftlefs defire to
the fair Country of *Meffena*, bordering upon them.
They therefore fwore fecretly, to follow the War,
'till the *Meffenians* were Conquer'd; they then fur-
pris'd *Amphia*, a Frontier, and put all to the Sword.
The *Meffenians* Army, an obftinate Force, fought
without Victory, ended by dark night. After this,
Friends came in on both fides, and three other Battles were fought; but in the laft, the *Lacedemonians*
were put to flight. Thus the War continued fo
long by the obftinacy of the *Spartans*, that their
Wives fent them word their Cities would become
difpeopled for want of Iffue; whereupon they fent
back their ableft young Men, promifcuoufly to accompany their young Women, whofe Iffue became
the greateft part of the Nation, and were called
Parthians. The *Meffenians* at length, by Oracle,
were order'd to Sacrifice a Virgin of the Stock of
Egyptus, of the *Arcadian* Royal Blood. *Ariftodemus*
the King, ripped up his own Daughters Belly, to
prove her a Virgin, contrary to her Lover's report;
which to fave her, faid fhe was with Child; yet the
Meffenians prevailed not. So that the miferable Father flew himfelf at the Grave, with whom the
Meffenians loft their Courage, and yielded after
twenty years rigorous Contefts. After thirty
years, the young Men of the *Meffenians*, of whom,

N 4 young

young *Aristodemus*, descended from *Ægyptus*, was Chief, finding their strength, and scorning such Masters; finding also the *Argives* and *Arcadians* firm, resolv'd to attempt the *Lacedemonians*, under the Conduct of *Aristodemus*, in the Fourth Year of the Twenty Third Olympiad. The *Lacedemonians* hast to quench the fire before it be too hot, but found their Servants their Equals; and *Aristodemus* refusing the Title of King, for his Valour became their General; and in the next Battle, assisted with *Argives*, *Arcadians*, and *Sicyonians*, put the *Spartans*, *Corinthians*, and others to flight; and after surprized a Town in *Laconia*, and vanquished *Anaxander* King of *Sparta*. But by a treacherous defection of *Aristocratus*, hired by the Enemy, the *Messenians* are forced, and slain, *Andania* the Chief Town, and others far from Sea forsaken, and the People forc'd to *Era*, a strong Mountain, which held the Enemy work for Eleven Years; wherein *Aristocratus* with three hundred Souldiers abroad, perform'd great things; Supriz'd and Sack'd *Amiclæ*, which was thrice taken, and still he escaped. Of which escapes that was admirable; that being cast with Fifty more into a deep Natural Cave, he died not of the Fall as the rest, yet without hope; 'till by a little light he spied a Fox eating on a dead Carcafs, and got it by the Tail, and follow'd it 'till he could no further, and then let it go, seeing light in the hole, and so wrought himself out with his Nails. The *Spartans* believed not them which reported he was escaped, 'till the flaughters he made of the *Corinthians* at *Era* assured it. Thus Eleven Years were spent about *Era*, which at last was enter'd in a stormy Night, through neglect of the Watch; which was discovered to the *Spartans* by a Slave fled from his Master into the City. So the *Messenians* were dispers'd, pers'd, and Built *Messina* in *Sicily*, and three hundred years after returned, by *Epaminondas*'s means.

§ 5. *Ardis* King of *Lydia* succeeded *Gyges* his Father Forty nine years, in the second of the twenty fifth Olympiad. He incroached upon the *Ionians* in *Asia*, took *Colephon*, and *Priene*; but the *Cymmerians* expell'd by the *Scythians*, Invaded *Asia*, won *Sardis*, and held it till *Alyattes*, this Man's Grandchild. *Phraortes* King of the *Medes*, the third Year of the twenty ninth Olympiad, the last of *Manasses*, succeeded his Father *Deioces*, who had Reigned fifty three years; who Commanded more absolutely than his Predecessor, and by a more State-like Severity and Ceremonies upheld Majesty, almost fallen. He desired not to enlarge his Dominions, but to Govern well his own; and differed so much from his Predecessors, that he seemed to be the first King of the *Medes*, as *Herodotus* reports. He was Founder of *Ecbitane*, now *Tauris*, and chosen by the Patrons of the Books of *Judith* to be *Arphaxad*, and so, must *Ben Merodach* be *Nebuchadnezar*. But the brief decision of this Controversie is the Book of *Judith*, which is not Canonical: For as Chronologers can find no time to place that Story, so Cosmographers are as much troubled to find *Japheth*'s Borders there set down, and *Phud* and *Lud*; so that for time and place, they are

Extra Anni Solisque Vias.

§ 6. Other Contemporaries, as *Numa Pompilius* in *Rome*, who succeeded *Romulus* after one Year. In the second year of *Manasses*, he brought the rude multitude of Thieves and Out-Laws, which followed *Romulus*, to some good Civility; by devising Ceremonies of Superstition, as things of great importance, learned of his Nymph *Egeria*. Which Superstitions himself Condemned, in his Books, found almost Six Hundred Years after

in

in his Grave, which were publickly burnt, as speaking against the Religion then in use. After forty three year, *Tullus Hostilius* succeeded in *Manasses* forty sixth, and Reigned thirty two years; for for the most part as *Numa*, in Peace. He made breach with the *Albans*, but doubting the *Tuscans*, their common Enemies, would make advantage of the Dissention, they put it to a Combate of three Brethren on either side; Cousin Germans, and of equal years and strength; but the *Horatij* of *Rome* prevail'd against the *Curatij* and *Alba*, where the *Latins* submit to *Rome*, and *Alba* not long after was demolished. *Hyppomanes* had Ruled seven years in *Athens*, in the entrance of *Mamasses*, and the three last Governours for ten years were in his time. In whose times I follow *Halicarnasseus*; who professing care in matching the *Grecian* years with the *Roman* Occasions, beginneth with *Rome's* Building, the first year of the seventh Olympiad, and the first of *Cecrops* in *Athens*. *Midas* now Reigned in *Phrygia*, &c. The *Scythians* invaded him; *Syracuse* in *Sicily*, Founded by *Archias*, *Miscellus*, and other *Corinthians*. *Nicomedia*, formerly *Astacus* in *Propontis*, enlarged by *Zipartus's* Navy of *Thrace*. *Sybilla* of *Samus* now lived, according to *Pausanias*. *Croton* on the Bay of *Tarentum*, built by *Miscellus*. *Gela* in *Sicily*, *Phaselis* in *Pamphylia*. *Chalcedon* in *Asia*, built by the *Magerenses*. The *Parthians* expelled *Lacedemon*, were Conducted by *Phalantus* into *Italy*, where they took *Tarentum*.

CHAP.

CHAP. XXIV.

Of Ammon, Josiah, *and the rest, to the Destruction of* Jerusalem.

§. 1. **A**MMON, Twenty two years old, Succeeded two years, and was as Wicked as his Father had been; his Servants slew him. *Josiah* Eight years old, succeeded Thirty one Years. He sought after the God of his Father *David*, and at Twelve years old made a worthy Reformation, fulfilling the Prophecy delivered at *Bethel*, to *Jeroboam*. By which History it appears, that *Bethel* and some parts of the Ten Tribes were come under the Power of *Judah* ; either taken in by *Hezechiah* upon the death of *Assurbaddon*, while the *Babylonians*, who loved him, were busie in *Assyria* ; or at *Manasses's* Inlargement: The *Babylonians* not yet fit to deal with the *Egyptian* so far off, to oblige *Judah* to them, were content with this Inlargement as necessary against the *Egyptians*. This may be the Reason *Manasses* Fortified himself after his return, which was not against the *Babylonians*, but the *Egyptians*, as appeared in *Josiah* his opposing *Necho* with such earnestness, as argueth a firm League with the *Babylonians*. That *Egypt's* Friendship was little worth, *Judah* had oft found, and payed for, by the *Assyrians* and *Babylonians* displeasure, for adhering to *Egypt* ; yet had it been a small matter upon his earnest Request to let him pass, if *Josiah* had not been obliged to the *Babylonians* by his Ancestors Covenant, to Offend and Defend ; neither had it been Wisdom to Encounter such an Army, offering no Violence. Whatever moved *Josiah*, it is likely he forgot (as the best do sometimes) to ask Counsel of God, and depended on the *Babylonians* too much, which could not please God.

God. The Conclusion was, that God for the Wickedness of the People, took away that good King,
who had stayed his Hand from Revenging himself
upon them, whose Miseries presently insued his
Death, so much bewailed of all.

§. 2. *Neco*, Son to *Psammiticus*, following his Fathers designs, who had made entrance into *Syria*,
being assisted by the extraordinary Valor of the
Greeks, and knowing how *Assyria*, stood in danger
by the Power of the *Medes*, intended with a Powerful Army to visit *Euphrates*, and strengthen the
Passages about *Carchemish*, or further to Invade *Syria*. Having therefore over-thrown *Josiah* in his
way, not intending to stay the Conquest of *Judah*, he
proceeded, and took *Cadytis*, perhaps *Carchemish*, and
became, in a manner, Lord of all *Syria*, saith *Josephus*, particularly of the *Phænicians*, whom he set
to Sail from the *Arabian* Gulf round about *Africa*,
by the *Cape* of *good Hope*. In his return from *Euphrates*, he took *Jehoahaz*, the younger Son of *Josiah*, whom *Jeremy* calls *Shallum*, whom the People
had made King, and put him in Bonds, and put *E-
liakim* in his place, calling him *Jehojakim*, and layed
a Tribute on the Land, but forbore the Conquest.
Jehoahaz was King but three Months; *Jehojakim* the
Elder Son of *Josiah*, Reigned Ten years, he was of the
Egyptian Faction, and of the behaviour of the worst of
his Ancestors, which had so Infected the Land, that
the Chief Priests also were defiled therewith. Yet the
Lord raised up Prophets which reproved him, among
whom *Uriah*, flying from the Tyrant which sought
his Life, is from *Egypt* sent back to death, contrary to the Custom of Nations.

§. 3. *Of the Kings of* Media *and* Babylon. §. *Merodach*, Son of *Baladan*, taking advantage of *Senacherib*'s Misadventure and Death, with the Assistance
of his Sons, made himself King of *Babylon*, but
kept in Action 'till *Assurhaddon*'s death, Eleven years,
so

so that he could not intend *Syria*, but was well rewarded then, by a great part of *Assyria*, if not by all, as some less probably think. Yet his little concern with the *Assyrian* Affairs all his long Reign, argues him busied at Home in setling his Purchases there; and having Amity with *Hezekiah*. *Ben. Mirodach* his Son succeeded Twenty one years, whose Governours (as I take it) captivated *Manasses*, in whose time *Psamniticus*, with his Greek Mercenaries, prevailed in *Syria*, which might procure *Manasses* his release, and it may be a part of the Kingdom of *Samaria*, which the *Babylonians* could not now intend.

Nabulassar his Son succeeded Thirty five years, whose works at home kept him from looking abroad; for *Phraortes* King of the *Medes*, Invaded *Assyria*, and Besieged *Ninive*, which it seems was not yet subject to *Babylon*; for *Nabonassar* repelled him not, but the *Scythians* Invaded *Media*, and forced him thence. *Phraortes* Son of *Deioces* King of *Media*, having inlarged his Dominions, attempted *Ninive*, which yet remained of her self well enough, saith *Herodotus*. Custom of Danger hardened the Un-war-like, whom sudden unknown Dangers amaze. *Ninive* had now been long exercised, so that *Phraortes* and his Family perished there.

Cyaxares his Son, a braver Man of War, won in Lesser *Asia*, all from *Halis* Eastward. He Besieged *Ninive*, and took it, saith *Eusebius*, whom I rather believe, than *Herodotus*, saying, the *Scythians* came upon him, which is not likely, for we cannot think him so improvident; but rather hearing they were to guard *Media*, he left the City, which about this time was destroyed, as we read in *Tobit*, a Book of sufficient Credit, for the Story of those Times. And sure we are, the Prophecy of *Nahum* was fulfilled by *Nebuchadnezzar*; and probable it is, that *Nabulassar*, after *Cyaxares* left it in weak case,
might

might feize upon it eafily, and put a Vice-Roy in it, which upon their Rebellion againft *Nebuchadnezzar*, were utterly deftroyed.

§. 4. The *Scythians*, about this time, made a great Expedition into *Afia*, of which *Herodotus* fpeaks much, and many Fabulous things ill agreeing with the time. Their firft Eruption muft needs be within the Reign of *Pfamniticus* King of *Egypt*, who met with them in *Paleftine*, and got them by intreaty and gifts to leave the Country. Before this they had wafted *Media*, and molefted *Affyria*, *Babylonia*, &c. and are faid to have Domineered in *Afia* Twenty eight Years, within the Compafs of the Reign of *Ardis*, *Sadiatts*, and *Haliatts*, Kings of *Lydia*, and the Twenty eight laft years of *Nabulaffar* King of *Babel*. What thefe Nations were, is next to be confidered. *Herodotus* tells us, the *Cimmerians* being driven out of their Country by the *Scythians*, invaded *Afia*, and that the *Scythians* purfued them into remote parts, and by chance fell on *Media* and *Egypt*, &c. But it is no uncommon thing for the *Greeks* to flander them, by whom their Nation hath been Beaten, as they were by thefe. For the *Cymmerians*, or *Cimbrians* are well known by their Conquefts of many Nations, to have been no fuch Cowards. Thefe were of the Pofterity of *Gomer*, who Peopled moft of the Weftern World, and whofe Reflux over-whelmed no fmall portion of *Greece* and *Afia*; of whofe Original, read *Goropius Becanus* his *Amazonica*, where we find the *Cimmerians*, *Scythians*, and *Sarmatians* were all one Nation, diftinguifhed by divers Names according to their Tribes, &c. *Homer* alfo fpake difgracefully of them for the fame caufe; for they had wafted his Country, as had the *Amazons*. As for the expulfion they write of, it was no more than fending out of Colonies into *Afia*, with an Army of *Scythians* to help to Plant them elfewhere, their own Country being

being over-charged. The *Sarmatians* also were their Companions, as their return by *Novogrod* in *Ruffia*, which was *Sarmatia*, sheweth. Such another Eruption they made above Five hundred years after. The *Cimmerians* being the first Company, held the way of the *Euxine* Sea on their Right hand, paffing through *Colchis*, entred *Pontus*, then *Paphlagonia*, where fortifying the Promontory, whereon the *Greeks* after built *Synope*, they there left the unferviceable men of their Train, under Guard. From thence to *Lydia*, *Phrygia*, and *Ionia*, the way lay open. In *Lydia* they Won *Sardis* from the King of *Ardis*, &c. The mifery of Wars is never fuch, as when Men are forced to feek a State which others poffefs ; when all is little enough for the one fide, and worketh the rooting out of the other. They which Fight for Maftery, are pacifyed with Tribute and Services ; but in thefe Migrations, the Affailants are fo unfatiable, that they need all the Defendants have, even to the fucceeding Infants Cradle. The mercilefs terms of this Controverfy, arms both fides with defperate Refolution, feeing all is at the ftake on both fides, to the utter Ruin of the one fide. Our *Britains* can witnefs the differenc of Conquefts, who loft but Liberty by the *Romans*, for the which they gained civil Acts, which before they never knew ; but by *Saxons* they loft all, to the eradication of the *Britains* Race. The *Danes* made the like attempt on the *Saxons*, with fuch continuance as bred acquaintance between them, neither being able to fubdue the other ; fo many *Danes* became peaceable Inhabitants in wafted parts, and the reft returned home. Such was (as I think) the end of the *Cimmerian* War in *Lydia*, which having continued long, made both fides willing to reft ; fo that upon fome Victory of King *Halyattes*, the *Cimmerians* were content with what they had gotten on the Eaft fide of the River *Halys* ; which henceforth became the Border of *Lydia*, on whofe Eaft fide, dwelt the *A-*

mazons.

mazons, that is, the *Cimmerians* and *Scythians.* Hereto ſerveth, that when *Cyaxares* of *Media* ſought Revenge on the *Scythians*, *Haliates* aſſiſted them, to prevent his encroaching Weſtward. *Herodotus's* Tale of this War about the *Scythian* Fugitives, is leſs probable. The *Scythians* and *Sarmatians* took to the *South*, as the *Cimerians* had to the *Weſt*, paſſing between*Caucaſus* and the *Caſpian* Sea through *Albania*, *Colthene*, &c. where now are *Servia* and *Georgia*, and entred *Media* in the time of *Phraortes*, who was glad to Compound with them, while *Pſammiticus* reigned in *Egypt*, and in the ſixth year of *Nabulaſſar*, from which their Twenty Eight Years Dominion ended in his Thirty fourth ; the *Medes* not venturing a ſecond Battel, thought nothing diſhonourable to remove ſuch troubleſome Gueſts, and therefore ſubmitted to a Tribute, and ſo got them to remove; who finding the Country more Pleaſant toward the *South*, were eaſily perſwaded. How *Babylon*, being in their way to *Egypt*, eſcaped, is uncertain ;yet'tis certain,that all thoſe parts of *Aſia* were Tributaries to them. *Pſamniticus*, to prevent their entring *Egypt*, (as a *Jealous* Husband of a fair Wife) which he would not be willing they ſhould ſee, met them in *Syria*, on the *South* of *Paleſtine*, and at their being at *Aſcalon*, and he at *Gaza*, and with fair words and rich Gifts ſo perſwaded 'em, that they returned to viſit their high Country Friends, and left *Syria* the more eaſy for him to deal with, while the Nations beyond *Euphrates* who had new work to entertain theſe Strangers with, returned. The *Scythians* flowing back, the way they came, grew an intolerable Burthen to all they light on, eſpecially the *Medes*, which there over-ſwarm'd, being Rich and near home, in a Climate beſt agreeing with their Bodies. Here they fell from exacting, the agreeed Tribute, to take what they liked ; yea All, from many ; whereby the Land was unmanured. *Cyaxares*, *es,* to remedy this oppreſſion, took this Courſe; that the *Medes* Feaſting the better part of the *Scythians,* made them drunk, and ſlew them, and recovered all; like as the *Danes* had been uſed in *England.* 'Tis like that this was done on the Chief Leaders, which forced the Multitude upon indifferent Conditions to return home, being yet ſtrong enough againſt the Encounters by the way. Others perhaps were ſetled in the Country before; others might go to their Countrymen in *Lydia.* At this time is reported the Story of the returned *Scythians,* which vanquiſhed their Corrival Slaves at home with Horſewhips; according to the Cuſtom of the *Muſcovian* Women ſending a Whip, which ſhe Curiouſly Worketh, to the Man which ſhall be her Husband, in token of Subjection.

§. 5. Contemporaries, beſides the Kings of *Egypt, Babylon, Medes,* and *Lydians,* of whom we ſpake: *Tullus Hoſtilius* Reigned in *Rome* 'till the twenty firſt year of *Joſiah: Ancus Martius* ſucceeded twenty four years. *Tarquin Priſcus,* a Stranger, was next, who being Tutor to *Ancus's* Children, was ſo gracious with the People, and ſoRich, that they choſe him King, the fourth year of *Zedekiah,* and Reigned thirty eight years. *Cypſilus* in *Corinth* expelling the *Bacides,* Reigned thirty years in Peace. *Periander* his Son ſucceeded; a Tyrant, who ſlew his Wife, and in Honour of her, ſtript all the Women ſtark naked, and burnt their Apparel to her Ghoſt. Yet the *Greeks* were then ſo Wiſe as to admire his Wiſdom, as one of the Seven Sages. *Draco* the Law-Maker of *Athens,* puniſh'd every Offence with death. *Solon* abrogated them. *Zeleucus,* Law-giver to the *Locrians,* in *Italy;* his Law put out the Eyes of the Adulterer; and to ſave one of his Sons offending that way, put out one of his own. He reſtored Womens immodeſt Attire, by allowing it to intice a Lover, not to go out of the Houſe by Night, but to

O play

play the Whore; nor to be attended with more than one Woman abroad, except they were drunken; which Difpenfations, Women were afhamed to claim.

§.6. *Jerufalem* in the third year of *Jehojakim* is Befieged by *Nebuchadnezzar*, the fecond year of his Reign with his Father; and, notwithstanding the affiftance of *Neco* King of *Egypt*, forced *Jehojakim* to become his Vaffal, and took *Daniel* and his Fellows Hoftages; but hafted home, not intending there to ftay, *Neco* coming with fuch difadvantage fo far from home, in a Country which loved him not. Befides, his Father's death called him to poffefs his own, before he fought other Mens. But the next year, which was *Nebuchadnezzar*'s firft, and *Neco*'s laft, they fought on the Bank of *Euphrates*, where *Neco* Fought his laft, and *Nebuchadnezzar* recover'd all *Syria. Paufanius* fucceeded *Neco*, but inferiour in Valour; he thought to reftore *Jehoahaz* his Prifoner, and caft out *Jehojakim*, but the Lord faid to the contrary. *Jehojakim* alfo rely'd on the *Egyptians*, 'till *Nebuchadnezzar* forced a Tribute on him; fo he fubmitted quietly three years; in his fourth year it feemeth that *Jeremiah* was firft Imprifoned.

Tyrus holding out againft *Nebuchadnezzar*, was in his feventh year Befieged, and in his fourteenth year taken; for her Captivity was limited to feventy years, and her Siege was thirteen. It was divided from the Main by a deep broad Channel, excelled in ftore of Ships, which *Nebuchadnezzar* wanted, and every Wind brought fupply from Foreign Parts, fo that it feared neither Force, nor Famine. But God, that had threatned *Tyre*, fent a King impatient of refiftance, to undertake fuch a piece of work, to ftop a vaft Channel in the Sea, ufing thereto the Wood of *Libanus*, not far off, and the Ruins of old *Tyre*, with the toilfom labour of many thoufands of Men, wherewith he prevailed at length.

length. But the wealthy Citizens fled by Sea to *Creet*, and left little Wealth for Booty; therefore the Lord promised them *Egypt*; see *Ezek.* 29. 18, 19. *Jehojakim*, upon what occasion is uncertain; (whether Mutiny among the Souldiers, or Rumour of the *Egyptians* coming against *Nebuchadnezzar*) renounced his Subjection, but was presently subdued by *Nebuchadnezzar*, and slain, and his Son *Jehojakim* or *Jeconias* put in his place, and after three Months, removed to *Babylon*, and *Mattanias* his Uncle established in his stead; and called *Zedekiah*, who took an Oath of subjection. In his fourth year he went to *Babel*, about some business, wherein it seems he was not satisfied; for upon his return, he began to practice with the Neighbouring Princes of *Moab*, &c. what year *Johanan* the False Prophet opposed *Jeremy*. *Nebuchadnezzar* hearing of *Zedekiah*'s practice, came in the dead of Winter, and Besieged *Jerusalem*; and though the year following he raised his Siege to meet *Hophra*, * yet upon the *Egyptians* * *Apries*, abandoning his Enterprize, he returned, and gave in *Herodo-* the City no rest, 'till he brake it up. *tus.*

Zedekiah escaping in the Night through a Vault under the Earth, is yet overtaken, &c. and his Eyes being put out, he was carried into *Babel*, but saw it not, as *Ezekiel* foretold, *Ch.* 12. 13. This was the eleventh year of *Zedekiah*, and eighteenth of *Nebuchadnezzar*, the year after the Temple was burnt; the four hundred thirty first year after the Building. What followed, is written 2 *Kings* 25. *Jer.* 39. & 52.

O 2   CHAP.

THE

HISTORY

OF THE

WORLD.

BOOK III.   Part I.

FROM

The Deſtruction of *Jeruſalem* unto
Philip of *Macedon.*

C H A P. I.

The time from the Deſtruction of Jeruſalem
to the Aſſyrian *Fall.*

§. I. **T**HE *Connexion of Sacred and Profane.*
Hiſtory. §. Before the *Grecian* Olympiads, and the Eaſtern Date from
Nabonaſſar, the Courſe of Time had
no beaten Path, as after it had more certain Marks ;
yet from *Jeruſalem's* Deſtruction, the former, with
O 3   the

the fucceeding Ages, are more clearly difcern'd in
their Connection.   The harm which fome have
found in the years of the overgrown Monarchies,
doth preferve their Names, which otherwife might
have been forgotten, but cannot fhew the Year of
fuch a King, in which any thing expreffed in Scripture was done.   Neither could any cartainty be
gathered from the late Kings of the *Affyrians*, &c.
if *Nebuchadnezzar's* Reign had not been precifely applied to the years of *Jehojakim*, and *Zedekiah*.
Hence have we the firft light to difcover how to
connect Sacred and Profane Hiftories; for *Judah's*
Seventy years Captivity begin under *Nebuchadnezzar*,
and ending the firft of *Cyrus*, directs us backward and
forward.   This firft year of *Cyrus*, is joyned with
the firft of the fifty fifth Olympiad.   And that he
Reigned twenty three year before his Monarchy, and
feven after, is apparent; and giving them four hundred and eight year between *Troy's* Fall, and *Iphetus's*
reftoring the Olympiads, we may arrive to the knowledge of the true *Grecian* Antiquities.   For other
Nations, let St. *Auguftine* be trufted.

§. 2. The Seventy Years of *Babylonian* Captivity
being our chief mark of direction, we are to inform
our felves truly therein.   Some begin from *Jeconias's*
Captivity, eleven year before *Zedekiah*; citing
Ezek. 40. 1.   *Beraldus* judgeth that it began the firft
of *Nebuchadnezzar*, and fourth of *Joakim*; citing
2 *Chron.* 36. and *Dan.* 1. *Matth.* 1. 11. but cannot
thus make it good.   Wretched *Porphyrie* fcoffeth at
St. *Matth.* 1. 11. not knowing *Jofias's* Sons had divers Names, as *Epiphanius* fhewed.   The Wretch
affirmeth the Book of *Daniel* was written long after
his death, at or near the time of *Antiochus Epiphanes*,
whom *Eufebius*, *Apollonius*, &c. have anfwered.
And the Seventy Interpreters Tranflated it out of
Hebrew, one hundred year before that.   *Jaddus* the
High-

High-Prieft alfo fhewed the Book to the Great *Alex-ander*, &c. True it is, the *Jews* afcribe it to *Ef-dras*, and equal it not to the Prophet, but put it a-mong the *Hagiographs*, or Holy Books; which are *Daniel, Pfalms, Job, Proverbs, Canticles, Ruth, La-mentations, Eccefiaftes, Hefter, Nebemiab,* and *Chro-nicles.* Our Chriftian Councils and Fathers acknow-ledge it Canonical; and our Saviour who cited no *Apocrypha,* cited it as a proof exceeding all.

§. 3. That the Seventy Years Captivity began at *Jerufalem's* deftruction, not *Jeconias's* Captivity, is clear; *Jeremiab* himfelf, explained himfelf, and *Daniel,* cited by fome to the contrary. Compare *Chap.* 25. 9, 11, 12. with *Chap.* 29. 10. where, in the firft place, he exprefly beginneth the Captivity of Seventy years, at *Jerufalem's* Deftruction; and thereof certifies the Captivity in the fecond place. So alfo it is underftood by themfelves, 2 *Chron.* 36. 19, 20, 21. So *Dan.* 9. 2. the Seventy years re-ferred to *Jerufalem's* Defolation.

§. 4. Touching the King's Reigning in *Babylon* thofe feventy Years, and the time of each, help us a little to the times before or after; neither it feems were moft of their Acts worth Recording. For as *Nebuchadnezzar's* latter times were either in delights, or madnefs, fo his Pofterity grew flothful, as Sons whofe Fathers have purchafed enough to their hands; yet let us confider of Men's Opinions therein, and judge as we fee caufe. The fureft Opinion, is theirs which follow the Scripture; which Name only *Ne-buchadnezzar, Evilmerodach,* and *Balthafar* and *Jeremy,* which feemeth to limit the Dominion of *Babel,* to Father, Son, and Grandfon. To qualifie this, I fee no neceffity, except Profane Authors were conftant and probable in more Succeffions, which they are not. *Jofephus* reckons five, citing *Berofus*; but far otherwife than doth *Jerom,* &c.

Anius Metaſthenes nameth five, of which, the three laſt were Brethren ; but neither he, nor the reſt, can qualifie *Jeremiah.*

§. 5. *Scaliger's* Opinion is here handled, and diſproved, beginning the ſeventieth year from *Jechonias's* tranſportation : and giving *Evilmerodach* but two years, *Balthaſar* one, of which he maketh four, ſpent in his protection, and maketh him a Son of *Nebuchadnezzar's* Daughter. But as *Jeremiah's* ſpeech of *Evilmerodach's* raiſing up *Jeconias,* argueth longer time, ſo his ſpeaking expreſly of *Nebuchadnezzar's* Sons in the Succeſſion. So *Daniel* employ'd in ſo high a Place by the King, and after falling to a private Life, could not have been forgotten of him in two year, or leſs. *Scaliger* alſo finds one *Nabonidus* after *Balthaſar,* and giveth him ſeventeen years, and maketh him *Darius Medus,* whom others make the ſame with *Balthaſar,* to make good *Beroſus,* whom *Scaliger* his chief Patron, herein forſaketh. His grounds are, one, out of *Daniel* 5. 31. where *Darius* is not ſaid to win, but receive the Kingdom ; makes no ſtrong concluſion, *&c.* His other is out of *Megaſthenes* in *Euſebius,* calling *Nabonidus* a *Mede,* but I find it not ; and if I did, I would little regard it, conſidering his other improbable Reports with it. Beſides, the Opinion agreeth hardly with Scripture, which ſaith, *the Kingdom ſhould be divided between the Medes and Perſians.* So that either *Darius* was not *Nabonidus,* or elſe bethink us what *Perſian* ſhared with him. Nay, both the Nations made the Empire, as *Daniel's* Ram ſheweth ; and the *Greeks* call the Wars made by *Xerxes,* the Wars of the *Medes.* So that the Notion of the Chronologers holding *Darius* Partner in *Cyrus's* Victories, was not well condemn'd.

§. 6. *Lyra,* and others, who hold thoſe only named in Scripture, to have reigned in *Babylon* during thoſe Seventy years ; I eſteem more conformable to Reaſon.

fon.   For the years of their Reign, it is clear, that
Evilmerodach began to Reign, 2 *Kings* 25. 27. *Jer.*
52. 31. in the Thirty Seventh year of *Jechonias's*
Captivity, from which, deduct *Zedekiab's* Eleventh
year, when the City was taken, there remained
Twenty Six of the Seventy.   How to diftribute the
other Forty four to the fucceeding Kings, is not fo
needful, as long as the total Sum is certain.   Yet
I will be bold to conjecture, as others have done,
giving to *Belthafar* Seventeen years, with *Jofephus* ;
fo there remain Twenty Seven, of which one may
be taken away for the Firft of *Darius* ; fo Twenty
fix remain for *Evilmerodach* : Befides *Jofephus*, all
that confound *Balthafar* and *Nabonidus*, give him Seventeen Years; and *Daniel's* being grown out of
Balthafar's Knowledge, who yet had ferved him his
Third year, argueth fome long time between.   That
Evilmerodach Reigned fome good time, is probable,
by *Jechonias's* favour under him ; and fome of great
judgment, have given him Twenty three years, and
more might be given as well as that.

§. 7. Touching the actions of thefe Kings. *Nebu-*
chadnezzar's former years were Victorious. In his Nineteenth year he won *Jerufalem* and proud *Tyrus*, *Efa.*
23. 15. The fame year *Egypt* was next aimed at, as
the faireft Mark ; but the petty Nations about *Ju-*
dab, who defired the Ruin thereof, were to be made
fure, for fear of incommoding his Return from *E-*
gypt, if he fucceeded not.   All thefe ill Neighbours
which imagined to gain by *Judab's* fall as *Tyrus* had,
and had followed the Camp as Ravens, were fuddenly oppofed by *Nebuchadnezzar*, as the Lord had
threatned, and brought into the Condition *Judab*
was in, *Efa.* 16. 14.

§. 8. *Nebuchadnezzar* having freed the Coaft behind him, through *Syria* and *Arabia*, leaving neither Friend to *Egypt*, nor Foe to himfelf, able to
give impediment to his Proceeding or Retreat, he
pre-

presently took it in hand, and according to our Three great Prophets, had a Victorious Conquest of *Egypt*, although some good Authors following *Herodotus* and *Diodore*, extenuate it to a Ravage without Conquest; and that *Apries*, or *Hophra* their King, was slain after in an Insurrection of his Subjects, and *Amasis* chosen to succeed. But *Herodotus* and *Diodorus* are herein contradicted by such Authority as Force our Belief, as *Esa.* 20. 4, 5, 6. *Jer.* 43. 10, and 44; and 46. 25, 26: So *Ezek.* 29. 20. 30. and 32. 31. So that *Junius*, who in one place took *Hophra's* Enemies to be *Amasis* and his Fellows, yet on *Jer.* 44. 30. he Confessed the *Egyptian* Priests had abused *Herodotus*. *Josephus* also herein is rather to be believed, reporting *Egypt's* Conquests, and slaying of the King by *Nebuchadnezzar*, who appointed another in his stead; all which is consonant to the Prophets.

§. 9. *Nebuchadnezzar's* Victories after the Conquest of *Syria*, more enlarged his Dominions than his former; for besides the Conquest of *Egypt*, we are bound to believe he Conquered *Phut*, and *Lud*, and other Nations, as it seemeth, even to *Mauritania*. Hitherto *Egypt* had flourished Fifteen hundred Eighty years; but from henceforth, Forty years under a Vice-Roy, and was long after in recovering strength, but never to her Antient Glory, *Esa.* 19. 11. *Ezek.* 29. 13. &c.

§. 10. *Nebuchadnezzar's* Actions are diversly dated, some from the beginning of his Reign, whose first year ran with part of *Jehojakim's* Third, when *Daniel* was carried Captive. Another date was from the beginning of his Empire, which was after the Conquest of *Egypt*, as his Dream, *Dan.* 2. 1. which could not be the Second years Reign, considering the third then being up of *Daniel*, before he stood before the King, as also that *Nebuchadnezzar* was yet no such King, as he was when *Daniel* declared the Dream, &c.

&c. After the Conquest of *Egypt, Ninive,* which Rebelled, was destroyed by him, as *Nahum* foretold ; whose Prophecy went between the destruction of *Egypt* and *Ninive.*

§. 11. *Nebuchadnezzar's* last Times are found only in *Daniel,* as his Buildings in *Babel, cap.* 4. 27. wherein he glorified so much ; and no marvel if *Josephus's* report out of *Berosus,* be true, of an Orchard supported by Arches, as high as Mountains, reared in Fifteen days. But his over-valuing his own Greatness, abased him as low ; and the Lord, for his presuming to erect an Image to be worshipped to his dishonour, whom he had before acknowledged, cast such contempt upon him, as never befel such a Man. For, after the Lord had convinced him by the miraculous cooling of his Furnace, and by a second Dream, warned him, and given him one year respite, he had Human Sense taken from him, *&c.* Upon his restoring, *Augustine* and others, held him saved.

§. 12. *Evilmerodach* succeeded, in whose Nineteenth year ended the Fortieth year of *Egypt's* Desolation, and now brake the *Babylonian* Yoak under *Amasis* their King. This fell out while *Astyages* the *Mede,* Grand-Father to *Cyrus,* held War with *Evilmerodach,* and had the better, which emboldened *Egypt. Astyages* died in the Ninth year of *Evilmerodach,* and left the *Medes* and *Persians* in Arms against *Evilmerodach,* whom also they slew.

§. 13. A conjecture how it might be that in *Nebuchadnezzar's* Seven Years of Madness, *Niglisar* might govern by his Wife *Nitocris's* means, *Nebuchadnezzar's* Daughter and *Labassardach* after him, but slain after Nine Months, presently before *Nebuchadnezzar's* Restauration.

CHAP.

CHAP. II.

The Perfians *greatnefs, how it grew.*

§. 1. THAT the *Medes* were chief in the o-
verthrow of *Babylon,* the infallible Witnefs of Two great Prophets, maketh good, *Efa.* 13
17. *Jer.* 51. 11. 28. according to which, *Julius A-
fricanus* proveth *Babel* was taken before *Cyrus* began
to Reign. So that the Empire loft by *Baltbaffar,*
the laft of *Belochus*'s Line, fell to *Cyaxares* or *Darius
Medus,* the laft of *Arbaces*'s Race, who fucceeded
his Father *Aftyages,* &c.

§. 2. *Cyrus,* to whom alone the *Greeks* afcribe the
Conqueft of *Babel,* was thought immediate Succeffor
to *Aftyages,* by fome who deny he had any other
Son than this *Cyrus* Son of *Mandane* his Daughter. *Viginer* alfo probably reafoneth, that *Aftyages*
had no fuch Son as *Darius,* being unknown to fo
many Authors there named. But Negative Arguments from Authors, are of no force and neceffity.
Either *Aftyages* muft be *Darius,* in *Daniel* 9. which
his Time will not fuffer, or another Succeffor before
Cyrus muft be granted, who for Life commanded
all. Yet in regard he was Old, and followed not
the Wars in Perfon, but *Cyrus* as his Lieutenant, did
all; the *Greeks,* who heard only of him, afcribed all to
him; as did the *Perfians,* in Honour to him, who
fhortly brought all to them.

§. 3. *Xenophon*'s Report of the Wars between the
Affyrians and the *Medes,* and *Perfians.* The *Affyrians* having command of fo many Countries, defired to bring under the *Medes* and *Perfians.* Knowing therefore their great ftrength, he perfwaded
Crœfus, the rich and ftrong King of *Lydia,* to join
with him, which he eafily yielded, for the quarrel

to

to the *Medes*, who had warred againſt *Alyattes* his Father. Theſe together compoſe an Army of Two Hundred Thouſand Foot and Sixty Thouſand Horſe, but are overthrown by *Darius* ; and *Cyaxares* King of the *Medes*, and *Cyrus* General of the *Perſian* Forces, and the *Aſſyrian* King ſlain ; ſo that many *Aſſyrians* revolted, and *Babylon* was glad, for her ſecurity, to get mercenary ſtrength, while *Cyrus* purſueth his Victory to leſſer *Aſia*, and took *Crœſus* Priſoner. After this followed the Attempt at *Babylon*, *Cyaxares* bearing the Charge, and *Cyrus* being Leader, &c.

§. 4. *Achæmenes* govern'd in *Perſia*, when *Arbaces* did the like in *Media*, and both joined with *Belochus* againſt *Sardanapalus*, and after held *Perſia* for himſelf, as the other did *Media* and *Babylon* ; yet *Arbaces*'s abſolute Command decayed 'till *Deioces* Onehundred fortys year after, when *Salmanaſſar* Reigned in *Syria* ; ſo that neither the *Medes* nor *Perſians* found it fit to ſtir. From *Deioces* to *Aſtyages*, there paſt above Ninety years, in which time *Phraortes* Reigned, but not like to have Conquered *Perſia*, as *Herodotus* Writ. For *Suſiana* was under *Daniel*'s Charge for *Nebuchadnezzar* ; who alſo would hardly have ventured into *Syria* and *Egypt*, leaving ſuch an Enemy on his Back. It ſeemeth, the Succeſſors of *Achæmenes* did little worth remembring, ſeeing in the *Perſian* Greatneſs, nothing was Publiſhed of their firſt Kings. *Xenophon* reports the Crown deſcended from Father to Son many Deſcents; and that *Cambyſes* begot *Cyrus*; ſo that the Story of *Aſtyages*'s giving *Mandane* his Daughter to a baſe Man, to diſable her Iſſue, whoſe Greatneſs he feared, is improbable. Two Races ſprung from *Achæmenes* ; the Firſt, according to *Reyneccius*, are *Darius*, *Cyrus* Firſt, *Cambyſes*, *Cyrus* the Great, *Cambyſes*,

byses, &c. Of the Second Race came the Seven Princes who overthrew the *Magi,* and chose *Darius,* Son of *Hystaspes,* one of them for King.

Persia, first called *Elemais,* of a Son of *Shem,* &c. Their City called *Persepolis,* in the Second Book of *Maccabees,* is called *Elemais* in the First Book, and now *Cyrus;* but Built in another place, for that which *Alexander* destroyed at the request of the Harlot *Thais.* The first Kingdom known to us, according to the Interpreters of *Gen.* 14. was *Chedorlaomer,* with whom *Amraphel* or *Ninus* joined in the War against the *Arabians.*

CHAP. III.

Of Cyrus *the First* Persian *Monarch.*

§. 1. CYRUS, saith *Strabo,* was so called of the River which watereth *Persia; Herodotus* saith, it signifies a Father; *Plutarch* saith, the Son *Esai* named him almost Two Hundred years before. He Conquered *Lydia,* and took *Croesus* before *Babylon,* which he won in the Fifty Fifth *Olympiad,* and in the Twenty Eighth *Olympiad,* upon a Rebellion, subdued it again.

§. 2. *Lydia* had *Lydus* the Son of *Atys,* her first King, which Family was extinguished; *Argon* descended from *Hercules,* was chose by the *Oracle,* and held Twenty two Generations, to *Candaulus* the last: *Gyges* succeeded him in Bed and Kingdom, which he left to *Atys* Father of *Sadiattes*

diattes, Father of *Halyattes,* who begat *Crœfus :* All their time was One Hundred Seventy years. *Crœ-fus* so inlarged his Dominion, that he was Inferiour to no King of that Age, commanding *Phrygia, Bythynia, Caria, Misia, Paphlagonia,* &c. He, in confidence of his good Succefs, envying *Cyrus's* Fame, and defirous to check his Profperous Undertakings, asked Counfel of *Apollo ;* Then *Darius,* who affured *Crœfus* paffing *Halis's* River, fhall diffolve a great Dominion. An Anfwer doubtful, becaufe the Devil was Ignorant of the Event.

§. 3. *Crœfus* thus refolved, defpifed all *Sandanes* his Confellor's Arguments to the contrary, as the Barrennefs of the Enemies Country, their hard manner of Living, War-like, Indefatigable and Profperous ; by whofe Fall he can gain only Fame, wherein he excelled ; and if he were Beaten, his Lofs could be hardly told, or foon, conceived. *Crœfus* proceeds with a powerful Army, but is ftaid at *Pterium,* a ftrong City of *Capadocia,* which he fought to force, while *Cyrus* advanc'd ; *Cratippus* anfwer'd *Pompey* well, That Kingdoms have their Increafe and Periods from Divine Ordinance ; and fo was it with thefe two great Princes, whofe Forces meeting, the *Perfians* had fomewhat the better, but Night parted them. *Crœfus,* doubtful of the next days Succefs, quit the Field to *Cyrus,* and with all hafte, got into *Sardis* ; and becaufe of Winter, fent home his Forces, not doubting any perfuit.

Cyrus finding the *Lydians* gon, followed flowly after, to avoid difcovering ; and having good Intelligence of *Crœfus's* proceedings, delay'd 'till the Forces were difpos'd to their Winter Garrifon ; when unexpectedly he invefted *Sardis,* and in fourteen

teen days forced it. _Crœsus_ thrusting in among the multitude, was ready to be slain, had not his dumb Son, forced by Passion, cried _Spare Crœsus_; who thereupon was brought to _Cyrus_, who judged him to be burnt. Being upon the heap of Wood, he cryed out, Θ _Solon! Solon! Solon!_ and upon urging to declare what he meant, answer'd, _That he found_ Solon's _words true, That no Man knew his own Happiness 'till his End._ _Cyrus_ hearing thereof, called for him (remembring his own Mortality) forgave him, and ever after used him as a King, and Companion. _Xenophon_ Reports, that _Cyrus_ used him so, without speaking of the purpose of burning; belike thinking it a Cruelty unworthy _Cyrus_, so to use his Great Unkle by his Grandmother, whose Brother he was. _Cyrus_ ever after so trusted him, that in his Journey to _Scythia_, he left him to advise _Cambyses_ his Son.

§. 5. _Cyrus_ after the Conquest of _Lydia_ (as it seems) Invaded _Scythia_, and taking _Amorges_, whose Wife _Spartha_ renewing the War, took _Cyrus_, and so by exchange, recover'd her Husband. He also reduc'd the _Phocians_ and _Greeks_ in lesser _Asia_, being fallen off; and having setled all his Provinces, prepared to attempt _Babylon_, as the height of his Designs; whereto he inforced Head and Hand. _Cyrus_ having spent ten years in ordering former Purchases, and preparing for _Babylon_, knowing the strength of it, being treble Walled, of great heighth, and surrounded with Waters unfordable, and victualled for twenty years, despaired to carry it by Assault, or to Famish it in short time, or without great and assur'd Guard, considering the vast circuit of the Wall, above forty eight Miles, of thirty two Foot thickness, and one hundred Cubits high. _Cyrus_ having considered these difficulties, with the inconveniency of lying long at the Siege with such a Multitude, and the doubtful Terms of Conquer'd remote

mote Provinces, with the dishonour of making shew to attempt, what in probability could not be compassed, contrived how to turn aside *Euphrates* by many Channels. *Balthazar* in the mean time, secure of any thing the Enemy could do, fell to Feasting, &c. when the Lord of Heaven, against whom he exalted himself, sent a Message by a Divine Hand-writing, which marred all their Mirth. The execution of that fearful Sentence came on as fast, when in the same night, *Cyrus* causing the Dams between the River and his Trenches to be cut down, *Euphrates* suddenly fail'd the City, and left the Besiegers a ready entrance, upon a secure People, drowned in their Cups. No Historian, if he had been present, could have better set out *Babel*'s Calamities in that surprize, than did *Isaiah* two hundred years before, and *Jeremy* above seventy years, whose Prophecies were now accomplish'd.

§. 6. *Cyrus* his last Wars and End are diversly reported. *Herodotus* and *Justin* tell us of his Wars with the *Massagets*, and his death by Queen *Tomyris*. But I believe with *Viginier*, that War was rather that which he had before with the *Scythians*; and that *Tomyris* was *Sparta*. *Ctesias* reports he was wounded in his War with *Derbician Scythians*, and died three days after; and by *Strabo*'s Report, he was buried in his own City *Pasagardes*, whose Tomb *Alexander* the Great opened, saith *Curtius*. There is no likelihood of any such overthrow of the *Persians* in *Scythia*, considering *Cambyses*'s present Journey into *Egypt*, and therefore I believe he died at home, as *Xenophon* reports, setting down his Oration to his Son, &c.

§. 7. *Cyrus* his Decree for building God's Temple, was, in true consideration, the noblest of all his Acts, as a Service to the Author of all goodness, accomplishing what the Lord had promised seventy years before, touching the return of the *Jews*, &c.

P   restoring

reſtoring the Veſſels of the Sanctuary, and re-building the Houſe of God. Yet was the Work hindred all the days of *Cyrus,* by the *Samaritans,* and Governours of the Provinces, who wrought upon *Cambyſes* in his Father's days; and after, upon ſuggeſtion that it was a Rebellious City, *&c.* He Reigned thirty, or one and thirty Years.

§. 8. *Cyrus* had two Sons, *Cambyſes,* and *Smerdis:* Three Daughters, *Atoſſa,* and *Meroe,* whom *Cambyſes* their Brother Married, and *Artiſtona* Wife to *Darius Hyſtaſpes,* as was *Atoſſa* after *Cambyſes's* death. *Codman* miſtakes her for *Heſter,* becauſe ſhe was called *Hadaſa* ; but nearneſs of Names confounds not the Perſon, where the one was the known Daughter of *Cyrus,* the other a *Jew* ; who though a while ſhe concealed her Kindred, yet ſhe after diſcovered it, *&c.*

CHAP. IV.

Of the Perſian *Affairs, from* Cyrus, *to* Darius.

§. 1. THE *Perſian* Kings are diverſly numbred; but *Euſebius,* and moſt Latin Authors follow the *Greeks.* *Krentzheim* hath refelled all the other ; and *Beucer* maketh it good by Scripture. *Cyrus* Reign'd in all thirty years, nam'd 2 *Chron.* 36. and *Ezra* 1. 1. and elſewhere. *Cambyſes* with the *Magi* eight years, named in *Daniel* 11. 2. *Darius Hyſtaſpes, Ezr.* 4. 5. he Reigned thirty ſix; then *Xerxes* twenty one years, plainly ſet out, *Dan.* 11. 2. *Artaxeres Longimanus* forty years, *Ezr.* 4. 7. called alſo *Artaſta, Ezra* 4. 7. and 7. 7. *Darius Northis* nine-

nineteen years, *Ezra* 4. 24. and 5. 6. *Nehem.* 12. 22: *Artaxeres Mriemon* forty three years, *Nehem.* 2. 1. Father to *Artaxerxes*, *Octius*, and *Arsames*, in whom the Line of *Cyrus* ended. *Octius* Reigned twenty two years, *Arsames* three ; *Darius* the last was of another Family, and Reigned six years. All these are by *Eusebius* fitted to the Olympiad.

§. 2. *Cambyses* succeeded his Father; like him only in desire to increase the Empire. In the fifth year of his sole Reign, the third of the sixty third Olympiad, he Invaded *Egypt*, for that *Amasis* denied him his Daughter; but *Psamneticus* Reigning after, is slain by *Cambyses*, six Months after *Amasis*'s death ; others give him six years.

§. 3. *Cambyses* also forced *Euelthon* King of *Cyprus* to submit; he destroyed the *Egyptian* Images and Temples, and sent to do the like to *Jupiter Ammon*, in *Lybia*, but the Devil by a Storm oppressed them with Sand, yet himself attempted it after in vain ; he also slew *Apis* the *Egyptian* Bull. But shortly after, upon a Dream that his Brother sate upon his Throne, he procured *Praxaspes* his Favourite to kill him. Intending to Marry his Sisters, he asked his Judges what Law permitted it, who answered, *Persian Kings are Lawless.* Yet he caused *Sisanus* a Corrupt Judge to be flaied alive, covering the Judges Seat with the Skin, and put his Son into the Office. He shot *Praxaspes*'s Son in the Heart, to shew his Father the Wine he delighted in had not taken away his Wits. Mounting his Horse in haste to *Persia*, hearing of *Semendis* a *Magus*, upon likeness to his Brother usurped the Crown, his Sword falling out, gave him his death's wound. He Built *Babylon* in *Egypt*, where *Latopolis* had stood, and *Meroe* in *Nilus* by his Sisters Name, whom he slew, for weeping for *Smerdis*.

§. 4. The Seven Princes descend from *Achæmenes*'s discovering the Fraud of the Imposture, with joyn-

ed

ed Forces rooted him out; and after Confultation, whether Popular Government, or a few Choice Men, or Regal, were beft, the Refolution was to make him King, whofe Horfe fhould Neigh firft after the Sun-Rifing. *Darius,* one of them, Confulting with *Oebarus* Mafter of his Horfe, caufed his Horfe to cover a Mare in the Suburbs the Night before ; who coming the next Morning by that place with the reft, made *Darius* Emperor, by his Horfe Neighing firft. *

Her. lib. 3.

CHAP. V.

Of Darius *the Son of* Hyftafpes.

§. 1. **D**Arius came of the fecond Race of *Achæmenes,* thus. *Cyrus* the Firft begat *Teifpius,* who begat *Arianes* Father of *Arfanes,* who accompanied *Cyrus* in *Scythia* ; where *Cyrus,* upon a Dream, grew Jealous of *Darius* ; but afterwards he followed *Cambyfes* into *Egypt,* Married two of *Cyrus*'s Daughters. *Reyneccius* gives *Hyftafpes* five Sons, *Herodotus* four.

§. 2. *Darius* made many equal Laws, gave his Subjects eafie accefs, and was fo mild, that many Nations offered fubjection ; yet he laid divers Taxes on them. *Babel* being revolted in the time of the *Magi, Darius* Befieg'd it, and by *Zopirus,* who for his fake cut off his own Ears and Nofe, fled to the *Babylonians,* and complained of *Darius*'s Cruelty. For diffuading the Siege of *Babel,* he is made their Leader, and recovers it.

§. 3. He gave order for Building the Temple, and made a Decree againft all that fhould hinder it, *Ezr.* 6.

Darius

§. 4. *Darius* having recovered *Babylon*, invaded *Scythia*, passing over *Ister*, or *Danubius*, by a Bridge of small Vessels, which he committed to the keeping of the *Ionians*, and *Ætolians* ; among whom *Miltiades* persuaded them to break it down, so to distress *Darius* ; but *Histiæus* Prince of *Milet* of *Ionia* dissuaded 'em. *Darius* entring the Desart Country of *Bessaravia*, found neither People, nor Relief ; the *Scythians* there being all Grasiers, and Horsemen, without any Town or Tillage, and living in Waggons, which at every station they set in order of a Town, as do the *Chrim Tartars* their Posterities at this day. *Darius* wearied with seeking, and seeing his Folly, sent to them, either to submit, or try his Valour : who for Answer, sent him a Bird, a Frog, a Mouse, and five Arrows. This dumb shew *Darius* took as a yielding him All, even the Elements in which these Creatures live, and their Weapons : But *Gobrias*, one of the Seven Princes, construed their meaning aright, as telling him he cannot escape their Arrows, except by flight, diving, or hiding himself. This they made good, by assailing his Camp, vexing it with continual Alarums ; and so fearless, forsook his Camp by Night, and hasted to *Ister*, whither yet the *Scythians* came before him, missing him as they came. They persuaded the *Ionians* to depart, assuring them the *Persians* should never hurt nor harm them ; which had proved true, if *Hystiæus* had proved firm, and stayed for them there.

§. 5. *Darius* escaping the *Scythians*, Invaded *Thrace*, and *Macedon*, transplanted the *Pæonians*, and possessed *Chalcedon*, *Byzantium*, *Perinthus*, &c. and the best part of *Thrace*. Then he sent to *Amyntas* King of *Macedon*, requiring his subjection by the Earth and Water, as the *Persian* manner was. He doubting his own strength, entertain'd the Ambassadors, who offering incivility to the Ladies at a Feast, were slain by the device of *Alexander* the King's

Son ; sending young Men in the Ladies Attire. *Darius* intending to revenge the Affront, was pacifyed by *Bubaris*, a principal Commander under *Darius*, to whom *Alexander* succeeded his Father, and had given *Gygea* his Sister ; who persuaded him how necessary the amity with *Macedon* was, in the intended War with the *Greeks*.

§. 6. The War with *Greece*, grew upon occasion of *Pysistratus*, who, in the time of the Annual Government, upon a division of two great Families in *Athens*, usurped the Government as in behalf of the People; who yet perceiving he aimed at a Monarchy, which of all Forms of Government, they could not brook, they forced him to fly the first and second time; but the third time, by hiring Forces he recovered, and Ruled Seventeen years after, and left it to his Sons, *Hyppias* and *Hypparchus*, the last of which was Murthered by *Hermodius* for his unnatural Lust to him. Hereupon *Hyppias* doubting himself, and falling to more severity than had been there used, they raise Armies with the *Lacedemonians* aid, and forced him to give over, and leave the City. He being Allied to *Æantides*, Tyrant of *Lampsacus*, was by him presented to *Darius*.

§. 7. These *Grecian* Colonies in the Sea Coast of *Asia*, after Five hundred years Liberty, were brought under by *Crœsus*, and fell with him under the *Persian* Yoke, and were by the Practise of *Histiæus*, put into Rebellion, because *Darius* had taken him to *Susa*, and they, under shew of Honour, held him, as doubting his greatness in *Ionia*. This he perceived to be practised with *Aristagoras*, his Cousin and Deputy in *Miletum*, to make a Breach, hoping to be sent to reduce them, as he was. For *Darius* hearing of this Revolt, and of the *Athenians* joining with them, was exceedingly provoked against *Athens*, being excited by *Hyppias*; as for the *Ionians*, he sent *Histiæus*, who promised what he intended not; but before his

coming

coming, *Artaphemes* had broken their Power, being Vice-Roy in *Lydia*; so that *Histiæus*, after vain attempts, was taken and lost his Head.

§. 8. *Darius*, who first pretended only against the *Athenians* and *Eritræans*, for assisting the *Ionians*, and Burning *Sardis*, seeing the good Success of the Forces against them, sent, and demanded Acknowledgments from all the *Greeks*, who generally refused, and forced the *Ægenits*, which had submitted, to renounce it. *Darius* prepares an Hundred Thousand Foot, and Sixty Thousand Horses, which, as they passed over the Sea, took the *Cyclad* Islands, and so advanc'd to *Eritria* in *Eubæa*, and sack'd it. From thence they pass into *Attica*, conducted by *Hippias* their King, Twenty Years after, who Incamped in *Marathon* toward *Athens*. The *Athenians* sent *Phidippidus* to the *Lacedemonians* for Succour, which he failed of; but in *Arcadia*, a Familiar Devil (supposed to be *Pan*) promised the Gods assistance, which much Incouraged the Multitude, who rely more on blind Prophecies, than solid Reason. The *Athenian* Forces were Ten Thousand and One Thousand *Platæans*, with which coming into the Field, the *Persians* scorned their small numbers, and thought them void of Understanding, to venter into the Field. But, in conclusion, the *Greeks* fighting for all they had, and the *Persians* for what they needed not, Necessity provok'd the one, and Confidence in their Multitude, making the other secure, the *Persians* are put to Rout, fly to their Ships, which will drive them too, when Courage was lost. Of the *Persians*, were slain in the Place, Six Thousand Three Hundred; of the *Greeks* One hundred Ninety two; which they say fell out by strange Sights, frighting the *Persians*. *Miltiades* carried the honour of this Victory; but having broken his Thigh in a Service which he sought against the Isle *Paros*; at his return, his ungrateful Citizens cast

him

him in Prison, where, in a few days, he ended his Life. *Darius*, after Thirty Six Years Reign, dyed.

CHAP. VI.

Of Xerxes, *Emperour of* Persia.

§. 1. XErxes succeeded, and inherited, with his Crown, a double War ; one with *E-gypt*, the other with *Greece* ; as terrible in Preparation, as ridiculous in Success; from which War, *Artaban*, Brother to the late *Darius*, dissuaded him: But *Mardonius*, Grand-Child to *Hystaspis*, as was *Xerxes*, and his Brother in-Law by Marriage of his Sister, persuadeth it. *Herodotus* tells of 1700000 Foot ; but *Trogus* makes it 700000 Foot, and 80000 Horse, besides Camels, Chariots, and other Beasts for Carriage. The Commanders were all Princes of the Blood, of which *Mardonius*, Cousin to the King, was chief; only the Immortal Regiment, which was ever supplyed with Ten thousand select *Persians*, was given to *Hydarnes*. Gallies Two thousand two hundred and Eight, and three thousand Vessels for Transportation.

§. 2. This World of an Army made their Rendezvous at *Sardis*, whose whole Company *Pythias*, a *Lydian*, entertain'd with Food, and presented the King with two Thousand Talents of Silver, and four Millions of Gold, wanting Seven thousand✗ which *Xerxes* made up, and gave all back again. Yet the Tyrant cut one of his five Sons into two parts, for whom the Father had intreated to be spared in this Expedition, to tend him in his Age. He cut Mount *Athos*, and five Cities in the half Island from *Thrace*. He also made a Bridge of Six hundred Seventy two

Gallies

✗ *Darici*

Gallies over the *Hellefpont*, over which all his Army paffed in Seven days, which he beheld in the Plains of *Abidos* from an high place. Here *Artabanus* put him in mind, *That Man's Life is fo much more miferable than the end, that the happieft man oft pleafeth himfelf more with the defire of Death than Life,* &c. and layed before him two great Dangers that might proceed from fuch a Multitude; at Sea, by Storm, having no Harbour to command, or able to receive them; at Land, the Country not able to feed them, *&c.* He only replyed, that great Enterprizes were never undertaken without great Perils; which is a good Refolution, if Neceffity inforce the Enterprife, which here it did not, *&c.* and fuch Multitudes are rather heavy Burthens than ftrong Aids, impoffible to be Marfhalled.

§. 3. *Xerxes* having Tranfported his Army into *Thrace*, being to pafs the *Straits* of *Thermopile*, of half an Acre between the Mountains, which divide *Theffaly* from *Greece*, was refifted by *Leonidas* King of *Sparta*, with three hundred Men, and three or four hundred *Greeks*, 'till a Fugitive *Grecian* taught the *Perfians* a Way by the Ridge of the Mountains, by which, part of their Army afcending, came upon their Backs. Yet *Leonidas*, with his Seven hundred Men, ftood to it, and flew twenty thoufand, and two of the Kings Brethren; though in the end, he and the reft were flain. This valorous Refolution, efpecially of the *Lacedemonians,* terrified *Xerxes*; fo that he asked Counfel of *Demoratus*, a Banifhed King of *Sparta*, who advifed to fend fufficient Force in three hundred Ships, to ravage *Lycaonia*, fo to divert the *Lacedemonians* and their Neighbours at home, while *Xerxes* fubdued the reft. *Achamenes* the Kings Brother advifed him to keep the Ships together near the Land Forces, confidering four hundred were caft away in a Storm. But the *Grecian* Navy lying at *Artemifium*, where the *Perfian* Armada

mada thought to inclose them, knowing they had sent two hundred Ships about, met them in the Night unlook'd for, and Defeated them. The other intending, by strong hand, to repair that loss, set upon the *Grecian* Navy, but had the worst, leaving both the place and Spoil to the Enemy.

§. 4. *Xerxes* being entred the *Phocians* Country, ravag'd it and the Regions adjoining; he sent also to pillage the Temple of *Delphos,* but was overwhelmed (they say) by two Rocks, which brake from *Parnassus.* Surely his Attempt was Impious, seeing he believ'd *Apollo* a God; so that the only Holy might give the Devil leave to defend himself against his own Servant which dishonour'd him. For, saith he, will a Man spoil his God? *Mat.* 3. 8. *Jer.* 2. 9, 10. Yea, the *Persians* had blamed the *Athenians* for Burning *Cybel's* Temple in the City *Sardis.* He proceeded to *Athens,* which was forsaken, and Burnt the Citadel and Temple.

§. 5. The *Athenians* had removed their Wives and Children to *Salamis,* &c. prising the common Liberty of *Greece* before private; yet the *Greeks* resolved to abandon *Salamis* and *Ægina,* had not *Themistocles,* Admiral of the *Athenian* Fleet, dissuaded them from it, as also from the purpose to fortify *Peloponesus* only, and abandon the rest of *Greece,* as not defensible; yet could he not prevail, 'till he threatned, that the *Athenians,* whose Ships were the Strength of the *Greek* Navy, would take their Wives and Children, and remove to *Italy,* and there plant themselves. The *Peloponesians* knowing how desperate the Case would be with them, were glad to yield.

§. 6. The *Persians* deliberate to offer the *Greeks* a Battle, which the King desired, and the Leaders, to give him content, seem to approve of it. But *Artemisia,* Princess of *Halicarnasseus,* advised the King to set forward to *Peloponesus,* to separate the *Greek* Navy, while every one would haste to defend his own,

and

and so single, were easily mastered, which conjoined, were too strong by their better Skill at Sea. The *Peloponesians* amazed at the approach, and fearing the Enemies March to *Peloponesus,* esteeming all *Greece* lost but that part, resolve to set Sail for *Isemus.* *Themistocles* knowing he had no spare time to bestow on Ears shut up by Fear, sent a trusty Messenger to tell the *Persians* of this intended flight; willing them with speed to send some Forces about the Island. The *Persians* thinking the *Athenians* did this to make their way for Favour, as meaning to fall to the King, followed the Advice. The *Peloponesians,* in the Morning, intending to weigh Anchor, saw the Enemy in their way, and so were forced to the Fight in the Straights of *Salamis,* where they had a memorable Victory; forcing the Enemies Ships to fall foul one upon another, and so could neither Fight nor fly.

§. 7. After the Victory, every Captain, by Scrutiny, was willed to write his Name which merited most, and every Man ambitious of the Honour, set his own Name first, and *Themistocles* next; Affection serving her self first, is then content to yield to Vertue next. *Xerxes* set a good Face on it, as intending a new Preparation; but the Princes which knew his Temper, discerned his faint Heart, especially *Mardonius,* Author of this War. He therefore to prevent the King's Indignation, went unto him with many fair Words, laying the fault upon the Cowardly *Egyptians, Phœnycians,* and *Cilicians,* which was no dishonour to the King, who had taken *Athens,* which was principally intended, and the most of *Greece.* Hereupon he desired the King to leave him three hundred Thousand men to finish the War, and himself, with the rest, to return to *Asia.* The King's Care liked well hereof, and made haste, hearing the *Greeks* intended to break his Bridge, as *Themistocles* had inform'd, under-hand, so to weaken the Army, and ease the Country. §. 8 *Mar-*

§. 8. *Mardonius* having undertaken to reduce *Greece*, removed to *Theſſaly*, and from thence, ſent *Alexander*, King of *Macedon*, with great Promiſes, to perſuade the *Athenians* to come in, which the *Lacedemonians* underſtanding, ſent likewiſe to perſuade them to remain firm. The *Athenians* Anſwer *Alexander*, renouncing Amity with *Xerxes* as long as the Sun kept his Courſe ; whereupon *Mardonius* haſted to *Athens*, which was again left to him void. From thence he ſolicited them with many fair. promiſes in vain ; yet the *Lacedemonians* grew cold in ſending Aid, 'till the *Athenians* grew to threaten a Courſe which would little pleaſe them. A Counſellor of *Sparta* thereupon ſaid, our Wall upon *Iſtonus* will little avail us, if *Athens* liſten to *Mardonius*; with which Speech, the *Lacedemonians* bethought. themſelves and diſpatched five thouſand *Spartans*, and gave orders for five thouſand more.

§. 9. *Mardonius*'s Army of Thirty thouſand was increaſed to fifty thouſand, with the *Macedonians*, *Thebans* and *Theſſalians*, againſt which, the Forces of *Greece* were One hundred and ten Thouſand; of which forty thouſand were weightily Armed. All theſe comfronted one another in a convenient place belonging to the *Platæans*, who gave it to the *Athenians*, upon the Oracles promiſe of Victory, if the Battle were fought on *Athenian* ground. In the end the Armies encounter each other ; *Mardonius* is ſlain, his Army deſtroyed, and *Artabaſus*, with three thouſand, flyeth to *Byzantium*, and ſo Shipped into *Aſia*.

§. 10. *Xerxes* being at *Sardis*, committed Sixty thouſand to *Tygranes* to keep *Ionia* and the Coaſt, where his two *Admirals* lay at *Mycale*, who perceiving the *Grecian* Fleet was coming, drew their Ships on ground, and fortifyed the places, and diſarmed the *Samians* among them, and ſet the *Miletians* far off, to keep the Streights, doubting them. The

Greeks

Greeks refolutely force them, and the *Samians* in the Fight, get what Weapons they can, and play the Devil againſt the *Perfians*, whoſe Example the *Ionians* follow ; ſo that the *Perfians* are overthrown, and of thoſe that fled, the *Milefians* had the ſlaughter ; this was the Evening of that Day, the Battel was at *Plataa*, which was the laſt that was heard of this mighty Army levied againſt *Greece*.

§. 11. *Xerxes* not regarding theſe Loſſes, was engag'd in the love of his Brother's Wife, who rejected him ; and after of her Daughter, Wife to his Son ; whereof did follow the Salvage Cruelty of *Ameſtris* his Wife, on his Brother's Wife, and his Murther of his Brother *Maſiſtes*, her Husband.

CHAP. VII.

The Greek *Affairs, from the* Perſian *Wars, to the* Peloponeſian, *of Twenty Seven Years.*

§. 1. THE *Greeks* having utterly defeated that *Perfian* Army of Seventeen Hundred Thouſand, and left a few thouſands of them, that the *Peloponeſians* ſent home, leaving *Xantippus*, and his *Athenians*, affiſted with the revolted *Iones*, who took *Seſtos* in the Streight of *Hellefpont*, between which, and *Abidos*, *Xerxes*'s Bridge had ſtood ; and in the Spring return'd home, taking their Wives and Children with them, out of the Iſlands where they had left them. The *Athenians* neglecting their private intereſt, fell preſently to fortifie their City ; which the *Lacedemonians*, doubting the *Athenians* power at Sea, diſſuaded ; but in vain, being held in ſuſpence with fair words, till the work was ended ; and then were anſwer'd, *That* Athens *knew what belonged to her ſafety, as they had ſhewed in the* Perſian *War, without direction from others.*

§. 2. The

§. 2. The *Athenians* sent out Thirty Ships, the *Lacedemonians* Twenty, the rest of *Greece* adding thereto, *Pausanias* of *Lacedemon* having the Conduct; who having possess'd themselves of many Principal Places in *Cyprus*, went from thence to *Thrace*, and recovered *Bizantium*, now *Constantinople*, from the *Persians*. After this, *Pausanias* beginning to play the Tyrant, is called home, and *Docres* put in his Place, who is also misliked, as indeed a good Commander might be, in comparison of the Wise and Virtuous *Aristides* Commander of the *Athenians*, much more Men of ill desert. The *Lacedemonians* being weary of following the War, of which the *Athenians* were eager, return home and take their ease, while the other got Honour, and had all the rest of the *Greeks* willing to be Commanded by the *Athenians*, and to bear what Charge they lay upon them for the common defence of *Greece*, gladly referring themselves to *Aristides*. But just *Aristides* could not prevent the *Athenians* making Slaves of their Fellows in short time; imposing Thirteen Hundred Talents a year upon their Confederates. *Timon* Son of *Miltiades* was General, who brought many Inhabitants of *Greece* into the *Athenian* Servitude; while neglecting to follow the Wars, chusing rather to bear the Charge than serve, grew weak as the other became strong. *Timon* having taken *Phaleis*, entred *Eryquidom* in *Pamphilia*, overthrew the *Persian* Army at Land, and took two hundred Ships, and forced Eighty Sail of *Phœnicians* to run on ground and perish. This forced the *Persians* to an honourable Peace with the *Athenians*.

§. 3. *Xerxes* becomes cruel to his Kindred, and those about him; which made his Uncle *Artabanus* to repose less safety in his Fidelity, than in the hope of a Crown, by destroying a Cruel Cowardly and Hated

ted Prince. Thus by means of *Millorldatus* an Eunuch, the King is murther'd, and his Son *Darius* charg'd with it, and put to death. But *Artabanus* is surpriz'd by *Artaxerxes*, and flain.

§. 4. *Artaxerxes* making Peace with the *Athenians, Themistocles* feeking to check the Peoples infolency in their *Democratical* Government, is Banished Ten Years, who for fafety fled to *Persia,* where, to avoid leading Forces againft *Athens,* he Poifoned himfelf.

§. 5. *Athens,* contrary to the Peace with the *Persians,* meafuring Honour by profit, thought to Surprize *Cyprus,* a convenient Seat for any State, which would Trade with *Syria, Egypt, Cilicia,* &c. But *Timon* with two hundred Sail, folicited by *Icarus* King of *Lybia,* to joyn in Conqueft; and shewing him *Egypt,* accepted the motion, fucceeded in the Attempt, to the taking two parts of *Memphis,* 'till *Magabazus* fent Forces to affift the *Persians* there; by which means, the *Athenians* were forced to *Profopotes,* and there flain, with lofs of all their Gallies, and fifty more fent to their affiftance.

§. 6. The *Athenians* in thefe fix years of *Egyptian* War held their own with advantage, winning the *Egyptian Phocis, Tanagra,* &c. fpoiled the Sea-Coaft of *Peloponefus,* and then made a Peace with them.

§. 7. *Artaxerxes Longimanus,* to whom moft good Authors give forty, and fome forty four years, was he which fo much favoured the *Jews,* as we fee in *Efdras,* and *Nehemiah;* which was that *Abafuerus* who Married *Hefter,* lived in *Sufa,* and Reigned from *India,* to *Æthiopia,* and therefore a *Persian.* Now as *Darius Hystafpes* his many Wives, the Honour he left *Atoffa* in, *Jojachim*'s being High-Prieft in the days of *Artaxerxes,* prove he was not *Hefters* Husband, fo much lefs was *Xerxes;* and *Mordocha* proveth he could be none of the fucceeding Kings of *Perfia.*

§. 8.

§. 8. *The* Greeks *prosecute their Civil-War, leaving the* Persians *in Peace for many Ages. Their* Egyptian *Expedition being come to nought, the* Lacedemonians *recover* Delphos, *which the* Athenians *regain, and commit to the* Phocians. *But the* Bæotians *recover their Liberty against the* Athenians, *as did* Eubæa, *and* Megaras, *and* Athens *seek Peace with* Sparta *for thirty years; but after six years Invaded* Samos.

CHAP. VIII.

Of the Peloponesian War.

§. 1. GReece was never under the Government of one Prince 'till *Philip* of *Macedon*, and *Alexander* his Son, and by them rather United than Subjected, as they were by the Kings following; who brought all *Greece* into servitude, except those Two which deserved it most, *Athens*, and *Lacedemon*, which distracted all by their private quarrels, drawing all the rest to side with them. *Lacedemon* having lived under one form of Government four hundred years, used only to War, as glorying only in Valour. The *Athenians* to the contrary, measured Honour, and all by Gain. The *Lacedemonians* were deliberate, grave, and resolute, for which, all other States of *Greece* followed them; the *Athenians* were eager, sudden in concluding, and hasty in execution; obeyed by force, and by means of their Ships, forced the Islanders to hard Tribute. The *Lacedemonians* being In-Landers, perceiving the *Athenians* to grow great, became jealous of them.

§. 2.

§. 2. *Athens* to enlarge her Command, uſed to protect the weaker States againſt the ſtronger, though having been their Colonies, as *Corcyra* was to *Corinth*. This Wrong *Corinth* complained of to *Sparta*, as others did; and when *Sparta* could not prevail by intreaty, they reſolve on Force, which *Athens* prepares for. The *Lacedemonians* exceed in numbers and qualities; the *Athenians* in many Ships, and abſolute Subjects.

§. 3. *Athens* the two firſt years had all the Country about waſted, and the Towns viſited with a grievous Peſtilence, by the throng of People and Cattle, fled thither. The *Lacedemonians* win *Platæa*, but cannot reſcue *Mytilene* from the *Athenians*, for want of Ships; their Confederates alſo grew weary, ſo that the *Lacedemonians* ſeeing how little hurt they can do to *Athens*, which was eaſily relieved by Sea, fall to build Ships, but to no purpoſe, wanting good Seamen.

§. 4. *Sparta* hearing that a Fleet of *Athenians* by contrary Winds ſtayed at *Pilus*, a Promontory, began to fortifie themſelves there, and haſted from *Attica*, to put off ſuch ill Neighbours from planting ſo near *Peloponeſus*; but finding the Garriſon not ſo eaſily to be forced, they poſſeſſed the Haven, put four hundred Men into the Iſland, and ſend part of the Fleet for Materials to ruine the Garriſon. The *Athenian* Fleet hearing of the Garriſons diſtreſſes, returned, and overthrew the *Spartan* Fleet, &c. The four hundred Men in the Iſland, the Magiſtrates of *Sparta* ſeek to recover, by ſending to *Athens* to treat of Peace, but in vain; for *Athens* weighed Honour by Profit, and held the advantage gotten; and in the end, by force took the *Spartans* in the Iſland Priſoners, and ſent them to *Athens*.

§. 5. The *Lacedemonians* in this Condition, labour for Peace, which the inſolent *Athenians* neglected, 'till the overthrow their Forces by the *La-cedemonians*

Q

cædemonians imployed in *Thrace*, had received, which made the *Athenians* more earneſt to effect a Peace ; eſpecially, conſidering, that beſide 'the *Athenian* Power, the *Argives* their ancient, and not to be neglected Enemies, were like to joyn with the *A-thenians*, the ＊Thirty years Peace being expired. The Peace at laſt is concluded, but Conditions im-poſſible ; for *Lacedemon* could not reſtore all the Cities which the *Athenians* had loſt by their means, as the Cities taken into their Protection, refuſed to return ſubject to their old Lords the *Athenians*. But before any quarrel grew, the *Spartans* enter into a ſtraighter Alliance with *Athens*, by a League Offen-ſive and Defenſive, to diſappoint the *Argives*. This League put all *Greece* in jealouſie that theſe two would prove Lords of all.

§. 6. The States of *Greece*, which had exceſſively admired the Valour of *Sparta*, ſeeing it now to ſeek Peace, upon Terms not ſo Honourable, grew to contemn it, as the *Corinthians*, *Thebans*, &c. who caſt their Eyes upon the great Rich City of *Argos*, and conceived great matters of it. This is the common baſe Condition of the moſt, who curiouſly ſearching into other Mens Vices, cannot diſcern their Virtues ; and comparing our beſt parts with their faults, are juſtly plagued with falſe opinion of that good in others, which we know wanting in our ſelves; the *Corinthians* beginning, complain that the *Lacedemonians* had left ſome of their Towns in the *Athenians* hands; the *Mantinians* follow, who feared revenge, for that they had drawn ſome *Ar-cadians* from the *Spartans*, to follow them. Theſe begin to enter League with the *Argives*, and other Cities of *Peloponeſus* follow. The *Lacedemonians* knowing the ſcope of this new Confederacy, ſend to *Corinth*, to ſtop the Matter where it began, charge-ing them with their Oath of old Alliance, which the *Corinthians* anſwer; ſaying the *Lacedemonians* had firſt

first broken in concluding with *Athens*, without care of restoring the Towns taken from *Corinth; &c.* The *Corinthians* thereupon enter League with *Argos*, and draw others; only the *Thebans* were not so forward, because *Argos* was a popular State. The *Corinthians* also, for further security, sought Peace with *Athens*, and obtained a Truce, but no League. But in conclusion, as *Athens*, had, by force, gotten an absolute command, and could perform what she promised, so *Lacedemon*, which had so many followers, but voluntary, could not do so ; as where they should restore *Panacty* held by the *Thebans*, for recovery of *Pylus*, they could not, and so gave discontent to *Athens*. There were also in *Athens*, *Alcibiades* a young brave Noble-man, and others, as also some in *Sparta* desirous of War, who promoted the breach of Peace what they could. *Alcibiades* therefore sent to *Argos*, which thought not now of superiority, as lately she did, but of Security, advising them to secure themselves by League with *Athens*. The *Lacedemonians* seeing that *Argos* took that course, sent to *Athens* to stay the proceeding, knowing the Combination was not for their Wealth ; but by a trick of *Alcibiades*, lost their labour.

§.7. The *Argives* presuming of their Allies, molest the *Epidaurians*, which the *Spartans* were bound to defend ; upon which occasion, the *Athenians* and *Spartans* collaterally infest each other, and the *Corinthians*, *Bæotians*, *Phocians*, *Locrians*, follow the *Lacedemonians*, who, in one Victory, recovered much Reputation ; so that the Nobles of *Argos* getting the uper-hand of the Citizens, made League with them, renouncing *Athens* ; but the People recovering, chased away their Nobles, and reversed all.

§. 8. *Athens*, in the intermission of open War at home, renew their hopes of subduing *Sicily*, and sent such a Fleet as *Greece* never set out, of which *Alcibiades* was one General. *Siracuse* is besieged, but re-

lieved

lieved by the *Lacedemonians*, and the Fleet block'd up in the Haven; neither could *Athens* relieve it through home Factions, whence *Alcibiades* was driven, to banish himself; and by this reason *Sparta*, in the absence of their Forces, Invaded *Attica*, the *Persians* lending *Money*. The *Lacedemonians* also by *Alcibiades*'s Advice (who fled to them) fortifyed *Decelia* near *Athens*, and all the Country about; Yet the *Athenians*, in their Obstinacy, sent another Fleet, which was quite vanquished in the Haven, and the Army, by Land, utterly over-thrown. This befell the *Athenians* deservedly by *Nicias*'s Resolution, who chose to venture little less than all the Power of *Athens*, rather than to incur the *Athenians* Censure upon Return, to be condemned unjustly, as other Generals had been; this Resolution cannot be commended, seeing an honest valiant Man should do what Reason directs, and measure Honour and Dishonour by a well-informed Conscience, rather than the malicious Report and Censure of others; yet it is excusable, considering the Peoples Injustice; and knowing an ill Fact is nothing so pernicious as an unjust Sentence, which begun upon one, becomes a President. But his fear to fly, as he thought to do, was ridiculous, because of an Eclipse that day, which made him defer it 'till twenty seven days after, with lamentable effect.

§. 9. The *Athenians*, after this loss had also their Subjects abroad rebellious, and which recovered their long lost Liberty. At home also the principal Citizens, wearied with the Peoples Insolency, changed the Government, procuring the Captains abroad to set up an *Aristocracy* in the Towns of their Confederacy, as four hundred usurped it at home. But the Army at *Samos* disliked that usurpation, and *Alcibiades*, who was fled from the *Lacedemonians*, who had honour'd him much, till his Virtue had bred him Envy, and was with *Tissaphernes*

the

the *Persian* Vice-Roy, with whom he was grown into such Favour, as he persuaded him to stay his Favour to the *Lacedemonians.* Yet his Revocation was not confirmed at *Athens,* 'till the four hundred wearied with the Troubles of the Times, and not prevailing with *Sparta* for Peace, resigned their Authority to Five thousand, which had been their Assistants, who presently agreed to the revocation of him and his Companions.

§. 10. After this, *Alcibiades* joining with the *Athenian* Fleet, after an Overthrow of the *Lacedemonian* Fleet, commanded by *Mindarus,* took *Cyzicus, Perinthus, Chalcedon, Bizantium,* and with this Honour returned to *Athens,* where he was made High-Admiral. But upon a loss of a great part of his Fleet by his Lieutenant in his Absence, fighting contrary to his Commandment, he was again forced to banish himself, to a greater loss to *Athens* than before.

§. 11. After this also the *Athenians* Ships in a discomfiture, were forced into the Haven of *Mytelene,* where they were beset, so that *Athens* were compelled to Man all their Vessels, to relieve them at *Argamusæ*; yet the ten Captains, which had the Victory of the *Lacedemonians,* were condemned at *Athens* unjustly, as after appeared.

§. 12. *Lysander,* with the *Peloponesian* Fleet, Besieged *Lapsacus* ; the *Athenian* Fleet of an hundred Eighty Sail came too late to relieve it ; and then put in at *Sestos,* and after at *Æges-Potamos,* from whence they daily braved *Lysander,* not a League off, and return to *Ages Potamos,* from whence the Men used to go by Land to *Sestos,* leaving the Ships. *Alcibiades* lived near, and saw their negligent endangering the Ships, and gave them warning, which they regarded not ; so *Lysander* came suddainly on them, and overthrew them, went to *Athens* with *Pausanias* and *Agis,* the Two Kings of *Sparta,* and Summoned the City, which refused 'till Famin Forced, which fell on them by the *Lacedemoni-*

ans

ans taking the Iſlands from them, which uſed to relieve them.   So all her Subject Cities are freed ; the Wall, to the Port caſt down; her Government reſtrained to her own Territories ; and ſhe to uſe but Twelve Ships, and to follow *Sparta* in all Wars. And ſo ended the *Peloponeſian* War, after twenty ſeven years. Her only hope of Recovery was in *Alcibiades*, whoſe death the *Lacedemonians* procured. *Lacedemon* abuſing this good Succeſs, grew Odious, ſo that many Cities of *Greece* combined againſt her, and *Thebes*, under the leading of *Epaminondas*, who trained up *Philip* of *Macedonia*, gave her a great Foil.

CHAP. IX.

Matters concurring with this War, and a while after.

§. 1. PERSIA after, had *Artaxerxes, Xerxes* the Second, and after him, *Sogdianus* his Brother (who ſeem to be the Sons of *Heſter*) but one year ; whom *Darius Nothus* ſucceeded, who ſlew *Sogdianus* as he had his Brother *Xerxes*.   He reigned Nineteen years.   *Amyrtæus* an *Egyptian*, Allyed himſelf with *Greece*, overthrew the *Perſian* Garriſons in *Egypt*, and Reigned ; while *Darius* aſſiſting the *Lacedemonians* with Money, by the Overthrow of *Athens*, recover'd what had been loſt in *Aſia* the leſſer, over which he made *Cyrus*, his younger Son, Lieutenant, but upon ſome diſlike, intended to have dealt ſharply with him, had not Death prevented.

§. 2. *Athens*, after her Overthrow, had Thirty Governours, called Tyrants, choſen to execute the Law, with ſupreme Authority. Theſe contriving

to

to retain that Power, put certain Seditious Fellows
to death without Law, which all Men approved,
confidering their Lewdnefs, but not that it might
prove their own cafe, if their Governours pleafe to
call them Seditious, as it fell out. For their Thirty fent to *Lacedemon*, to defire a Garrifon, pretending to cut off the Seditious ; but by entertaining the
Captain to his liking, they grew bold with the
Chief Citizens, and fhed much Blood. *Theramenes*
one of them, fhewing his diflike, after they had chofen Three thoufand Citizens of their liking, to affift in the Government, with priviledge, in queftion of Death to be tryed by Law, and not at
Commandment of the Thirty ; they call *Theramenes*
in queftion, as without the priviledge, and put him
to death.

§. 3. After this, the Tyrants Out-rage made many good Citizens fly to *Thebes*, where *Thrafybulus*,
and about Seventy more, refolve to free *Athens* of
the Tyrants, and take *Phyla*, a ftrong place in the
Territory of *Athens*, which the Tyrants, in vain,
fought to recover, their ftrength encreafing to a
Thoufand, with which they got *Pyræus*, the Suburbs of *Athens* on the Port, and flew Seventy of
the Three Thoufand which came to expect them,
and *Critias* the chief Tyrant. The Tyrants fend
for Aid to *Sparta*, and *Lyfander* is fent with Forces,
and *Paufanias* followed, not to overthrow *Thrafybulus*, but after fome fhew, to work Peace, which
he did, fending the Thirty, and others that were
the caufe of the Tumult, to *Sparta*.

C H A P. X.

Cyrus *the Younger, his Expedition into* Persia.

§. 1. **A**Rtaxerxes *Mnemon*, or the mindful, succeeded in *Persia*, Established by his Father ; who also at his Mother *Parasali*'s earnest intreaty, pardoned his Brother *Cyrus*'s aspiring,
and Established him Vice-Roy in *Lydia*, and those
parts.

§. 2. *Cyrus* after such Disgrace from his Brother,
who spared his Life only for his Mothers importunity, of whose Favour he presumed ; knowing also
the Affections of his People, and presuming upon
the *Lacedemonians* formerly aided by him ; thought
his Interest to the Crown worth prosecuting. He
sends to *Sparta*, which commands their Admiral to
be at his command ; he seized on some Towns
subject to *Tissaphernes* ; furnished the *Grecian* Captains with Money to List Souldiers to be at his Command ; then making a shew of Besieging *Miletus*, he
calls over his *Grecian* Forces, and suddainly set forward toward *Persia*.

§. 3. *Tissaphernes* posting to the Court, his News
caus'd great Exclamations and Fear, in which the
King gathered his Army of Nine hundred Thousand,
with which yet he durst not venture the Tryal. The
Greeks, which follow *Cyrus* are, with difficulty allured over *Euphrates*, &c. but being over, resolved
to find out *Artaxerxes*, who was retiring to the utmost Border of his Kingdom, had not *Teribazus*,
one of his Captains, dissuaded him.

§. 4. *Cyrus*, with his Army of One hundred thousand, drawing toward his Brother, who had
Intrenched Forty Miles in Length, Thirty Foot
broad, and Eighteen deep, and yet left it ; at length
when he thought he had been fled, was forced suddenly

denly to Arm. The *Greeks* not ufed to incounter
fuchMultitudes, began to diftruft their own Courage;
yet upon the On-fet, found they had to do with fo
many contemptible Cowards, who fled without confideration. *Cyrus*, glad to fee it, and being thereupon adopted King, yet defires to appear worthy
of it, put himfelf with Six hundred Horfe, upon a
Squadron of Six thoufand which fled before him;
and being left by his Followers which purfued the
Enemy, he again fpying the King in the midft of
his Troops, brake in with a *Jew*, and pierced the
King's Curace, but was prefently flain, and his Head
and right Hand being cut off,were fhewed on a Spear
Point, recalled thy flying *Perfians*, who before were
crying on *Cyrus* for Mercy. After this, the King
and *Tiffaphernes* met, and followed the *Greeks*, which
knew not of *Cyrus's* Death; who feeing the King
following, turned to him. And he, wheeling about,
left them, and took an Hill, from which they forced him, and then returned to their Quarters.

§. 5. *Artaxerxes* could not rejoice in his Succefs,
when he thought what Report the *Greeks* would
make of the bafenefs of his People, which might incourage the *Greeks* to vifit his Country with more
Force than he would like. The next Morning
therefore, when they knew from *Ariæus* of *Cyrus's*
end, he fent *Phalinus* a *Greek* unto them, to require
their Arms, and to fue for Mercy; which they fcorn-
ed, *&c.*

§. 6. The *Greeks*, next Night, came to *Ariæus*, a
principal Commander under *Cyrus*, who tarried
for them; but Four hundred Foot and 40 Horfe, all
Thraconians, fled to the King *Ariæus*, who being offered by them to make him King,wanted the Courage
to venture for it,but was glad to covenant with them
for mutual affiftance in returning,which he directed.
The next day they lighted on the King's Army,which
gave them way; yea the King fent to them about a
Peace,

Peace, and appointed them a place where to have
Victuals.

'§.7. *Tissaphernes* cometh to them like a Fox to
entrap them, pretending his Love to them, being
Neighbour to *Greece*, and promising his Mediation
to the King, if they will send a mild Answer; and
to Conduct them home. Hereupon a League is sworn
betweeen them, and he returned to the King, and
after Twenty days came back to them, and set forward. The *Greeks* grew jealous of his long stay,
and would not have staied, had not *Clearchus* their
General persuaded them, relying too much on *Tissaphernes*'s Oath. *Tissaphernes*, after some days
March together, found opportunity upon *Clearchus*, seeking to assure him of the *Greeks* good Will
to him (which he seemed to doubt) to draw all
their Captains to his Camp, promising to tell them
which of them it was which sought secretly to raise
dissention between them. Thus having drawn them
into his Snare, he sent *Clearchus*, and other four
Colonels to the King, but slew the rest; then he
sent *Ariæus* as from the King, to require them to
yield, but in vain.

§.8. The *Greeks* amused at the loss of their Leaders,
neglected to consult what Supplies to make, 'till
Xenophon, whose Learning supplyed the want of Experience, awaked them; who thereupon is intreated
to take the charge of *Proxenus*'s Regiment and those
Captains; *Xenophon* made Slings, took Fifty Horses
out of the Carriages, and set Men on their backs;
taught the Archers to shoot compass, which they had
not used; and thus kept off the *Persian* Archers.
Thus their Valour made them way through all
difficulties; so that *Tissaphernes* fell to his surest
course, to distress them by burning all the Country
before them.

§. 9. The

§. 9. The *Greeks* paſſing through the *Carduchi*, a Fierce Swift People, and skilful Archers with the Sling, were much troubled with them ſeven days; and came to *Centriles*, which runneth between them and *Armenia*, where Forces were layed to hinder their Paſſage; but finding a Ford, they chaſed away the *Perſian* Subjects, and left the *Carduchi*, which ſeem to have Inhabited the Mountain *Niphates*, not far from *Tygris* Spring; contrary to *Ptolomy*, who placeth them far Eaſt, upon the River *Cyrus*, in *Medea*.

§. 10. The *Greeks* being come to *Armenia*, paſſed Sixty Miles to the heads of *Tygris*, and as far beyond peaceably, 'till *Teribazus* encountred them at the River *Teleboa*. He Governing for the *Perſians*, pretended to favour the *Greeks*, and made a Covenant with them; but in their ſecurity lying in wait for them, was diſcovered by a Souldier, taken by the *Greeks*, who found him out on the ſudden, and made him leave his Rich Pavilion behind him. Thence they went to the Northward, near the Fountains of *Euphrates*, where they found ſtore of Victuals, &c.

§. 11. The *Greeks* came to the River *Phaſis*, and paſſed thoſe Nations, the *Phaſians*, and *Chalybeans*; the firſt fled with all Proviſion into ſtrong Holds, of which one was forced, and yielded ſtore of Cattle. The Fierce *Chalybeans* afflicted them much, and fought with them hand to hand; the *Scythians* uſed them kindly at *Gmias*, whoſe Governour led them to Mount *Moſchici*, whence they ſaw the *Euxine-Sea*. Then they came to *Trabiſond*, or *Trapezus*, a Colonie of *Greeks* in *Colchos*, whoſe People uſed them with Hoſtility, which was well requited, while they reſted at *Trapezus*.

§. 12. The *Greeks* at *Trabiſond* deſiring Shipping for their Men's eaſie Travel, which the *Lacedemonian* Admiral who lay there promiſed to provide.

But

But lying long in expectation of Ships, and Victuals failing, they sent their Sick, with Women, Children, and Baggage by Sea; and the Army being Eight Thousand Six Hundred Men, went by Land to *Cerasus*, a *Greek* Town, as was *Cotione* their next Lodging, both Colonies from *Sinope*, as was *Trapezus*. Here the Inhabitants Discourtesie made the Souldiers to use violence, which the *Sinopians* took ill, and threatned Revenge. *Xenophon* excused it by necessity, which if it would not serve, he shewed how little he fear'd them; upon which considerations they yielded.

§. 13. *Xenophon*, while Ships are preparing, intended to build a City thereabouts; which being discovered, they most disliked the Design; and *Sinope* and *Heraclea* much feared it; and to prevent it, promise both Ships, and Mony. The Ships are sent without Mony, which made the Captains fear a Mutiny, having held the Souldiers in hope of it; but upon coming of *Cherisophus* from the *Lacedemonian* Admiral, with a few Gallies, and promise of Mony at their arrival in *Greece*, they set out from the Port of *Sinope*.

§. 14. The *Greeks* drawing homeward, thought fit to chuse an Absolute Commander, desiring *Xenophon* to take it upon him, which he refused, knowing the trouble of leading Voluntaries. *Cherisophus* accepts the offer, but was soon deposed, for not favouring their intent to surprize *Heraclea*, which had been friendly to them. For four Thousand four Hundred of them being *Arcadians*, and *Achæans*, chose new Leaders, and forsook the rest; but had been overthrown in *Bithynia*, if *Xenophon* and his Company had not come in.

§. 15. *Xenophon* forceth the *Persians* and *Thracians* in *Bithynia*, and ravages that part about Cape *Calpas*, and carries the Spoil to *Chrysopolis* near *Chalcedon*, and

and Sold it. *Tissaphernes* doubting their coming into
Phrygia, procured the Admiral of *Sparta* to lead
them out into *Europe*, and so ended that famous
Expedition, which opened the way for *Greece* to
visit *Persia* the second time, to the translating of the
Empire.

CHAP. XI.

Of the Greeks *Affairs*, under the Lacedemonians *Command.*

§. 1. **G**Reece understanding the effeminate Baseness of the *Asiaticks*, desired an undertaking of that huge unweildy Empire; but were hindred by home Distractions through the *Theban* War;
which called the *Lacedemonian* Power out of *Asia.*
Xenophon's retreat from *Babylon*, to *Greece*, four
thousand two hundred and eighty one Mile, in one
Year and three Months, through Enemies Countries,
I know not whether any Age hath parallel'd ; *Conon*
the *Briton* with six Thousand Men, came home thro'
all the breadth of *Italy*, and length of *France*, in
despight of the Emperor *Theodosius*; which Retreat
was like, rather than equal.

§. 2. *Timbro* the *Grecian* General in *Asia*, receiving *Xenophon*'s Men, took in Towns whichfell from
Tissaphernes, but for his Oppressions is deposed, and
Dercillidas a *Spartan* succeeded;who bearing a grudge
to *Pharnabasus*, and not favoured by *Tissaphernes*,
the other *Persian* Governours in lower *Asia*, upon appointment with *Tissaphernes*, entred *Æolis*, and in
few days subdued it ; wasted *Bithynia*, took *Atarne*,
a strong City, and *Cheronia*, with Eleven Towns in
it. Then he was Commanded from *Sparta*, to attempt *Caria*, the Seat of *Tissaphernes*. In defence
whereof,

whereof, *Pharnabafus* joyned with *Tiſſaphernes*, by which means the *Greeks* were over-match'd, being forſaken by the *Ionians* and Iſlanders; yet *Tiſſaphernes* feared to Fight, well remembring *Xenophon*'s Retreat; and ſo contrary to *Pharnabazus*'s Councel, a Truce is concluded.

§. 3. The *Lacedemonians* being now at leiſure, reſolve to revenge ſome private Wrongs done by the *Eleans*, who were Precedents of the *Olympian* Games, and accordingly forced them to free the Cities which had been ſubject to them, and overthrew their Walls. This pretence of Liberty, was their uſual ground of Wars; though after that, they made the ſame Towns little better than Vaſſals to *Sparta*.

§. 4. *Ageſilaus* newly made King of *Sparta*, ambitious of the honour of Victory againſt the *Perſians*, with a great Army ſet forward to *Aulis* in *Bæotia*, to Sacrifice there, as *Agamemnon* had done long before; but the *Thebans*, Lords of that Country, interrupted him. *Ageſilaus* reſented this Contumely, purſued his Enterprize, and landed at *Epheſus*, where *Tiſſaphernes* entertained him with a Treaty of Peace; ſeeking only to gain time for the better ſupplying himſelf with Men and Mony; which being come, he ſent to *Ageſilaus* to be gone, or to maintain his Poſt by force. *Ageſilaus* anſwer'd, *He was glad he had to deal with an Enemy, which by Perjury deſerved vengeance from Heaven.* So ſeeming to prepare for *Caria*, where *Tiſſaphernes* was prepared for him, he went directly to *Phrygia*, which he plundred, 'till *Tiſſaphernes*'s Cavalry came up, whom he could not well repell for want of Horſes, and therefore returned to *Epheſus* to furniſh himſelf with them; and as ſoon as the Seaſon ſerved, he entred and took *Bæotis* in *Tiſſaphernes*'s Country, overthrew his Cavalry in the Plain of *Meander*, for want of their Infantry, and took their Camp, which was very Rich. The King his Maſter diſtruſting him, and

and feeing how odious he was to the *Greeks,* thought
fit for procuring Peace, to take off his Head by *Ti-
thraustes,* whom he fent to fucceed him. Which
being done, he fent to *Agefilaus,* to certifie the
Author of the War was dead ; and that the King
was content that the *Greeks* fhould enjoy their Liberty, paying his Tribute. The Anfwer is referred
to the Council of *Sparta,* and 'till it came, *Agefilaus*
is content for Thirty Talents, at his requeft, to
transfer the War againft *Pharnabafus.* Thus thefe
Lieutenants valu'd not the King's Affairs further
than in their own Provinces ; the foolifh Cuftom of
thofe Kings being to be guided by Eunuchs, and
Concubines, Rewarding or Punifhing the Provincials, as they got, or loft.

§. 5. *Agefilaus* wafteth *Phrygia,* took *Pharnabafus's*
Palace, and drove him out of his Camp, *&c.* *Pharnabafus* feeketh fome good Compofition, reprefent-
ing the many good Offices done to the State of *Sparta* in the Wars with *Athens.* *Agefilaus* replieth,
That having War with his Mafter, they were forced to offend him ; but if he would revolt from the
King, they would Eftablifh him a free King over his
Province. *Pharnabafus* anfwering plainly, That
while his Mafter trufted him, he would be their
Enemy ; but if the Charge were taken from him,
he would fhift fides, and come over to them. So
Agefilaus removeth out of *Phrygia,* having made a
violent Enemy, of an honourable Friend.

§.6. *Tithrauftes* perceiving *Agefilaus* defign'd not
to leave *Afia,* took a wife Courfe, and fent Fifty
Talents to be difperfed among the Principal of
Thebes, and caus'd the *Argives* and *Corinthians* to
raife War againft *Sparta,* whom they formerly hated. The Quarrel is framed, from the *Locrians*
paying a Rent to the *Thebans,* which the *Phocians*
claimed, and for which they made a Diftrefs by violence ; whereupon the *Thebans* invaded *Phocis* in
Hoftile

Hoftile manner, which flyeth to *Sparta* for aid. The *Spartans* fend *Lyfander* to raife Men about *Phocis*, and to attend *Paufanias* the other King, with Forces out of *Peloponefus* ; but *Corinth* refufed to aſſiſt. *Toebes* knowing how many Succours *Lacedemon* ſhould have, even of thofe which affected them little, fent to *Athens* to beg aſſiſtance, and obtained it by *Thrafibulus*'s means ; who in the time of the Thirty Tyrants, being Baniſh'd, was courteouſly uſed at *Thebes*, while *Paufanias* ſtayed for the Confederates. *Lyfander* was ſlain at the Siege he layed to *Halyartus* ; whither after *Paufanias* came, and that the *Athenian* Aid was come to the *Thebans*, he departed ; for which he was Condemned, and fled to *Tegea*.

§. 7. The *Thebans* upon this Succeſs, had the *Argives*, *Corinths*, *Eubæans*, and others, come into Confederation ; ſo that *Sparta* feeing the danger, fent for *Agefilaus*. *Pharnabafus* confidering how much the *Greeks* Diviſion imported the King his Maſter, as before he had advanced the *Lacedemonians* Sea-Forces to the Overthrow of the *Athenians*, ſo now he feeketh to raife the *Athenian*, and break the *Lacedemonian*, who for three Talents had fold his Favour: He therefore furniſh'd *Conon*, and the *Athenians* with Eight Ships, and gave him Command of a great Navy, with which he deſtroyed the *Spartan* Fleet at *Cnidus*, in requital of the loſs of the *Athenian* Navy at *Ægos Potamos*, furpriz'd by *Lyfander*. *Conon* thus return'd to *Athens*, with a ſtrong Navy, and much Gold.

§. 8. The *Lacedemonians* for ſome years ſupport their Reputation by ſome Victories gotten by *Agefilaus*, 'till *Iphicrates* the *Athenian* General, gain'd a great Victory over them at *Lechæum*, and that by *Pharnabafus*'s perfuaſion ; promiſing them to Rule by their own Laws. The Cities in *Afia* expelled the *Spartan* Governours, *Abidos* only excepted ; and

Thra-

Thrasibulus the *Athenian*, with a Fleet had taken *Bizantium*, *Chalcedon*, *Lesbos*, &c.

§. 9. The *Lacedemonians* not able to maintain War againſt Men as good as themſelves, aſſiſted with *Perſian* Treaſure, crave Peace with *Artaxerxes*, offering to leave the *Greeks* in *Aſia* to him, and ſet the Iſlands and Towns in *Greece* all free; ſo that *Greece* ſhould never be able to moleſt the King. This Offer was not accepted, ſo War is continued in *Aſia* againſt *Strutha*, the King's Lieutenant there, and in *Greece* among themſelves; but by means of *Antalcidas*, the King, they made Peace.

§. 10. *Olynthus*, a ſtrong City in *Thrace*, grew formidable to their Neighbours, having ſubjected divers Cities, which made the reſt, even in *Macedon*, to crave aid of *Lacedemon*, which brought it under; and in their way *Thebes* is ſurprized by Treaſon.

§. 11. *Thebes* recovered by a Plot layed by certain Baniſhed Citizens, and *Phylladas* a Scribe of the Town; who, at a Feaſt promiſing to bring them the Choice Women of the Town to the Embraces of the Attenders, brought the Baniſh'd in Womens Attire, being come ſecretly, who ſlew them, and freed the City.

C H A P. XII.

Thebes *Flouriſhed from the Battle of* Leuctra, *to that of* Mantinæa.

§. 1. THE *Lacedemonians* were Stout and Grave in all Proceedings, but diſhonourable in neglecting all Reſpects, which hinder'd the Commodity of *Sparta*, which often brought them ſhame and loſs, when the execution was committed to weak conceited Men. Thus *Thebes* began to hold

R   them

them hard to it, and *Athens* began to surround *Peloponesus* with their Navy. But *Athens* seeing *Thebes* to incroach on her weak Neighbours, of which, some were Dependents on them, whom yet they could not succour, being engaged in such Wars, resolve to make Peace in *Greece*, according to the Form *Antalcidas* brought from *Persia.* The *Thebans* being sent to, agree, and meet at *Sparta* with the rest; where being required to subscribe to the freedom of the *Bœotians, Epaminondas* required that *Sparta* should do the same for *Laconia*, being no more subject to *Sparta*, than *Bœotia* to *Thebes. Agesilaus* hating *Thebes*, did thereupon, passionately dash the name of *Thebes* out of the League; and in haste sent *Cleombrotus*, one of their Kings, with all his Power, who was slain at *Leuctra*, and the Flower of the Army; after which loss, *Sparta* never recover'd it self; but *Thebes* grew to such Command, that in a short time, they brought Seventy Thousand strong to the Gates of *Sparta*.

§. 2. The *Athenians* taking upon them to manage the Peace, calling the Deputies of all the Confederated Estates, conclude the general Liberty of all Towns small and great. The *Mantuans* hereupon build their Town which *Sparta* had forced them to demolish, and allie themselves with such *Arcadian* Towns as most hated *Sparta*. But by a Faction among the *Arcadians*, the *Lacedemonians* are called in, and *Agesilaus* led them, but effected little. *Epaminondas* of *Thebes* assisted, with divers other Countries, which followed *Thebes*, joyning with the *Arcadians*, ravag'd *Laconia*, where since the *Dorians* entred, Six Hundred past, where never Enemies set foot, yet durst not the *Lacedemonians* come out of *Sparta* to succour it; so he re-built *Messene*, long ago destroyed by *Sparta*, calling home the old Inhabitants.

Sparta

§. 3. *Sparta* after this, required no more the leading of the Army, or other Precedency, only the *Athenians* yielded them the Leading by Land every Five Days fucceffively with them; a conclufion of vain Ambition, as the next Invafion of *Peloponefus* fhewed. And this Example bred the like emulation in the *Arcadians*, who thereupon will have their turn to lead with the *Thebans*; which Infolency bred fufpicion in the *Thebans*, and Hatred in the reft; fo that in the next Enterprize of the *Spartans* upon them, their Conceits overthrew them.

§. 4. The *Arcadians* misfortune rejoyced the *Thebans*, as without whofe aid Enterprizes proved ill, and by whom the *Lacedæmonians* were kept under; the *Theffalians* were protected, and the *Macedonian* quarrels fo moderated, that *Philip* Son of *Amyntas* was committed to them as an Hoftage. In this Reputation (little fhort of a general Command of all *Greece*) they fent Famous *Pelopidas* to *Artaxerxes* for his Alliance, which he granted, rejecting the contrary Suits of the other *Grecian* States, who had been very incommodious to him, and his Predeceffors, where *Thebes* had always fhewed good affection to *Perfia*. Befides, as they were no Seamen, and fo the lefs to be doubted in *Afia*, fo their ftrength might fecure him againft the reft, who now might much moleft him in the Revolt of all his Maritime Provinces, by fending them aid, without which he eafily reduced them; for the time fet by Divine Providence for the *Perfians* Fall was not yet come. The *Thebans* thus made Protectors of the common Peace by the King, yet got nothing, the other Eftates refufing.

§. 5. *Thebes* being grown by the mutual envy of *powerfull* *Athens* and *Sparta*, which being brought low, are glad to combine againft her; all the other Eftates of *Greece* are divided between them. The

Arca-

Arcadians had renounced the *Lacedemonians*, their old Leaders, and are become doubtful Adherents to the *Thebans*, without whose consent they had made Peace with the *Athenians.* *Epaminondas* therefore with the *Thebans* thought to invade *Peloponesus*, before the *Arcadians* turned Enemies, and while *Corinth* in their way stood Neutral, and the *Arcadians* were yet in disorder, and had sent to *Thebes* to complain of the Captains in *Tegea.* This Complaint was answered, *That their Peace with Athens was the Cause*; but Epaminondas *would come by them, and prove their Fidelity by their aid in his intended War.* The *Arcadians* amaz'd at this Answer, send to *Athens* for help, and to *Sparta*, offering to help against the Invasion; who kindly accepted it, not standing upon point of Leading.

§. 6. *Epaminondas*, besides great Forces raised out of other parts of *Greece*, had all the strength the *Argives* and *Messenians* could make; and while he stayed at *Nemia*, intercepted Intelligence that the *Athenian* Forces which he meant to encounter, would come by Sea. Thereupon he decamp'd, and march'd to *Tegea*, who with the most of *Arcadia* declare themselves his. The common Opinion was, that *Epaminondas* would first attempt the revolted *Arcadians*, therefore the *Lacedemonian* Captains fortifie *Mantinæa*, and send for *Agesilaus* from *Sparta*, with the small Forces that were there; so that *Epaminondas* with speed and secrecy marching to *Sparta*, had surpriz'd it, had not *Agesilaus* returned with precipitation, upon Intelligence by an unknown Fellow. *Epaminondas* disappointed of this hope, is presented with another; conceiving the *Mantineans* now fearing no danger, would disperse themselves abroad in the Fields about their Harvest; and thereupon sent his Horsemen before to interrupt them. But the *Athenians* coming thither, think to meet their Confederates, rescued the distressed *Mantineans* in in the Fields, and prefently after came all the *Bœo-tians* Power, and the *Lacedemonians* and their Friends were at hand.

§. 7. *Epaminondas* failing in both thefe Attempts, to prevent the decay of the Terrour of his Name in *Peloponefus*, refolved to check their Courage in the firft growth, and to leave a Memorable Chara&ter of this Expedition. Having therefore warned his Men to prepare to fight for the Sovereignty of all *Greece*, he made fhew to the Enemy by in-, trenching, to decline them, fo to allay their heat, and breed fecurity, wherein he might fuddenly ftrike amazement in them, by breaking in, as it hapned. The *Thebans* had the Honour of the Day, by forcing all their Enemies out of the Field, but loft their incomparable Commander *Epami-nondas*, by the ftroak of a Dart in his Breaft, of which he died when the Truncheon was pulled out ; but firft advifed the *Thebans* to make Peace, as wanting a General, when he heard that *Lobidas* and *Diophantes*, two Principal Men of War were flain. Thus died the Worthieft Man that ever *Greece* bred, and hardly matched in any Age or Country.

§. 8. The *Mantinean* Battle was the greateft that had been ever in the Country of Natives, in which all *Greece* were interefled, which never had better Souldiers, or braver Commanders. The iffue made all willing of a General Peace, wherein was concluded every Eftate fhould enjoy what it then held, and none forced to depend on other ; the *Meffenians* being included in this League, for which the *Lacedemonians* refufe it. After this, *Athens* and *Sparta* had leifure to feek Wealth in foreign Wars, as did *Agefilaus*, who fent to affift *Tachos* King of *Egypt*, defcended from *Amyrtæus*, who rebelled againft *Darius Nothus*. But *Agefilaus*

Trayte-

Trayterously fled from the King, to his Rebels, so that he was forced to flye to *Persia*, and *Nectanebus* succeeded, who Rewarded *Agesilaus* with two Hundred and Thirty Talent of Silver; with which, returning home, he died.

THE

THE
HISTORY
OF THE
WORLD.

BOOK IV. Part I.

Of the *Macedonian* Kingdom, from *Philip*, to the Race of *Antigonus*.

CHAP. I.

Of Philip, *Father to* Alexander *the Great.*

§. 1. **M**acedon at this time was little valued
by the *Greeks*, whose Glory in their
Persian Victory did so pamper them,
that they neglected all Nations but
themselves, especially the *Macedonians*, lately weak-
ned by Neighbouring Princes, in the time of *Amyntas* Father of *Philip*. But it fared with the *Greeks*,
as it commonly falleth out with Men of Note in the
World, that they often fall by the hands which
they least fear; and they considered not, that all

R 4   great

great Alterations are sudden and violent, in which
it is ever late to repair decayed Banks; when inraged Rivers are once swollen; *Greece* was far from
care to repair their Fences between them and this
Inundation, that they rather brake them down, by
wasting each other; so that as *Orosius* said, the
Cities of *Greece* lost all Command, by striving each
of them to Command all. *Macedon*, so called, from
Macedon Son of *Osiris*, bordereth on the North;
whose Kings were from *Temenus*, of the Race of
Hercules, and *Argives* by Nation. *Caranos* of *Argos*
Planted a Colony there, upon surprize of *Edessa*, a-
bout six years after *Arbaces* became King of *Medes*.

§. 2. *Philip* the Second, the youngest Son of *A-
myntas* II. Educated under *Epaminondas* in *Thebes*,
where he was in Hostage, escaped thence in the
first year of the Hundred and Fifth Olympiad,
which was three Hundred Ninety and Three years
after the Building of *Rome*: Being returned to *Macedon*, invironed with many Enemies, he took upon
him to Command, as a Protector of his young
Nephew, Son of *Percidas* his Brother, late King;
but his fruitful Ambition soon overgrew his Modesty,
and was easily persuaded by the People, to take
upon him the Absolute Rule, as the necessity of the
State required a King both Prudent and Active;
for as the King of *Thrace* sought to set *Pausanias*,
and the *Athenians Argaeus*, the Sons of *Æropus* the
late Usurper, so the *Illyrians* and *Pannonians* made
daily incursions on all sides. *Philip* to ease himself
of these heavy burthens, corrupted the *Pannonian's*
Men of War with Mony, and brought the *Thracian*
King from *Pausania*, and then made head against
the *Athenians*, and *Argaeus*, whom he overthrew,
and forced the *Athenians* to desire Peace.

§. 3. *Philip*

§. 3. *Philip* had now leisure to look Northward, invaded his bordering Enemies, and slew *Bardilus* King of *Illyrium*, recovering what he held in *Macedon*, and forced the *Pannonians* to Tribute. Then hasting to *Thessalia*, his South Neighbour, he took *Larissa* upon the River *Peneus*; but before he would proceed with *Thessaly*, he made sure of the entrance out of *Thrace*, winning *Amphipolis*, seated upon the bordering River; he also recovered *Pydna*, and *Crenidus*, which he called *Phillipi*. He also entred League with the *Olynthians*, his Father's mortal Enemies, and gave them *Pydna*, yet not designing they should hold it, or their own.

§. 4. *Philip* by the *Phocian* or Sacred War, in the second year of the hundred and sixth Olympiad, was drawn into *Greece*. This War grew by occasion that the *Phocians* having Plowed up one piece of ground belonging to *Delphos*'s Temple, were by the *Thebans* prosecution fined a great Summ at the General Council of *Greece*, and for refusing, are Condemned to the Sword. The *Phocians* hereupon plunder'd *Apollo*'s Temple, which yielded them Ten thousand Talents; with which they hired many Men, but after three Victories, were beaten by the *Thebans*, *Thessalians*, &c. In the mean time, *Philip* at the Siege of *Methon* lost an Eye; shortly after his Forces were overthrown in *Thessaly*, by the *Phocians* and *Thracians*, whom in the next Battle he defeated, slew six thousand, and took three thousand, and freed *Thessaly* of the Tyrant *Lycophron*, who had by force taken the City of *Pheres*.

§. 5. *Philip* after this quarrel'd with the *Olynthians*, a powerful People, who had a contest with the *Macedonians*, for protecting two of his half Brethren against his Sword; for his Quarrels were balanced by his Ambition, which made all things lawful, that any way served his turn; whether Murther of Brethren, breach of Faith, corrupting by Mony, esteem-
in g

ing no place strong, where his Ass laden with Gold could enter.

Therefore having overthrown them twice, and forced them to keep their City, he corrupted two Citizens, which gave him entrance ; where he slew his Brethren, and sold the Citizens for Slaves. Thus he Conquer'd more by Corruption and Fraud, than by Force ; as did *Philip* of *Spain.*

§. 6. *Philip* at the Request of the *Bœotians,* sent them aid against the *Phocians,* sufficient to retard, but not to end the War, so to weaken the strength of *Greece. Artaxerxes Ochus* also sent them One Hundred and Eighty Thousand Crowns ; but upon further request of his own presence, whom they promise to give entrance into their Territory, he went with Power sufficient to give Law to both Parties. Upon whose coming, *Phatlecus* the *Phocian* Leader, fearing to shock with him, made his Peace with him, and with a Regiment of Eight Thousand Men withdrew into *Peloponesus,* and left the *Phocians* to his mercy, who made them Slaves.

§. 7. *Philip* after this slew many Thousands of the *Illyrians* and *Dardanians,* brought *Thrace* to Tribute, but was forced to leave *Perinthus* and *Bizantium* reliev'd by *Athens, Chios,* and *Rhodes* ; and when he sought Peace with *Athens,* they refuse it, upon *Demosthenes*'s Eloquent persuasions. Putting up this Affront, he supplied himself, by taking Seventy Merchants Ships ; and with new Forces entred *Scythia,* with *Alexander* his Son, but prospered not.

§. 8. *Philip* after Eight Years spent Northward, was again called by the *Greeks* against *Amphissa,* who refused to obey the Decree of the *Amphyctians,* or General Counsel of *Greece.* To this Enterprize he needed no drawing on, but forthwith entred *Phocis,* won *Platæa,* and subdued all the Region. *Athens,* by persuasion of *Demosthenes,* drawing the
Thebans

Thebans to joyn, rejected *Philip*'s reafonable Conditions of Peace, and put their Freedom to the chance
of one Battle at *Cheronia*, wherein they were overthrown; yet *Philip* attempted not their City, as he
put a Garifon in *Thebes*, &c. Shortly after at *Corinth* he is chofen, and ftiled firft Commander of all
Greece, by the general States; whereupon he raifed
an Army of great ftrength againft *Perfia*, Commanded by *Attalus* and *Parmenio*, who tranfported
it into *Afia*, while he intended the Marriage of
Cleopatra his Daughter, to *Alexander* King of *Epirus*. At this Marriage-Feaft he was flain by one
Paufanias, of his Guard, for not doing him right
upon *Attalus*, who had made him drunk, and then
procured his Carnal abufing, *&c.* *Olympias* encouraged the Murther of her Husband. *   *Juft.L.9.*

§. 9. *Alexander*'s Greatnefs was fo well founded by
his Father, that the finifhing it with eafe was more
glorious to him, than the beginning was to *Philip*; for
befides his fubduing that Famous Nation of *Greece*,
he left him many Choice Commanders, as worthy of
Crowns as himfelf.

CHAP. II.

Of Alexander *the Great.*

§. 1. **A**Lexander fucceeded *Philip* his Father after
Twenty Five Years Reign; being a
Prince no lefs Valiant by Nature, than by Educa-
tion, enriched with all forts of good Learning. He
entred upon his Reign Four Hundred and Seventeen
Years after *Rome*'s Building, being Twenty Years
Old; which young Years encouraged his Neigh-
bouring Nations to confult about recovery of Li-
berty, which he prevented with much Expedition.
For

For after Revenge of his Father's death, and freeing his own Nation from all Exactions, and Bodily Slavery, and winning with Clemency, such as feared his Disposition to Cruelty, and using Austerity to such as contemned his Youth, He made a Journey into *Peloponesus*, and so well exercised his Spirits among them, that by the Councel of the State of *Greece*, he was Elected General against the *Persians*, which Enterprize possessed all his Thoughts. But the *Persian* Gold having guilt *Demosthenes*'s Tongue, he persuaded the *Athenians*, with the *Thebans* and *Lacedemonians*, to stand for their Ancient Liberty, and gave it out that *Alexander* was slain. Indeed Policy, as it is now a-days, defined by Falshood and Knavery, holding, that devised Rumours and Lyes, tho' they serve the turn but for a day or two, are greatly available; but in all my Observations, I have found the Success as ridiculous as the Invention; for Men finding themselves abused by such Baits, at other times neglect true Reports, which much concerneth them to believe. *Alexander* much grieved to have his Thoughts diverted, and time lost from his *Persian* Enterprize, made such expedition, that he brought the first News himself of his preparation to *Athens*, which, as upon a sudden fainting, presently submitted, and easily pardoned, by persuasion of *Alexander*'s desire to see *Persia*; as Wise Men are not easily drawn from great Purposes, nor by occasion easily put off. Then he subdued the Nations bordering North of *Macedon*; but yet could not get out of *Europe*, 'till he had demolish'd *Thebes*, which attempted his Garison in the Citadel, and obstinately refused to yield up the Authors of their Rebellion.

§. 2. *Alexander* having without cause given, put to death his Mother-in-Laws Kinsmen, advanced by his Father, and some of his own, whom he suspected; took also with him into *Asia* such Tributary Princes as he doubted, by unjust Cruelty to secure
all

all things; yet the End fell out contrary to the Policy which Ambition commended to him; all his Planting was soon rooted up; whom he most trusted, were the most Traiterous, and his Mother, Friends, and Children fell by as merciless a Sword as his own, and Confusion left his dead Body in the Grave. He passed into *Asia* with Thirty Two Thousand Foot, and Five Thousand Horse, all Old Souldiers, which he landed near *Troy*; where at the River of *Granick*, he was forced to climb up the deep Bank, guarded against him with many Thousand *Persians*; of whom he slew Twenty Thousand Foot, and Two Thousand Five Hundred Horse. But this slaughter must be taken rather on the Back than the Breast; for had they stood to it, *Alexander* must needs have lost above Twenty Thousand Foot, and Two Thousand Five Hundred Horse, especially if the *Persian* Horsemen had fought fiercely; and the *Grecians* in *Darius*'s Pay fought it out to the last Man, as *Plutarch* Reports.

§. 3. *Alexander*'s Souldiers were greatly encouraged by winning this Passage; and all the Country so terrified, that all the lesser *Asia* yielded without a Blow. For in all Invasions, where the Invaded are beaten, upon great advantage of place, they will easily be perswaded that such an Enemy upon equal terms can hardly be resisted; the Assailant therefore in such Cases of defending Places, is to be opposed with the ablest Forces; yet fewest Places of great circuit are so fenced, wherein one Entrance or other is not to be forced by an able Enemy; as the *Alps*, wherein *Francis* the *French* King found entrance to *Milan*, though the *Switzers* guarded them; *Xerxes* forced the entrance at *Thermopylæ*; *Cyrus* the younger, and *Alexander*, found the Gates of *Taurus* open into *Cilicia*; *Julius Agricola* found Fords into *Anglesey*, which made the amazed *Britains* submit, &c. It was therefore well done of *Alexander*, to pass the
River

River in the Face of their Enemies, without seeking an easier Passage, beating off the Enemy in their strength, leaving no hope of Succour to their Followers, in so unable Protectors. After this, *Sardis, Ephesus, Trallis,* and *Magnesia,* yielded themselves, and so enjoyed their own Laws; but he demolish'd *Halicarnassus,* for its obstinate resistance. Then he entred *Caria,* and restored *Ada* the Queen, expelled by *Darius's* Lieutenant, and *Lycia, Pamphylia, Pisidia,* and all the Sea-Coasts of lesser *Asia,* and then entred *Celenas* on *Meander,* and so through *Phrygia* toward the *Euxine-Sea,* and so to *Gordium,* where he cut the Gordian-Knot asunder. He also expelled the *Persians* out of the Isles of *Lesbos, Scio,* and *Coas,* which he committed to two of his Captains, to clear the Sea-Coast on his back, and then remov'd to *Ancira* on the River *Sangarius,* as is *Gordium,* and so to *Paphlagonia.* Here he heard of the death of *Menon, Darius's* Lieutenant, which much heartened him, being the only Captain he respected of all his Enemies. For so much hath the Spirit of some one Man excelled, as it hath undertaken and effected the alteration of the greatest States, as the erection of Monarchs, Conquest of Kingdoms, guiding handfuls of Men against Multitudes of equal bodily strength, contriving Victories beyond all hope and Discourse of Reason, converting the fearful Passions of his own Followers into Magnanimity, and the Valour of his Enemies into Cowardize. Such Spirits have been stirred up in sundry Ages to erect and cast down, and to bring all Things, Persons, and States, to the same certain ends which that Infinite Spirit of the Universe, Piercing, Moving, and Governing All Things, hath ordained, as which is seen in this King's Undertaking, *&c.* who not meeting with a Spirit like his own, was opposed only with difficulties of Passages, and tedious Journies; and certainly the things performed by *Xenophon,* discover as brave a Spirit as *Alexander's,* working no

less

less exquisitely, though the effects were less material, as were the Forces and Power of Commanders by which it wrought. But he who would find the exact Pattern of a Noble Commander, must look upon such as *Epaminondas*, that in courting Worthy Captains, better followed than themselves, have by their singular Vertue over-top'd them, that would not have yielded one foot to another. Such as these seldom obtain to great Empires, seeing it is harder to master the equal Forces of one hardy well-order'd State, than an unweildy Empire of many servile Nations ; and that only Brave Roman *Cæsar* is the Example, whose exquisite managing attained the Greatness.

Alexander hasteth to the Streights of *Cilicia*, to prevent *Darius*, which *Arsenes* the Governour had left to a weak Guard, which abandoned it, when he pretending to waste the Country, withdrew himself further off; so the Province came easily into *Alexander*'s Power.

§. 4. *Darius* approached with his Army of more than Two Hundred and Ninety Thousand of divers Nations, saith *Curtius*; Four Hundred Thousand after *Justine*, and Six Hundred Thousand in *Plutarch*. *Curtius* describeth the manner of his coming with such Pompous Riches, Gorgeous Apparel, a Pageant of his Gods, Train of Ladies attending his Mother, Wife, Children, with their Nurses, Eunuchs, Concubines, all sumptuously Apparel'd; with Six Hundred Mules, and Three Hundred Camels laden with Treasure, &c. Such was the Train of this May-game King ; so unmarshalled, effeminate, unarmed, but with Gold and glittering Garments, as would have encouraged the nakedest Nation in the World against them. We find by common Experience, that no discourse of Magnanimity, National Vertue, Religion, or Liberty, and whatsoever else is wont to encourage Vertuous

Men,

Men, hath any force with the Common Souldier, in Comparison of Spoil and Riches. Rich Ships are Boarded upon all difadvantages, Rich Towns furioufly affaulted, and plentiful Countries willingly invaded. War is willingly made, and for the most part, with good fuccefs againft the Richeft Nations. For as the needy are adventurous, fo Plenty is wont to fhun Peril ; and Men which are well to live, do rather ftudy to live Wealthy, than care to dye Honourable ; for no Man hafteth to the Market, where nothing is to be bought but Blows. This Battle at *Iſſus* is no where well defcribed ; but we may guefs what refiftance was made, if it be true that *Curtius* faith, that of the *Perfians* were flain Two Hundred Thoufand, and of the *Macedonians* but Two Hundred and Eighty ; of which number, *Arianus* and others cut off almoft half ; fo that it feemeth thefe died rather by over-labour, in killing, than being killed. *Darius* found it true now, what *Charedemus* a Banifhed *Athenian* told him near *Babylon,* That his rich delicate confufed Multitude, would be more fearful to the Countries through which they fhould pafs, than to the Long-trained *Macedonians,* againft whom it were fitter to oppofe a competent number of *Grecians* of equal Courage, having fuch abundance of Treafure to do it ; for which unpleafing Difcourfe, the poor *Greek* was flain, &c. Defperate is that Princes fafety, whofe Ear judgeth what is profitable, to be too fharp, and will entertain nothing that is unpleafant. For Liberty in Council is the life of it, which vanifheth if it be taken away. The like Advice was given by the *Grecians* which ferved under him, which he fet light by, who intreated him not to fight in the Streights, but to retire into the Plains of *Mefopotamia,* where he might environ all the *Macedonians,* and to divide his Army into Parts, not committing the Whole to one ftroak, *&c.* But that Infinite Wifdom of God, which worketh diverfly,

doth

doth often in the alteration of Kingdoms and
States, take Understanding from Governours ; not
to discern of Counsel. *Alexander*, by Advice of
Parmenio, stayed in a place where *Darius* could bring
no more Hands to fight than he, and utterly overthrew him, took his Treasure, Wife, Mother, Children, and Train of Ladies, which the *Grecians* had advised to leave at *Babylon*; and *Darius* casting off his
Crown, hardly escaped. Yet, after this, he writ to
Alexander about ransoming his Women, and some
proud Conditions of Peace, which he scorned. *Alexander*, after the Victory, made *Parmenio* Governour
of all *Phœnicia*, which presently submitted ; *Zidon*'s
Kingdom, committed to *Hephestion*, he gave to a
Day Labourer of the Royal Blood, who desired he
might bear his Prosperity, as well as he had done
his Adversity.

§. 5. *Alexander* coming near *Tyre*, received from
them a Crown of Gold, and store of Victuals and o-
ther Presents ; but could not be admitted into the
City as he desired, to offer Sacrifice to *Hercules*, 'till
he erected a Cause-way from the Main, Eight hundred Furlongs to it, which he did in Seven Months.
He put Eight Thousand to the Sword, Crucifyed two
Thousand on the Shore, and made Thirteen Thousand Slaves, for that they had barbarously drowned his Messengers. The Government he gave to
Philotus, Son of *Parmenio*.

§. 6. *Darius* sendeth again to stay his passage on
toward the East, laying down the difficulties, threatning to compass him in the Plain Countries, and offering him his Daughter and many Kingdoms for
Dowry : *Alexander* answered, he offer'd him what
was his own ; that he was to give, not to take Conditions ; and disdained all resistances at Rivers, having past the Sea. *Parmenio*, full of Years, Honour
and Wealth, told *Alexander*, if he were *Alexander*,
he would accept his Offer : *So would I*, said he, *If I*

S   *were*

were Parmenio. *Alexander* proceeded to *Gaza*, defended by *Belis* for *Darius*, with much Reſolution,
where he buried many *Macedonians* in the Sands,
and was wounded in the Breaſt ; yet took the Town
and cauſed *Belis* to be drawn about it, being weak by
many Wounds, defending that Cruelty by *Achilles's*
uſage of *Hector*. From thence he went to *Jeruſalem*,
where *Jaddus* the High Prieſt in his Robes met him,
whom he fell down before, remembring he had in
Macedon ſeen ſuch a Prieſt, which profeſſed the ſame
God, and incouraged him in his purpoſe for *Perſia* ;
ſo he gave the Jews what Immunities they deſired.

§. 7. *Alexander* turned from thence towards *Egypt*,
where *Aſtaces*, Lieutenant unto *Darius*, delivered
Memphis into his Hands, with 800 Talents of Treaſure. There doating after Deities, he took a deſperate Journey to viſit *Jupiter Hamon*, through the
dangerous Sands, that the lying Oracle, might acknowledge him *Jupiter's* Son, and ſo to be Worſhipped. Many prodigious Fables feigned hereabout,
look like thoſe of the *Spaniards* in the *Weſt-Indies*.
Curtius's deſcription of the place diſproved. It is
Two hundred Miles from any Sea in the *South* of the
Lybia, having the *Naſſamons* on the Weſt.

§. 8. *Alexander* returneth to *Memphis*, where he
committed the Provinces of *Egypt* to ſundry Governours, according to his Maſter *Ariſtotle's* Rule,
That great Dominion be not committed to any one.
Then he gave order for building of *Alexandria* ;
heard *Pſammonis* the Philoſopher who brought the
haughty King to confeſs, *That God is the Father of all
Men, but acknowledgeth good Men for his Children.* From thence he led his Army towards *Euphrates*, where *Mazæus* abandoned the defence of the
Paſſage ; from whence he Marched towards *Tygris*,
ſo violent in its Current and deep, that it had been
eaſie to repell them, who could not uſe Bows or
Darts, wading together Arm in Arm to withſtand
the

the Current. *Mazæus* having cowardly forsaken the Advantage of the Ford, which no Valour of his Enemy could have easily won, presents himself with some Companies of Horse, setting Fire on the Provision of the Country, but too late, for *Alexander's* Horse-men saved much.

§. 9. *Darius's* Forces, by *Curtius's* Report, were Two hundred Thousand Foot, and Fifty thousand Horse; *Arrianus* makes them Fourteen hundred thousand in all; it is probable they were about four hundred thousand, with which Multitude they thought to overpower their few Enemies in the Plains of *Assyria*; but Skill and Practice do more toward Victory, than rude Multitude. *Alexander's* Army, upon occasion of an Eclipse of the Moon, are affrighted, but are incouraged by *Egyptian* Astrologers. For it had been contrary to all Rule, to have an Army afraid to Fight. *Darius* offered great Conditions of Peace, in vain.

§. 10. *Alexander* is advised by *Parmenio*, to Assault *Darius's* Camp by Night; that the sight of the Multitude might breed no Terrour; which Counsel is a good ground of War, as oft as few must fight with many; but *Alexander* will have Day-Light to witness his Valour. Then he gave his Army Rest and store of Food before the Battle, according to the Rule of War, which saith, Men well refreshed will stand the better to it; for Hunger fights more eagerly within, than Steel without. His Forces, according to *Arrianus*, were Forty thousand Foot, and Seventy thousand Horse; which I take to be his *European* followers, besides *Egyptians*, *Syrians*, *Arabians*, *Scythians*. Of these, *Curtius* saith, three hundred only were slain, and Forty thousand *Persians*; others differ. So that as in the former two, so in this Battle what can we judge, but the *Persians*, upon the first Charge, ran away; else had every one but cast a Dart or a Stone, the *Macedonians* could not have

bought

bought the Empire so cheap ; neither could they have past the River so easily, if Sixty thousand had been Armed with Spades only.

§. 11. *Darius* after the Rout of his Army, recovered *Arbela* that Night, with his Treasure, intends a retreat into *Media*, while the *Macedonians*, as he supposed (but was deceiv'd) would attempt *Babylon*, *Susa*, &c. Rich Cities. *Alexander* pursueth, and enters *Arbela*, and possesseth the Treasure, while *Darius* flyeth, and then took his way to *Babylon*, which *Mazius* and the Captain of the Castle, rendred with the Treasure. Here he rested thirty four days, spent in such Voluptuous Pleasure, as made the *Macedonians* forget the Hardness of their Military Discipline. Here he erected Bands of One thousand, called *Chiliarchs*, bestowed on such as in the late War had best deserved. This City and Territory he left in Charge with Three of his own Captains, gracing *Mazeus* with the Title of Lieutenant. Then he entred the Province *Satrapene*, and so to *Susa* on the River *Euleus* in *Persia*, which *Abulites* gave up with Fifty thousand Talents of Silver Bullion, and Twelve *Elopha*'s, which he committed to some *Macedonians*, giving *Abulites* only the Title of Lieutenant ; as he did after to *Teridates* of *Persepolis* ; observing well, That Traytors to their own Kings are never to be trusted alone in great matters, wherein Falshood may redeem their lost Estate. Vassals of Fortune love only their Kings Prosperity, not Person.

§. 12. *Alexander* advancing toward *Persepolis*, was much worsted by *Ariobarzanes* at the *Streights* between the Mountains, which divide *Susiana* and *Persia*. But by a *Lycian* which lived there, he found another way, and came suddainly upon *Aribbarzanes*, and forced him ; who not finding entrance into *Persepolis*, returned with a second Charge upon the *Macedonians*, and was slain. *Teridates*, another of

Darius

Darius's trusty Grandees, sends to *Alexander* to make haste to *Persepolis* before the People pillaged the Treasury, which at that day, was the Richest in the World. This place *Alexander* committed to *Nicarides*, a Creature of his own, and left the Body of his Army there, while he with a Thousand Horse, and some choice Foot, not able to stand still, would in the Winter see the parts of *Persia* covered with Snow; when his Foot-men were impatient of that extreme travail, he left his Horse to bear a part with them: But I rather commend him who seeks wisely to prevent Extremities, than rash People which vaunt what they have indured with Common Souldiers. *Cæsar*'s first care was for Victuals; and he which will describe that Beast (War) must begin at his Belly, said *Coligni*. *Alexander* returns to *Persepolis*, where he smother'd all his Reputation in Cups, and Familiarity with Harlots, of which, *Thais* caus'd him to burn that sumptuous City *Persepolis*.

§. 13. *Darius*, in *Media*, having about Forty thousand Souldiers, which he design'd to encrease in *Bactria*; hearing of *Alexander*'s Approach, resolves to Fight, *&c*. *Nabarzanes* and *Bessus*, Governour of *Bactria*, Conspire against him, and draw away Thirty thousand of his Souldiers, neither durst his *Persian* Cowards (tho' offer'd the assistance of Four thousand *Greeks*, led by *Patronus*.) defend him from *Bessus*, who took and bound him, and put him in a Cart covered with Hides, and set forward to *Bactria*, in hopes, either by delivering him to *Alexander*, to make their Peace, or killing him to become King; but failed in both; God not induring so strange a Villany. *Alexander* hasting after with Six thousand Horse and other selected Companies, best Armed, and for speed, mounted also on Horse-back, hearing by such as daily forsook *Bessus*, what was done, pursued as in Post; so that *Bessus* finding *Darius* unwilling to take Horse and fly with him, wounded him

S 3   to

to death, and the Beasts which drew him, and left him alone. *Polystratus*, a *Macedonian* Priest, Thirsty with pursuing, while he stay'd at a Water discover'd the Cart, and found *Darius* bathing in his own Blood, at point of Death, and took Commendations from his Mouth to *Alexander*, to revenge him; and refreshed him with Water, &c.

§. 14. *Alexander* hearing of *Darius*'s Death, persuaded the *Macedonians* to pursue *Bessus*, and leaving some Forces in *Parthia*, enters *Hyrcania*, with some resistance of the *Mardons*. He passed the River *Zioberis*, which begins in *Parthia*, runneth under the ledge of Mountains, which part *Parthia* and *Hyrcania*, and after three hundred Furlongs, riseth again, and falleth into the *Caspian* Sea. In *Zadracarta*, called *Hyrcania* by *Ptolomy*, he rested Fifteen days, where *Patapherne* and other great Commanders of *Darius*, submitted to him, and were restored; especially he graced *Artabasus* for his Fidelity to his old Master, &c. he also, to his dishonour, accepted *Nabarzanes* the Traytor.

§. 15. *Thalestris* or *Minothea*, Queen of the *Amazons*, visited *Alexander*, and made suit to him for his Company, 'till she were with Child by him, which she obtained and departed. *Plutarch* citeth many for this Report, which yet is rather a Tale than true, not being mention'd by *Alexander* in his Epistle to *Antipater*, and laughed at by King *Lysimachus* of *Thrace*, a follower of *Alexander*. Here in a digression, he citeth *Pomponius Mela*, *Solinus*, *Ptolomy*, *Pliny*, *Claudian*, *Diodorus*, *Herodotus*, *Ammonius*, *Marcellinus*, *Plutarch*, to prove there were such *Amazons* of old. And to justify his own Report of such now in the South part of *America*, he citeth *Fra. Lopez.* his *Indian* History, *p. 2. cap. 28.* and *Ulrichus Schnidel* and *Ed. Lopes* in Disc.

§. 16. *Alexander* having begun at *Persepolis* to fall into the *Persian* Luxury, now took on him *Persian* Robes,

Robes, and Greatness to be Adored, to esteem Clemency as Baseness, Temperance, a poor humour, fitter for a Teacher of Youth than an incomparable King. His Court and Camp grew full of shameless Courtisans and Sodomy; Eunuchs and all other shameless Manners of the vanquished *Persians*, which he had detested, but now exceeded that Monster *Darius*, from whose Tyranny he vaunted, he had deliver'd many Nations by assistance of the Gods he served, which detested the *Persian* Vices. His nearest Friends grew ashamed of him, crying out he had more impoverished the *Macedonians* in their Virtues than inriched them in their Victories, and made them more Slaves than the Conquered. *Alexander* understanding hereof, sought to pacify the wiser sort with Gifts; and gave out that *Bessus* had assumed the Title of King of *Bactria*, and raised a great Army, so perswading them to go on. Coming to pass over an inaccessable Rock, he forced away the Guarder by the Smoke of a Pile of Wood, taking the advantage of the Winds; as in *Guicciardine* three hundred *Spaniards*, were smothered by firing withered Grass.

§. 17. *Alexander* at the entrance of *Bactria*, taketh the way of *Hyrcania*, and thence Northward towards the *Mardi*, on the *Caspian*, and so over the Mountain *Coranus* into *Aria*, East of *Bactria*, where the City *Artaconna* yielded after some resistance. Here upon a Treason of *Dimnus* and others, against *Alexander*, *Philotas* is suspected for not acquainting *Alexander* with it, after that *Cebalius* had discovered it unto him; but upon Examination, his error of Concealment, for want of opportunity to tell the King, was for his Father *Parmenio*'s sake, and his own good Service, and his dead Brother Pardoned. But upon *Craterus* his Enemies instigation, pretending piety for the King's preservation, the Prince swallowed his Promise, and made his

Enemies

Enemies his Judges. *Alexander*, the Evening of the same Night he had appointed for *Philotas's* apprehension, called him to a Banquet, and difcourfed familiarly with him, as of old ; but being in the dead of the Night apprehended and bound, he cried out, O Alexander ! *the malice of mine Enemies furmounts thy Mercies, and is more conftant than the word of a King.* Among other Circumftances urged by *Alexander,* this was not the leaft ; that in Anfwer to a Letter written to him by the King, of the Honour given him by *Jupiter Hamon,* he faid, *He could but joy that he was admitted into the Fellowfhip of the Gods ; yet he could not but grieve for thofe which fhould live under one which would exceed the Nature of a Man.* Hereby *Alexander* gather'd he envy'd his Glory ; for fo the Monfter Flattery perfuaded Princes, of the Men which cannot approve in them things to be abhorred. *Philotas* the next day is brought bound like a Thief, to hear the King's Oration againft him ; his Father the Greateft Captain in the World, and his Brethren flain in his Service, which fo oppreft him with Grief, that he could utter nothing but Tears, Sorrow, having wafted his Spirits. But when he would have anfwered in the *Perfian* Tongue, which all underftood, the King departed, faying, *he difdained his own Country Language.* Thus all are encouraged to exceed in hatred againft him, feeing the King's refolution, fo that his Defence availed not. Though none of the Confpirators upon torment accufed him ; yet by refiftlefs and unnatural Torments, devifed by *Craterus, Cinus, Hepheftion,* and others, he accufed himfelf, in hopes to be flain out-right ; but was deceived, though he confefled not what he knew, but what they beft liked. Of this kind of judicial Proceeding * St. *Auguftine* complaineth. * So *Seneca* speaking of *Alexander's* Cruelty, faid, Cruelty is no Humane Vice, it is unworthy fo mild a Spirit ; it is

* *De Civ. Lib.* 19.

a

a beaſtly Rage to delight in Blood, and changing a
Man into a Salvage Monſter.   The like End had all
the accuſed : Only *Parmenio* yet lived, who with
great Fidelity had ſerved both the Father and the
Son, opened the way into *Aſia*, depreſſed *Attalus*
the King's Enemy, in all hazards led the Vanguard,
prudent in Councel, ſuceſsful in Attempts, beloved of the Men of War, as he who had purchaſed
of the King the Eaſt Empire, and all his Glory.
This Man being in *Media*, muſt be diſpatched by
Polydamas his beſt beloved Friend, leaving *Cleander*
and others who murthered him, reading the King's
Letter.   Thus ended *Parmenio*, who had performed
many notable things without the King, who did nothing without him worth praiſe.

  Alexander after this ſubdued the *Araſpians*, and
Aracoſians, and came to the foot of *Taurus*, where
he built another *Alexandria*, which he Peopled with
Seven Hundred ancient *Macedonians*: *Beſſus* for-
ſakes *Bactria*, of which *Artabazus* is made Governour, and *Alexander* followed him over *Oxus* into
Sogdiana, where he loſt more Men by drinking in-
ordinately after great want, than in any Battle with
the *Perſians*.   At this River *Beſſus* might eaſily have
diſtreſſed him, being forced to paſs over his Army
with Hides ſtuffed with Straw and ſowed together ;
but *Spitamines*, *Dataphernes*, *Catanes*, &c. Commanders of his Army remembring how he had ſerved
Darius, laid Hands on him, bound him, and with a
Chain about his Neck, led him like a Maſtiff Dog
to *Alexander*, who gave him to *Oxatres*, *Darius*'s Brother to torment.   Shortly after he came to *Maracanda*, which *Petrus Perondinus* takes to be *Samar-
chand Jamerlanes*, a Regal City, which was Seventy
Furlongs compaſs.   But upon the Rebellion of the
Bactrians and *Sogdians*, ſtirred up by *Spitamines* and
Catanes, he left the place, which they recovered,
while he was buſy in ſubduing others, againſt whom he
                                        employed

employed *Menedemus*. In the mean time, *Alexander* Marched on to the River *Jaxartes* (not *Tanais*, as *Curtius* and *Trogus* miftake it, being two thoufand Miles from *Sogdiana*) upon which he Built a City of his Name, fixty Furlongs in compafs, which while the Citizens fought to hinder, as prejudicial to their excurfions, fome Sixty *Macedonians* were flain, and One thoufand one hundred hurt in paffing that great River to repell them. *Menedemus* the mean while with 2000 Foot and 300 Horfe are flain by *Spitamenes*, who flies into *Bactria*, and leaveth *Sogdiana*, where *Alexander* kills and wafteth without mercy. Here he received fupply of Nineteen thoufand, out of *Greece*, *Syria* and *Lycia* (as oft before from thence and other parts) with which he repaffed *Oxus*, on whofe South he built Six Towns near one another for mutual Succour. But he is troubled with a new Rebel, *Arimazus* a *Sogdian*, who with Thirty thoufand, maintain'd the Top of an Hill which *Alexander* could not Win, 'till three hundred choice young Men crept up to the Top thereof, upon promife of Ten Talents to the firft, Nine to the Second, and fo to the reft in proportion, of which Thirty two were loft; thus Wit effecteth what Force could not.

§. 19 *Alexander* having committed *Maracanda*, and the Countries about it to *Clytus*, flew him foon after, for that in a drunken fit, he derided the Oracle of *Hamon*, and objected to the King, the death of *Parmenio*. Thus in Cups, the one forgot whom he offended, the other whom he flew; which when he was recover'd, he would have revenged on himfelf, but for *Califthenes*'s perfuafion, remembring too late, he had deferved as much as any, and had faved his Life: Drunkennefs both kindles and lays open every Vice; it removes Shame, which gives impediment to bad Attempts, &c. *Spitamenes*, fhortly after, was murdered by his Wife, and *Dataphernes* is fent bound by the *Dalians* to *Alexander*; who proceeded
                                                      ed

ed into *Gabara*, where he loft a Thoufand in a Tempeft, and the reft fuffered Hunger, Cold, Lightnings, &c. So he came to the *Cohortans*, which welcomed him with Feafting, and a Prefent of Thirty fair Virgins, of which one was *Roxane*, afterward his Wife. Here he tore *Califthenes* afunder on a Rack, without any proof, for *Harmolaus*'s Treafon : But indeed, for Reafoning at a Drinking againft Deifying *Alexander*, propounded by a Parafite, and heard by the King, ftanding behind a Partition; *Seneca* calls this Act, his eternal Crime, which no Virtue or Felicity can redeem; for whatfoever can be fpoken to his Praife, is not anfwerable to this Reproach; *He flew* Califthenes.

§. 20. *Alexander* with Twelve Thoufand Foot and Horfe, entred the *Indian* Borders, where, after a few days, *Nifa*, built by *Bacchus*, was delivered; from whence he went to *Dedala*, and fo to *Arcadera*, abandoned by the Inhabitants, fo that they failed of Victuals, and were forced to divide the Army. Here he took *Nora*, &c. and came to *Indus*, where *Hepheftion* had prepared Boats, and had perfuaded *Omphis* King of the Country, who offered his Service to *Alexander*, and prefented him with Fifty Elephants. *Abiafaris* hearing thereof, made his peace with *Alexander*, fo that *Porus* only retained, the other Enemy of *Omphis*. *Alexander* fent to command his Homage at the Border of his Kingdom : He anfwered he would attend him there, but for other acknowledgment, he would take Counfel of his Sword. *Porus* attends him on the Bank of *Hydafpes* with Thirty thoufand Foot, Nine hundred Elephants, Three hundred Armed Chariots, and a great Troop of Horfe. The River was Four Furlongs broad, and fwift, and deep, with many Iflands, of which one was well fhaded with Wood, where *Alexander* ftaid, and fent *Ptolomy* up the River, with a great part of the Army, which *Porus* fuppofing to be the Whole, removed,

ved, to oppose their coming over, while *Alexander*
recovered the further Shore without Resistance, and
advanceth towards *Porus*, who a while, took him to
be *Abiasares* his Confederate, come over the River
to aid him. But finding it to the contrary, he sent his
Brother with Four thousand Men, and a hundred Armed Waggons, having four hundred Armed Men in
them, but of small use, by reason of late Rain,
and the *Scythians* which Galled their Horses, and made
them overturn the Waggons. *Perdicas* charg'd the
Indian Horses, and made all to retire, which made
Porus move forward with the gross of his Army, that
the scatter'd parts of his Vant-guard might recover
his Rear, *&c.* The Elephants much molested the *Ma-*
cedonians; 'till being inraged by the galling of Arrows
and Darts, they turned head upon their follower's
Foot, *&c.* After a long and doubtful Fight, *Porus*,
sore wounded, and Abandoned by his Men, and o-
ver-matched in Numbers, and skill of Leaders, fell
into the Conquerors hands, who restored and, inlarged his Kingdoms.

§. 21. *Alexander* having overthrown *Porus*, and
hearing by these *Indian* Kings, that one *Agamenes*,
beyond *Ganges*, commanding many Nations, was the
powerfullest King of all these Regions, and able to
bring into the Field, Two hundred thousand Foot,
three hundred Elephants, twenty thousand Horse, and
two thousand armed Chariots, was much inflamed to
proceed, but all the Art he had, could not perswade
the Souldiers thereto; only they are content to follow him to the South, having *Indus* for his guide.

So he returned to *Acesines*, intending to lay up
his Fleet, where it encountreth *Hydaspes*, by which
two Rivers, he built two Cities, *Nicæ* and *Bucepha-*
lon. Here he intended a fourth supply of six thousand Horse-men, and seven thousand Foot out of
Thrace, and twenty five thousand Rich Armour from
Babylon, which he distributed among the Souldiers.
                                                     Here

Hereabout he won many Towns, received One hundred Embassadors from an *Indian* King, with a Present of three hundred Horses, one hundred thirty Waggons, and one thousand Targets. Sailing Southward by many obscure Nations, among them he built another *Alexandria*, and took, among many other places, one called *Samus*, whose Inhabitants fought with poisoned Swords. Being come to the out-let of *Indus*, he sent to discover the Coast along toward the Mouth of *Euphrates*. After part of Winter spent here, he marched in Eighteen Days to *Gedrosia*, in which Passage, his Army suffered such Misery for want of Food, that not the fourth part returned alive.

§. 22. *Alexander* came to *Carmania*, and drawing near *Persia*, he fell to imitate *Bacchus*'s Triumphs in Cups, which Swinish hateful Vice, always inflamed him to Cruelty. For the Hang-man followed the Feast, saith *Curtius*, and *Apastes*, a Provincial Governour, was slain by his Commandment. Here *Cleander*, and his Fellows employed in the Murder of *Parmenio*, brought him a supply of Five thousand Foot, and one thousand Horse, but upon complaint of their Out-rages, *Cleander* and the rest, with six hundred Souldiers, were commended to the Hang-man, to the joy of all. *Alexander* removed and came to *Pasargada*, where *Cyrus* was buried, and was presented with many rich Gifts by *Orsines*, a Prince of the Race of *Cyrus*, whom *Alexander* put to Death, by the practice of *Bagoas* one of his Eunuchs, because he was neglected of him; the Accusation that he had robbed *Cyrus*'s his Tomb, was from Two loose Fellows. *Phrates* also was slain upon suspicion of his Greatness; so headlong was he become to shed Blood, and believe false Reports. *Calanus* an *Indian* Philosopher, burnt himself, being Seventy three years old, fore-telling *Alexander* of his own Death shortly after. *Alexander* removed to *Susa*, where he Married

Statira,

Statira, Darius's Eldest Daughter, and her Sister he gave to *Hephestion,* and Eighty Persian Ladies to his Captains; and at the Marriage he gave Six thousand Cups of Gold to so many Guests. *Harpalus* his Treasurer in *Babylon* having been lavish of the Treasure, fled away with five thousand Talents, and six thousand hired Souldiers, but was taken and slain in *Greece,* to *Alexander's* great Joy. Great discontentment grew in his Army, knowing his purpose to send his decay'd Souldiers to *Macedon,* and to detain the rest, whom he labour'd to pacify in vain, 'till their Passions were evaporated; when the inconsiderate Multitude may be led as a Whale, with a twined Thread, is drawn to Land after some tumbling. *Craterus* is sent with those which were Licensed to return, and made Lieutenant of *Macedon, Thrace* and *Thessaly,* which place *Antipater,* now sent for by the King, had held with great Fidelity. *Antipater* could see no reason of his removal, but a disposition in the King to send him after *Parmenio.* With this *Antipater,* the King, for all his great courage, had no great Appetite to grapple; for Jealous Princes do not always stand in doubt of every ill affected, though Valiant Man, but where there is a Kingly Courage compounded of Hardiness and Understanding; this is often so fearful to Kings, as they take leave, both of Law and Religion, to free themselves of such. · *Alexander* after this, went to *Media* to set things in Order, where *Hephestion,* his greatest Favourite dyed; on whose Monument, he bestowed Twelve thousand Talents. The King took Methods to make all Men weary of his Government, seeing Cruelty is more fearful than any Adventure that can be made against it. *Antipater* therefore came not, nor sent any Excuse, but free'd himself by his Sons, *Cassander, Philip,* and *Lollaus,* who waited on the King's Cup. These, at a drinking Feast, in a Carouse in *Hercules's* Cup, gave him a Draught

of

of Drink ſtronger than *Hercules* himſelf; ſo he quitted the World within a few days. Princes ſeldom find advantage by making their Miniſters over-great, and thereby ſuſpicious to themſelves. For he which doth not acknowledge Fidelity to be a Debt, but that Kings ought to purchaſe it of their Vaſſals, will never pleaſe himſelf with the Price given; only the Reſtorative indeed that ſtrengthens it, is the Goodneſs and Vertue of the Prince, and his Liberality makes it more diligent. *Antipater* had Govern'd two or three Kingdoms Twelve years, and peradventure knew not to play another part, as *Cæſar* which forgot the Art of Obedience, after long governing the *Gauls.*

§23. *Alexander's* Cruelty and Pride is inexcuſable; his Drunkenneſs no leſs. *Auguſtine* juſtly derided his lamenting want of Employment, when he ſhould have no more to Conquer; as if well to Govern the Conquered, would not ſufficiently buſie his Brain. His Valour, a Thouſand in his Army Matched. His Liberality *Seneca* Taxeth, and his Speech about a Kings gift is Fooliſh. Compared with other troublers of the World. *Cæſar,* and others after more glorious; for he never undertook Warlike Nations.

CHAP. III.

Aridæus, his Reign after Alexander.

A*Lexander* in his ſtubborn Pride, refuſed to eſtabliſh any Succeſſor; eſteeming none Worthy; and the greateſt Ambition of his Followers Learned of their Maſter to endure no Equals; a Leſſon ſoon taken out by Spirits reflecting upon their own Worth, wanting the Reverence of a greater Object. Thus the Queſtion of the Succeſſion became difficult. *Alexander* having no Iſſue but by *Barſinoe*

a

a *Persian*, and *Roxane*, of mean Condition, both excepted againſt as of Conquered Nations. *Ptolomy*, the Son of *Philip*, who gave his Mother *Barſinoe* great with Child to *Lagus*, is of opinion, the Rule ſhould reſt in the Captains, to order it by Voices. *Ariſtonus* another Captain, propounded *Perdicas*, as deſigned Succeſſor by *Alexander*, who at the point of death, left his Kingdom to the worthieſt, and delivered his Ring to him; who had ſucceeded his Favourite *Hepheſtion* in Favour and Place, he being urged by many, to take the Royal Eſtate upon him, not content with the Souldiers acclamation, of a counterfeit Modeſty, put it off, looking that every one of the Princes would intreat him, that ſo his Acceptance might be the leſs Envied: But as he which feigns a ſleep may be eaten with a Wolf; ſo *Meleager* his Enemy, took advantage of his Irreſolution, and acted againſt him; concluded, that whoever were Heir to the Crown, the Souldiers ought to Inherit the Treaſure, to that which he invited them, who were nothing backward in ſharing it.

§. 2. *Aridæus*, a Natural Brother of *Alexander*, in this Uproar, is named by ſome one, liked by many, and produced, and commended by *Meleager* to the Army, which changeth his Name to *Philip*, inveſteth him in *Alexander*'s Robes, and proclaims him King, contrary to the Mind of many of the Nobles, who yet by the interceſſion of the Ancient Captains, are reconciled, though neither ſide meant faithfully. For *Meleager* now Governing the King, who was no wiſer than *Alexander*'s Chair in which he ſate; attempted to kill *Perdicas*, who underſtanding of their coming which are ſent to do it, rebuked them with ſuch Gravity, that they departed honeſter than they came. The Camp hearing of this Attempt, fell into an Uproar, which the King their Creature could not appeaſe, 'till offered to reſign unto them; ſo upon the King's motion, after ſundry Embaſſies between

him

him and his Nobles. *Meleager* is joined with *Leona-tus* and *Perdicas* in Government of the Army; so much Love is protested, where none is meant. For presently after, upon Rumors against *Perdicas*, purposely raised, as if they proceeded from *Meleager*, to make him guilty of seditious Rumours, if he should give way thereto; He, to prevent the danger, persuades *Perdicas* to a general Muster, for cleansing the Army by punishing seditious Persons and other Offenders, not in the least intending his special Friends, and such as followed him, when he disturbed the Election of a King, by calling away Souldiers to the sharing of the Treasure. The manner of this Muster is solemn, having the Horsemen, among whom the King must ride, the Elephants, the *Macedonian* Foot, and Mercenaries set in Batalia in distinct parties, so as to skirmish by way of Exercise. The *Macedonian* Pikes (called the *Pha-lanx*) led by *Meleager*, is placed at disadvantage, and so charged by the Horse-men and Elephants, as afforded no Jesting; and the King being now in *Per-dicas*'s possession, must command to be delivered to death, such of the Infantry as *Perdicas* required. Thus Three hundred of *Meleager*'s Friends and Follow-ers, are cast to the Elephants to be slain; and *Me-leager* flying to a Temple for Sanctuary, having too late discovered the Design, was there also slain. The Princes held a new Counsel, divide the Provinces among themselves, leave *Aridæus* the Office of a Visitor, and *Perdicas* his Protector, and Commander of his Forces; and gave *Aridæus*, a Captain, the Charge to bury the Corps of *Alexander*, at *Alexandria* in *Egypt*.

- *Alexander*, in his life time, knowing the factious quality of the *Greeks*, had commanded that all the banished should be restored, thinking, by them, to have a sure Party in every City; but by that proud Injunction, contrary to their Laws, lost the Hearts of the rest, who esteemed it a beginning of open Ty-

T   ranny.

ranny.. The *Athenians* and *Ætolians* who oppos'd
this Decree, upon *Alexander*'s Death, Proclaim
War againſt the *Macedonians*, and by *Leoſthenes* their
Captain, who called in the *Ætolians*, overthrew the
Bœotians which ſided with *Antipater*, Lieutenant to
Alexander. *Antipater* doubting his own ſtrength,
ſent to *Craterus* in *Aſia*, whoſe coming into *Macedon*, had ſo troubled his Thoughts but a Month before. So vain are the Hopes and Fears of Men, which
decree all by mortal Wiſdom, ſhunning and perſuing
their Deſtiny afar off, even when it ſeems near at
hand. *Craterus* and the Captains in *Aſia*, neareſt to
Europe, are ſolicited to make haſte ; for *Antipater*
could raiſe in *Macedon* but Thirteen Thouſand raw
Souldiers, and ſix hundred Horſe, beſides the *Theſ-
ſalian* brave Troops. Whereas *Leoſthenes* brought
into the Field twenty two thouſand Foot, and two
thouſand five hundred Horſe, beſides many Auxila-
ries which came in. But before *Craterus* came, *Antipater* ventred a Battle, which he loſt, and was forced into *Lamia*, a fortifyed and well provided Town
to endure a Siege, which *Leoſthenes* preſented him
with:

§. 4. *Perdicas*, Protector of *Aridæus*, had no peculiar Province, but greater Forces than any, with
which, and his Marriage with *Cleopatra*, *Alexander*'s
Siſter, he hoped for greater Matters. He firſt ſubdued *Cappadocia*, which had never ſubmitted to *Alexander*, and committed it to *Eumenes*, whom he
truſted above all Men.

§. 5. *Antipater* having in vain expected his *Aſian*
Succours, offered to yield upon Terms of Reaſon, but
Leoſthenes will have an abſolute yielding ; which the
other, having been his Commander, refuſed ; ſo the
Siege is delayed 'till the *Ætolians* grew weary and
departed, ſo that the Trenches were thinly Mann'd.
Upon this advantage, *Antipater* ſallied out, and ſlew
many, and *Leoſthenes* himſelf ; but yet was not relieved

lieved of the Siege. *Leonatus*, in the mean time, is perfuaded to haften to it with twenty Thoufand Foot, and Two thoufand five hundred Horfe out of *Phrygia* the leffer, which he willingly undertook for *Cleopatra*'s fake, which fent for him to *Pella* in *Macedon.* But *Antiphilus*, who fucceeded *Leofthenes*, raifed his Siege, and went to meet him before *Antipater* and he joined, and obtain'd a great Victory, and the greater by *Leonatus*'s Death. The vanquifhed *Macedonians*, too proud to fly, and weak to renew the Fight, betook them to high grounds, 'till the day following, when *Antipater* came, who alfo kept the high ground as if he meant not to fight, which moved many *Greeks* to depart. This inftability (incorrigible in Volunteers) was the more inexcufable. *Craterus*, with a ftrong Army, at length is come, and joineth with *Antipater*, making between them Forty thoufand heavy Armed, Three thoufand light, and Five thoufand Horfe ; of which number, the *Greeks* wanted one thoufand five hundred Horfe, and Eighteen thoufand Foot, who loft he day, with the flaughter only of Five hundred Men. So the *Greeks*, not fubject to one General, defiring to preferve their own Eftates, betrayed their Country's liberty by a carelefs defence, while *Theffaly* feeks her Peace.

§. 6. *Antipater*'s gentle Conditions to fuch as were forward to feek Peace, drew on the reft ; only *Athens* and *Ætolia* are plotting to profecute the War, begun by them more bravely than wifely, 'till *Antipater* is come to their Doors, when wanting wherewith to refift, they feek Peace, abfolutely fubmitting, as *Leofthenes* had proudly required of *Antipater*, who now overthrew the Popular Eftate, raifed a Democracy of Nine thoufand of the moft confiderable Perfons, tranfmitted the tumultuous into *Thrace*, and flew *Demofthenes.*

§. 7. *Antipater* giveth his Daughter *Phila* to *Craterus*, and after the Marriage, both go againft the

Ætolians, who had conveyed their impotent People and Goods, into places of great fafety, of which, that rough Mountainous Country yields many, and the reft fortify their ftrong Cities. Here the two great Commanders are kept in play, 'till News out of *Afia* made them defire very earneftly to be gone, giving them what Conditions they pleafed. This *Afiatique* Expedition grew from *Perdicas*'s Plot, to bring *Aridæus* into *Macedon*, defigning by his prefence to make void the Offices of his Vice-Roys, that fo himfelf, who Adminiftred all under the Titular Majefty of *Aridæus*, might obtain *Cleopatra*, and thereby, both Greatnefs and a good Title. *Antigonus*, Governour of *Phrygia*, whom he difcerned no way proper for his purpofe, is called in queftion for Life, but efcaped with his Son *Demetrius*, and came to *Antipater*.

§. 8. *Perdicas* perceiving his intentions were laid open, refolves to make them good with the Sword; and firft he will begin with *Ptolomy* of *Egypt*, leaving *Eumenes* upon the *Afiatique* Coaft, to withftand *Antipater* and *Craterus*. *Ptolomy* having won the Egyptians with his fweet behaviour, and added the Dominion of *Cyrene*, hearing of *Perdicas*'s coming to the *Camels Wall*, a little town in *Egypt*, put himfelf into it, and bravely kept it againft him. *Perdicas* removeth to a place over againft *Memphis*, where in vain attempting to pafs over *Nilus*, three thoufand, of his Men were drowned and devoured by *Crocodiles*, and fuch as fell into *Ptolomy*'s hands, were faved alive, whom he ufed courteoufly, and buried the dead, caft up by the River. The Captains hearing of this his Humanity, fell to mutiny, thinking it unreafonable to make War on fo Virtuous and Honourable a Perfon, to fulfil the pleafure of a Lordly Ambitious Man, ufing them like Slaves. *Pithon*, formerly made Governour of *Medea*, being prefent, and hating *Perdicas* for a difgrace offered him by the other,

(which

(which caused many *Greeks* to be slain, who had
yielded to him upon his Promise) drew a hundred Captains, and a good part of the Horse, entred upon *Perdicas*'s Tent, and slew him, who could
endure no Greatness but his own. *Ptolomy* the next
day, came to the Camp, and was joyfully received,
and offered the Protectorship, which he modestly
refused, and procured it for *Pithon.*

§. 9. *Eumenes,* being left by *Perdicas,* to withstand
Antipater, Alcetas, Brother of *Perdicas,* refused to assist him as his Brother Commanded : *Neoptolemus*
pretended to be willing, but being Summon'd, came in
a Hostile manner, as he promised *Antipater,* and was
shamefully disappointed and put to flight, leaving his
Foot-men, which upon *Eumenes*'s Charge, submitted and took Oath to serve him. *Neoptolemus* being
come to *Antipater,* persuades *Craterus* to march against *Eumenes,* assuring him, that upon his appearance,
all the *Macedonians* with *Eumenes,* would revolt. *Eumenes* fearing *Craterus*'s presence might be of ill consequence to him, peremptorily forbad the admitting either Messenger or Trumpeter ; and placed in his Battle
against *Craterus* such as knew him not, charging the
Leaders to run on without giving leisure to speak.
Craterus, to incourage his Men, promiseth the Spoil,
like him who sells the Bears Skin before he's caught:
Eumenes had the day, in which both *Craterus* and *Neoptolemus* lost their Lives; but his own *Macedonian*
Souldiers were incensed against him, hearing of *Craterus*'s death ; which he also much resented.

§. 10. *Pithon,* Protector of King *Aridæus,* was
so interrupted by *Euridice,* the King's Wife, Daughter of *Amyntas, Philip*'s Elder Brother, and of *Cyna,
Alexander*'s Sister, (a Lady of a Masculine Spirit,
well understanding her place) that he gave over his
Office, which she thought to supply, having been
trained up in the Art of War, by *Cyna* a Warlike
Woman. The Souldiers disappoint her and *Pi-*

thon, who hoped to have been intreated by them to
hold, and chose *Antipater,* who in a few days, arrived at the Camp with his Army, and took it upon
him, as the only powerful Man then living, of all
Alexander's Captains, whom all acknowledge their
Superior. *Antipater* taketh the King, Queen and Princess into *Macedon,* leaving *Antigonus* General of the
Royal *Army,* against *Eumenes,* and Ruler of *Asia,*
during the War, and besides his former Provinces,
gave him the Rule of *Susiana.*

§. 11. *Antigonus,* Lieutenant of *Asia,* being to
subdue *Eumenes, Alcetus* and *Attalus,* began
with *Eumenes,* seeking to Corrupt his Army by
Letters, but failed therein by *Eumenes's* cunning,
who made shew as if he writ them to try their faith
to him: Then *Antigonus* dealt with the Captains,
of which one brake out untimely; and another, called
Apollonides, held close 'till the Battle, and then turned to *Antigonus,* with such of the Horse-men as he
could persuade, being their General ; but *Eumenes*
overtook him, and cut him off, though he lost the
Battle. *Eumenes* not able to keep the Field, wished
his Men to shift for themselves, and retained only five
hundred Horse and two hundred Foot, with which
he tired *Antigonus* in following. At last he entred
Nora, a strong and well provided Fort, bordering
on *Cappadocia,* where they parted without
agreeing ; so *Antigonus* leaveth *Nora* besieged,
and with his other Forces, entred *Pisidia,* and overthrew *Alcetus.*

§. 12. *Ptolomy,* while other Princes were quiet in
their Government, sent an Army and won *Syria,* and
Phænicia, and took *Laomedon* the Governour thereof Prisoner. *Antipater* being Eighty Years Old, re-
posing great Confidence in *Polyspercon,* one of *Alexanders* most Ancient Captains, committed to him the
Protectorship and Government of *Macedon,* doubting his Son *Cassander's* sufficiency ; he also gave
charge

charge that no Woman should be admitted into the Administration of the Empire, and so dyed.

§. 13. *Polyspercon*'s skill was greater in War, than in the high Office he now undertook; being a man of an Inferior Wit, fitter to assist than command in Chief. The better to Countenance his Injunctions to the Governours of Provinces, he and his Council thought fit to call the Queen of *Olympias* to Court, whom *Antipater* suffered not in *Macedon*. But *Cassander*, Son of *Antipater*, (who thought himself the better Man) was not satisfyed with the Captainship of a Thousand; his Ambition soared high, when he considered the Love of those which commanded the Garrisons, and all the Rulers in the Cities so of *Greece*, so placed by his Father. Besides, he had that Interest in Queen *Euridice*, that was due only to her Husband, all which would not serve to bear out an open Rebellion. *Cassander* therefore finding what *Ptolomy* had done in *Syria*, and what *Antigonus* aimed at since *Antipater*'s death (for whose sake he presumed upon them) and seeing their occasions needed a Civil War, he went to *Antigonus* in *Asia*, and writ to *Ptolomy*.

§. 14. *Polyspercon*, upon *Cassander*'s departure, to disappoint him of his hopes from *Greece*, decreed in Council, to restore the popular Government in their Cities, and discharge the Garrisons, and Banish or kill the Governours placed by *Antipater*. Thus he dishonours the Man that raised him; overthrew worthy Men, placed as Friends to the State of *Macedon*; and gives away *Macedon*'s Command of *Greece*, if he means as he pretends, &c.

§. 15. *Athens* by this Decree, in all haste, cast out their Governours, *Phocion* and others, who fly for their Lives; but cannot remove the Garrison, commanded by *Nicanor*, a trusty Friend to *Cassander*. He possessing one of the Havens, found means to take the other, called *Paræus*, to their great dis-

courage-

couragement; but by *Alexander* the Son of *Polyspercon*, coming with an Army, are wholly misled, as if he came to aid them, whereas he came to get what *Nicanor* held, if he could perswade him thereto. *Phocion* and his Fellows fly to *Polyspercon* for Patronage, but he finding he could not get the Key of *Athens*, as he sought, without offending the other Towns of *Greece*; to cover his intent, as meaning well to *Athens*, he sent *Phocion* back into *Athens*, who wickedly put him to death, being above Eighty Years old; who had been chosen forty five times Governour, without seeking it; whose Integrity was approved, whose Counsel the City never repented, nor private Man for trusting him: *Philip* and *Alexander* honoured him; but could fasten no Gifts upon him: *Athens* never after bred a worthy Man.

§. 16. *Cassander* with such Forces as *Antigonus* lent him, entred *Pireus*, which drew *Polyspercon* headlong into *Attica* with an Army, but for want of Victuals departed, leaving *Alexander* with some Forces to hinder *Nicanor*, 'till he in *Peloponesus* attempted *Megalopolis*, which affected *Cassander*. But the Town furnished with Fifteen thousand able Men, was so defended, and his Elephants so galled in their Feet with Nails driven through Boards laid, and lightly covered in the Way, that he prevailed not; and wanting Provision to stay long, he forsook the Siege. After this, his Admiral *Clitus* after an Overthrow given to *Nicanor* in *Propontis*, is in the second Encounter (*Antigonus* having furnished *Nicanor*) utterly defeated, which made *Athens* submit to *Cassander*, as did other Cities.

§. 17. *Antigonus* lying before the Fort *Nora*, when he heard of *Antipater*'s death; knowing *Eumenes*'s sufficiency, and fidelity to *Perdicas*, thought no Man fitter to be employed in his designs. He sent therefore a Friend to them both, to deal with him to take an Oath of Fidelity to *Antigonus*, which he refused,

refufed, except *Olympias* and the Children of *Alexander* were put in, which was yielded to; fo he departed. *Antigonus* had before this taken on him
(as Lieutenant of *Afia*) to remove Governours of
Provinces, as *Aridæus* of *Phrygia*, and *Clitus* of *Lydia*,
which repaired to the Court for Relief, but all failed in *Clitus*'s overthrow at Sea.

§. 18. *Antigonus* now commanding the moft of the
Leffer *Afia*, was able to enter *Macedon*, and
feize the Court, but doubted the Reconciliation of
Caffander and *Polyfpercon* thereby; he alfo knew *Eumenes*'s fidelity to the Royal Blood. Againft him
therefore he bent with Twenty thoufand Foot and
Four thoufand Horfe, hoping to furprize him in *Cilicia*.
Eumenes a *Thracian*, of all the old Souldiers, was only
faithful to the Royal Blood; the Court therefore
gave him Commiffion to raife an Army againft
Antigonus, requiring the Provincials to affift, and
the old Silver-fhield-bands to follow him.

§. 19. *Olympias*, the Old Queen, intending to remove *Aridæus*, and place *Alexander*, Son of *Roxane*,
joining with *Polyfpercon*, enters *Macedon*, taketh *Euridice* and *Aridæus*, forfaken of all that followed her
at the fight of *Olympias*; both are Murdered, and
a hundred of *Caffander*'s Friends, with *Nicanor* his
Brother.

§. 20. *Caffander* lying at the Siege of *Tegea* in *Peloponefus*, hearing thefe ill Tidings, compounded with
Tegea and fhipt his Army into *Theffaly*; the *Ætolians* keeping the Streights of *Thermopylæ* by Land, in
favour of the Queen. *Caffander* leaveth *Callas* with
part of his Forces to divert *Polyfpercon*, carrying the
reft to Befiege *Pidna*, a ftrong Sea-Town, where
Olympias lay with the Court. *Æacides*, King of
Epyrus, her Coufin, hafted to her Succour, but upon
Difficulties of paffages, held by *Caffander*'s Men, his
Subjects refufe to proceed, and upon his feeking to
inforce them, banifh him and join with *Caffander*.

Polyfper-

Polyspercon. now is the Queen's only hope, which also failed; for by *Callas*'s means, corrupting of the Souldiers, he was glad to make a swift Retreat for want of Men. The Miseries of the Besieged by Famin and Mortality was so great, that she is forced to yield to *Caffander*, upon promise of Life; and procured *Aristonus*, to whom she had committed *Amphypolis*, to yield up the Town, which he did, and was killed by private Enemies procured to it by *Caffander*. *Olympias* is then called into publick question in an Assembly of the *Macedonians*, and condemned for the Murders committed by her under Title of Justice, and shortly after put to death. *Caffander* after his death, Celebrated Funerals for *Aridæus* and *Euridice*; Married *Theffalonica*, Daughter of King *Philip*, taken in *Pidna*; built the City *Caffandria*; committed *Roxane* and *Alexander* to close Prison; Re-edified *Thebes*, and restored it, &c.

C H A P. IV.

Of Antigonus's *growth in* Asia.

§. 1. E *Umenes*, with the *Argyraspides* or Silver-Bands, took his March towards the East, with his Commission to take Possession of those Countries, having small Assurance of his Silver Shields, whose Captains scorned his direction: Yet *Ptolomy* and *Antigonus* could not withdraw them. *Python* and *Seleuchus*, who govern'd *Medea* and *Babylon*, as he went, refused to let him pass, 'till they were forc'd to fly; so he came to the East, where *Peucestes* and other Lords receive him; yet
through

through Opinion of Self-worthiness, contended for Superiority; but by his Wisdom and Command of the Kings Treasure, he gained many of the most powerful.

§. 2. *Antigonus* followed, taking *Python* and *Seleucus* with him, to force the Enemies further off from the King's Treasure in *Susa*; but passing over *Coprates* by small Vessels, when the greater part was over, *Eumenes*, who kept a Bridge on *Tygris*, came with a Thousand Horse, and four Thousand Foot, and finding them disordered, forced most of 'em into the River, and drowned them, and slew the rest, except four Thousand which yielded in the sight of *Antigonus*, who with *Python* turned to *Media*, leaving *Seleuchus* to Besiege *Susa* Castle.

§. 3. *Eumenes* desired to lead the Army into the Province left by *Antigonus*; but *Peucestes*, Governour of *Persia*, drew them thither, using all means to win the Souldiers, which *Eumenes* prevented by a feign'd Letter from *Orontes*, Governour of *Armenia*, reporting *Olympias* had slain *Cassander*, and sent *Polysperçon* with a great Army to join with *Eumenes*; which News bred much fruitless joy. *Antigonus* brings his Army out of *Media*, to all their amazements; yet *Eumenes* then sick in an Horse-Litter, set his in a good form of Battle; and though he were inferiour to *Antigonus* by a third part, except Elephants, he held it out, and *Antigonus* was glad the next Night, to steal away into *Media*.

§. 4. *Antigonus*, in the dead of Winter, being within Nine Days Journey of his Enemy, passed through a difficult Wilderness, forbidding all use of Fire by Night, to prevent his being discovered, which was observed for some time, but broken at last, and so discerned. *Peucestes* and the rest, as Men amazed, fly; *Eumenes* stays them, promising to protract *Antigonus*, 'till their Forces be drawn up. Then taking some choise Captains, he disposed them on Tops of Hills, looking

ing towards *Antigonus,* keeping many Fires thereon. *Antigonus* thinking he was discovered, and fearing to be forced while his Men were tired, turned aside to places convenient for Refreshment; but upon Advice, finding that he was deluded, he sent, thinking to be revenged on them who were gone. All the Eastern Army was come, except the Elephants, which he sent to cut off, forcing the Horse-men which came with them, and had overthrown the Elephants, if brave Troops sent by *Eumenes* to look after them, had not come in unexpectedly.

§. 5. *Eumenes* having obtain'd the honour of an Expert General, got therewith the hatred of *Peucestes* and the other Commanders, which conspire his death; but conclude to spare him 'till after the Battle with *Antigonus*; which argued their Malice against his meer Virtue. *Eudamus,* who had charge of the Elephants, whom he had obliged, and others of whom he used to borrow Money when he needed not, to make them the more careful of his Life, certifyed him of the Treason. Hereupon he made his Will, and burnt his Writings of Secrets, and considered what he should do. To make his Peace with *Antigonus,* were contrary to his Faith given to *Olympias,* and the Princes, *&c.* He therefore resolved to withstand the Enemy, and after to look to himself, *&c.*

§. 6. *Eumenes*'s Souldiers not knowing the cause of his Perplexity, encouraged him, only desiring him to draw 'em up in Battalia, and they would play the Men. *Antigonus* had the advantage in Horse, but his Footmen advanced heavily, being to encounter the old Silver Shields, who had beaten them so oft, as now also they slew five thousand of them without the loss of a Man. *Antigonus*'s Horse and Elephants had the better; the rather by *Peucestes,* who drew off one thousand five hundred Horse, and departed. But while all the charge lay on *Eumenes, Antigonus*
sent

fent Companies of Horfe about unto *Eumenes*'s Carriages, unfeen by reafon of the Duft, and furprized them; for the Night growing on, they return'd to their Camps.

§. 7. *Eumenes* finding the Silver Shields difcontented for the lofs of their Carriages, comforted them with hopes of Recovery, the Enemy being weakened by their Valour, and unable to draw the Carts through the Wildernefs of Mountains. This availed not, for *Peucefles* was gone, and other Captains would fight no more; *Teutamus*, one of the Silver-fhield Captains, to win the Love of the Bands, dealt fecretly with *Antigonus*, intreated the reftoring of the Booty, which was all the Old Souldiers had for many Years fervice. The crafty Man anfwered, that if they will deliver *Eumenes*, he will do more for them; which they prefently performed, and villanoufly betrayed their worthy General, whom his Ambitious Adverfary, defpairing to win, flew. This was the end of the Wifdom, Fidelity, Valour, and Patience of him whofe Courage no Adverfity could leffen, nor Profperity his Circumfpection: But his Virtue, Wit and Induftry, were all caft away, by leading an Army without power to command; befides, God's purpofe to caft down that Family he fought to uphold. *Antigonus* buried him honourably, burnt one of the Captains alive that betrayed him, and committed all the Silver Shields to a Leader, to carry them into far Countries, with charge to Conjure fuch perjured Wretches, never to come near *Greece*.

§. 8. *Antigonus* and *Python* return to *Media*, where while *Python* by Gifts fought to win the Souldiers, which he only wanted, to become chief; *Antigonus* difcerning it, took him in his fecurity, condemn'd and flew him. Goes into *Perfia*, *Peucefles* entertain'd him obfequioufly, but loft his place.

§. 9. *Antigonus* vifiting *Seleuchus* in *Babylon*, hath Kingly Entertainment, and *Sufa*'s Caftle with the

Perfian

Persian Treasure and Riches; yet calls for a further
Accompt. *Seleuchus* doubts the meaning of his Friend,
of whom he never deserved well, and so fled to *Ptolomy* in *Egypt*.

C H A P. V.

Civil Wars between Alexander's *Captains.*

§. 1. **A**Ntigonus's Riches and Power made him formidable, and caused *Ptolomy*, *Cassander*, and
Lysimachus to combine against him, notwithstanding his Embassadours, by whom he intreated the
continuance of their Amity. In their Answer they
require a share of the *Eastern* Treasure, increase of
Cassander and *Lysimachus*'s Dominions, and restoring
of *Seleuchus*. He roundly replyed, that he would
not share his Victories with them who afforded him no
succour, and injoy'd what they had thereby, being by
his Arms freed from *Polyspercon*.

§. 2. *Antigonus* prepareth for War, Guards the
Sea Coast to hinder *Cassander*, and invaded *Syria*,
setting Workmen on *Lybanus* to build a Navy, takes
Joppa and *Gaza*, and forces *Tyrus* by Famine to yield,
upon Condition, that *Ptolomy*'s Souldiers might depart with their Armies. *Ptolomy* kept close in his
Country, not being able to Incounter the other in the
Field; but sent a Fleet of One Hundred Sail with *Seleuchus* to strengthen *Cyprus*, by which also *Caria*, held
by another *Cassander*, took a Resolution to hold out.

§. 3. *Greece* was desired on both sides, as an aid of
much Importance, where *Antigonus* by his Treasures
gained the *Lacedemonians*, and others of *Peloponesus*. He
also sought to make *Cassander* odious for the Death
of *Olympias*, and Imprisoneth *Roxane* and her Son;
forcing *Thessalonica*, building *Cassandria*, and re-edi-
fying

fying *Thebes* in ſpite of *Philip* and *Alexander.* Upon
theſe Reaſons he required the Army to declare *Caſſander* a Traitor, except he reſtored *Roxane* and her
Son, and ſubmitted to the Lieutenant General (himſelf) and that all the Cities of *Greece* ſhould be ſet
free : His regard of the Royal Blood was not ſoon
to be abated, but 'twas the Liberty of *Greece*
which induced *Ptolomy* to decree the like. *Antigonus* to make ſure work, gave *Alexander*, Son of
Polyſpercon, Five Hundred Talents to make War in
Peloponeſus ; But he at the perſuaſion of one ſent
from *Caſſander*, kept the Treaſure, and had the
Lordſhip of *Peloponeſus* put into his hand, making a
League with *Ptolomy* and *Caſſander.* But this Honour he enjoy'd not long, being ſlain by the Treaſon
of the *Sycionians*, hoping thereby to become free, but
were ſubdued by *Cretiſipolis* his Wife, &c.

§. 4. *Antigonus* with his Five Hundred Talents
having bought an Enemy, ſtirred up the Factious
Ætolians; but *Caſſander* curbed them, and won from
them *Ptolomy*'s Fleet, Commanded by *Polyclitus*, who
upon *Alexander*'s defect from *Antigonus*, left *Peloponeſus*, and returned homewards ; hearing of the
Rhodian Fleet, led by *Theodatus*, Admiral to *Antigonus*, he cunningly ſurprized it, not one eſcaping.
This ill News brought *Antigonus* and *Ptolomy* to
meet about ſome compoſition, but to no effect.

§. 5. *Lyſimachus* Overthrew *Seuthes*, a King of
the wild *Thracians*, with the Cities which Rebelled,
and ſlew *Pauſanias*, and took his Army ſent by *Antigonus.* *Philip* alſo, Lieutenant of *Caſſander*, waſted
the *Ætolians*, and drove moſt out of their Country,
and ſlew *Æacides*, King of *Epirus*, lately Reſtored.
Antigonus in the mean time won *Caria* : ſent Armies
into *Peloponeſus*, and other parts of *Greece*, beſtowing
Liberty on whom he took ; and making ſhew to
come over into *Macedon*, forc't *Caſſander* to haſt
thereto, and to leave many places weakly Guarded,
which his Army freed.   §. 6.

§. 6. *Antigonus*'s Presence in lesser *Asia*, gave life
to his Affairs there and in *Greece* ; but *Ptolomy* took
advantage of his Absence in *Syria*, visited *Cyprus*,
recover'd it, and left a Lieutenant in it, and in return made Ravage in *Caria*, and *Cilicia*, and drew
Demetrius Policartes, Son of *Antigonus* to the rescue,
and departed to *Egypt* ; where, with *Seleuchus*, he raised a Royal Army for recovery of *Syria*. *Demetrius*
being return'd, and hearing of *Ptolomy*'s coming, is
advised to give way, and not to Encounter two such
Generals ; but he rejects the Council as a cold Temper of aged Men, and will needs stand them at *Ga-*
za, *Ptolomy* hath the odds, but wanted Elephants,
which he supplied with a Palisade sharpned to gall the
Beasts, and Overthrew *Demetrius*, who fled to *Azo-*
tus Thirty Miles off : Won *Gaza*, and the best part
of *Syria*.

§. 7. *Seleuchus Nicanor* now took leave of *Ptolomy*
with Eight Hundred Foot, and Two Hundred Horse,
too small a Garrison to keep, much less to win one
of those great Cities in the East ; but Men enough
to enter where the Hearts of the Inhabitants are already gain'd. *Seleuchus*'s Name, whose Government
the *Babylonians* had found so good, was sufficient to
them to put all the resistance upon *Antigonus*. Men,
wishing them ill to speed. The defection grew so general, that the *Antigonians* durst stay in no strong
Town ; only they held a Castle full of Hostages, and
Prisoners which *Seleuchus* took, and so the Possession
of *Mesopotamia*, and *Babel*. *Nicanor* left in *Media*
by *Antigonus* with an Army, came with Ten Thousand Foot, and Seven Thousand Horse. *Seleuchus*
having but Four Hundred Horse, and above Three
Thousand Foot, drew them into a Marsh near
Tygris, which *Nicanor* thinking to be a flight, grew
less careful to Fortifie his Camp, and so was surprized the first Night, and lost all, with *Susiana* and
Media. Now began the Æra, or Date, of the *Greeks*;
used

uſed by the *Jews, Chaldeans* and *Syrians,* whoſe firſt Compleat Year at *Babylon,* was accounted from the end of the 438th of *Nabonaſſer,* ſaith *Gauricus.*

§. 8. *Ptolomy* having taken *Gaza,* ſent *Demetrius* all his Goods,Pages and Servants freely, with a cour-teous Meſſage, that their War was upon Terms of Honour, not Perſonal hatred. This inflam'd *Deme-trius's* earneſt deſire of Requital,which made him ga-ther all the Force he could, and ſend to his Father for ſupply ; againſt which, *Ptolomy* ſent *Cilles* with part of his Army, which was ſuddenly Surpriz'd by *Demetrius,* through *Cilles's* careleſs Marching, as a-gainſt a beaten remnant. Thus *Demetrius* repaired his Honour, and requited his Enemy, by reſtoring *Cilles,* and many other Friends with rich Preſents. *Antigonus* haſteth into *Syria* to embrace his Son, and perfect the recovering of it upon his Son's Foundati-on ; but *Ptolomy* now at leiſure returns to *Egypt,* Diſ-mantling the Principal Cities as he went ; thus all fell to *Antigonus* preſently : So eaſily did the Provin-ces accept ſtrange Lords, as Sheep and Oxen change Maſters, having no Title to their own Heads. Theſe People of *Syria, Egypt, Babylon, Aſſyria, Perſia,* were of no ſuch manly Temper, as at this time the States of *Greece* were, who took all occaſion to recover Li-berty, which theſe little eſteemed : So that the *Per-ſian* Nobles never ſtrove to recover Liberty after *A-lexander's* Death , but tamely ſubmitted to the Captains and Officers of the Army. The Reaſon hereof *Machivel* gives from the Form of Go-vernment : For where the Subjects are kept as Slaves, as in *Turkey,* a Conqueſt is eaſily obtained : But where Ancient Nobility are in due eſteem, it is hard to get all, and harder to keep, as in *France.* In the *Per-ſian* Empire all the Princes depended upon the meer Favour of the King, ſo that even his Brethren are his Slaves, as are all the *Baſſaes* in *Turkey.* Adding here-to want of Convenient Liberty in the People, who

U like

like *Esops* Afs, think Enemies cannot load him more heavily than his Mafter, and if they find the Conquerours Yoke more eafy, they will not haftily fhake it off ; as the *Gafcoigns* under the Government of *England*, heartily affected our Kings.

Antigonus fent Forces into *Arabia*, which at a Mart, furpriz'd the *Nabotheans* ; but in their return with the Body, were all flain, except Fifty Horfe out of Six Hundred, and not a Footman of Four Thoufand efcaped. *Demetrius* fent to revenge it, but was glad to make Peace ; and returned, and then was fent againft *Seleucus* with Fifteen Thoufand Foot, and Three Thoufand Horfe, but did nothing but Ravage about *Babylon*, *Seleucus* being in *Media* : Neither durft *Antigonus* carry the War beyond *Euphrates*, left *Syria* and *Afia* the lefs fhould be loft, having ill-affected Neighbours.

§. 9. Thefe Ambitious Heads, upon a flow advancement of their hopes grew dull and willing to breath, till occafion might better ferve, and agreed for the prefent, Firft, That each fhould retain what he had in prefent poffeffion. Secondly, That *Alexander*'s Son by *Roxane*, coming to Age, fhould be made King. Thirdly, All *Greece* to be fet free. The Second Article moft concerned *Caffander*, who was fure by it to lofe all, whatever fhift the other made, who meant not to lofe by it : But he by Murdering *Roxane*, and her Son, to make himfelf an odious Security, did thereby free them alfo from all accompt to any Superiour Lord. *Antigonus* pretended the Liberty of *Greece* ; but *Ptolomy* to provoke the *Greeks* to ftir in it, fent a Fleet along the Coaft of *Afia* to moleft *Antigonus*, and feeing them not much concern'd at it, he entred *Peloponefus* to embolden them to take Courage. But long Servitude had well ne're extinguifhed the Ancient Valour of the Nation, and their many former unfortunate Attempts, had fo fpent their Spirits, as that they fate ftill, expecting it fhould fall in their Mouths :

mouths; yet *Cratisipolis* yielded *Sicyon* and *Corinth* into his hand. When he saw the *Greeks* witheld the promised supply of Mony and Victuals, he renewed his former Friendship with *Caffander*. Now *Polyspercon* had in his hands another Son of *Alexander's*, by *Barsine* a *Persian*, called *Hercules*, whom he design'd to bring into *Macedon*, against whom *Caffander* prepared an Army, which yet he could not trust against the only Child of *Alexander*, and therefore attempted the treacherous old Villain, who for the Lordship of *Peloponesus* murdered his Pupil. *Antigonus* in the mean time slept not, but was working upon a business which would give a specious Title to the Empire; this was by matching with *Cleopatra* the Sister of *Alexander*, then lying in *Sardis*; But *Ptolomy* for all his many Wives, which was his Dotage, had prevented him in her Affection, which had induc'd her to take a journey into *Ægypt*, but the mischievous practice with the Governour prevented it by her secret Murther. Thus was the whole Race of *Philip* and of *Antigonus Alexander* extinguished by the justice of God for the Cruelty of those bloody Princes; and the ambitious Designs of those Tyrants founded in innocent Blood, were soon after cast down, overwhelming themselves and their Children in the Ruins thereof.

§. 10. Royalty is now extinguished by *Antigonus's* last infamous Murder, which he thought to over-shadow with the Glory of the freedom of *Greece*; for effecting whereof, he sent *Demetrius* with a strong Army of Two Hundred and Fifty Sail, and Five Thousand Talents, with Charge to begin at *Athens*, which he did; as also to *Megera*, for which the *Athenians*, who had forgot to employ their Hands, adulterate the Eloquence of their Tongues to base Flattery; decree the Titles of Kings and Gods, the the Saviours of *Athens* to *Antigonus* and *Demetrius*; chose a Priest, and cause the Ambassadors, to be sent to them as to *Jupiter*, *Theori*, or Confulters with the Gods.

§. 12. *Antigonus* calls his own Garifon from *Imbros*, and fet it free, and called *Demetrius* to *Cyprus*, kept by *Menelaus*, Brother of *Ptolomy*, whom he worfted, and forced him to *Salamis*, to whofe relief *Ptolomy* hafted with One Hundred and Forty Gallies, and Two Hundred Ships, with an Army; *Demetrius* Encounters them with One Hundred and Eighteen, but better furnifhed, with which he overthrew and put *Ptolomy* to flight with Eight only; fo *Cyprus* was yielded. After this, *Antigonus* and *Demetrius* made themfelves Kings, as did *Ptolomy*, *Lyfimachus*, and *Seleucus*.

CHAP. VI.

The Wars between the New Kings, 'till all were confumed.

§. 1. **A**Ntigonus hoping to fwallow up all thefe New Kings, chofe to begin with *Ptolomy*, the ftrongeft, againft whom he prepared Eighteen Thoufand Foot, and Eight Thoufand Horfe, with Eighty Three Elephants, all which he led in Perfon, and a Navy of One Hundred and Fifty Gallies, and One Hundred Ships under *Demetrius*. He departed from *Antigonia* in *Syria*, Built by himfelf; and paffing the Defart with no fmall danger, at Mount *Caffius* by *Nilus*, he faw his Navy in diftrefs, fore beaten, and many loft and driven back to *Gaza*. Being come to *Nilus*, he found all Paffages fo fortified, as by no means, though with great lofs he could force them; befides the falling away of his Souldiers, which pafs'd over to *Ptolomy*; fo that had he not refolved to return, *Ptolomy* had driven him out of

Ægypt

Ægypt with small Attendance. To save his Credit, all these misfortunes were laid on his Councel.

§. 2. *Antigonus* for the future, will follow his Affairs after another manner, by cutting the Branches, before he hew down the Tree; he will begin with the Dependents of his Enemies, whom the Confederates must either forsake, or come into the Field for their relief, where Military Power and the advantage of Provisions promised him Victory. The City of *Rhodes* had stood Neuter, and was grown Rich by Trade, and kept a good Fleet by Sea, but in this troublesome time their Affection was to *Ægypt*, this *Antigonus* made an Argument of his Quarrel, which he began with some petty Injuries, 'till he prepared for an Enterprize upon them, which he committed to *Demetrius* ; who so terrified the Citizens, that they offered him their assistance against all Persons. *Demetrius* knowing this offer proceeded not from Love, required a Hundred Hostages, and command of their Haven, with Conditions fitter for a Conquered State, than an assisting Neighbour, this restored the *Rhodians* to their lost Courage, who resolve to defend their Liberty to the last Man; to which end they Enfranchize their able *Bondmen*, wisely making them Free-Fellows, rather than themselves would become their Fellow-Slaves. Thus they endured a whole Years assaults, besides Famine, wherein *Ptolomy* with hazard relieved them oft ; but by the *Greeks* Ambassador's intreating Aid against *Cassander*, he is persuaded to give over, and took an Hundred private Hostages. The *Rhodians* presently erect Statues for *Lysimachus*, and *Cassander*, and make a God of *Ptolomy*.

§. 3. *Demetrius* chaseth *Cassander* beyond the Straits of *Thermopilæ*, and recover'd all that *Cassander* held there; the like he did in *Peloponesus*, setting all Free, and translateth *Sicyon* to another place, and called it *Demetrius*. Then he was proclaimed General of all *Greece*, and *Athens* decreed all his

Com-

Commandments ſhould be held Sacred, and juſt, with
God and Men. *Caſſander's* Caſe now oblig'd him to ſeek
Peace for *Macedon*, but *Antigonus* will have abſolute
ſubmiſſion, which made *Caſſander* ſollicit the Confederates, *Lyſimachus*, *Ptolomy*, and *Seleucus*, who ap-
prehending the common danger, agree to joyn Forces againſt a common Enemy. *Lyſimachus* with part
of *Caſſander's* Forces begins and paſſeth the *Helleſpont*,
makes hot War in *Aſia*, which *Antigonus* haſteth to
oppoſe, but cannot force *Lyſimachus* home, who
ſtayed for *Seleucus's* coming, and made him ſend for
Demetrius, &c.

§. 4. *Seleucus* is come, and joyned with *Ptolomy's*
Forces and *Lyſimachus*, making Sixty four Thou-
ſand Foot, Ten Thouſand Five Hundred Horſe,
Four Hundred Elephants, and One Hundred armed
Carts. *Antigonus* had Seventy Thouſand Foot, Ten
Thouſand Horſe, and Seventy Five Elephants; they
met at *Ipſus* near *Epheſus*, where the only memorable Thing was, that *Demetrius* encountred young
Antiochus, Son of *Seleucus*, and ſo purſued him in
flight, that *Seleucus* interpoſeth his Elephants between
Demetrius and *Antigonus's* Phalanx, and with his
Troops of Horſe ſo forced it, that many ſoon
revolted, and left him to death. Thus Princes
commonly ſucceed, who are more fear'd by their E-
nemies, than lov'd by Friends.

§. 5. *Demetrius* finding all loſt, made a ſpeedy
retreat to *Epheſus*, with Four Thouſand Horſe, and
Five Thouſand Foot, thinking long to be at *Athens*,
the Worſhippers of his Godhead, not knowing they
had repealed his Deity, 'till he met their Meſſengers,
not as *Theories*, to Conſult at their Oracle, but as Officers to prohibit his entring their City; which
ſhameleſs Ingratitude more afflicted him than all the
reſt; yet he ſpake them fair, 'till he recovered his
Ships out of their Haven. In the mean time the
Confederate are dividing his Father's Provinces, of
which

which *Seleucus* ſeiſed on *Syria*, and part of *Aſia* the leſs, whereat the reſt repined, and conſulted to op-poſe his Greatneſs in time, whereof he was not igno-rant, knowing the Law of State ought not to permit the over-growing of Neighbours. Therefore to ſerve his turn of *Demetrius* againſt *Lyſimachus*, he Married his Daughter *Stratonica*; but to ſave the life of his Son *Antiochus*, who was paſſionately in love with her, he gave her to him. The like Alliance was between *Ptolomy* and *Lyſimachus*, *Demetrius* and *Caſſander*, *De-metrius* and *Ptolomy*, yet not bound to each other, but for the preſent, as it hath been with Chriſtian Kings, whom neither Bed nor Book can make faithful in their Covenants. Yet *Demetrius* had this advantage by *Seleucus*'s Affinity, that he got *Cilicia* from *Pliſtar-chus* Brother to *Caſſander*, who yet was pacified by *Phila* their Siſter, Wife to *Demetrius*, who alſo about that time married *Ptolomy*'s Daughter; yet *Seleucus* had rather have *Demetrius* further off, having a mind to *Cilicia* (as *Ptolomy* had to *Cyprus*) and offered rea-dy mony for it, but in vain, for *Demetrius* had already found there Twelve Thouſand Talents of his Fathers.

§. 6. *Demetrius* with Three Hundred good Ships entreth *Attica*, beſiegeth the City of *Athens*, which *Ptolomy* ſought to relieve, but could not; ſo by ex-tream Famine it was yielded, but was ſpared notwith-ſtanding all their unthankfulneſs; yet he put a Garri-ſon in it to keep them honeſt by force. Then he went to *Peloponeſus*, againſt *Lacedemon*, but was haſtily cal-led away into *Aſia*, where *Lyſimachus* had won many Towns from him, and *Ptolomy* beſieged *Salamis* in *Cyprus*, where his Mother and Children remained. Yet hearing of *Caſſander*'s death, and that his Sons *An-tipater* and *Alexander* fought for the Kingdom, and that *Antipater* had furiouſly ſlain their Mother *Theſſalo-nica* for affecting his Brother, he choſe rather to go to aſſiſt *Alexander*, who deſired aid of him, and *Pyr-rhus* King of *Epirus*.

U 4 §. 7.

§. 7. *Pyrrhus* Son of *Æacides* an Infant, at his Father's death, was conveyed unto *Glaucias* King of *Illyria*, who at Twelve Years old set him in his Kingdom; out of which six years after he was forced, and went to serve *Demetrius*, who married his Sister, and after the Overthrow at *Ipsus*, became Hostage to *Ptolomy*, upon his reconciliation with *Demetrius*. In *Ægypt* he got the favour of *Berenice*, *Ptolomy*'s principal Wife, and Married her Daughter, and was restored to *Epirus*. He being requested of *Alexander* to aid him against *Antipater*, for reward took *Ambracia* by force, *Acarnania*, and much more, leaving the united Brethren to divide the rest. *Demetrius* also being come after all was done, is discontented, and pretending *Alexander* had plotted his death, slew him at a Feast, and seized on his part of the Kingdom. At which *Antipater*, who had Married *Lysimachus*'s Daughter, was so inraged, that his Father-in-Law to quiet him took away his troublesome life. Thus the House which *Cassander* had raised with so much Treachery and Royal-Blood, fell on his own Grave before theEarth was throughly setled. *Demetrius* after this access of Dominion, grew to such dissoluteness in Wine, Women, and Idleness, that he would not endure the trouble of Petitions, and doing justice, so that the People grew weary of his idleness, and the Souldiers of his vanity. Having lost all he had in *Asia* and *Cyprus*, but his Mother and Children, which *Ptolomy* honourably sent him home, he went against *Thebes*, and won it twice; then he went against *Pyrrhus* with two great Armies, of which one led by *Pentauchus* was overthrown, and he beaten by *Pyrrhus*, upon Challenge hand to hand; which loss offended not the *Macedonians* so much as the young Princes behaviour pleased them, seeming to see a lively figure of *Alexander* in his best qualities. This esteem of *Pyrrhus* was

increased

increased by the dislike which he had of *Demetrius*, for his Insolency, and Cruelty to his Souldiers, of whom he said, *The more of them died, the fewer he had to pay.* In the end he grew sensible of their general hatred, which to prevent, he intended a War in *Asia* with a Royal Army of almost One Hundred Thousand Foot, and Twelve Thousand Horse, and a Navy of Five Hundred Sail, of which many exceeded all former greatness. *Seleucus* and *Ptolomy* doubting the issue, are earnest with *Lysimachus* and *Pyrrhus* to joyn against him, who accordingly invade *Macedon*, *Lysimachus* entring that part next him; and when *Demetrius* went against him, *Pyrrhus* broke in on his side, and took *Berrhœa*, which News put all the Camp in a consternation, few forbearing seditious Speeches, and many desiring to return home. But he perceiving their design to go to *Lysimachus* their Countryman, led them against *Pyrrhus* a Stranger, thinking so to pacify them, wherein he was deceived. For though they were as hasty as he to meet with *Pyrrhus*, yet was it not to fight with him, but to submit to him; insomuch that many ran over to his Camp, and persuaded him to shew himself to the *Macedonians*, who would Salute him King. To try this, he rode forth in view of the Camp bare-headed, but was persuaded to put on his Helmet, whereon he wore two Goats Horns, by which he was known; whereupon all throng'd about him, some wishing *Demetrius* to be gone, who in disguise stole away. So *Pyrrhus* entred *Macedon* with Triumph, where *Lysimachus* met him, and shared the Kingdom with him, each hoping upon better opportunity to work his Fellow out of all.

· §. 8 *Demetrius* had left *Antigonus* his Son in *Greece*, with a great part of his Forces: with these he Besieged *Athens*, but was pacified by *Crates* the Philosopher, and so went into *Asia* with Eleven Thou-

sand

sand Souldiers to attempt *Lydia* and *Caria*, held by
Lysimachus, where he was successful till *Agathocles*,
Son of *Lysimachus*, forced him to seek a Kingdom in
higher *Asia*, and yet left him not so, but pursued
him over *Lycus*, where he lost so many, that he was
forced to flye with the rest into *Cilicia*, from whence
he writ Mournful Letters to *Seleucus*, who durst not
trust him, till after some inconsiderable Victories, he is
left with a few Friends, who persuaded him to yield
to *Seleucus*, by whom he is put into a foggy Island
under sure Guard, where he spent Three Years
merrily, and there Dyed.

§. 9. *Ptolomy* about the same time Died also, who
beside other Princely Virtues was mindful of his
word, which in those times was a rare Commendation. *Ptolomy Philadelphus*, who had Reigned with
him Two or Three Years, succeeded: *Ptolomy Ce-*
raunus offended, and fled to *Seleucus.* The *Macedo-*
nians after Seven Months revolt from *Pyrrhus* to *Lysi-*
machus, who Reigned alone Five Years, when the City
Lysimacha fell by an Earthquake, after which himself
having Poisoned *Agathocles* his Son, by instigation of
a Mother in Law, in a War with *Seleucus* in *Asia* was
slain. *Seleucus* surviving all *Alexanders* Hero's, as
Heir of all the Conquered World, passed over into
Maccedon, and took possession of *Europe*, where within Seven Months *Ptolomy Ceraunus* Treacherously
flew him, being Seventy Seven Years Old. *Pyrrhus*
the Epirot, was now become equal to any of those
Old Commanders in the Art of War, yea *Hanibal*
preferred him before them all. *Supra*, §. 7.

CHAP.

CHAP. VII.

Romes growth, and setling of the Eastern State.

§. 1. ROMES Greatness beginning now to
encounter *Greece*, it is convenient here
to make a compendious relation of her growth from
Tullus Hostilius, who having Reigned Thirty Two
Year was burnt, together with his House, by Lightning. *Ancus Martius* Grandchild to *Numa* succeeded, who Walled the City, and built a Bridge over
Tybris, and after Twenty Four Years dyed, leaving
his Children in Charge with *Incumon* a *Corinthian*,
his Favourite, who had fled from *Cypselus* King of
Corinth, and dwelt in *Tarquinii*, from whence he
was called *Tarquinius*. He Reigned Thirty Eight
Years, and was slain by *Ancus Martius*'s Sons; but
by the coming of *Tarquin*'s Wife, *Servius Tullus*,
her Daughters Husband, was made Governour for a
time, under pretence her Husband was Sick; in
which Government he continued by force Forty
Four Years, and then was slain. *Tarquinius Superbus*
is Proclaimed King by *Tullia* his Wife, Daughter to
Servius, who forced her Coach over her Father's dead
Corps. He took *Oriculum, Susa, Pometia*, and the *Gabii*;
but for the Rape of *Lucretia* by *Sextus Tarquinius* his
Brother, he and all his Family were expell'd by *Junius
Brutus*, and *Collatinus* her Husband; that manner of
Government was changed from a King to two yearly
Consuls, or Providers for the City, wherein these
two began. Their first War was with *Porsennus*
King of *Hetruria*, who came to *Rome* by force, to
restore *Tarquinius*; but was so long resisted by *Hora-
tius Cocles*, upon the Bridge, 'till being overpower'd
by Numbers, he was forc'd to leap into the River *Tibris*
with his Armour on, and so terrified by *Mutius Sca-
vola*'s resolution, burning his own hand for killing
the

the Secretary inftead of the King, that he entred into League with *Rome. Brutus* being flain in this War
was mourned for a whole year by the Ladies, as the
Champion of their Chaftity. *Mamilius Tufculanus,*
Son-in-Law to *Tarquinius,* with his *Latines,* renewed
the War ; againft whom, *Aulus Pofthumus* in a new
Office of *Diĉtator* was fent, who overthrew them.
After Sixteen Years of Confuls, upon a tumult of
the People, the Office of Tribunes was enaĉted, to
follow the Peoples Caufes as Solicitors. Then follow the Wars with the *Volfci* and *Æqui,* in which,
T. Martius got the Surname *Coriolanus,* for winning the City *Corioli* ; but was after Banifhed, for
raifing the rate of Corn too high. *Coriolanus* flyeth
to the *Volfci,* whom he incenfed, and was with *At-
tius Tullus* employed againft *Rome,* and fo far prevailed, that when neither force nor intreaty would
ferve, his Wife and Mother were fent, whofe for-
rowful deprecations prevailed. Not long after,
Three Hundred and Six *Fabii*'s undertaking the
War againft the *Veii* in *Hetruria,* were flain, and
left but one Infant of the whole Family ; of whom
(it is faid) came *Fabius Maximus.* In procefs of
time, the Confuls and other Magiftrates are abrogated, and Ten Men ordained, who Enaĉted Laws,
and Two Years after, are forced to refign to Confuls. After that, they fubdued the *Veients* and
Falifci yielded to *Camillus* in reverence to his Juftice upon the Schoolmafter of their Town, who
having decoy'd out many Principal Men's Children,
yielded them up to him for Hoftages, whom he
fent back bound, with his Scholars whipping him.
He alfo won the City of *Veij,* after Ten Years
Siege ; but upon unequal divifion of the Spoil, ungratefully they Banifhed him. While he lived at
Ardea, the *Gauls* invading *Hetruria,* as they roved
over the Country, being offended with the *Roman*
Ambaf-

Ambaffadors, went to *Rome*, which was abandoned before their coming; and, fet it on fire, and had taken the Capitol, defended by *M. Manlius*, but for the gagling of Geefe. After Seven Months Siege *Brennus* agreed to depart for One Thoufand Weight of Gold, which while they were weighing, *Camillus* with an Army came upon them, and forced them away. At this time they had Military Tribunes.

§. 2. *Rome* Three Hundred Sixty Five years after its Building, re-eftablifhed Confuls, Enacting that one fhould always be a *Plebean*, when fhe began War with the *Samnites*, dwelling between *Apulia*, and *Campania*, whom they invaded, and forced to fubmit to *Rome* for protection. This War continued Fifty Years, and drew the *Hetrurians* into it, in which time the *Latines* claimed freedom in *Rome*, which bred a quarrel, wherein the *Latines* were overthrown. The *Sabines* were after fubdued, and won *Tarentinus*, after which the *Apulians*, *Lucanians*, *Meffapians*, and *Brutians*, who drew the *Samnites* to rebell, fent for *Pyrrhus* out of *Epirus* to affift them.

§. 3. *Pyrrhus*, forfaken by the *Macedonians*, impatient of Peace, accepted the Conditions of thefe Confederates, hoping to enlarge his Empire toward the Weft, as *Alexander* had to the Eaft, and then to live Magnificently, as he anfwered his Counfellor *Cynea*, who replied, *He might do fo, if he could be content with his own.* *Pyrrhus* carrieth an Army of almoft Thirty Thoufand choice Souldiers to the *Tarentines*, who were nothing forward in provifion for War; which while he was employ'd about, *Levinus* the *Roman* Conful drew near, wafting the *Lucans*; fo that *Pyrrhus* was forc'd with his own and. fome weak affiftance of the *Tarentines*, to try the *Roman* Valour. But feeing them come on fo bravely, he he offered to arbitrate a Peace between them and the *Tarentines* ; but was answered, *They neither chose him their Judge, nor feared him their Enemy.* *Pyrrhus* upon view of their Camp, perceiving he had to deal with Men well-trained, set a strong *Corps du Guard* upon the passage of the River, which when he saw them force, he thought it time to bring on his whole Forces before all the Army was come over, and all little enough, while Spear and Sword were used. But when his Elephants came in, the *Roman* Horse quickly turned head, and the Foot at the sight and first impression of those strange Beasts fled with such consternation, that they left their Camp to the Enemy. Yet *Pyrrhus* by this trial finding the *Romans* could better endure many such Losses, than he such Victories, sent *Cyneas* to persuade an Agreement with the *Romans*, which they refused, as long as he was in *Italy*. This Answer inflam'd *Pyrrhus* with desire to enter into League with that gallant City, which refused to treat of Peace, except he first left *Italy*. They come therefore to a second Battel, which he obtain'd by his Elephants, but with such loss of the Flower of his Army, that he desired any occasion to be gone with Honour.

§. 4. *Pyrrhus* waiting an opportunity to leave *Italy*, hath two occasions offered ; and first from *Madecon*, where *Ptolomy Ceraunus* (who had murthered *Seleucus* his Protector) was slain by the *Gauls*, who came out of the Country with those who took *Rome*, and passing through many Countries, and making long abode in *Pannonia*, at length came to *Macedon*, under one *Belgius* ; after whom came *Brennus* another Captain, with One Hundred and Eighteen Thousand Foot, and Fifteen Thousand Horse, which *Sosthenes* with the *Macedonians* avoided, by shutting up the Cities. At the same time also the *Cicilians* sent to *Pyrrhus* for aid against the *Carthaginians*, which occasion

casion he took, and with Thirty Thousand Foot, and Two Thousand Five Hundred Horse entred *Sicily*, expell'd the *Carthaginians*, won *Erex* the strong City, and in *Syracusa* began to play the Tyrant. But being again called into *Italy* by the *Tarentines* against the *Romans*, he was beaten by the *Carthaginians* Gallies, and after that forced out of *Italy* to *Epirus*, by *M. Curius* the Roman.

§. 5. *Antigonus* Son of *Demetrius Poliorcetes*, with an Army, Navy, and Treasure came into *Macedon*, while *Brennus* with most of his *Gauls* was gone to plunder the Temple of *Delphos*, leaving Fifteen Thousand Foot, and Three Thousand Horse. These went to *Antigonus*, requiring him to buy his Peace; to whose Embassadors he shewed his Riches, Navy, Camp, and Camels. This being reported at their return, inflamed the *Gauls* to hasten thither; of whose coming *Antigonus* having intelligence, left his Camp, and put himself and all his Men into a Wood, so the *Gauls* finding him gone, hasted to the Seaside, supposing him fled. Part of *Antigonus*'s Army having recovered their Ships, espying the *Gauls* presumptuous disorder, taking their time, suddenly went on shoar, and set upon them with such Resolution, that after the slaughter of many, the rest yielded to *Antigonus*. This Success bred in the Barbarians a great reputation of *Antigonus*, but his own Men had no better opinion of him than of one who crept into Woods at sight of the Enemy.

This appeared shortly after, when *Pyrrhus* being returned to *Epirus* with a small Army of Eight Thousand Foot, and Five Hundred Horse, came to make Devastations in *Macedon*, in hope to force *Antigonus* to compound with him for his Peace. At his entrance Two Thousand of *Antigonus*'s Souldiers Revolted to him, and many Cities yielded, by which good beginning, he took Courage to attempt *Antigonus*

gonus and his Army for the Kingdom. *Antigonus* had no inclination to fight with him, but to weary him with protracting time ; but *Pyrrhus* so forced a Streight, in which he overtook him, that he slew most of the *Gauls, Antigonus* not taking any care to relieve them ; which the Captains of the Elephants fearing to be their own case, yielded. Then *Pyrrhus* went to the Phalanx, which could not be Charged but in Front, which was very dangerous ; but perceiving they had no desire to fight, he drew near to them in Person, persuading them to yield, which they presently did ; so *Antigonus* with a few Horse fled to *Thessalonica*, but is forced by *Ptolomy* Son of *Pyrrhus*, who pursued him, to fly to *Peloponesus*.

§. 6. *Pyrrhus* having gotten the Kingdom of *Macedon*, beaten *Antigonus* and the *Gauls*, he thought himself without match in any of the Kingdoms of *Alexander's* Conquests. He therefore raised an Army of Twenty Five Thousand Foot, Two Thousand Horse, and Twenty Four Elephants, as against *Antigonus* in *Peloponesus*, to free such Cities as he held there, but indeed to restore King *Cleonymus* to *Lacedemon*, but made shew of all Friendship to them. This dissimulation the *Lacedemonians* had used 'till none would trust them ; and yet now they were not hurt by *Pyrrhus's* use of it, by reason of his deferring the assaults, 'till they had fortified the Town, which was never done before. He assailed the Town three days together, and had won it the second day, but for a Fall his wounded Horse gave him, and the third day relief came unto them ; so that despairing to carry it, he was content to go to *Argos*, whither one Faction of the City called him, promising to render it, as the other Faction called *Antigonus* ; but both sides repented it when they were come, and desired their departure, which *Antigonus* assured them by

Hostages ;

Hostages; *Pyrrhus* promised, but design'd it not.; for by Night his Complices opened him a Gate at which his Army entred, 'till the Elephants came, which stop'd up the Gates, from whence grew the Alarum; the Citizens arm, and put the Souldiers in the dark to great confusion, they being ignorant of the Streets; yet *Pyrrhus* gain'd the Market-place. *Antigonus* came to their rescue, and *Pyrrhus* is slain by a Slate cast from an House, by a Woman, whose Son was fighting with him.

X   THE

THE

HISTORY

OF THE

WORLD.

BOOK V. Part I.

From the fetled Rule of *Alexander*'s Suc-
ceffors, 'till the *Romans* Conquer'd
Afia, and *Macedon*.

CHAP. I.

Of the Firft Punick *War.*

§. 1. **C**Arthage had ftood above Six Hundred
Years, when fhe contended with *Rome*
for *Sicily*; it furpafs'd *Rome* in *Antiquity.* One Hundred
and Fifty Years, as well as in Dominion, which extended from the Weft part of *Cyrene*, to *Hercules's-
Streights*, Fifteen Hundred Miles; wherein ftood
Three Hundred Cities. It commanded *Spain*, and
all the Iflands in the *Mediterranean*, South-Weft from

Sicily; it had Flourished about Seven Hundred and Thirty Years when *Scipio* took it; who carried off One Million Four Hundred and Ten Thousand Pounds, besides the Souldiers part. It was oft Rebuilt, and Invincible while it Commanded the Sea, which almost compass'd it; 'twas Twenty Miles in Circuit, and a treble Wall. Without the Walls, and between them, were Streets with Vaults for Three Hundred Elephants, and Stables for Four Thousand Horse, with room for Provender and Lodging for the Horse-Men, and Twenty Thousand Foot, which never troubled the City, as it is at this day in *China*. The Castle of *Beyrsa* in the South-side, was two Miles and a half in compass, with an *Arsenal*, under which the Ships and Gallies did Ride. The Form of the Common-Wealth was like that of *Sparta*, having Titular Kings, and Aristocratical Senators; but in latter times the People usurpt too much; which confusion in Government, with their too great trust to Mercenaries, together with Avarice and Cruelty, occasion'd their ruine. They exacted from their Vassals one half of the Fruits of the Earth, besides Tributes; made merciless Officers by exactions to augment the Treasure, and put to death, without Mercy, him who offended ignorantly, nay even their Captains upon ill Success, which made them often desperately to hazard all. The Year after *Tarquin's* expulsion, *Rome* sought a League with *Carthage*, agreed the *Romans* should Trade in no part of *Africk*; but no Haven in *Italy* to be shut against *Carthage*, &c. Their Care was to keep the *Romans* in continual War in *Italy*, that *Sicily* destitute of aid from thence, might more easily be brought under by them. This made them offer Succours to *Rome* against *Pyrrhus*, to prevent his interrupting their attempts in *Sicily*; at which time the League was renewed, especially against *Pyrrhus*, who then defeated the purposes of *Carthage* for that time. Some time before, a Troop of *Campanian*

panian Souldiers, who had ferved under *Agathocles*, and were entertained in *Meffana* as Friends, with perfidious Cruelty flew thofe that had trufted them, and poffeffed their Cities, Wives, Lands, and Goods, and called themfelves *Mamertines*, who afterwards molefted the Neighbours, but were oppofed by the *Syracufians*, and Befieged. But unable to hold out, and being divided, one fide refolves to give themfelves to *Carthage*, the other to *Rome*. The *Carthaginians* readily lay hold of the Offer, fend Forces, and had the Caftle furrendred. But the contrary Faction drawing that fide to agreement, expelled the Captain, for which he was Crucified at home as a Coward and Traytor. *Carthage* hereupon befieges *Meffana*, and the *Syracufians* joyn with them by Sea and Land; while *Appius Claudius* the *Roman* Conful, with an Army paffing the Streights of *Sicily* by Night, put himfelf into *Meffana*, fending to the *Carthaginians*, and *Hierom* King of *Syracufe*, requiring them to depart from their Confederacy; which Meffage being flighted, occafion'd the *Punick* War.

§. 2. *Rome*'s undertaking the defence of *Rhegium* with a Legion of Four Thoufand *Roman* Souldiers, whom they had requefted for their defence againft *Pyrrhus* and the *Carthaginians*, prov'd bafely treacherous; for thefe Confederating with the *Mamertines*, plunder the City, even as the *Mamertines* had formerly done at *Meffana*. The *Romans* upon Complaint hereof, fent Forces which vanquifhed them, and put all to death, reftoring *Rhegium* to its former Liberty, to the high commendation of their Juftice; but when the *Mamertines* came to be confider'd, tho' they had given example and aid to their Legion at *Rhegium*, yet Profit prevailed againft Juftice, which they ufed to pretend, and their care to hinder *Carthages* further footing in *Sicily*, perfuaded them to defer the punifhment of the Villains, whofe Fellows they had deftroyed.

ſtroyed. *Appius Claudius* being ſent unto them of *Meſ-ſana,* ſally'd out on that ſide *Hierom* kept, and worſted him, and the *Syracuſians,* who had fooliſhly joyned with *Carthage,* againſt whom they muſt have ſought aid at *Rome* if *Meſſana* had been won. *Hierom* knowing ſuch another Bargain would have made him Bankrupt, departed, and the next day the *Carthaginians* ſucceeded ſo ill, that they left Camp and Country to the *Romans,* who Confederated with this Neſt of Thieves and Murderers, with whom no League was juſt.

§. 3. *Sicily's* Dominion is now become the Prize for which *Rome* and *Carthage* contend; concerning which Iſland the general Opinion of Antiquity is, that it was a Demy Iſland adjoyning to *Italy,* near *Rhegium,* and ſeparated by Tempeſts, others ſay by Earthquakes, others by Tides. It excells all the Iſlands of the Midland Sea in bigneſs and fertility, and is formed like the Greek Δ *Delta,* or a Triangle. For Fertility *Cicero* calls it the Granary of the Commonwealth, and Nurſe of the vulgar ſort, furniſhing their greateſt Armies with Leather, Apparel, and Corn. About *Leordium* and other parts Wheat groweth of it ſelf. It had Six Colonies, and Sixty Cities; it bred *Archimedes,* the Mathematician, *Euclid* the Geometrician, *Empedocles* the Philoſopher, and *Diodorus* the Hiſtorian. It was Peopled by *Sicans* out of *Spain,* after the firſt Inhabitants which were Giants, and the *Sicans* were caſt out by the *Siculi* from *Italy,* driven out from the place in which *Rome* ſtands, by the *Pelaſgi;* from theſe *Siculi* it beareth the name. After them came the *Morgetes* out of *Italy,* who were expelled by the *Oxnotrians,* &c. The *Trojans* came after, and then the *Phenicians,* which built *Parormus,* or *Palmero.* The report of Giants which firſt Inhabited the Iſland, I could reject, did not *Moſes* make us know that ſuch were the firſt Planters of the Countries about *Iſrael;* and did not

not other Authors confirm it, as *Auguſtine, Tertullian, Procopius, Iſidore, Nicephorus, Pliny, Diodorus,* &c. Yea *Veſpuſius* in his ſecond Navigation into *America,* ſaw the like there. And I wonder at this the leſs, ſeeing the ſame is written of all Nations that is written of one, touching their ſimplicity of Life, mean Suſtenance, poor Cottages, Cloathing of Skins, Hunting, Arms, manner of Boats ; in all which, as we are altered from the firſt Simplicity, to extream Curioſity, and exceſs in Building, Diet, Apparel, ſo have we as monſtrous Perſons for Oppreſſion and all Vices; all which as Time bred and increaſed, ſo ſhall it overthrow all Fleſh at laſt.

The *Greeks* Plantation in *Sicily* was by *Theocles,* who being driven upon it by an Eaſt Wind, at his return reported to the *Athenians* the excellency of the place, and upon their neglect, perſuaded the *Chalcidians* that were needy and induſtrious, who ſent a Colony of *Eubæans,* which built *Naxus.* *Archias* with his *Corinthians* followed, and built a part of that which was after called *Syracuſe,* adding three other parts as they encreaſed; and poſſeſſing moſt of the Sea-Coaſt, forced the *Siguli* into the Mountains at *Trinacia.* The *Chalcidians* alſo got *Leontium, Catana,* and *Hybla,* which they called *Megara;* as the *Rhodians* and *Cretians* did *Gala,* and their Poſte-did built *Agrigentum.* The *Syracuſans* alſo built *Arxa, Caſemeria, Camerina, Enna,* &c. as the *Meſſaniaus* took *Zancle,* changing the Name.

Agrigentium from popular Government, was by *Phaleris* brought to *Tyranny,* who after Thirty One Years was ſtoned to death, and their liberty was recovered, 'till *Thoro* long after Uſurped *Gela,* forced *Naxos, Zancle,* and *Leontium,* and giving aid to the Magiſtrates of *Syracuſe* againſt the People, was choſen Prince in the Second Year of the Seventy Second Olympiad. He aiding *Thoro* his Father-in-Law, of *Agrigentum,* againſt *Terillus,* of *Himera,*

ſlew

flew One Hundred and Fifty Thousand, led by *A-milcar*, in defence of *Terillus*. The *Carthaginians* well beaten seek his Peace, which is granted, on Condition, no more to Sacrifice Children to *Saturn*, but to pay Two Thousand Talents, and Two Armed Ships, whereto they added a Crown of Gold worth One Hundred Talents of Gold; so much are some Natures improv'd by hardship. His Subjects loved him exceedingly, yea his Dog burnt himself, with his Body at his Funeral. *Hierom* his Brother succeeded, a Cruel Rude Covetous Man, but improv'd by *Simonides*, became a Studier of good Arts. His Brother *Thrasibulus* succeeded, who after Ten Months Tyranny, was forced by the Citizens to restore their Liberty, and was Banished; so *Syracuse* kept her Liberty almost Sixty Years; and was in some manner acknowledged of all the *Greek* Cities, by freeing them from *Ducetius* King of the *Sicilians*, except *Trinacia*. But *Leontium* being oppressed by *Syracuse*, sought aid from *Athens* the Sixth year of the *Peloponesian* War, which sent One Hundred Gallies, and other Forces, which invaded *Syracuse*, winning and losing, 'till both sides wearied agree, and *Leontium* is admitted into equal Fellowship, and the *Athenian* Captains sent home, whom their City banish for gaining nothing in *Sicily* as they expected. Shortly after fell out the most memorable War that ever *Greece* made; there *Athens* aided *Egesta*, oppressed by *Seleucus*, and *Leontium* and *Catana* wronged by *Syracusa*, whom the *Lacedemonians* succoured. *Alcibiades*, *Nicias*, and *Lamachus* are sent from *Athens*, but did little the first Summer, and *Alcibiades* is discharged, and new Supplies on both sides are sent the next Spring; but *Syracuse* is almost blocked up yet with *Lamachus*'s death, before the Succors from *Sparta* and *Corinth*, led by *Glippus* and *Pithon*, came.

But

But after their coming *Nicias* was broken, and forced to write for new Supplies; which were sent with *Euremedon* and *Demosthenes*, who the same day invaded the *Syracusians* with more haft than Success; having such loss, as they determined to return to succour *Athens* then in distress. *Nicias* on the contrary persuaded them to stay, upon intelligence the Town could not hold out long; but had not the Moon been Eclipsed, the suspicion whereof caused them to defer it, they had departed. But their Superstition cost them dear, even the utter loss of all in two Sea-Fights in the great Haven, and in their retreat by Land toward *Camerina*, in which Forty Thousand are overthrown, *Nicias* and *Demosthenes* taken, and miserably murder'd; for contrary to the Endeavours of *Glippus* and *Hermocrates* the *Syracusian* Commander, to save them, they were barbarously murdered by the cruel Multitude, &c. The *Egestanes* now fearing the *Syracusians*, apply themselves to *Carthage*, to whom they offer their City; and *Hannibal* with Thirty Thousand Men is sent, who in revenge of his Father's and Uncle's Death won and sack'd *Himera* and *Seleucus*, and buried Three Thousand *Himerans* where *Amilcar* was slain. *Hermocrates* after his good Service is by malice of his Enemies, Exiled by the ungrateful Multitude, being in *Greece*, who being returned, began to repair *Silenus*, but upon persuasion of his Friends in *Syracuse*, attempting to take a Gate, was slain.

Dionysius, Son-in-Law to *Hermocrates*, being made Prætor, and Commander of the *Syracusian* Armies, behav'd himself so well, that he got the good will of the People and Men of War; and began early, being but Twenty Five Years Old, that he might play the Tyrant long. He obtain'd his first Favour by accusing the Noblemen, whom the baser sort desire to reign over; then he got of them Six Hundred Men to guard his Person, as *Pisistratus* at *Athens* had done,

done, againſt the malice of his Enemies; and to gain
the Souldiers, he gave them double Pay, and procured the reſtoring of many Baniſhed Men, who thereby were made his own. Then he made himſelf abſolute Lord by poſſeſſion of the Citadel, in which
was great Proviſion, and under which the Gallies
Moored; what he deſign'd by this the Chief Citizens diſcerned it, though the People would not ſee.
Yet after a Foil given at *Gela* by the *Carthaginians*
(which the Men at Arms thought he was willing to)
they left him, and haſting to *Syracuſe*, in hope to free
the City of him, they forced his Palace, ranſaked his
Treaſure, and abuſed his Wife; all which he revenged, being at their heels, ſparing none that he ſuſpected. Then he grew ſo doubtful, being the
greateſt Robber that ever State had, that he truſted
not a Brother to enter his Chamber unſearched; yet
being at the War, the Citizens rebell at home, ſo
that with much difficulty he recovered the Citadel,
and ſo the Command of the City; and when the multitude were gathering in Harveſt he diſarmed the Citizens. Afterwards he went into the Field with
Eighty Thouſand Foot, and Three Thouſand Horſe,
and ſent his Brother *Leptines* with Two Hundred
Gallies to Sea, and Five Hundred Ships of Burthen,
which overthrew Fifty Ships of War, Five Thouſand
Souldiers, and many Ships of burthen brought by *Himilco* from *Carthage*, while many Cities alſo yielded
to *Dionyſius*, who yet loſt a great part of his Army
at *Egeſta*. *Himilco* finds half his Army with *Mago*
by Sea, which met again with *Leptines*, and ſlew
Twenty Thouſand, and took One Hundred Gallies,
which made *Dionyſius* haſten home, whom *Himilco*
follows with ſpeed, beſieging him by Sea and
Land; but the Plague having taken away One Hundred Thouſand of his Men, and other numbers ſlain
by the City with the *Lacedemonian* aid, he craved
Peace, which the other ſold for a great Summ, and
on

on Condition to leave such as were not *Carthagini-*
ans ; but when he was out at Sea the Tyrant followed,
and slew many. *Mago*, who stayed behind to strengthen the *Carthaginians* in *Sicily*, received Supplies of
Eighty Thousand Men, which did nothing but make
Peace with *Dionysius* ; who march'd into *Italy*, where
he took *Rhegium*,, and used much Cruelty therein.

Afterwards in another Battle with *Mago* he slew
him, and Ten Thousand *Africans* ; but *Mago's* Son
slew his Brother *Leptines*,, and Fourteen Thousand
Men, which made him now buy his Peace : Shortly
after he died, after Thirty Eight Years Tyranny,
and his Son *Dionysius* succeeded, with his Father's
disposition ; tho' to gain favour he dissembled, freed
many Prisoners, and remitted many Taxes; but slew
his Brethren by another Mother, the Sister of *Diony-*
sius a Valiant Just Man. This Man had so prevail'd
with him as to hear *Plato*, whom he had sent for, by
whose Wisdom he began to be reform'd, but continu'd it not. After this, his Flatterers procure *Di-*
onysius's Banishment, persuading the King, *Diony-*
sius sought to weaken his Mind by Philosophy, and
by offer which he had made to furnish the King with
Fifty Gallies, to make himself Master of the Kingdom. *Dionysius* was well beloved in *Greece*, where
he gathered Eight Hundred brave Followers, whom
he carried to *Syracuse* ; while the Tyrant was in *Italy*,
he entred without resistance, and recovered the Cities Liberty, though the Tyrant held the Castle.
After this the Worthy Man had the Reward which
popular Estates use to give, and was forced to abandon the City, but returned twice from *Leontium* to
assist them against the Castle, which gall'd them ;
and at last recovered the Castle, and was after murthered by *Cratippus*, who shortly after was slain by
the same Dagger. *Dionysius* after this recovered
the City, and made many flye to *Icetes*, Tyrant of
Leontium, who, with the *Carthaginians*, force *Diony-*
sius

sius into the Castle, and besieged him. After comes *Timolion* with Forces from *Corinth* to free the City, who with the *Carthaginians* forsake *Icetes*, wins the City, and hath the Castle rendred by *Dionysius*, which he beats down, calling it the Nest of Tyrants. *Syracuse* wasted by former Wars, is new Peopled with Ten Thousand *Greeks* by *Timolion's* means, who also overthrew *Asdrubal*, but *Amilcar* coming with Seventy Thousand *Africans*, with Two Gallies, and One Thousand Ships of burthen, vanquish'd *Icetes*, and slew him and his Followers; suppres'd all the Tyrants in *Sicily*, and died in Peace and Honour. *Sicily* after Twenty Years Peace from *Timolion's* death, falls under the Tyranny of *Agathocles*, who rising by degrees in the Field, came from a Beggar to be Prætor, and after Tyrant of *Syracuse*. Being Prætor, and in League with *Amilcar* the *Carthaginian*, he entertain'd Five Thousand *Africans*, and many old Souldiers, pretending to besiege *Herbita*, but indeed sets upon the Senators, the Rich, and all his Enemies, dividing the Spoil among the Poor, and giving liberty to the Souldiers to Plunder, Murther, and Ravish, calling it a violent Remedy for the violent Disease of the Commonwealth; pretending now to reduce the Oligarchy to the ancient and indifferent Democracy. But having left none fit for Magistracy, he knew that those whom he assisted in their Murders and Outrages would need his aid to protect them, and therefore would make him King, which accordingly they did. This *Amilcar* was content with, in hope that upon his wasting the Island all would fall into the *Carthaginians* hands; but the *Carthaginians* upon complaint send another *Amilcar*; upon which, the former chose rather to destroy himself, than to give an account to *Cartbage*. *Agathocles* before the *Carthaginians* came, had made the better part of *Sicily* his own, and defeating the first Supplies that they returned, and so encountred the second,

cond, brought by *Amilcar*, by which he grew presumptuous of that which failed him. One misfortune is
enough to overthrow a Tyrant, without great circumspection ; as it was with him, who after one great Defeat was glad to retire home, and being there besieged
with that wicked Rabble which had been Execution-
ers of his Tyrannous Entrance, he to prevent the Famine which was like to follow, Shipped himself with
as many as he thought convenient, leaving the City.
Antander his Brother went to Sea when the *Carthaginian* Fleet was going out to seize on certain Ships
coming with Provision ; these seeing *Agathocles*, made
toward him, who hasted toward *Africa*, while the
Provision got into the City; but before he got to Land
the *Carthaginians* Fleet is fatigu'd by endeavouring to
overtake him, and was beaten and routed by him. Being landed, after many plausible Speeches to his Company, as if he were Master of all the Riches in *A-
frick*, he burnt all their Ships, except one or two, to
use for Messengers. In this heat of resolution he
winneth two Cities, and demolish'd them, to the
great amazement of *Carthage*, who sent out against him
Hanno and *Bomilcar*, which were his profess'd Enemies, of whom *Agathocles* cut *Hanno* and his Followers in pieces, the other looking on. This Success drew
an *African* King to joyn with him, as did *Ophellas*
King of the *Cyrenians*, to whom he promised to deliver what he wan in *Afriok*, but indeed treache-
roufly murthered him, and entertain'd his Army.
After this he made a start to *Sicily*, and appeased
some Eruptions, returned to *Africa*, pacify'd his
Souldiers in mutiny for want of Pay, and might have
brought *Carthage* to buy Peace, and give over all in
Sicily, if his thoughts of the Conquest of *Carthage*
had not deceived him, by an impression, which as
light an accident as a flash of fire caused to vanish ;
for upon two Fires in the Night, kindled by accident, both Armies fled, each afraid of other. *Agathocles*

thocles in the dark, falling on his *African* Souldiers, which he took for Enemies, loft four Thousand, which so discouraged him, that he endeavour'd secretly to steal away ; which being understood of the Army, they slew his two Sons, and made their Peace with *Carthage*. *Agathocles* returning to *Sicily*, grew more cruel, exceeding *Phalaris*, but in the end is driven to seek Aid of the *Carthaginians* against those that he had banished, which took Arms against him, whom he subdued by their help, for which he restored to them all the *Phœnician* Towns he held in *Sicily*, and they suppli'd him with Corn and four hundred Talents of Gold and Silver. After this he went into *Italy*, subdued the *Brutians*, made the Ifle *Lipara* buy Peace for a hundred Talents of Gold ; but in his return with Eleven Ships laden with Gold, all was loft, and all the Fleet but his own Galley, which brought him to a more miserable end, by grievous torment in his Sinews and Veins, over all his Body, in which he was forsaken of all, and dyed basely as he began. His fellow Souldiers after that, Trayterously possessed themselves of *Messana*.

§. 4. *Hierom*, Tyrant of *Syracuse*, is followed home with the Wars by *Appias Claudius*, but thought it Wisdom to buy Peace for a hundred or two hundred Talents ; neither could *Carthage* be justly offended, seeing they made no haste to his Relief, knowing the City not able to hold out now, as in their attempting it ; besides, that *Rome* sought only their Friendship, whereas *Carthage* strove for a command of them.

§. 6. *Hierom*, a just and good Prince, beloved of his Subjects, as he sought their good, sided with *Rome*. *Lucius Posthumus* and Q. *Mamisius*, remove the Army to *Agrigentum*, which *Carthage* had stored with all manner of Ammunition, and Fifty Thousand Souldiers, between whom, upon a Sally made by the Besieged, was a Fight, which made the one side keep

in,

in, and the other ftrongly to Intrench before and behind.   *Hanibal* in the City fends for Succour to *Carthage*, which imbarks an Army under the Command of
Hanno, with certain Elephants, who landing at *Hi-
raclea*, furprifed *Erberus*, where lay the *Roman* Provifion, which lofs had diftreffed the *Romans*, but that
Hierom fupplied them.   *Hanno*, after that, affails
them, and by pretending flight of his Horfe-men,
drew them further to the place where he lay cover'd,
and fo flaughter'd many :   But in his fecond Affault,
he loft the day, and fled to *Heraclia*, whither fhortly after, *Hanibal*, with the remainder of his Army,
breaking in the Night through the *Romans* Camp efcaped. The *Romans* who came into *Sicily* with no other intent but to Succour the *Mamils*, and keep the *Carthaginians* from their own Doors, now afpire to the
Command of *Sicily*, and peradventure to vifit *Carthage*.   This is the Difeafe of Mortal Men, to covet
the greateft things, and not to enjoy the leaft ; the
defire of what we neither have nor need, taking from
us the fruition and ufe of what we have already.
The *Romans* fend two new Confuls, *Lucius Verus*,
and *Titus Octacilius*, fo the Inland Town became
theirs, and as many Maritime places were Commanded by *Carthage* ; which was the caufe the *Romans* determined to raife a Fleet, which before this, knew
not how to move an Oar.   Having now built one
hundred and twenty Gallies, and trained Men to row :
C. Cornelius, one of that Years Confuls, with Seventeen of them paft over to *Meffena*, and taking Pleafure therein, went to *Zippara*, whereof *Hannibal*,
Governour of *Panormus*, having Intelligence, fent and
furprifed the Conful and his Gallies ; and flufh'd with
this fuccefs, himfelf, with Fifty, went to furprife the
reft, but came off with great lofs. *Cornelius* is redeemed,
and *Duillius* his Fellow, is made Admiral ; who, confidering the Advantage of the *Carthaginian* light
Gallies, in rowing away from the heavy ones of the
Romans,

Romans, deviſed an Iron to grapple when they met, and ſo got the Advantage, which an heavy ſtrong broader Veſſel hath of weaker and lighter, which are in danger of ſplitting; neither are they ſo ſteady, which is no ſmall help in Fight, wherein the beſt uſe of the Hand is in them which beſt keep their Feet.

§. 7. *Rome* proceeds in War by Sea, ſends a Fleet to *Sardinia*; and *Hannibal* had obtained a Fleet at *Carthage,* which now Anchored in *Sardinia* Haven, which the *Romans,* coming ſuddenly, ſurprized, and *Hannibal* eſcaping hardly, was hanged at his return; For in War it is too much to offend twice. But *Amilcar* lying in *Panormus,* ſent *Hanno,* upon Intelligence of the *Roman* diſorder in *Sicily,* who, unlooked for, ſlew four thouſand of them. *Panormus* was the next which the Conſul Beſieged, but could not draw the *Carthaginians* into the Field, nor force the great City ſo ſtrongly guarded; ſo they left it, and took the Land Towns. *C. Attilius,* Conſul next Year, was beaten and loſt Nine Gallies of Ten, but by coming up of the reſt of his Fleet, the *Carthaginians* loſt Eighteen. Upon this, *Rome* built a Fleet of three hundred and Thirty Ships, and *Carthage* another of Three hundred and fifty, to try who ſhould Command the Seas; the *Romans* one hundred forty thouſand, and the *Carthaginians* one hundred and fifty thouſand Men aboard. Both Navies met, but *Attilius* had the better, taking ſixty three and ſinking Thirty, with loſs of twenty Four; which fell out by *Amilcar's* ordering his Gallies, ſo as that himſelf being forced and not able to recover to join with his other Squadrons, that Squadron of the *Romans* which forced him, fell back and helped their Fellows.

§. 8. The *Romans* repair their Fleet, ſet forward to *Africa,* landing at *Clypea,* a Port Town, which yielded, and ſo gave them an Haven, without which all Invaſions are fooliſh. *Amilcar* is alſo come to *Carthage,* and defence is prepared, while

while *Mantius*, one of the Conſuls, with all the Navy, is called home, with two thouſand Captive *Africans*, leaving but fifteen thouſand Foot, five hundred Horſe, and forty Gallies with *Atilius*. He Beſieged *Adis*, where, to hinder him, *Amilcar*, *Hanno*, and *Beſter*, are ſent with an Army, who deſigning to weary him with lingring, place themſelves on the top of an Hill. *Regulus* diſcovering the advantage that neither the *Carthaginian* Horſe nor Elephants could do ſervice there, ſet ſtoutly upon them, and forc'd them to leave their Camp to the Spoil, after which they proceed to *Tunis*, ſixteen Miles from *Carthage*, to the great Terrour of that City, which being incumber'd with Multitudes, fled into it from the *Romans*, could not long keep Famine out, which would let in the *Romans*. *Atilius* finds this Advantage, but doubting they will hold out 'till his Year expire, and ſo the next Conſuls ſhall have the Honour, he treats of Peace with *Carthage*, that he may reap his own Fruit; Ambition ſeeking only to gratify it ſelf ; but *Atilius*'s Conditions were ſo unworthy, that the *Carthaginians* diſdain'd 'em, changing Fear into a Couragious Reſolution to defend their Liberty to the laſt Man. To ſtrengthen their Reſolution, *Xantippus*, a *Spartan*, a very expert Souldier, with a great Troop of *Greeks* formerly ſent for, came, who ſhewing the Errours of the Commanders in the former Over-throw, to the Senate, is made General of Twelve thouſand Foot, four thouſand Horſe, and one hundred Elephants, which were all the Forces which *Carthage* could raiſe at home, to fight for Liberty, Lives and all. But ſuch as uſe Mercenaries, as they did, are ſtronger abroad than at home, as we ſee in their other Armies of one hundred and forty thouſand, and one hundred and fifty thouſand at Sea, *&c.* *Xantippus* ſo ordered this Army in a Level Ground, that he utterly overthrew the *Romans*, took *Atilius* and five hundred others, and ſlew all the reſt but two

Y   thouſand,

thousand, &c. Thus one wise head overmatch many Hands. *Atilius*, upon his word, went to *Rome* to treat about Exchange and Ransome of Prisoners, which he dissuaded, considering the loss *Rome* should take thereby; and returning to *Carthage*, dyed by Torture, as a Malicious obstinate Enemy, whose vainglorious Frowardness rather than necessity of State, the *Romans* afterwards slighted, and made the Exchange; losing all he had gotten, and more; as did the *Flanderkins* at *Gaunt*.

§. 9. *Carthage*, by this Victory, recovered all in *Africa*, but *Clypea*, kept by the *Romans*, to whose Succour three hundred and fifty Gallies. are sent, which being encountred by two hundred from *Carthage*, they took one hundred and fourteen of them, and taking on board their Besieged Men at *Clypea*, return from *Sicily*, hoping to get all there that *Carthage* held. The Pilots persuade them to put into Harbour, the Season threatning a Storm, urging that the South of *Sicily* hath no good Ports; but these Men being Conquerors, desperately oppose the Elements, and near *Cameria*, all their Fleet but Eighty three were cast away, which was the remainder of their late Victory. The *Carthaginians* hoping to recover command at Sea, send *Asdrubal* with two hundred Gallies, with all the old Souldiers, and one hundred and forty Elephants, which land at *Lilybæum*; while the *Romans* make a hundred and twenty Ships, which; with the remainder of their Wrack, they sent to *Panormus*, and surrounded it by Sea and Land, and take it. Then they visit *Africk* again, make some Spoil, but in return between *Panormus* and *Italy*, Neptune spoiled them of all that *Mars* had given, with the loss of a hundred and fifty Ships; so that now the Sea hath devoured four hundred and six Ships and Gallies, and made them resolve to keep the Land; and upon Experience of *Atilius*'s loss by Elephants, they dread fighting in Champain Countries. But finding how impossible

possible it was to succour the places they held in *Sicily* by Land-Marches, against the speedy Passage of the *Carthaginians* by Sea, they change their minds.

§. 10. *Cætilius* with half of the *Roman* Army in *Panormus*, is attempted by *Asdrubal* and his Forces, from *Lilybæum*, who sending his Elephants before against a Legion which came by Appointment, to draw them on under colour of retireing, 'till they came to a Trench which they could not pass; where being repell'd by the Souldiers in it, inraged, they turn on their own Foot and disorder them. *Cæcilius* seeing the advantage, brake out, slew many and took the Elephants. *Rome* hereupon, hoping at once to end the Fourteen Years War of *Sicily*, prepare a new Fleet of two hundred Sail, which is sent to *Lilybæum*, the only place of Importance in the *Carthaginians* Hands. This *Himilco*, with a Garrison of ten thousand, held against them; and *Hannibal*, Son of *Amilcar*, is sent with ten thousand more, which he led into the City in despite of all resistance. During this Siege, a *Rhodian* undertook, with a very swift Gally, to enter the Town through the *Roman* Fleet, and performed it, coming back again to *Carthage*; after the *Rhodian*, others performed as much, which made the *Romans* sink so many Ships with Stones, that the Passage was block'd up, so that at his next coming he was taken, with another *Carthaginian* Gally. *Lilybæum* begins to be distressed by continual watching and labour; but in this Despair, some of the *Roman* Engines are thrown down by a violent Storm, and burnt by a *Greek* Souldier; which the *Romans* would not repair, but resolve to starve the Defendants. *M. Claudius* a Consul, arrives with ten thousand, and re-inforced the Army, and propounds the Surprize of *Drepanum*, a City on the other side of the Bay, which all imbrace, and being imbarked, Arrive. *Adherbal*, a Valiant and prudent Warriour, exhorting his Men to Fight abroad rather than to be shut

up at home, puts to Sea ; the Conful's Fleet being
more in hafte to furprize than in order to defend,
is forced into a Bay in which he wants room to range
himfelf.   In this ftreight he forceth his way out with
Thirty Gallies, and fled, leaving Ninety four Ships
to his Enemies Entertainment. *L. Junius* a Conful,
is fent from *Rome* with fixty Gallies to take the
Charge, who met the remainder of the Fleet at
Meffana, except fome in *Lilybæum* Port, and made
up a hundred and twenty Gallies, and eight hundred Ships of Burden, and at *Syracufe,* fent the
Queftors or Treafurers with half the Provifion of
fome Gallies for Convoy. *Adberbal,* upon this Victory, not being fecure, fends *Carthalo* with a hundred Gallies to try what he can do in *Lilybæum* Port,
who furprized, took and burnt all the Gallies in it ;
and Coafting along the *South,* met with Conful *Junius*'s Victuallers, forced them into a Road full of
Rocks, where *Carthalo* took fome of them, waiting
for the reft who could not ftay long in fo dangerous
a place. Whilft he is thus waiting for them the Conful is difcovered, againft whom he went out, who is
alfo glad to take into a dangerous Creek. *Carthalo*
takes a ftation, fit to watch which will ftir firft ; but
difcerning a Storm at hand, he made hafte to double
the Cape of *Pachinus,* and left the Conful to the boifterous South Wind, which utterly wrackt all his
Gallies, *&c.* *Rome* at the Report hereof again re-
nounces the Sea, refolving rather to truft to their Legions upon firm Land.

§. 11. *Junius* the Conful to regain the Honour he
had loft at Sea, refolves to attempt *Erix* on the
Mount, which he took, and Fortify'd as being fit for
a Garrifon between *Lilybæum* and *Panormus.*   Shortly
after in the Eighteenth Year of this War, *Amilcar,*
firnamed *Barcas,* Father of *G. Hannibal,* is fent with
a Fleet and Army, with which he fo wafted the *Locrians* and *Brutians,* that he repayed the *Roman* Spoils.

In

In *Sicily* he settles himself between *Panormus* and *E-rix*, and three Years molested the *Romans* ; and after found way into *Erix* before the Guards, either at the bottom or on the top of the Hill, knew it, and there he kept them in play almost two Years. *Rome* now knows no way to be rid of this obstinate Warriour, 'till they command the Sea, which requires a Fleet, and (they having wasted the common Treasure) the private Citizens must make it good. It is decreed, and two hundred Gallies are by the *Rhodian* Pattern raised and committed to *C. Luctatius Catullus*. *Hanno*, Admiral of the *Carthaginian* Fleet, well furnish'd as he thought, for them at *Erix*, but neither with fit Mariners nor stout Fellows, as soon appear'd. For *Catullus* the Consul having well exercised his Men in rowing, he lightned his Gallies, and stored all of them with choice Land Souldiers, which *Hanno* was so deficient in, that at the first Encounter he had fifty stem'd, seventy taken, and ten thousand made Prisoners. *Carthage* thus utterly discourag'd, sends to *Amilcar*, referring it wholly to his Wisdom what to do, who considering the present necessity, sent to *Luctatius* to treat of Peace, who, upon the same consideration of *Romes* present Poverty, agreed on Conditions, which were sent to *Rome*, who sent Commissioners to conclude the Peace. *Carthage* is expell'd out of *Sicily*, restores Prisoners, and payed three thousand two hundred Talents in Twenty Years.

Y 3   CHAP.

CHAP. II.

What pass'd between the First and Second Punick Wars.

§. 1. THE *Carthaginians* thus quit of *Sicily* and the Iflands about it, have now leifure to think how to help themfelves in a following War, rather than to be content with the prefent Peace; for that the Conquerors give and the Conquered receive Laws. But *Rome* forgot in this Affair what had been anfwered a Senator, demanding what Peace *Rome* may hope for, or be affured of, if they quitted the prefent Advantage over them? It was Anfwered, *if the Peace you give us be good and faithful, it will hold; if it be ill, it will not.* The Senate approved the Anfwer as manly and free; for who will believe that any People will endure an over-hard Condition longer than Neceffity compells. They therefore grofly flatter themfelves, to think that the *Carthaginians,* inferiour neither in Power or Pride, will fit down with lofs and difhonour any longer than they are deprived of the means and opportunity of Revenge. But when the Army of the *Carthaginians* was to be tranfported home, which *Amilcar* committed to *Gefco,* who confidering the great Sums *Carthage* did owe the Souldiers, more than the City was able to pay, they fent them over in fmal Numbers, to be difpatched and fent away before the Arrival of others of their Fellows. The Governors on the contrary put them off, 'till all were come; and to avoid the diforders of fuch lawlefs Gueft, fent them to *Sicca* to prevent their coming to *Carthage.* Then *Hanno* is fent to perfuade them to be content with part of their Pay, confidering the Poverty of the City. They which had expected the uttermoft Farthing with fome donative, hearing this, are inraged, and refolving to demand their due nearer home, remove to *Tunis,* not far from *Carthage,* which

which now began to see her Errours against that old Rule,

> *Have special care that valiant Poverty,*
> *Be not opprest with too great Injury.*

Many other Errours, besides the first gathering together so many in Arms whom they went to wrong, were committed, as thrusting out their Wives and Children, who might have been Hostages, and to send Senators, daily promising to satisfie all demands. By these shiftings, the Souldiers perceive the City's fear, and thereupon raise other demands besides Pay. The Commotion increased, and they are requested to refer all to any that had commanded in *Sicily*; and they chose *Gesco*, who had made a quiet end but for two seditious Persons, *Spendius* and *Matho*, who prevail with the *African* Souldiers, putting all in uproar; neither could *Gesco's*, offering to pay the whole stipend, pacify them, who now seek a Quarrel rather than Money. They therefore chose *Spendius* and *Matho* Captains, and upon further Speech which *Gesco* made, which discontented them, they cast him and those that came with him into Bonds, and lay violent Hands upon the Treasure he brought for them. *Matho* and *Spendius* send Embassadors to solicit all *Africk*, easily stirred up against *Carthage*, which now must hear of their Oppressions, in exacting half their Corn, Tribute, and were extreme in punishing small Offences: For Adversity hath been told of her Errors. Now all that are able fly to Arms, and the very Women bring forth their Jewels, so that besides seventy Thousand *Africans* which came in, their Treasure vastly encreased.

§. 2. Tyranny must use the help of Mercenaries, which commonly are as false, as the War against Tyrants is Cruel. Tyranny is a violent Form of Government; respecting the Commanders pleasure, and not the good of Subjects. Violent it is, seeing no Man can yield willing Obedience, where his Life and Well-

Y 4 fare

fare is not regarded. Tyrants which are moſt Cruel ſeem mild ſometimes to ſome for their own advantage; but in large Dominions, where they cannot take ſuch particular knowledge of Men, he who cannot endure the face of one ſo honeſt, as will put him in mind of moderation, will not bound his deſires. The ſweetneſs of Oppreſſion from a few, inflames his appetite to ſpare none, ſeeing there is no cauſe to reſpect one more than other; and Covetouſneſs is never ſatisfied. Having ſqueez'd from all, yet believing every one could have ſpared more, and he knows many pretend want without cauſe; and therefore deviſeth new tricks of Robbery, which pleaſe him as much as the gain, devouring the recreation of his Spirit: He knows he is hated for it, and therefore ſeeks to turn hatred into fear, by cruelty againſt the ſuſpected, whether juſtly or no, ſo that the Conſpirator can be no more fearful of his Tyranny than the Inocent. Wherefore thinking upon his own ſecurity, he muſt diſarm all, fortifie himſelf in ſome ſtrong place, and take a guard of luſty Souldiers, not of Subjects, leſt any one grow to the feeling of the common miſery; but of Strangers, which neither have Wealth nor Credit at home. To make theſe his own, they ſhall be permitted to do as he doth, to Rob, Raviſh, Murder, and ſatisfy their own Appetites.

§. 3. *Carthage* calls us back to proceed with her Mercenaries in Arms againſt her, at the Siege of *Utica* and *Hippagreta,* ſeated on the Weſtern Haven of *Carthage,* the reſt of their Forces encamped at *Tunis. Hanno* is ſent with power againſt them from *Carthage*; whoſe ſudden coming made them forſake their Tents, to flye to a rough high ground to avoid his Hundred Elephants; but perceiving he was entred the City, they return, force his Camp with great ſlaughter, took his Proviſion, and poſſeſſed all Paſſages from *Carthage.* The *Carthaginians* upon this loſs ſend *Amilcar* with Ten Thouſand Men and Seventy

Venty Elephants more, whose Passage over the
Bridge of *Macra* or *Bagradas* the Mercenaries having
taken by *Hanno*'s oversight, *Amilcar* was forc'd to take
his opportunity formerly observed by him, when the
Rivers mouth us'd to be stop'd with Sand and Gravel, and so passed over, to the Enemies amazement,
which yet took heart by the coming of Fifteen Thousand Men from *Utica*, besides Ten Thousand which
guarded the Bridge.   Their Army now far exceeded
his; they wait their advantage, but with some dif-
order, which *Amilcar* espying, made haste in his
March as if he had fled, which drew the Enemy to
follow confusedly, as to a Victory; but by his wheeling about upon them Six Thousand of them were
slain, and Two Thousand taken. After this, *Nar-
vasus* who led Two Thousand *Numidian* Horse,
sent to the Mercenaries, and came over to *Amilcar*,
as being a Man of Honour; with whose assistance
Amilcar set upon *Spendius*, and slew Ten Thousand,
and took Four Thousand Prisoners, whom he kindly
treated. *Matho, Spendius*, and other Leaders,
to prevent the falling away of their Men by allure-
ment of *Amilcar*'s lenity to such, procure a general
consent to put *Gesco* and his Fellows to death, so to
make them odious to *Carthage*; and decree further
to kill all *Carthaginian* Prisoners; which execrable
fury and desperation, was like the Councel of *Achito-
phel*. *Utica* and *Hippagreta* now fall from *Carthage*,
and slew their Garrison, so that *Hanno* comes to joyn
with *Amilcar*, but by reason of the animosity between
them, the common Cause is little promoted ; so by
judgment of the Army *Hanno* was sent home, and
Hannibal succeeded him.

The Mercenaries with Fifty Thousand Men are
come near *Carthage*, but too weak to assault it or famish it, having the Sea open, by which it received Succour from *Syracuse*, and *Rome* made overtures of like
assistance. *Amilcar* is at their backs, keeping them
in ;

in; and when they durſt not leave their higher ground for fear of *Amilcar*'s Elephants, and *Narvaſus*'s Horſes, *Amilcar* to prevent what Deſperation might put them to, ſhut them up with Trench and Rampart; ſo while they expect aid from *Matho* at *Tunis*, Famine forced them to eat their Priſoners, and then one another. In this extremity they force *Spendius* and Two others to go to *Amilcar* to ſeek Peace, which was granted, upon condition he ſhall chuſe any Ten, and the reſt to depart in their Shirts. *Amilcar* choſe *Spendius*, and the two with him, and with his Army goeth to chuſe the reſt; which the Mercenaries thinking to be to aſſault them, ran the two Armies in confuſion, and were all ſlain to the number of Four Thouſand. *Amilcar* proceeds to *Tunis*, in the Siege whereof *Hannibal* is taken by *Matho*, and Crucified as *Spendius* had been; upon which loſs, *Hanno* is ſent upon a feigned reconciliation with *Amilcar*, which ſhortly after overthrew *Matho*, and ended that War of two Years and four Months.

§. 4. *Carthage* being endangered by her *Sicilian Mercenaries* at home, was alſo troubled with Mercenaries in *Sardinia*, which murthered the Governour; againſt whom another *Hanno* was ſent, with as many Mercenaries as *Carthage* could ſpare; who alſo ſlew *Hanno*, and joyned with the firſt, and expelled all the *Carthaginians*. Then looking to ſucceed in Command of the Iſland, the Inhabitants withſtood them, and expelled them; neither would the *Romans*, invited by them, undertake it; as they likewiſe refuſed to accept *Utica* offering it ſelf. This might have ſerved for an example of Roman Faith to Poſterity, if they had not thruſt themſelves into it after *Carthage* had ended her home Wars, and prepared for *Sardinia*, which the *Romans* pretending to be againſt *Rome* it ſelf, made the Quarrel to proclaim War;

War; which forced *Carthage* in her prefent weaknefs to renounce her Right in *Sardinia.*

§. 5. *Carthage* having found her own Punick Faith and Dealing at the hands of *Rome,* learned how neceffary it was to make her felf ftrong, or refolve to fubmit to *Rome*; and becaufe the *Roman* jealoufie forbad them to attempt any thing in the Midland-Sea, they refolve upon an Expedition to *Spain,* which they commit to *Amilcar,* who in Nine Years fubdued moft of the Country, and was then flain in Battle with the People which then inhabited *Portugal.* *Afdrubal* his Son-in-Law fucceeded, enlarged their Dominions, and built *Carthagena* in the Kingdom of *Granado.* *Rome* grew jealous, but knows not how to ground a quarrel, having no acquaintance in *Spain.* They fend to *Afdrubal,* requiring him not to pafs over *Iberus,* hoping his Refolute Spirit would give them a ground to work upon, but are deceived, by his appearance to conform to their will. The *Saguntines* on the South of *Iberus* perceiving how *Carthage* gave way to *Rome,* entred Confederation with her; which the *Carthaginians,* now grown ftrong, thought to be an ill example, and to their prejudice, and remembring old injuries, prepare againft the *Saguntines.*

§. 6. *Greece* during the firft *Punick* War after *Pyrrhus*'s Death, had fomewhat recover'd her Liberty through the diffentions in *Macedon,* which after *Pyrrhus,* was eftablifhed in *Antigonus* the Son of *Demetrius,* and his Iffue, as *Ægypt* was in *Ptolomy*'s, and *Afia* and *Syria* in *Seleucus.* *Antigonus* being after *Pyrrhus* driven out by *Alexander* the Son of *Pyrrhus,* was reftored by his own Son *Demetrius,* who alfo expelled *Alexander* the *Epirot* out of *Epirus.* *Demetrius* alfo got his Father poffeffion of the Citadel of *Corinth,* which was the entrance by Land into *Peloponnefus.* *Demetrius* fucceeded *Antigonus* in *Macedon* Ten Years, and left *Philip* a young Son, his Uncle *Antigonus*

tigonus being Protector, who held it for life, and by
the diffentions of *Greece* got no.lefs Authority therein than old *Philip* had done by the fame means. The
Achaians in his time were grown the moft powerful
People of *Greece,* unto whom many other Cities united themfelves, by means of *Aratus* a *Sicyonian,* who
having freed *Sicyon* from the Tyrant which held it,
for fear of *Antigonus,* entred the League. He alfo
furprized the Citadel of *Corinth,* and the *Magarians*
fell from him, and joyned with *Achaia,* as did other
States. *Aratus* freed *Argos, Megapons,* and *Hermi-
on* from their Tyrants, and by Mony gain'd the Captains of the Garrifon in *Athens.* Now alfo the *Ætolians* grew powerful, but after Devaftations made in
Peloponnefus, they were glad to beg affiftance of *Achaia*
againft *Demetrius,* yet ungratefully they fought to
fet the *Lacedemonians* againft them, and drew in *Antigonus. Lacedemon* at that time was in a weak Condition, but by *Cleomenes* one of their Kings, was
raifed to fuch hopes, that he was fo bold as to claim
the Principality of *Greece. Aratus* feeing the danger of
Achaia by the *Lacedemonians* rifing, which he knew
not how to ftop, ufed means to *Antigonus,* giving
him hopes of the *Achaians* fubmitting to him. But
it had been more honourable if *Aratus* had ended
the War, withdrawing *Achaia* to yield to *Cleomenes,*
feeing he had fo freed his Country of further trouble,
and the *Macedonian* Command. But as difdain at
the *Lacedemonians* rifing over them carried them to
Antigonus, fo *Aratus* that wrought it, loft his Honour and Life by the *Macedonians,* who might have
been Fellows, with *Cleomenes,* with whom *Ptolomy*
joyned, and left the *Achaians,* with whom he had
been in League. After this, *Cleomenes* gave them
fuch an overthrow, that they fought Peace, which
was willingly yielded upon fair Conditions, that *Lacedemon* fhould lead in the Wars, and will reftore
all Perfons and Places taken. *Aratus* oppofed this

all

all he could, so that *Cleomenes* proceeded with his War, and many Cities became his ; whereupon *Aratus* hasteneth *Antigonus,* who promiseth help, if he may be put in possession of the *Corinthian* Citadel, which *Aratus* promised, and sent his Son for Hostage. The *Corinthians* importune *Cleomenes* to prevent this, which he sought to do by all fair offers to *Aratus,* which he rejected, surrounding it with Trenches, but all in vain, for upon the danger of losing *Argos,* *Cleomenes* went to rescue his Garrison there, and in the mean time *Corinth* yielded to *Antigonus,* who following *Cleomenes,* disappointed him at *Argos* also, and after took in many other Places, so that *Sparta* shortly lost all again to *Antigonus,* whom *Aratus* honoured even as a God, offering Sacrifice to him at his being at *Sicyon,* which Example the other Cities of *Achaia* followed. For though *Cleomenes* performed many brave Services, and put many Affronts upon *Antigonus,* yet at length in a Battel at *Selasia* he was overthrown, and all his Forces broken, and himself returning to *Sparta,* persuaded the little remainder to yield to *Antigonus,* and so departed from them, embarking for *Egypt,* where *Ptolomy* lovingly entertain'd him. Thus ended the Glory of *Lacedemon,* which as a Light ready to go out, had with a great, but no long blaze, shined more brightly of late than in some Ages past ; and *Cleomenes* a generous Prince, but his Son *Leoniaus,* who had wretchedly brought worthy King *Agis* his Fellow, with his Mother and Grandmother unto a bloody end, slew himself in *Ægypt,* and had his own Wife and Grand Children murdered by the vicious young Prince *Ptolomy Philopater.* *Antigonus* after this entred *Sparta,* whereinto the force of the Enemies could never make way before, where he kindly treated the Citizens, and left them to their own Laws ; but he could not stay, the *Illyrians* wasting *Macedon,* whom he overcame ; but by straining a Vein died soon after. *Philip* the
Son

Son of *Demetrius*, a Boy succeeded in *Macedon*, as did *Antiochus* the Great in *Asia*, and *Ptolomy Philopater* in *Ægypt*, who was young also, *&c.*

§. 7. *Rome* subdued *Sardinia*, and *Corsica*, and the *Illyrians*, while *Carthage* is Conquering *Spain*. The *Illyrians* Inhabited the Country now called *Slavonia*, whom *Demetrius* King of *Macedon* hired to rescue the *Macedonians* so distressed by the *Ætolians*, yet strive for dividing the Booty before the Town was won, as did the *French* at *Poictiers*, and *Agin-Court*. But the *Illyrians* ended the Controversie, slew many, and took more, and divided their Baggage. The *Illyrians* proud of worsting the stoutest of the *Greeks*, *Tuta* their Queen gave them liberty to rob at Sea whom they could, Friend or Foe, and sent an Army by Sea and Land, which invaded *Epirus*, and took *Phænice* by the Treachery of Eight Hundred *Gauls* entertain'd there, being driven out of *Sicily* by the *Romans* for the like Treachery. Lying here, they made prize of many *Italian* Merchants, and being called home take a Ransom of the *Epirots* for the Town and Prisoners, and returned home. *Rome* sent to *Teuta* requiring satisfaction for the *Italian* Merchants; but she refused, and answered, Kings use not to forbid their Subjects to get by Sea what they can. And when one of the *Roman* Ambassadors replied, That their manner was to revenge such private injuries, and would teach her to reform her Kingly manner, without all regard of the common Law of Nations, she slew him. The *Romans* to revenge this injury, who can take no satisfaction but with the Sword, sent an Army by Sea, and another by Land. Touching the Law of Nations concerning Ambassadors, it seems grounded on this; that seeing without Mediation there would never be an end of War, it was thought equal to all Nations by light of Nature, that Ambassadors should pass safely between Enemies; yet if any State lay hand upon their

Enemies

Enemies Embassador not sent to them, but to solicite
a third Nation against them; or shall practise against
the Person of the Prince, to whom he is sent,
this Law will fail him. *Teuta* sends out a great
Fleet, Commanded by *Demetrius Pharos*, of which,
part took *Corcyra*, an Island in the *Adriatique*, the
other Besieged *Dyrrachicum*, when the Queen called
home *Demetrius*, I know not why; but so as he
chose rather to yield *Corcyra* to the *Roman* Conful, and the *Illyrian* Garrison, and went with him
to *Appolonia*, not far off, which *Pintus* calls *Sissopo-
lis*; where the other Consul, with Land Forces,
met, and went to *Durazzo* and rais'd the Siege.
From thence they enter *Illyrium*; and put the
Queen to flight to *Rison* and profecute the War,
force her to seek for Peace, to quit the better
part of *Illyrium*, which they commit to *Demetrius*, and to pay Tribute for the rest to *Rome*.

§. 8. *Rome* took the next Arms against the *Gauls*
in *Lumbardy*, a fierce unadvised People; more then
Men at the first onset, but less than Women after;
by whom *Italy* had many Alarms, but few Wars; especially when *Rome* had to do with other great Enemies, as *Pyrrhus* or *Carthage*, when they might have
said little to it. The *Romans*, three Years before
Pyrrhus had set upon the *Gauls* at home, upon a
slaughter in the *Senones*, a Tribe of *Gauls* made of
Lucius Cæcilus and his Army at *Arretium* in *Hetruria*,
and had expelled the *Senones* and placed a Colony of
Romans. This made all the Tribes of the *Gauls*,
with those which dwelt on both sides of the *Alps*, to
enter into League, to prevent their own expulsion;
the *Insubrians* Inhabited the Dutchy of *Milan*, &c.
who also hired the *Gessates* on *Rodanus*, and made an
Army of fifty Thousand Foot, and twenty Thousand,
Horse, all choice Men, besides the *Seno-Galli* before
expelled. The *Cenonians* and *Venetians* adhere to
Rome, and which, upon that occasion, caused a view
of

of all their own and Allies Forces to be taken, set down by *Polybius,* where may be seen the Power of *Rome* in those days ; Seven hundred Thousand Foot, and seventy Thousand Horse : But all Heads are not fit for Helmets. The one Consul with his part of the Army, which was four Legions, and thirty thousand Foot of the Allies, and two thousand Horse, met them in *Tuscany,* where, by a plain stratagem of shew, to flag the Gauls, they slew six thousand ; but upon the coming of *Lucius Emilius* the other Consul, they resolve upon Retreats. This had been Advantagious before the Enemy had been in Sight, but extreme dangerous in head of the Enemy, and all in Fear ; as the *French* found at *Naples,* and the *Gauls* now, who being follow'd by one Consul, and met by another ; is forced and lost forty thousand and their Courage, and in a short time all they had in *Italy.* Thus the *Romans* spent twenty Three Years Peace with *Carthage.*

C H A P. III.

Of the Second Punick War.

§. 1. **H**Annibal about twenty six Years old, chosen General of the *Carthaginian* Forces in *Spain,* is envied by *Hanno* and his Party, neither being able to Tax the Virtue of their Enemies, nor recommend themselves by any Service to the Common-Wealth; except in dissuading from War, and cautious Advice not to provoke the *Romans.* But the Senate and People, who knew the *Romans* Oath was no Security to *Carthage,* unless she would become their Subject, did the more highly esteem him, as *Amilcar* his Father who had saved them. Knowing therefore the Peace continu'd but 'till *Rome* could find Advantage, they wished the beginning of the

War,

War rather while their State was in good Condition, than to stay 'till being fallen into distress, the Enemy should begin it. *Hannibal* well understood this, as also the advantage in getting the start, and therefore thought long 'till he was dealing with them, before they should have notice of his purpose, which could not be conceal'd if once he came to Action; besides the hinderance by slow and timerous proceeding therein. Before therefore he would provoke the *Romans* by attempting *Saguntum*, he wisely ended the Conquest of all that lay between, as the *Olcades* near *Tagus*, and *Vaccai* in Old *Castile*, where they took *Salamanca*, and *Arbucala*. But the Spring following, all that had escaped, joyning with the *Toletans*, to the number of One Hundred Thousand able Men, stayed *Hannibal* on the Banks of *Tagus*, which runneth by *Lysbourn*, supposing his accustom'd Courage would now neglect discretion, as he seemed to do at other times. But he that is as a Chrystal for every Eye to see through, makes himself an Ass for every Man to ride or drive; whereas wise and honest Men, in that which is Just and Virtuous, are like Coffers with double Bottoms, which shew not all at once. Before he was General, he was of all Men the most venturous, which doth not always become a General; and therefore he now dissembles Fear, and draweth back from the River, as fearing to ford it, by that means to draw his Enemies into it. But when he saw them pushing disorderly into the swift Stream, he turned his Camels to entertain their Landing, and pressing in with his Horse above and beneath upon them, made a great slaughter, which amazed the *Spaniards* on that side the River of *Iberus*. The *Saguntines* post their Ambassadors to *Rome*, who proceed *Roman* like, with deliberation, sending Ambassadors to and fro, while *Hannibal* prepareth, and found out also a pretence like that which the *Romans* made use of with the *Mamertines*, for the *Turdetani*

Z   injured

injured by the *Saguntines*, implored his help. The *Romans* were as glad of the Quarrel, but were not yet ready, and therefore temporize 'till they could raise an Army to remove the Seat of War to *Saguntum*. In the mean time *Demetrius Pharius* whom the *Romans* had made their *Illyrian* King, rebelled; against whom *Æmilius* was sent, but before his Landing in *Illyria*, *Hannibal* sat down before *Saguntum*; where by a Sallie made by the Citizens, he was dangerously wounded, but before it was long he put them all to the Sword; many shut themselves in their Houses, and then fired them. * *Rome* storms at the News, and will be revenged. She sends to *Carthage* to know whether *Hannibal* had their allowance; which question *Carthage* calls insolent, and gives them an impertinent answer; forgetting, as *Polybius* thinks, to charge *Rome* with breach of Oath in taking *Sardinia* from them: But in the end both sides resolve upon War, as that which both desire. This is plain dealing, and no wrangling about breach of Covenants, which they only stand about, who are unwilling to fight. For Kings understand the obligation of a Treaty by the Condition of their own advantage, and commonly the best advised begin with the Sword, and then with the Trumpet, as the *Arrogonois* with the *French* in *Naples*, and *Philip* the Second of *Spain* with *England*, taking all our Ships in his Ports. *Hannibal* besides the forwardness of *Carthage*, had also been sworn by his Father to pursue *Rome* with immortal hatred, being but Nine Years old, which I doubt not but some Kings not at peace with us, were charged with by their Predecessors, to declare themselves our Enemies when their Coffers were full.

§. 2. *Hannibal* upon this resolves to visit *Rome*, instructing *Asdrubal* his Brother about the Government of *Spain*; and sends as many Troops of *Spaniards* into *Africk*, as there were *Africans* in *Spain*,

to

* See Cap. 4. §. 8.

to be Pledges each Nation for other, *viz.* Thirteen
Thousand Eight Hundred and Fifty Foot, and One
Thousand Two Hundred Horse, with Four Thousand young Men of Quality out of the best Cities,
to be Garrison'd in *Carthage,* and with his Brother
he left Fifty Seven Gallies, Twelve Thousand *Africans,* and of other Foreigners Two Thousand, and
Twenty One Elephants. Then he sends to the *Py-
rene* Mountaineers and *Gauls* for a quiet passage, and
in the Spring passeth over *Iberus* Ninety Thousand
Foot, and Twelve Thousand Horse, with which he
Conquer'd *Spain* on the East of that River, and left
one *Hanno* with Ten Thousand Foot, and One Thousand Horse to Govern it. At the Borders he dis-
missed the *Spaniards* that desired it, and so with Fifty Thousand Foot, and Nine Thousand Horse, he
entred *Gaul,* and by fair words and gifts passed to
Rhodanus, where the *Vivaretz* to be rid of them gave
way and directed him; yet he was put to some
trouble on the other side, and in passing over his
Elephants on Boughs of Trees covered with Turffs,
and towed over. Then the *Cisalpine Gauls* in *Piemont* and *Milan,* lately revolted from *Rome,* and
came over to him, and gave him Guides over the
Alps; yet was he exceedingly molested by the *Sa-
voiards,* and put to loss both of Carriages and Men,
besides Fifteen Days tedious March over the Mountains in the beginning of Winter.

§. 3. The *Cisalpine Gauls* before *Hannibal's* coming had revolted from *Rome,* and besieged the *Roman* Commissioners in *Modena,* when they could not
force *Cremona* and *Placentia,* two *Roman* Colonies;
but seeming weary, and desirous of Peace, *Rome* sent
Ambassadors, whom they detain. *Manlius* the Prætor, who lay in those parts with an Army, coming
to relieve the Besieged, is overthrown by the *Gaul's*
Ambush in a Wood, and *Atilius* his fellow Prætor
sent with another supply was beaten, &c. *Rome* not

dream-

dreaming that the *Carthaginians* after so many indignities slavishly endured, would grow so brave as to
look into *Italy*, had sent *Titus Sempronius*, one of their
Consuls, with an Army, and Two Hundred and Sixty
Quinqueremes into *Africk*, and *P. Cornelius Scipio*
the other Consul, with an Army into *Spain*, hoping
to find *Hannibal* there. But he hearing at *Massilia*
that *Hannibal* was past over *Rhodanus*, sent his Brother *Cnius Cornelius Scipio* with the greatest part of
the Forces to try *Asdrubal*; and himself with some
choice Men hastened after *Hannibal* by Sea to *Pisa*,
and so to *Lumbardy*, where he gathered together the
broken Troops of the beaten Prætor.

§. 4. *Hannibal* after Five Months tedious Journey,
and having past the *Alps*, hath but Twenty Thousand
Foot and Six Hundred Horse left of those he muster'd
at *Rhodanus*, as the Monument he raised in *Juno's*
Temple witnesseth, besides the *Gauls*, *Lycurgians*, &c.
lately joyned. In *Piemont* he forced the City *Turine*,
which had refused his Alliance, which drew many
Gauls and others to joyn with him, and prepared o-
thers which yet held off, hearing of the Consul
Scipio's coming; which wavering made both Generals to hasten the Trial. *Ticinum* was the place
where they exhort their Armies, and where *Hannibal* set before his " the desperate fight of his *Savoy*
" Captives which he had used so miserably, that
" he who was slain by his Fellow thought he succeed-
" ed well, though he which overcame had Liberty,
" with an Horse and Mony. This he shewed his
" Souldiers was their case, whose Life without Vi-
" ctory will be a bondage worse than Death, but
" with Victory will be well rewarded. *Scipio* encouraged his Men by the Victories of their Ancestors
even over the *Carthaginians*; that these were but a
declining Troop of Rebels, feeble by hard travel, and
many wants. In the Battle *Scipio* was dangerously
wounded, and left in the place, if his Son (after Sirnamed

named *Africanus* had not brought him off. The Conful feeing his Horfemen beaten, and the reft difcouraged, made his retreat to *Placentia*. *Hannibal* after two Days got over *Ticinum*, and prefented himfelf before *Placentia*, but no Man looks out; whereupon the Conful's *Gauls* fell from him to *Hannibal*, who fent them home with kind ufage, the better to perfuade their Nation to confederacy. The Conful fteals away in the Night, but had been overtaken by the *Numidian* Horfmen, if they had not ftayed to plunder his Camp, while he recovered the Bank of *Trebia*, where he fortified himfelf, expecting his Fellow Conful. The *Gauls* come over dayly to *Hannibal*, who is in want of Victuals, but relieved himfelf by taking *Chaftidium*, in which all the *Roman* Store and Ammunition lay, which was betrayed to him. *Rome* hearing of thefe Difafters, will revenge it by *Sempronius* the other Conful, with his Armies at *Ariminum*, which being brought to *Trebia*, where *Scipio* lay of his Wounds, *Sempronius* will have the honour of the day before the other recovers, or his Office now almoft out fhould expire; neither can he be diffuaded. *Hannibal* by the *Gauls* in their Camp underftanding it, conceal'd his Brother *Mago* within an Ambufh in a low place overgrown with Reeds, who preffing the Enemy in the Reer, while the other charged them in Front and Flank, Twenty Six Thoufand of the *Romans* were flain. *Sempronius* erred, Firft, Fighting in a Champion Country, to the advantage of *Hannibal*'s Elephants. Secondly, in not difcovering the Ground. Thirdly, In leading his weary hungry Men through the River, immediately to fight with frefh and well-fed Men.

§. 5. Winter is wellcome to the beaten *Romans*, who kept themfelves warm in *Cremona* and *Placentia*, whom yet *Hannibal* kept waking, *&c.* The *Lygurians* joyn with *Hannibal*, and put into his hand two *Roman* Quæftors, or Treafurers, two Colonels,

and

and five Sons of the Senators, of which he kept the *Romans* in miserable Bondage, but sent home their followers. Having wearied those *Gauls* where he wintred, when the Year was well advanc'd he pass'd the *Appenine* Mountains with such difficulty, that he chose to take through the Fenns, in which he lost his Elephants, and the use of one Eye with the severity of his March, and so came to *Aretium,* where wasting all the Countries, about Sixteen of which he set on fire just by *Flaminius* the Consul, an hot-headed popular Orator, who intending to quench it with *Carthaginian* Blood, fell unadvisedly into *Hannibal*'s Troops, between *Cortona,* and the Lake *Thrasamene,* where he and Fifteen Thousand of the *Romans* were slain, and Six Thousand escaped to the Mountains; where being discover'd, they stay'd not, but yet were overtaken by *Maharbal,* to whom they yielded upon promise of Liberty, which Condition *Hannibal* would not allow, being made without him; a trick learned of the *Romans* to break Covenants. Now he had Fifteen Thousand *Italian* Prisoners, of which the *Romans* he kept to hard meats, but freed the rest, in hopes to make the *Italians* his Allies; but an ancient Reputation is not so soon lost. *Servilius* the other Consul not knowing what was done, sent *Centronius* with Four Thousand Men to encrease the Army; but *Maherbal* intercepted them, slew half, and the rest yielded, the News whereof made *Servilius* hasten to the defence of *Rome.* Thus we discern the fruits of popular Jealousie in changing the Commanders in War yearly, which endangereth the growth of the Empire. For the best Wit in the World cannot inform it self in the compass of one year of all the good helps requisite to the prosecution of War to the best effect, as *Cæsar* did in *Gaul* by Ten Years continuance.

§. 6. *Rome* amazed at this success, and the imminent danger, flye to an old Remedy long out of use, and

and create a Dictator, whofe Office was above a Conful, and fcarcely fubject to any controul. The People as having Supream Authority, chofe *Fabius Maximus*, the beft Man of War in the City, who chofe *M. Minutius Rufus* Maiter of the Horfe, which is as his Lieutenant. *Fabius* began with Reformation in Religion, a commendable beginning if the Religion had been good. The *Sybil*'s Books were herein confulted, which directed Vows to *Mars*, a Sacrifice to *Jupiter*, and a Temple to *Venus*, which Trumperies prove the Books written by an ill Spirit. *Fabius* fets out with four Legions, and received *Servilius*'s Army, and fent him to Sea to purfue the *Carthaginian* Fleet, which had intercepted the Supply fent to *Scipio* in *Spain*. *Hannibal* in the mean time refrefhed his Men, armed the *Africans* after the *Roman* manner, and fo Coafted toward *Apulia*, not to take any City by long Siege, which breaks the force of a great Army; but feeking to weaken the *Romans* reputation, defired to be Mafter of the Field, which would foon open the Gates of Cities. Therefore he prefented. *Fabius* Battel as foon as he faw him, but he would not bite; knowing the difference between old Victorious Souldiers and Novices, whom he would acquaint with dangers, and to look upon the Lyon afar off, before they fet foot upon his Tail. *Minutius* had a contrary difpofition, fiery, like *Flaminius*, taxing *Fabius* with Cowardife; but that moved not this well-advifed Commander, who knew the danger of purfuing misfortune, which wafteth it felf by Suffering, fooner than by Oppofition. It is the Invading Army that defires Battel, and *Hannibal*'s was alfo Victorious, therefore *Fabius* fuffered him to fall upon the Rich Territory of *Campania*, himfelf keeping the Hills, being much weaker in Horfe. But Winter drawing on, *Hannibal* cannot ftay in the wafted Country, and could not get into a frefh, but muft pafs by the Dictator, who prefumed he now

had

had him faſt, but was deceived; for *Hannibal* in a
dark Night tying Faggots to the Horns of Two
Thouſand Kine, and ſetting them on fire, drove
them over the Hills; which terrible ſight caus'd *Fabius* to keep his Trenches, leſt he ſhould be circumvented, ſo *Hannibal* paſs'd by. *Fabius* is call'd home
about ſome matter of Religion, leaving the Army
with *Minutius*, yet with peremptory Charge not to
fight; but *Minutius* finding the Army of one mind,
reſolved to fight, though it were death to tranſgreſs
the Dictator's Charge. His Succeſs in the Encounter
was good, having taken ſuch advantage that he dared
Hannibal in his Camp, and came off with the better.
The Army applauds *Minutius*, but the People of
Rome more, and by motion of *Metellus* a Tribune,
ſeconded by *Terentius Varro* a Popular Fellow, Enemy to the Nobility, and who had been Prætor the
laſt year, *Minutius* is joyn'd in equal Authority
with *Fabius*: When they met *Fabius* divided the Army with *Minutius* by Lot, which the other likes not
ſo well as to Command the whole by Courſe, but
took his Lot, and incamped a mile and a half from
the Dictator, as deſirous to have occaſion to Fight,
as *Fabius* to the contrary. *Hannibal* deſign'd to try
Minutius's Courage the next day, and in the Night
conceal'd an Ambuſh of Horſe and Foot in ſpacious
Caves in the Vallie, and early in the Morning gave
occaſion to *Minutius* like the former, which he gladly
took, but ſucceeded worſe, and had loſt all, if *Fabius* had not come to reſcue him.

§.7. *Fabius* is commended by the principal Citizens; but the inferiour ſort cry out againſt his cold,
protracting the War, doing nothing of Conſequence
all his year. *Terentius Varro* took advantage to put
in for the Conſulſhip, which far exceeded his own
worth, without the favour of the Multitude, which
ſupply all his wants, eſpecially having *Bibilus Herennæus* a Kinſman, Tribune of the People, who by his
Place

Place might speak what he pleas'd to assist him. This bold Orator inveighed against the Nobility, as the Causes which drew *Hannibal* into *Italy*, who now could not be expelled without a *Plebeian* Consul. The Fathers labour to hinder this, first by choice of a Dictator, which held not; and by an *Inter-Regnum*, which was a Government of Ten of the Fathers for Five Days; in which the heat of the Multitude might be assuaged, and all begin again; but after five Days no other but *Terentius* will be heard of; so that to bridle this violent Person, *Lucius Paulus Æmilius* a Worthy Honourable Man is chosen the second Consul, and a great levy of Men, which made up the Army under the old Consuls Eighty Thousand Foot, and Six Thousand Horse. While this preparation and other businesses are ordering at *Rome*, *Hannibal* who Wintred at *Geryon* in *Apulia*, took the Castle of *Canne*, where much of the *Roman* Provision lay, but *Servilius* the old Consul could do nothing 'till the new came. At their departing, *Fabius* gravely exhorted *Æmilius* not only to play the Man against the *Carthaginians*, but also in bridling the rashness of his Collegue; who answer'd, He would do his utmost for his Country, but would rather adventure upon the Enemie's Sword, than the Citizens malice.

§. 8. *Æmilius* with his Collegue being come to the Camp, took occasion to encourage the Souldiers by the Consideration of old Victories against the *Carthaginians*, and other more warlike Nations, the present great numbers, even all that *Rome* could make. *Hannibal*'s Success was by Slight, not Valour; and they saw how destitute he was of the helps they had. They conceive all this, and the happiness of following such a Leader as they knew him to be; but mistook him, as if they should lose the Patience of waiting a Convenient Season, and only presume upon their advantage. But indeed there hapned an inconvenience, than which few are more dangerous, when they consider not the dissention

sention of their Chief Commanders, while *Varro*
upbraideth *Æmilius*'s Advise to decline such an Opportunity, to savour too much of *Q. Fabius*; and
Varro's hast by *Æmilius* is compared to *Flaminius.*
Varro in his Day of Command removed into the
Plains chose by *Hannibal*; *Æmilius* the next Day in-
trencheth, and will not stir, and sent part of the
Army to the East of the River *Aufidus*, intrenching
them. The want of skill in *Varro*, and his obstinate
Resolution against his Fellow Consuls prudent Coun-
sel, was great in suffering the Roman Army to be
drawn along by *Hannibal* to fight in a place of the
Enemies most advantage for his Horse, and in ran-
ging his Army in form, good against Elephants,
which the Enemy had not, but unprofitable against
Horse, in which the Enemies had the advantage.
The Battle began by *Asdrubal* upon *Æmilius*, whose
Roman Gentlemen were over-matched in number and
Horsemanship by the boisterous *Gauls* and *Spaniards*,
who forced them to give back, so that *Æmilius* put
himself on foot among the Legions, while *Asdrubal*
pursued, and slew almost all his broken Troops; the
Equites riding about him, who rescued him, did also
alight with him to help their distressed Foot, which
Hannibal esteemed a yielding. *Terentius Varro* his
Collegue in the Left Wing, is troubled with *Hanno*
or *Maharbal*, when Five Hundred *Numidian* Horse
came in and threw down their Arms in token of
yielding, whom he order'd to rest behind the Army
'till all were done. But these crafty Adventurers
Arm'd under their Cloaths with short Swords, spy-
ing their time, fell on the hindermost of the *Romans*
to their great terrour, which, *Asdrubal* having slain
the *Roman* Troops, highly increas'd, by joyning with
these *Numidians*, and so forced *Terentius* to trust to
his Horses heels. The *Numidian* Light-Horsmen
pursue him, while *Asdrubal* with the *Gauls* and *Spanish* Horse fall upon the backs of the *Roman* Foot,
disorder'd

disorder'd by *Hannibal*, who had environ'd them on
three sides; they being in a manner surrounded, a
miserable slaughter was made of them, wherein it is
probable that *Æmilius* dyed, and not that he got
out wounded, as *Livy* reports; he was found with
Lentulus in his flight, offering him his Horse, which
he refused. All the *Roman* Army, except Four
Thousand Foot and Two Thousand Horse, fell in this
Slaughter with *Æmilius*; as for *Terentius*, he escaped to *Venusia*, with Seventy Foot almost, and about
Two Thousand became Prisoners to the *Numidians*.
The *Roman* Camps were a while defended, but in
the end yielded, Eight Thousand of which became
Prisoners, though *Livy* tells us but of Three Thousand Foot, and Three Hundred Horse taken Prisoners. *Hannibal* lost but Five Thousand Five Hundred Foot, and Two Hundred Horse; and had he
pursued his Victory, as *Maharbal* persuaded, and
forthwith marched to *Rome*, it is little doubted but
the War had ended, as he was told, *He knew how to
get, but not to use a Victory.*

§. *Hannibal* having plunder'd the *Roman* Camp,
made head toward *Samnium*, where many Towns
seemed to favour *Carthage*, of which *Cossa* opened
to him, where he layed up his Baggage, and left
Mago to take in other places, while himself hasted
into *Campania*; where, as in all Cities of *Italy*, so
especially there, the multitude generally affected
him, for his sending home all their Citizens, whom
he had taken with much Civility. This Fruitful
Country of *Campania*, and *Capua* the Head, had design'd to open to him in *Fabius* the Dictator's days,
if his nearness had not hindred it, which after the
Victory at *Cannæ* was taken away; yet having Three
Hundred principal Gentlemen serving at *Sicily* under
the *Romans*, whom they desire to recover before they
fall off, they sent Ambassadors to Consul *Terentius*
to sound him, formerly offering their Service. But
he

he little bewailing the *Romans* misfortune, which had now loft all, faid, *Campania* muft now not help *Rome* only, but alfo make good the War againft the *Carthaginians.* The *Campanians* hearing this of their Ambaffadors, prefently make a League with *Hannibal*, only *Decius Magius* oppofed it to *Capua* where *Hannibal* came, and Condemned him as a Traytor; but to prevent the envy of his Execution, fent him to *Carthage.* Other Towns depending upon this, ran the fame courfe; though the next Cities, as *Nola, Nuceria,* and *Naples* ftood out for *Rome,* which yet was at this time in extream fear of *Hannibal's* coming, fo that *Terentius* was called home to name a Dictator. At his coming it was wifely done to give a good welcome, to cover their fear, and prevent the lamentations of the multitude, which would have bred contempt of the Governours, and not out of Greatnefs of Spirit, as *Livy* would have it. *M. Junius* is named Dictator, and *T. Sem, pronius* Mafter of the Horfe, who prefently raifed four Legions, and One Thoufand Horfe, being forced to prefs Boys. To thefe were added Eight Thoufand fturdy Slaves, encouraged with promife of Liberty upon deferts; Men alfo in Debt, and others in danger of Death for Capital Offences, are freed, if they will ferve in this War. To Arm thefe, they took down the Spoils of Enemies heretofore hung up in their Temples and Porches. About this time Ten Agents fent by the Prifoners to Treat with the Senate about their Redemption, came, with whom *Carthalo* is fent by *Hannibal* to found their difpofition to Peace, whom they will not fee, neither will redeem their Prifoners; pretending their Folly in not efcaping by flight as others did, but their wants was the true Caufe; for when fuch as efcaped came, they condemned them to ferve in *Sicily,* till the War ended, becaufe they had fled. The Dictator takes

the

the Field with twenty five Thousand Men, with whom he spent his time in *Campania* I know not how, while *Hannibal* made many idle Journeys between *Nola* and *Naples* ; but *Nola* was forc'd to call for *Marcellus* a *Prætor*, with his Legion to hinder the Multitude from opening to *Hannibal*. Failing thus of *Nola* he got *Nucera* by composition ; and returning to *Nola*, knowing the Affection of the Multitude, he sought to draw *Marcellus* out, but was out-witted by him. After this, hearing the Dictator was about *Casiline*, he went to seek him, not liking his being so near *Capua*, where he design'd to Winter ; there he attempted *Casilines*, and won it by composition, and upon the Inhabitants departure, put in seven hundred *Carthaginians* for defence of the Campaign, and went to Winter at *Capua*.

§. 10. *Mago*, Son of *Amilcar*, is sent to *Carthage*, to make report of *Hannibal's* proceedings and Victories, and demand Supplies, which *Hanno*, his old Enemy hindred what he could ; yet it was agreed to send him Forty Thousand *Numidians*, forty Elephants, and a great store of Silver ; and in *Spain* to levy twenty thousand Foot and four Thousand Horse ; which Aid was not so well compleated ; for only the Elephants and some of the Money was sent. So *Asdrubal's* Journey out of *Spain* into *Italy* was much talked of, but not performed 'till many Years after, when *Rome* had recovered her self. Thus *Hanno's* contrivance to remove the War out of *Italy* into *Spain*, to force *Emporiæ* and expel the *Romans*, was but to oppose *Hannibal*, in retarding the Supply agreed upon, to which the sparing *Carthaginians* were easily persuaded, but repented it too late ; not seeing now that the safety of *Carthage* and *Spain* lay upon the Success in *Italy*.

§. 11. The *Roman* Victories in *Spain* by *Scipio* against *Asdrubal*, reported by *Roman* History proved improbable ; and the Actions of *Scipio* there briefly run

run over ; among other Arguments of improbability, that *Scipio* vanquifh'd *Afdrubal* is that Objection of *Fabius,* cited and unanfwer'd by *Livy*; if *Afdrubal* were Vanquifh'd, how could he invade *Italy* with more than fixty Thoufand? In running over the particular Actions of *Scipio* in *Spain,* I will not infift upon any that are uncertain. After *Curius Scipio* had done Wonders by Sea and Land, and taken in one hundred and twenty Eftates, and driven *Afdrubal* into a Corner to hide himfelf ; and that the *Celtiberians* had flain fifteen Thoufand, and taken four Thoufand, *Publius Scipio* came in with Supplies to help his Brother. Thefe again beat *Afdrubal* by Sea and Land ; fo that he is forced to write to *Carthage* for Succours ; but without any he is commanded to lead his Army forth into *Italy*, which Journey he prepared for, by great Impofitions upon the Spaniard, raifing much Treafure. But he cannot fo pafs, for at *Ibera* the *Romans* beat him, take and pillage his Camp, and upon this event, all *Spain* falls off from him, fo that he hath fmall hopes of fafety in *Spain*, and much lefs of Travailing into *Italy*. Of thefe Exploits, Advertifements are fent to *Rome*, and Letters to the Senate, that they have neither Money, Apparel nor Bread for Fleet or Army; fo that for want they muft leave the Province. Thefe Contents of the Letters fuit not well with the Advertifements of fuch Exploits ; and came unfeafonably to *Rome*, fcarce able, after the lofs at *Cannæ*, to help it felf at home. Yet forfooth, they are fupplyed, and again beat *Afdrubal* twice, tho' he had fixty Thoufand Men, and with fixteen Thoufand, flew forty fix Thoufand. But according to *Livy*, the next Year, tho' all *Spain* had been twice gotten from the *Carthaginians*, and that they loft fo many thoufands, and plunder'd of the Treafure gathered by *Afdrubal*, yet is he able to purfue *Publius Scipio*, and fet down by him at *Mons Victoriæ*, and after removeth to *Illiturgis*, which he Befiegeth

fiegeth, but is again beaten by *Curius Scipio*, who, with one Legion of five Thoufand enters the Town, and flew the next day twelve Thoufand *Carthaginians* more, and took three Thoufand Prifoners; and at *Auringes* flew eight Thoufand. After all this, the *Romans* take *Saguntum*, and deftroy the *Turdetans*, which argueth the *Carthaginians* were too weak to difturb them, or rather, the *Romans* took it by furprize; for as the many Sieges made by the *Carthaginians*, argue them Mafters of the Field, fo the *Romans* confuming a whole Year after, in gaining the *Celtiberians*, and that by exprefs Condition of a great Sum of Money, to make War againft the *Carthaginians*; yet if we will believe it, thefe *Celtiberians* had fome Years before given Hoftages to *Scipio*. With the accefs of thirty Thoufand *Celtiberians*, the two *Scipio*'s feek out the fo oft beaten *Carthaginians* (if all former Reports were true) not far off nor fo broken, having three Armies led by *Afdrubal*, Son of *Amilcar*, *Mago*, and *Afdrubal* Son of *Gefco*; *Curius Scipio* undertakes the firft; *Publius Scipio* makes hafte to the other two, being Five Days March off, left they fhould run away upon the Report of their Fellows overthrow. But *Publius Scipio*, with two parts of the *Roman* Army, is met with, and forced to keep his Trenches; and yet not fafe in them, fteals out by Night, leaving *Fonteius* his Lieutenant with a few to keep the Camp, while he hoped to intercept feven Thoufand five hundred *Sueffetans*, but being purfued by the *Numidian* Horfe, was flain. His Brother, twenty feven days after, meeting with *Afdrubal*, is forfaken of his *Celtiberian* Mercenaries, after a violent Flight in which he is overtaken, loft his Life, fome few efcaping to *T. Fonteius*, if it may be believed, confidering the plainnefs of the Country. After this, *L. Martius*, a *Roman* Gentleman, gathers together the fcatter'd Souldiers, and fome Companies out of Garrifons, making up a pretty Army, with which he wrought Wonders, by

report

report of *Valerius Antias*, &c. *Martius* magnifieth his Service by News at *Rome*, and ftileth himfelf *Propretor*, at which the Senate is offended, and fend *Claudius Nero* with twelve thoufand Foot, and one thoufand one hundred Horfe, where he found almoft all the *Spanish* Friends fa'ln off: But we muft believe that he boldly advanced toward *Afdrubal*, Brother of *Hannibal*, and took him in fuch a ftreight, as that he offered to quit *Spain* if he might do it peaceably; yet was he called home, and *Publius*, Son of *Publius Scipio* fent Pro-conful into *Spain*. This *Publius Scipio* was a Man of a Noble Prefence, fingularly well Condition'd, efpecially in Temper, Continence, Bounty, and all Virtues which procure Love. To pafs by the feveral Accounts of this Man given by Hiftorians; if this one were true, that in all *Rome* no Man was found which durft defire the place 'till this *Cornelius Scipio*, but that twenty four ftood up at the fame time, then were not the Wonders reported of *L. Martius* like to be true. This Proconful with *Junius Sillanus* Propretor, lands at *Emporiæ* with ten Thoufand Foot and one Thoufand Horfe, and Marcheth to *Tarracon*, and as foon as Winter was ended, attempted *N. Carthage*, which he furprized, and therein many Hoftages of *Spain*, which he kindly fent home, and fo drew many to his Friendfhip. Yet *Afdrubal* ftayed not his Journey to his Brother in *Italy*, leaving *Mago* and the other *Afdrubal* in *Spain*. The *Roman* Hiftorians tell us, that *Scipio* beat him into *Italy*, with many incoherent relations of the *Spanish* Affairs.

§. 12. *Hannibal*, as we heard, after the Battle at *Cannæ* wintred at *Capua*, not attempting *Rome*, left not carrying it without a long Siege, he fhould be forced, for want of Victuals, to rife; which might difhearten his Men and the States of *Italy* which had joined him. His expected Supplies from *Carthage* came all to a few Elephants, with fome excufe for the reft, rest, especially for want of a convenient Haven to Land in.: Yet he took the Field, designing to gain some good Haven Town ; to which end he sent *Hanno* to the *Lucans* but with ill success, losing Two Thousand Men, yet *Hammilco* with the *Locrians*, assisted with the *Brutians*, wan *Pretilia* by force, and *Cosentia*: *Croton* was left them, and *Locri*-yeilded, but *Rhegium* held out. *Rome* at this time was brought so low, that when the Messengers from *Petilium* upon their Knees sought succour, the Senate willed them to provide for their own safety. At the same time their *Prætor Posthumus Atomus* with Twenty Five Thousand, was cut in pieces by the *Gauls* in a Wood through which they must pass, whose Trees before their coming were so cunningly sawed, that a little force would throw them down : So that after they were in, the *Gauls* about the Wood beginning, one Tree cast down another, and overwhelmed the *Romans*. About the same time *Philip* King of *Macedon* entred into League with *Hannibal*, of mutual and Personal assisting ; the one in Conquest of *Italy* for the *Carthaginian*, the other of *Greece* for *Philip* : But predisposing of Kingdoms is justly controuled by the Divine Providence. The *Romans* understanding this League, sent M. *Valerius* the *Prætor* to employ *Philip*, more in *Greece* than would give him leave to visit *Italy* ; which he so well effected by stirring up the *Ætolians*, old Enemies to *Macedon*, that he was chosen Consul at *Rome*, and *Sulpitius* sent in his stead. *Philip* being thus incumbred in *Greece*, and seeing *Carthage* was careless of supplying him with a Fleet, which he wanted, after he had forced the *Ætolians* to submit, he hearkned to the *Romans*, who desired his Friendship, which he esteemed much to his Honour.

§. 13. The *Carthaginians* undertaking so many Enterprises at once, and following them by halves, was an errour ; but their neglect of supplying *Hannibal*,

when

when he had as great an opportunity as a Conquerour could defire, argued his Enemies at home, durft not truft him with the Power which might injure themfelves. *Hannibal* therefore is forced by neceffity to feed his *Italian* Friends with Hopes, trifling about *Nola, Naples,* and *Cuma,* about which latter *Gracchus* a Conful over-reached the Magiftrates of *Capua,* who had Confpired to take the Senators of *Cuma* at a Sacrifice, but was himfelf furprifed by *Gracchus,* who flew above TwoThoufand, and immediately after OneThoufand Four Hundred more of *Hannibal's* Men, at this Siege of *Cuma. Hannibal* not able to make good all his Garrifon Towns, and continue ftrong in Field, was forc'd to pafs from place to place, waiting occafions till his fupply came. In the mean time *Hanno* in a Journey againft *Beneventum,* with Seventeen Thoufand Foot, and Twelve Hundred Horfe, is met by the Conful *Gracchus* with an Army, confifting of Slaves, who upon promife of Manumiffion, fought fo valiantly that they forced *Hanno* to flie but with Two Thoufand. Thus *Rome* began to repair her breach made at *Canna*; yet her Treafury was empty: For all the Fruits her Ground could yield, were hardly able to feed their own Armies: No not *Sicily,* and *Sardinia.* Now *Afdrubal* is expected out of *Spain* : *Macedon* is feared, which mortal dangers could not be avoided, but with expence of Treafure. Hereupon the People are Affembled, and *Quintus Fabius* the *Prator,* opened to them the publick Wants, and how to fupply them; which the People undertook. Then followed the two Cenfors, who Cenfured all diforders in the City, or about the Wars paft; and thus by Pruning the Branches the decayed Root recovered.

§. 14. *Fabius Maximus,* one of the Confuls, having Befieged *Caffeline* in *Campania,* after *Marcellus,* the other Conful was come, who finding it fo obftinately defended, would have left it, as no great
Enter-

Enterprife, if *Marcellus* had not replied, that Things
undertaken by a great Commander, ought to be pro-
fecuted. So the Siege being continued, he forced them
within to feek Peace. But as the Befieged were going forth according to Covenant, *Marcellus* takes a
Gate, entreth, and puts to the Sword, or taketh
all but Fifty, which ran to *Fabius* for Protection: This
needed a *Roman* Equivocation to juftifie it. Many o-
ther fmall Towns of the *Samnites*, and fome of the
Lucans, and *Apulians*, were recovered, and Twenty
Five Thoufand of the Enemies put to the Sword. The
new Conful next was *Quintus Fabius*, Son to *Maximus Gracchus*, who was Conful the other Year: Thus
the Father became Lieutenant to his Son. *Fabius*
entred *Arpi*, by Scalade in a ftormy Night; yet was
fo refifted by a *Carthaginian* Garrifon, that they left
the Town by Compofition: Divers other places returned to the *Roman* obedience: But *Tarentum* in the
mean time was betrafed to *Hannibal* who entred the
Town; but the Citadel was held by the *Romans*. The
next Year the City of *Rome* Armed Twenty Three
Legions, of which many were Boys, under Seventeen
Years Old, and *Fulvius Flaccus*, with *Appius Claudius*
Confuls, Befiege *Capua*, who fend to *Hannibal* to relieve them, which Charge was committed to *Hanno*,
who made good Provifion which the Peafants fhould
have carried to *Capua*, but by their negligence, *Fulvius* took it with Two Thoufand Waggons in *Hanno's*
Camp, in his abfence, where were Six Thoufand flain,
and Seven Thoufand taken. In the mean time the
Metapontines, and *Thurines*, yielded to *Hannibal*: And
Gracchus late Conful was flain, being appointed to
keep *Beneventum*, for fecuring the Confuls at the
Siege of *Capua*. But *Hannibal* diflodged them, followed *Claudius*, and upon his return fell upon *Penula*
with almoft Sixteen Thoufand Men, of which fcarce
Two Thoufand efcaped; and *Fulvius* à *Prætor* with
Eight Thoufand in *Appulia*, was fo furprized by *Ma-*

go, that he carried away but Two Thousand. The
Consuls renew the Siege of *Capua,* which sendeth to
Hannibal, then at *Brundusium,* and have a comfortable Answer, but came not till Want began to pinch
them. But being come, he took one of their Forts, and
fell upon the Camp; the Citizens also issue out, and
{ *Claudius* hath his Deaths wound, yet can he not
raise the Siege. Then inraged with himself, he resolves to Attempt *Rome,* hoping so to raise it; which
the Senate understanding, refer it to the Generals,
whether to stay or come home; and they agree that
Fulvius with Fifteen Thousand Foot, and One Thousand Horse should go to *Rome. Hannibal* hasteth
with Ten Days Provision, and *Fulvius* is not long
after him; but when his Provision was spent, he
made as much haste away, having only frighted the
timerous multitude. *Fulvius* also returns to *Capua,*
where *Belstar* and *Hanno* are closely Besieged, and
can by no means draw on *Hannibal,* whose Spirits
were spent more by Domestick Treachery than *Roman* Force. *Capua* in desperate Case, having twice
rejected mercy, after Twenty Seven chief Senators
had purposely Poison'd themselves at a Supper, open
the Gates to the *Romans,* who tooke severe revenge
on all but Two poor Women, who were found not
guilty, the rest were either slain, sold, or banished.
Other *Capuan* People that submitted sped not better,
Capua was new Peopled, but never incorporated, but
Governed by a Magistrate sent yearly from *Rome.*

§. 15. *Sardinia* during the Wars in *Italy,* was
drawn to a Rebellion by the *Carthaginians,* who
encourage *Harsicoras* and *Hostius* his Son, Popular
in the Island, promising them aid against *Mutius* the
Prætor. The *Romans* hearing thereof, sent *T. Manlius,* who in his Consulship had won the Island, with
Twenty Two Thousand Foot, and Twelve Hundred
Horse, as their commendable manner was to suport
in their Provinces those Men and their Families,
, which

which had firft fubdued them. *Manlius* foon after his Arrival, in one Day overthrew *Hyoftius*, who in his Father's abfence would needs venture upon the old Soldiers, who flew above Thirty Thoufand Men, *Afdrubal* the bold, and other *Carthaginians* came foon after, and made *Manlius* leave *Cornus*, which he had Befieged, and go to *Calaris*, where in a Battle he flew Twelve Thoufand, and took Three Thoufand. *Hyoftus*, *Afdrubal*, and the reft dy'd, and the Rebellion ended. *Sicily* alfo grew troublefome after the Battle at *Canna*, when old *Hierom* King *Siracufe* dying, left his Kingdom to *Hyeronifmus* a Grandchild, fifteen Years Old, under tuition of fifteen Principal Men, of which *Andronodorus* that Married *Demarata*, Daughter of *Hiero*, defigning how to be the only Man, applyed himfelf to the King, pufhing him on to affume the Government, wherein he quickly exceeded and turned Tyrant. He affected not the *Romans* as his Father had done, defpifing the prefent weaknefs of *Rome*, and cafting an Eye upon the prevailing Fortune of *Carthage*, entred League with them upon Condition, that *Sicily* fhould be his. But while he was bufie herein, his Tyranny produced Treafon againft his Perfon, which took effect at *Leontium*, where he was flain. *Andronodorus*, pufh'd no by his Wife, endeavoured to become Tyrant; but finding it yet too hard to compafs, applauded the Peoples liberty, and fo by them is chofen chief *Prætor*. He finding *Themiftius* who Married the Sifter of *Hieronymus*, affected as himfelf, (as he was alfo Wiv'd) dealt with him, and drew him to take his part: But being too free in communicating their defign, 'twas difcover'd to the Senate; fo that entring into the Senate, both were flain, and their Wives alfo, for affecting Royalty. Then new *Prætors* are chofen in their place, called *Epicides* and *Hippocrates*, Born in *Carthage*, but of *Syracufan* Parents; both which *Hannibal* had ufed in the League with *Hieronymus*; who being in Office, oppofed the *Roman* League. But finding the People afraid of *Marcellus*, who alfo required the City to expel them, they ftirred up the *Leontines* to take their Liberty as *Syracufe* had done; for feeing the Tyrant was flain there, it was no reafon they fhould remain Subject to *Syracufe*. When *Marcellus* heard that *Leontium* revolted from *Syracufe*, he offered his help, and won the Town in a day: So the two Ringleaders fled to *Heberfus*, but the Citizens were pardoned; tho' the contrary Report bred a mutiny againft the *Roman Prætors* Cruelty among the *Syracufan* Mercenaries. Thefe being led by their *Prætors* to *Herbefus*, *Epicides* and *Hyppocrates* came out with Olive Branches to the Army, wherein Six-Hundred *Creets*, whom *Hannibal* had ufed well, took Protection of them, and at *Megara* by a counterfeit Letter of *Hyppocrates* to *Marcellus*, from *Syracufe*, intreating him to make away their troublefome Mercenaries, the Army was in fuch Uproar that the *Prætors* fled for Life. So the Army was led by *Hyppocrates* to *Syracufe*, who let him in; where he flew whom he lifted, fet Slaves and Prifoners free, as is ufually done by Tyrants, and thus the two Brethren became Lords of *Syracufe*. *Marcellus* hearing of the alterations, hoping by his fuccefs at *Leontium*, to make fhort work at *Syracufe*, prefently Befieged it by Sea and Land, omitting no violence and terrour in two or three Affaults; but was beaten off, not fo much by virtue of the Defendents, as by the skill of that Noble Mathematician *Archimedes*, who at *Hiero*, at the late King's requeft, framed fuch Engines of War as did the *Romans* more mifchief than could have been done by Cannon, either by Sea, or Land; for they caft among them great Stones and Timber, and by an Iron Graple would take up a Galley by the Prow and fhake out all the Men, &c. *Marcellus* not knowing which way to turn, and loath to give over, refolved to famifh the Town, which was a defperate piece of work,

confider-

considering the large Haven and their *Carthaginian*
Friends, who even then had sent *Himilco* with twenty five Thousand Foot, three Thousand Horse, and
twelve Elephants, and *Bomilcar* with a Fleet had
Victualled the City.   Upon *Himilco's* Landing, many
Towns yielded, which forced *Marcellus* to rise with
a great part of his Army to prevent him of other
places, as he did, but came too late to *Agrigentum*,
which *Himilco* had gotten. Winter coming on, *Mar-*
cellus leaving sufficient Force before *Syracuse*, went
to *Leontium*, where Studying how to save his Honour, which his leaving the Enterprize would im-
peach, he falls on another Point of Dishonour, to prevail by Treason; which yet succeeded not.   In the
end a Fugitive out of the City informed him of a
Feast to be held to *Diana*, for which there was plenty of Wine: Upon this, in the Night he scaled the
Walls, and took some part of the City, which was
divided by Walls, like four or five Cities. The
Souldiers and Citizens after this offer to compound,
which *Marcellus* liketh, but once or twice it is interrupted, and being at a stand, *Marcellus* in the time of
the Treaty corrupted one of the Captains of the
Town, which was a Mercenary *Spaniard*, by whose
Treason he entred the Town, and had a Booty no less
than that of *Carthage*. In this surprize *Archimedes*
was slain, whose death *Marcellus* lamenteth, and Buried him Honourably. This under-dealing of *Mar-*
cellus was not approved at *Rome*, considering *Hie-*
ro's benefits; and that the Citizens when at Liberty
favoured *Rome*, but were now over-ruled by
Tyrants and Mercenaries: Yet the Senate thought
not good to restore the Booty, nor give over the
the Dominion: Nevertheless, it was not so well with
Syracuse before as after, considering their Factions,
Conspirators, Tyrants, Murders, Banishments, *&c.*
which yet Justifieth not *Rome's* injustice more than
him which stole the Cup from a sick Person, because

he

he was always drinking in it. After this all *Sicily* yeilded, except *Agrigentum,* &c. held by *Epicides, Hanno,* and *Mutines* a *Numidan,* a Wife and Valiant Man, by whom *Marcellus* was much interrupted ; yet was his Virtue fo envied by *Hanno,* that he took his Charge from him. The *Numidians* were fo Incenfed with this Indignity to their Country Man, that they left *Hanno,* and committed themfelves to *Mutines* difpofition, who entring into Intelligence with *Valentine Levinus* the *Roman* Conful, newly come, delivered *Agrigentum* into his hands, and affifted in the Conqueft of all the reft.

§. 16. *Rome* wanting Money to pay off the Souldiers, and to mannage the War againft *Hannibal,* and that in *Sicily,* when *Marcellus* and *Livinus* were chofen Confuls ; they propofed that the Confuls fhould bring in all the Money they had, that the Senators do the like, referving of Gold or other Plate only a Salt-feller, a Cup, a Ring, and fome pieces of Art, as Toys for their Wives and Children. This example the Gentlemen and Commonality followed cheerfully; all holding it equal, that every private Condition fhould run the Fortune of the Common-wealth; which if once ruin'd, in vain could any particulur Man hope to injoy the benefit of his proper fubftance. Upon this *Marcellus* was fent againft *Hannibal,* and *Livinus* into *Sicily,* where he finifhed what *Marcellus* left. *Hannibal* by long hard Service and wanting Supplies from *Carthage,* grew unable to keep the Field, and fufficiently to Garrifon his Towns, this made him Demolifh the places he could not Defend ; which aleniated many, fo that *Salapia* yielded to *Marcellus,* and betrayed a Regiment of *Hannibal's* beft *Numidian* Horfe. *Hannibal* in this ftrait hears of *Mafaniffa* with five Thoufand *Numidians* fent to *Spain,* and *Afdrubal's* coming to *Italy,* which News made *Hannibal* then keep what he could, and the *Romans* to recover ⸗hat they can. *Hannibal* by great Marches came

unlook'd

unlook'd for to *Fulvius*, a *Roman Prætor* at *Hardonia*, flew him, Twelve Tribunes or Colonels, and feven Thoufand more; others fay thirteen Thoufand, burnt the Town, and removed the Inhabitants. Afterwards *Marcellus*, who thought himfelf the only *Roman* fit to Incounter *Hannibal*, met with him, and loft fix Enfigns and three Thoufand Men; but the next day *Marcellus* flew eight Thoufand *Carthaginians*, loft three Thoufand, and had fo many wounded, that he could follow *Hannibal* no further. *Quintus Fabius Maximus* now Conful, befieged *Tarentum* Garrifoned with *Brutians*, whofe Captain in Love with a Woman in the Town, was drawn by a Brother of the Woman's to betray it; fo all were put to the Sword, even the *Brutians*, contrary to his word, that it might be thought he won the Town by Affault, not by Treafon: But it faved not his Reputation. *Claudius Marcellus* and *C. Crifpinus* Confuls the next Year, whom *Hannibal* entertained with many Skirmifhes, declined a fet Battle, till he might join with his Brother *Afdrubal*; but watching all advantage, he took them in his Ambufcade, as they came to view a place with fmall Forces, where they intended to Incamp. Here *Hannibal* had placed in Covert fome Companies of *Numidians*, who incompaffed them, flew *Marcellus*, wounded *Crifpine* to Death, and giving honourable Funerals to *Marcellus*, fent his Afhes in a Silver Pot to young *Marcellus*. *Crifpine* confidering that *Hannibal* had *Marcellus*'s Ring, with which he might deceive fome Cities, fent warning all about thereof; even as a Letter in *Marcellus*'s Name came to *Salapia* to prepare for his coming thither, which *Hannibal* followed with *Roman* Fugitives, which fpake Latin to the Watch, and bad them open to the Conful. The Gate was opened, and when fix Hundred Men were entred, the Port-Cullis were let down, and *Hannibal* out-witted in his own Stratagem. After *Crifpinus* death, *Claudius Nero*, and

M. Livius

M. Livius succeeded Consuls : Of which two, *Livius* had been many Years before condemned and expelled by the People ; for which indignity he refused the place, till with much importunity he was overcome. Thus as Men in fair Weather break the Branches of the Palm Tree, under which they shelter themselves in Storms ; so do the ungrateful with Men of Merit, (as *Themistocles* reprov'd the *Athenians.*) The two Consuls take their way, *Livius* to meet *Asdrubal*, *Nero* to follow *Hannibal*, to hinder their Marches ; knowing the mischievous effects of a Conjunction of two *Malevolent* Planets. It seemed that *Livius* was too weak to oppose *Asdrubal*, and therefore *Nero* took six Hundred Foot, and one Thousand Horse, and in six Days long Marches came to him : But *Asdrubal* perceiving the increase, thought to decline a Battle by removing over the River *Metaneus*, had not *Nero* followed and forced him to it, in which *Asdrubal* was slain, and fifty six Thousand with him, saith *Livy* ; but *Polybius* numbers but ten Thousand. After this Victory *Nero* hasted to his Camp with *Asdrubal*'s Head, which he threw before the *Carthaginians*, and freed some Prisoners which might make Report of the Victory in *Hannibal*'s Camp, so to strike a terrour into it. Here the Tide began to turn on the *Romans* side, and so increased that no Bounds could contain it ; and *Hannibal*'s hopes decayed daily. From this thirteenth Year of the second *Punick* War unto the eighteenth, in which it ended, little is delivered worthy of Memory.

§. 17. *Publius Cornelius Scipio,* after *Asdrubal*'s departure into *Italy*, had to do with *Hanno*, lately sent to succeed *Asdrubal*, whom *M. Syllanus* shortly after took Prisoner : *Asdrubal* Son of *Gesco*, and *Mago*, left by *Asdrubal* Son of *Amilcar*, remained to make head, who prepared seventy Thousand Foot, four Thousand Horse, and thirty two Elephants to keep the Field. *Scipio* makes up his Legions with

some

some Auxiliary *Spaniards*, and seeks out the Enemy with forty five Thousand Foot, and three Thousand Horse, whom he fed well the day before, and early next Morn provoked the empty *Carthaginians* to Battle, as *Hannibal* had served his Father at *Trebia.* *Asdrubal* wholly depended upon this Battle, in which he was worsted, whereupon *Artanes* with his *Turde-tans* fell to the *Romans* ; and the other *Spaniards* being confirmed in the Report of the *Carthaginians* ill suc-cess at *Metaurus* in *Italy*, never did them good ser-vice after. *Asdrubal* perceiving this, hasteth toward the Sea, but is overtaken by *Scipio*, and charged so fu-riously, that he with seven Thousand took themselves to a strong piece of Ground, from whence himself stole by Night to the *Gades*, whither *Mago* and *Masanissa* followed, and their Army dispersed : So all the Towns, except three, submitted to *Scipio*, who the Year after took them ; only *Astapa* was burnt with all the Riches therein by the Inhabitants, who slew themselves, except such as desperately broke out up-on the *Romans* Camp and so were slain. *Asdrubal* leaves *Mago* at *Gades*, and Saileth to *Syphax* King of the *Masæsuli*, a People of the *Numidians*, hoping to perswade him to be a Friend to *Carthage* ; but *Scipio* meeting him there drew him to the *Roman* side, which he soon forsook. *Scipio* returns to *Spain*, and hav-ing taken Revenge of the three Cities which held out, he celebrated Funeral Games at New *Carthage* for his Father and Unkle, which was performed by Du-els of Slaves ; as also such as had Quarrels for Title of Land, which Friends could not compose.

Scipio being dangerously sick, is reported Dead ; whereupon *Mandonius*, and *Indibilis*, two *Spanish* petty Kings rebel, hoping to make themselves great : and part of the *Roman* Army discontented with the little benefit they had got by the *Roman* Conquest fell to spoil, drive away their Colonels, choos-ing two base Leaders. *Scipio* sent new Colonels, which

which with fair words and promise of Pay brought
them to *Carthagenia*, where exemplary Justice is done
upon the two Leaders and their Accomplices; the
rest having sworn, Obedient receive Pay. *Mandonius* and
Indibilis pursued by *Scipio*, submit, and are pardoned,
but their former Power leſſened. *Maſaniſſa* pro-
miſeth to ſerve the *Romans*; and *Mago* by direction from *Carthage*, leaveth *Gades*, when he had Robbed it, to go to *Hannibal* in *Italy*, having Treaſure
ſent to raiſe an Army: So *Gades* preſently yielded to the *Romans*, and *Scipio* gives up the Province
to a Succeſſour, and is choſen Conſul.

§. 18. *Publius Cornelius Scipio*, and *Publius Licinius
Craſſus* are choſen Conſuls. *Scipio* had *Sicily* decreed
for his Province, with leave to make War in *Africa*
if he thought fit: Which *Quintus Fabius Maximus* oppoſed; nevertheleſs *Scipio* proceeds; But
was not allowed to Preſs Souldiers for *Africa*,
but what *Fabius* and other Ancient Senators ſhould
allow of. Beſides his *Roman* Forces, *Italy* ſent him
ſeven Thouſand Volunteers and all manner of needful Proviſion: In *Sicily* he found two Legions ſent
thither from the Battle at *Cannæ*, and Preſſed three
Hundred Horſe. Notwithſtanding all which he had
like to have been hindred in this Expedition upon
complaint of the *Locrians*, whoſe Town he had gotten from the *Carthaginians* by their aſſiſtance, who
were much oppreſſed by the Governours put in by
him. But the Commiſſioners ſending into *Sicily* to examine matters, found him ſo well prepared for *Carthage*, that they quickened his March. He ſent *Lælius* into *Africk* to make diſcoveries, who met with
Maſaniſſa revolted from the *Carthaginian* ſide to the
Roman, for an injury they did him about *Aſdrubal's*
Daughters being Betrothed to him, but by them given
to *Syphax* a more mighty *Numidian* Prince. *Lælius*
underſtood the State of *Africa* by *Maſaniſſa*, whom
Syphax had driven out of his Country, and by perſuaſion

suafion of *Sophonisba* renounced the Alliance of *Rome* to join with the *Carthaginians* her Country-men. This troubled *Scipio* and made him haften to *Africa,* left the Senate hearing thereof fhould ftay his Journey, to which he had been induced upon hopes of his affiftance. He Lands in *Africa,* is met by *Mafanif-fa* and Incamped before *Utica. Afdrubal* was with *Syphax* his Son in Law, to whom the *Carthaginians* fend to call him Home, being chofen their General, and to intreat *Syphax* againft *Scipio,* who lay before *Utica. Afdrubal* makes a Levy of thirty Thoufand Foot, and three Thoufand Horfe; and *Syphax* brings fifty Thoufand Foot, and ten Thoufand Horfe, with which they March toward *Scipio,* who diflodged to a place fit for his Navy, where he defigned to Winter, and there Fortified his Camp. *Afdrubal* and *Syphax* Incamp near to him, but carelefly, prefuming upon their Numbers. While they lay thus, *Scipio* endeavours to draw *Syphax* from the *Carthaginians,*and he tries to perfuade *Scipio* to a Peace; this is in debate while *Scipio,* learns how weak the Enemies Camp was, and how it might be fet on fire; whereupon he breaks off the Treaty of Peace, pretending his Counfel would not agree to it. Setting therefore all things in order for fuch a bufinefs, he fent *Lælius,* and *Mafaniffa,* to begin with *Syphax* who lay fartheft off; and when he faw the Flame,he drew on to *Afdrubal's* Camp, which was in confufion, running to help *Syphax* ; but immediately they found the like Flame in their own Camp. Great was the flaughter, in which but few efcaped, with *Syphax* and *Afdrubal.* After this new Levies are made, and a fecond Battle fought, and the *Romans* obtain a fecond Victory. *Afdrubal* flying to *Carthage,* and *Syphax* home, whither *Mafaniffa* and *Lælius* purfue him.

Scipio takes in many Towns, fome by force, others by furrender, for all the Subjects of *Carthage* wavered; and *Carthage* it felf durft not exact Taxes of them whom

they

they had so often overburthened. It is therefore decreed to Fortifie the City, to send for *Hannibal*, and to set out the Fleet against that of *Scipio* before *Utica*; who perceiving it, haftened thither from *Tunis* to defend them; so they returned, having gotten only six empty Hulks from the *Romans*. In the mean time *Masanissa* recovers his Kingdom, and with *Lælius* proceeds against *Syphax*, who quickly raised as great an Army as his first, which he also lost as soon, with himself and his Kingdom. For being taken, *Masanissa* carried him bound to *Cirta*, his chief City, which presently opened, where *Sophonisba* yielded her self, intreating she might not be delivered to the *Romans*; which suit her Youth and excellent Beauty so recommended, that *Masanissa* Married her presently. *Lælius* and *Scipio* were afterwards offended with this Marriage, and perfuaded *Masanissa* to give her over, for fear she should draw him into the same courses she had drawn *Syphax*. *Masanissa* to prevent her falling into the *Romans* hands, sent her a Cup of Poison with which she ended her Days: And he presently after to prevent the effects of Melancholy for that fact, is comforted by *Scipio* with a Crown, and Proclaimed King.

§. 19. *Carthage* hearing this bad News, and seeing *Scipio* returned to *Tunis*, are so astonish'd, that they send Thirty of the Princes which were of the Privy Council of the City unto *Scipio*, to beg Peace prostrate, kissing his and his Councils Feet, humbly acknowledging their fault in breaking the former Peace. *Scipio* considering the poor case that *Rome* was in, and the Wealth and Strength of *Carthage*, accepted the submission, on Condition *Carthage* should call home her Forces in *Italy*, relinquish all the Islands, deliver up all their Ships of War but Twenty, all Prisoners and Fugitives, meddle no more with *Spain*, pay a great Sum of Mony, and certain Hundred Thousand Bushels of Corn. These Articles are approved, a

TRUCE

Truce granted, 'till they send to *Rome*, and *Masanissa* sent home to his new Kingdom, as if all were ended; but it appeared after their Ambassadors were come to *Rome*, they only sought to gain time 'till *Hannibal* were come, by whom at least they hope to get a better Peace; the Senate therefore refer all to *Scipio* : But before their return, *Carthage* had seiz'd on the *Roman* Ships, with Provision from *Sicily*, scatter'd by storm, and sought to surprize *Scipio's* Ambassadors in their return from *Carthage*.

§. 20. *Hannibal* after his loss at *Metaurus* remained among the *Brutains*, expecting aid from *Carthage*, and his Brother *Mago* with Forces raised in *Gaul* and *Liguria*, who also solicited the *Hetrurians*, which caused the *Romans* to employ Three Armies in those Three Countries. *Mago* near *Milan* met with the *Roman* Forces, with which he fought, like a Son of *Amilcar*, but with the *Carthaginian* Fortune, losing Five Thousand, and himself wounded to death, was forced to retire to *Liguria*, where he found Ambassadors to call him home immediately, which he obeyed, but died by the way. *Hannibal* receiv'd the like Message of return, which he heard with such impatience, that he gnash'd his Teeth, and hardly refraining from Tears, he cried out, that not *Scipio*, but *Hanno* had overthrown the *Barchines* with the ruine of *Carthage*; so he departed, as if it had been to Exile. *Rome* being certain of his departure, appoint an Holy-day for Thanks to the Gods ; but *Quintus Fabius* rejoyc'd little, being in doubt of the issue in *Africa*.

§. 21. *Hannibal* Landed in *Africk* at *Leptis*, almost an Hundred Miles from *Carthage*, that marching along he might gather Horses, which he wanted ; and *Scipio* sends to *Masanissa* and the *Roman* Company with him to make speed to him, who brought Four Thousand Horse, and Six Thousand Foot. *Lælius* also is returned with the *Carthaginian* Ambassadors from *Rome*, at which time M. *Babius* kept the Camp in *Scipio's* absence. He laid hands on the Ambassadors,

and

and fent word to *Scipio*, who orders their good u-
fage, and fends them home; to fhew that the *Carthaginians* were lefs honourable than the *Romans*: Yet he
made more cruel War upon them than before, Sacking the Towns he took, refufing all Compofitions.
Carthage hearing this, hafted *Hannibal* to fight; who
thereupon Encamped at *Zama*, fent Spies into *Scipio's*
Camp, who being taken, were carried up and down
to fee what they would, and fo fent back. *Hannibal*
at this, admir'd his Enemie's brave Courage, and
fent to defire an Interview, which *Scipio* granted;
but being met, refufed to yield to the Peace which
Hannibal propounded, feeing the Conditions of it
were gainful to them, who had fo lately broke a
Peace made upon other Conditions. So they brake
off, and prepare for Battle, which was the next day
to try both Skill and Courage, efpecially of thefe
brave Commanders. They are both in the Field
early, fet their People in order, and exhort them to
Fight; a Noble Match, and feldom feen, whether
we regard the two Generals, their Cities, the import
of the Battle, and the Armies; though *Hannibal* was
over-matched in number, and goodnefs of Horfes,
and had only his Rereward of trained Men, which
were thofe brave Souldiers which had follow'd him in
Italy; all the reft being untrained boifterous *Barbarians*, except Four Thoufand *Macedonians*. The
iffue was the overthrow of the *Carthaginians*, of
whom Twenty Thoufand were flain, and as many
taken, with the lofs of Fifteen Thoufand *Romans* and
upwards: Yet the fingular Skill that *Hannibal* fhewed
in this his laft Fight, is highly commended by *Polybius*, and was acknowledg'd by *Scipio*, as *Livy* reports. *Hannibal* with a few Horfe came to *Afdru-
mentum*, whence being fent for, he went to *Carthage*,
where he tells them plainly, there was no way left
but fuch Peace as could be gotten. Prefently after,
Vermina Son of *Syphax*, who held a good part of his
                                        Father's

Father's Kingdom, coming to help when all was loft, was encountred by part of the *Roman* Army, which flew Fifteen Thoufand, and took Twelve Hundred. *Scipio* being come to *Tunis,* is Adored by Thirty *Carthaginian* Ambaffadors, in more pitiful manner than before, but lefs pitied for their former Treachery. Neverthelefs *Scipio* confidering the tedious Siege of fo ftrong and large a City, and the defires of the other Confuls to get the Honour of ending what remained, he was content to hear them, and to propound fuch Conditions as he thought good : As delivery of Prifoners, Fugitives, and Renegadoes, all their Gallies but Ten, and all Elephants ; make no War without Licence from *Rome,* reftore to *Mafaniffa* what they held from him, or his Anceftors; find Corn for the Army, and pay for Auxiliaries 'till the Peace was Concluded ;, pay Two Hundred Talents yearly, for Fifty year, and One Hundred Hoftages of Choice Men for obfervance of Conditions. The Conditions were declaim'd againft at *Carthage,* but upon *Hannibal's* Speech, Neceffity forced them to yield, and fend to *Rome,* who fent Ten Commiffioners to joyn with *Scipio* to Conclude the Peace, though the Conful *Lentulus* oppofed, defiring to follow the War in *Africk.* At their coming to *Carthage* all is agreed upon, and the firft Two Hundred Talents to be paid out of private Mens Purfes. This was grievous to them, and made fome Senators weep, whereat *Hannibal* laughed, as being no caufe to weep, in confideration of other Conditions, which touched their Freedom more, tho' lefs felt by them, and would make them hereafter confefs that it was the leaft part of their Mifery for which they now fhed Tears. *Scipio* having concluded at *Carthage,* and brought *Mafaniffa* into the Army; and Honour'd him, he confign'd over to him all the Towns of King *Syphax* which the *Romans* held, and fo left *Africk,* and Landed in *Sicily,* from whence he went

through

through *Italy* with part of his Army, in Glory no less than Triumph, with the greatest joy that ever any did, and had the Title of *African* given; which kind of Honour from a Conquer'd Province, grew afterwards in use for less Merit.

C H A P. IV.

Of Philip King of Macedon, Father of Perseus, subdued by the Romans.

§. 1. SImilitude in Worldly Events, ariseth from limitation of Matter, to which Nature is confin'd, which being *finite*, cannot always produce variable effects, especially in Actions which seem to depend on the Will of Man, which is over-ruled with the same Affections. The *Assyrians* invading the *Medes*, and not prevailing, within a while were subdued by them; thus it fell out between the *Persians*, and *Greeks*, and the *Romans*. For after *Pyrrhus* the *Epirot* had braved the *Romans*, and that they found their Virtue was a Richer Metal than the shining Valour of *Greece*, it was not long before they durst venture upon *Greece*, having beaten him, which in a Year made himself Lord of it, and of *Macedon*. *Teuta* the *Illyriana* Queen wasting *Greece*, without the least provocation, gave the first occasion, that *Rome* sought acquaintance with *Greece*, offering to Protect it. *Philip* King of *Macedon*, set up *Philip* Son of *Demetrius*, about Seventeen Years Old, who succeeded King of *Macedon*, and Protector of *Achæa*, and most part of *Greece*, two Years before the second *Punick* War began. In the beginning of his Reign, the *Ætolians* addicted only to War, Invaded the *Messenians* and other parts, and *Peloponesus* twice; of which complaint was made to *Philip*, then

at

at *Corinth*, and the *Lacedemonians* are accused as favouring it in spite of the *Achæans* and *Macedonians*. The *Ætolians* declining to appear, War is decreed against them ; and the *Lacedemonians* seem to be excused, but are not trusted. *Philip* prepareth, and draweth those *Illyrians* from the *Ætolians*, which aided the Invasion : The *Achæans* Proclaim the War, and send to other States to do the like: But the *Epirots*, *Lacedemonians*, and *Messenians* put it off ; and in the end the *Lacedemonians*, who had long Conspired to shake off the *Macedonians*, concluded a League with the *Ætolians*, and chose new Kings, which they had not done since *Cleomenes* Departed ; of these, *Lycurgus* was one, who bribed the *Ephori* to Elect him. He Invades the *Argives*, takes two Cities from them ; and gains upon the *Arcadians*. *Philip*, while the *Ætolians* are busie in *Peloponesus*, brings his Army to their Borders with the *Epirots*, where to procure a Peace, which the *Epirots* desire, he spent so long a time as broke the Force of his Army, with which he might have ended the War. While he was busie in *Ætolia*, the *Ætolian* Prætor *Scopos* over-ran *Thessaly*, broke into *Macedonia* as far as *Dium*, which he rased ; the *Dardanians* also Bordering on the North of *Macedon*, hearing of his absence in *Peloponesus*, brake into Spoil, as their manner was, which drew him Home. *Demetrius Pharius* chased out of his Kingdom by the *Romans*, met him, and was entertained as his Chief Counsellor : After which, he stole a Journey into *Peloponesus* in Winter, while the *Ætolians* and *Eleans* were abroad, and Surprised Two Thousand, took many Towns from the *Eleans*, and *Ætolians*, and their Confederates, and so went to *Argos*.

§. 2. *Philip* is drawn by *Apelles* a Counsellor, left by his Uncle *Antigonus*, to incroach upon the Liberties of the *Achæans*, who finding it opposed by *Aratus*, he contrives to bring him into disgrace with

Philip. The King, by the grave admonition of *Aratus*, and the example of *Amphitamus*, an *Elean* Captain, discovers *Appelles*'s Malice, who failing of his defire, defigns to be King himfelf, as the Spider made a Web to take the Swallow which drove the Flies out of the Chimney. He enters upon a Plot againft the King how to check the good Succefs of his Proceedings, and draws *Leontius* one of the *Targenteers*, and *Megale* the King's chief Secretary, into the Confpiracy : But the Reward of their Treafon was their own Ruin. After this a Peace is Solicited by feveral Embaffadours, to which *Philip* condefcended by perfuafion of *Demetrius Pharius* ; who alfo perfuaded him to a League with *Hannibal.*

§. 3. *Philip,* upon the Peace of *Greece,* prepares for *Italy* to affift *Hannibal* againft the *Romans,* whom *Pharius* hated for expelling him out of his Kingdom, which they had forgiven him.

§. 4. *Philip* before his *Italian* Expedition, thought fit in Policy to bring the *Greeks* Affociates under a more abfolute Form of Subjection, as *Apelles* had formerly advifed ; but *Demetrius Pharius* could better obferve the Kings humours, and without Contention fupplanted *Aratus* with the leaft Appearance, which *Apelles* could never do by more forceable means. In a Faction between the Nobles and Commons of the *Meffenians, Philip* was intreated to compofe the difference, of which occafion he was glad, defigning to affume the Government into his own hands. But being difcovered, he pretended a Sacrifice in the Caftle of *Ithome,* and purpofed to feize upon it, which *Demetrius* called a *Kingly point* not to be neglected, for fo he fhould hold the Ox by both his Horns ; meaning that *Ithome* and *Acrocorinthus* were the two Horns of *Peloponefus.* Yet *Philip* asking *Aratus* his Judgment, he was told by him, *that in taking that Caftle he fhould lofe his ftrongeft Caftle, which was his Credit;* upon which he gave over his purpofe ; but,

with

with secret disgust of *Aratus* and his Son. Next he seized on *Oricum*, a Town of the *Epirots*, his followers, and besieged *Apolonia*, and so instead of setling the Country, he kindled that Fire which could never be extinguished till it laid hold on his own Palace. After that, he Invaded the *Messenians* with open Force, but in vain; in which Attempt he lost *Demetrius*; and afterwards out of a Tyrannical humour, the worse he sped, the more angry he grew against those who seemed not to favour his injurious doings, as particularly against Old *Aratus* and his Son, whose Poisoning he procured. This was the recompence *Aratus* got for bringing the *Macedonians* into *Peloponesus* in spite of *Cleomenes* his Countryman, and a Temperate Prince.

§. 5. The *Achæans* upon *Aratus*'s Death chuse *Philopœmen* Prætor: By whom they were perswaded to cut off their Expences in Bravery of Apparel, Houshold-stuff, and dainty Fare, and bestowed it upon Armies: As also he altered their Weapons and manner of Fighting, and fitted them for Hand-service. At this time *Machanidas Lycurgus* Tyrant of *Lacedemon*, who entred the Country of the *Mantinæans*, was Courageously received by *Philopœmen*, and slain with his own hand, and four Thousand with him, and as many taken Prisoners.

§. 6. *Philip* having made Peace with the *Romans* and *Ætolians*, prepares to invade *Attalus* King of *Pergamus*, Son of *Attalus*, the younger Brother of *Philetarus* the Eunuch, the Treasurer of *Lysimachus* King of *Thrace*, from whom he fled for fear of his Tyranny, and seized upon *Pergamus* and nine Thousand Talents of *Lysimachus*'s, and Reigned twenty Years, as *Eumenes* his Brothers Son did after him twenty two Years, and *Attalus* after him, an active Prince, Bountiful and Valiant. He made use of the *Gauls*, then setled in *Asia*, in that part which is called *Galatia*;

latia ; and Quarrels with *Prusias* King of *Bithynia*, whose Ancestors began to Reign some Generations before the Great *Alexander.*

§. 7. *Prusias* having Married the Daughter of *Philip,* intreated him to come over into *Asia* to Conquer *Cios* for him ; and not having any cause of Quarrel, he besieged the Town, took it, omitting no Cruelty to the Inhabitants, contrary to his promise made to divers Embassadours from the *Rhodians* and other Estates, to whom he became odious. *Attalus* considering to what end *Philip*'s violent Ambition tended, joining to the *Rhodians*, fought with him at Sea, where he sustained far greater loss than they, and in the end was forced Home, they pursuing him.

§. 8. *Attalus* and the *Rhodians* solicite *Rome* against *Philip* : So did *Aurelius* their Agent in *Greece* ; but *Rome* was not in Condition till *Hannibal* was Vanquished, when the River of *Styx* was dried up, that is, when the necessity of Peace with *Philip* was taken away. *Attalus*, and the *Rhodians* meet the *Roman* Embassadour, while *Philip* winneth *Abidos* in *Asia.*

§. 9. *Rome* hearing the Calamity of *Abidos* resembling that of *Saguntum*, could not ground a Quarrel thereon, but thinking of another *Saguntum* at *Athens* a Confederate, formerly wronged by *Philip*, and imploring their aid, which yet the People denied, till *P. Sulpicius* the Consul told them that *Philip*'s preparation was indeed for *Italy*, if he could win *Athens.* This feigned pretence prevailed, and the Consul is sent ; who took not the way to *Macedon*, but Landed at the River *Apsus*, between *Dyrrachium* and *Apolonia*, where he began the War, and sent *C. Claudius* with Twenty Gallies and Souldiers to relieve *Athens*, against certain Pyrates, or Robbers by Sea and Land.

§. 10. *Claudius* groweth weary of standing like a Scare-Crow to save all the *Athenian* Fields from Spoil,

Spoil, and understanding that *Chalcis* in *Eubœa* was negligently Guarded, Sailed thither in the Night, and took it by Scalado, Plunder'd it, and set it on Fire, Consuming the Kings Magazines of Corn and other Provision of War. *Philip* hearing the News at *Demetrias*, twenty Miles off, marcheth speedily; but finding them gone, he Posteth to *Athens* in hope to surprise it in the Night, but they had Intelligence of his coming: So after a Skirmish before the return of *Claudius*, he departed to *Corinth*; and thence to an Assembly at *Argos*, called against *Nabis* Tyrant of *Lacedemon*, which had Invaded them after *Philopœmen* was out of Office and gone to *Crete*. Here *Philip* by coming, would have drawn the *Achæans* to break with the *Romans*, but was discover'd, and so parting made no other Attempt against *Athens*, having failed, except in demolishing some Temples of admirable Workmanship in *Attica*. *Sulpicius* Encamped near *Apsus*, sent his Lieutenant *Apistius* to the Borders of *Macedon*, who took *Antripatria*, and put it to the Sword and Fire, and other Towns, and returned to their Camp; by which Success, divers of the Neighbours which affected not *Philip*, offered Friendship to the *Romans*. The *Ætolian* Parliament was at hand, whither the *Macedonians*, *Romans*, *Athenians*, &c. send to persuade them to their Party: The *Macedonians* set out the true scope of the *Romans* pretensions of Friendship, by their Subjecting of *Messana* and *Syracuse*; the *Athenians* make a sorrowful rehearsal of the outrages done them by *Philip*; the *Romans* plead their former League with *Ætolia*, and threaten those that join with *Philip*: Which sheweth their meaning, however they pretend to assist their Friends: Which in the Conclusion is referred to *Dorymachus* their Prætor.

§. 11. *Philip* and the Consul met in the Borders of *Macedon* toward *Illyria*, and had divers Skirmishes, in which the *Romans* by an Ambush had a

great

great loſs at firſt, but by *Philip*'s ſtay to pick up
ſtraglers, he was overtaken by the *Roman* Legions,
which forc'd him to flye, and he hardly eſcaped, his
Horſe being ſlain, and he forced to accept his Subjects Horſe, who was after ſlain. The King recovers his Camp in the Night, taking his way Home:
But was overtaken, and put to a loſs before he could
recover *Macedon*, which was Invaded by the Borderers. The *Ætolians* hearing of *Philip*'s ill ſucceſs, Invade *Theſſaly*, and cruelly Plunder'd a few Towns;
but *Philip* finding them diſperſed, ſlew many of them.

§. 12. *Rome* thinking her ſelf ſafe at Home by
keeping War abroad, found more trouble than they
expected by the *Gauls*, Governed by one *Amilcar* a
Carthaginian, who took their Colony of *Placentia*, a
good ſtrong Town, which neither *Hannibal*, nor
Aſdrubal could force. Upon this, they ſent to *Carthage*, but the *Carthaginians* diſclaim *Amilcar* and Baniſh him, and ſent Corn to *Rome*, and to the Army
in *Macedon:* King *Maſaniſſa* would alſo have lent
them Two Thouſand *Numidian* Horſe, but they were
content with half the Number. The *Gauls* at the
Siege of *Cremona* are Overthrown, *L. Junius* and *A-
milcar* ſlain, and the Work againſt the *Gauls* made
eaſie for them which follow.

§. 13. *Rome* was not wont to trifle, but to bid
the Enemy Battel, or force them to it as ſoon as they
could, but now they learn of *Greece* to War by Ne-
gotiations. Their Treaſure was yet empty, and
they in Debt to the Citizens; yet weary of making
ſlow Proceedings by Confederates, they increaſe
the *Macedonian* Army at leaſt eight Thouſand Foot,
and eight Hundred Horſe, which they committed to
Quintus Flaminius the new Conſul. This augmen-
tation was requiſite, for that *Attalus* deſired to be
ſpared, being Invaded at Home by *Antiochus* ; which
they condeſcended to promiſe to, and Mediate Peace
between them, both being Loving Friends. But all this
ſhew

shew of Friendship with *Antiochus*, was but till they had made safe way through *Macedon*, as after appeared. *Quintus* being come, finds *Philip* and *Villius* the old Consul, Encamped one against the other in the Straits of *Epirus*, by the River *Apsus*, where he stayed long, seeking passage over the Mountain Guarded by *Philip*. During this delay, the King and Consul Treat of Peace, but in vain ; for that the Consul required the freeing all *Greece*, and Namely *Thessaly*, which had been Subject to *Macedon* ever since *Philip*, Father of *Alexander*. Ater this, the Consul was guided by an Herdsman, sent by a Prince of the *Epirots* which loved the *Romans*, so that *Philip* with the loss of two Thousand Men is forced Home through *Thessaly*, which he wasted as he went ; as did the *Ætolians*, and the Consul made a gleaning and took some Cities, and for want of Provision returned by *Phocis*, an Allie of *Macedon*. In the mean time the Consuls Brother, Admiral of the Navy with *Attalus*, and the *Rhodians*, wan two Cities of *Eubœa*, and besiege *Cenchrea* the Haven and *Arsenal* of *Corinth*. This quickened the *Achæans* desire to forsake *Philip*, having had so many motives by his injuries done them, and their having so brave a Leader of *Philopœmen*. In the end they hold an Assembly at *Sicyon*, whither their Emballadours on both sides come with their Adherents, where at last they decree to forsake *Philip*, and join with their Enemies. After this *Philip*'s Lieutenant lying in *Corinth*, was drawn by the multitude in *Argos* to assist them, so they cast out the *Achæan* Guard, and accepted *Philip* for Patron ; who thereupon had some hopes of a good end upon a Treaty. The Consul also considering his Office would Expire before he could end the War, is willing to enter into it, that he might have the Honour of the Peace. After two or three meetings, demands and offers being made, *Philip* refers himself to the Senate of
Rome,

Rome, which the Conful liked; and Embaffadours from all parts meet; but upon *Philip's* Embaffadours denial to have warrant to yield *Corinth*, *Dolchis*, and *Demetria*, all was dafht. *Philip* to be revenged of the *Achæans*, made League with the Tyrant *Nabis* of *Lacedemon*, and to oblige him, he gave *Argos* into his hands, which fo lately had given it felf to him from the *Achæans*. The Tyrant the next day Pillaged all the rich Men; and to pleafe the Multitude, he made equal divifion of the Land, as Tyrants ufe to do: and prefently made a League with *Quintius*, who continued General againft *Philip*.

§. 14. *T. Quintius* being continued General of the *Macedonian* War, with twenty fix Thoufand feeketh out *Philip*, who had a proportionable Number, and found him in *Theffaly*, near the City *Pheræ*, where though *Philip* defigned not that day to put all to the Fortune of Battel, yet being drawn on by the good Succefs of a Skirmifh, and the advantage of the Hill *Cynófcephalæ*, or Dogs-heads, he chofe his Ground. But by reafon the Mountain was full of Knobs like Dogs heads, he could Marfhal but one part of the Army, leaving the reft to follow in order as they could. By this roughnefs they could keep no order fit to make any Impreffion, or good refiftance, and fo were broken by *Quintius's* right Wing fent to them up the Hill: Of which Wing a Tribune and twenty Enfigns, or about two Thoufand Men turning down the Hill on the left hand, fell on *Philip's* Phalanx, or fquare Battel with Pikes in the Rear, and put all to flight, when *Philip* thought the day his own. So he loft eight Thoufand flain, and five Thoufand Prifoners.

§. 15. *Quintius* made hafte to *Lariffa* a City in *Italy*, which opened to him; fo all the Warlike *Archarnamians* left *Philip*, and gave themfelves to the *Romans*: The *Pæreans* alfo rife againft *Dinocrates* the Kings Lieutenant, and recover'd the Province. *Philip*

lip confidering his prefent neceffity, thought it Wifdom to yield to it, and firft fent, and then went
to *Quintius* to Treat about a Peace, for which a
day was appointed for all the Affociates, in which, as
the infolent *Ætolians* too much infulted over *Philip,*
and fought his utter Subverfion, fo *Quintius* as gene-
roufly oppofed them. *Philip* yielded to all that
Quintius required, and four Months Truce is a-
greed to by all but the Infolent *Ætolians* ; and the
determination referred to the Senate of *Rome.* The
new Confuls oppofe the Peace as fraudulent ; which
made the Senate wave it; but the Tribunes refer it to
the People, by whofe Sovereign Authority it was concluded. The Conditions were to remove all Garrifons out of *Greece* by a fet day ; yield up Captives,
Renegados, Ships of War, except five leffer and one
great one ; and pay a Thoufand Talents ; and for
performance he had already given his Son *Deme-*
trius an Hoftage, and four Hundred Talents. Great
was the joy at the conclufion ; but the *Ætolians* are
diffatisfied, and the *Bæotians* ftill favour the *Mace-*
donians : Some alfo fear the *Romans* will prove the
worfe Neighbours ; not knowing the *Romans* defign againft *Antiochus.* But to prevent all bad Rumours, *Quintius* at the *Ifinian* Games Proclaimed
freedom from Garrifons, and Liberty of their own
Laws, to the *Corinthians, Phocians, Locrians, Eubæ-*
ans, Achæans of *Pithiotis, Magnetians, Theffalians*
and *Perrhubians,* which the *Greeks* applauded with exceeding Thanks. He alfo fent to *Antiochus* by his
Embaffadour then prefent, requiring him to keep from
the free Cities of *Afia,* and reftore to *Ptolomy* and
Philip what he held of theirs, and not to pafs into
Europe with an Army.

CHAP.

CHAP. V.

Of the Roman Wars with Antiochus, and his Adherents.

§. 1. *SEleucus Nicanor* flain by *Ptolomy Cerannus,*
Anno 4. *Olymp.* 124. *Antiochus Soter* his Son
fucceeded Nineteen Years, to whom *Berofus* the *Chaldæ-*
an Dedicated his *Affyrian-Hiſtory,* which is notoriou-
fly falſified by Fryar. *Annius.* He neglected revenging
his Fathers Death, who had ſo loved him that he gave
him *Stratonica* his own Wife, being ſick for her. *Antio-*
chus the God, as the flattering *Meleſians* called him for
freeing them from *Timarchus* the Tyrant, fucceeded
Fifteen Year. His firſt Wife was *Laodice,* to whom
he took alſo *Bernice* the Daughter of *Ptolomy Phila-*
delphus, King of *Egypt,* and ſo compounded the War
between them ; but falling into the hatred of *Laodice,*
ſhe Poiſoned him for it, when her Son *Seleucus*
Callinicus was ready to Reign : She alſo murthered
Bernice, and her Son, two or three Years after *Pto-*
lomy's Death, but the Brother reveng'd it.

Ptolomy Philodelphus, Son of *Ptolomy* the firſt King
of *Egypt,* after *Alexander,* began to Reign with his
Father, and continued Forty Years : He was firſt de-
rived from *Alexander*'s Succeffours which made
League with *Rome,* and his Off-ſpring, the laſt of
thoſe Royal Families they rooted out. He ſet at
Liberty all the *Jews* which his Father made Slaves
in *Egypt,* and ſent rich Gifts to God's Temple in
Jeruſalem, and requeſted of *Eleazer* the Books of
Holy Scripture, and ſeventy two Learned *Hebrews*
to Tranflate them into *Greek,* to furniſh his Libra-
ry in *Alexandria,* of which *Genebrard* thinks *Jeſus,*
Sirach was one, whom *Janſenius* proveth then living.
Joſephus Antiq. li. 12. c. 2. reports one *Ariſtæus*
writ the Hiſtory thereof.

Seleucus Callinicus began his Reign with his Father's

ther's Murder, which coſt his Mothers Life, ſhe being ſlain by *Ptolomæus Evergetes* in revenge of his Siſter who Invaded *Seleucus*, but was called Home by Domeſtick Troubles. *Seleucus* perceiving himſelf not beloved of his Subjeʃts ſought not to gain them by merit, but by force prepares a great Fleet againſt them, whereon all his hope relyed, which God overwhelmed in the Sea, and himſelf hardly eſcaped. His Subjeʃts hoping he would become a new Man, in Commiſeration offer him their Service, which ſo revived him, that he raiſed an Army againſt *Ptolomy*, who overthrew him; which made him ſend for aid to his Brother *Antiochus Hierax*, or Hawk (for he cared not on whom he Preyed,) who was but fourteen Years Old, and was extream Ambitious. Before he came, *Seleuchus* made Peace with *Ptolomæus*, but had no Peace of his Brother, who overthrew him: But ſhortly after overthrown himſelf by *Eumenes* King of *Pergamus*, Son of *Attalus*, and forced to flye away, was taken up in *Capadocia* by *Artamenes*, who deſigned to betray him, which made him take his Wings to *Egypt*, where *Ptolomy*, knowing his perfidious Nature, impriſoned him; whence eſcaping by means of a Harlot, he fell into the hands of Thieves, who murthered him. *Seleuchus* at this time going to ſubdue the *Baʃtrians* and *Parthians*, was taken Priſoner by *Arſaces* Founder of the *Parthian* Kingdom, who yet releaſed him; but returning Home, he broke his Neck by a fall from his Horſe, after twenty Years Reign. *Seleuchus Ceraunus* ſucceeded his Father Three Years, and was ſlain by Treaſon, leaving *Antiochus* his Brother to ſucceed; and *Achæus* to Govern the Army.

§. 2. *Ptolomæus Evergetes*, who ſuceeded *Philadelphus*, yet Reigned, having Married *Berenice*, Daughter of *Magas* King of *Cyrene*, added it to his Kingdom, and as he thought, the Countries of *Cæloſyria*, *Paleſtine*, &c. His, and his Succeſſours Wars with the *Seleucidæ*, were Prophecied of by *Daniel*. *Onias ſias* the High Prieſt had provoked him, by detaining covetouſly twenty Talents Tribute; but was pacified by *Joſephus* a *Jew* ; and having Reigned Twenty ſix Years; Dyed in the 1̤3̤9̤ *Olympiad.*

Antiochus, ſcarce Fifteen Years Old when he began his Reign, which laſted Thirty ſix Years, in his Minority was wholly Governed by one *Hermias* an Ambitious Man,who incited him unſeaſonably to War againſt *Ptolomæus,* for recovery of *Cœloſyria,* &c. while *Molo* the Kings Lieutenant in *Media* Rebelled. *Xenætas* is ſent with Forces into *Media,* which are overthrown, while *Antiochus* lay in the Valley of *Marſyas,* between *Libanus* and *Antilibanus,* ſeeking to paſs into *Cœloſyria.* Hearing therefore the News of *Xenætas,* he haſtens into *Media,* which he recovered from *Molo,* whoſe left Wing Revolting to the King, *Molo* with divers of his Friends, to ſhorten the work, killed themſelves, and ſo prevented the Hangman with their own Swords. After this came the joyful News of his Queen's being Deliver'd of a Son. Fortune being thus bountiful, *Antigonus* Marches againſt *Artabanes* King of the *Atropians,* who being very Old and Timerous yielded to whatever he Propos'd. *Antiochus* in the *Eaſt,* thought good to viſit his Borders between the *Caſpian* and *Euxine* Sea, in which Journey his Phyſician informed him againſt *Hermits,* of whom himſelf was grown Jealous, and therefore conſented to his killing. About theſe times *Achæus* rebelled, in hope the King would periſh in his Expedition ; yet *Antiochus* more intending the recovery of *Cœloſyria,* neglected him till he had gotten *Seleucia,* firſt called *Antigonia,* founded by *Antigonus,* and after won by *Seleuchus,* and then by *Ptolomy.* Such is the vanity of Men, who think to eternize their Names, not by works of Vertue, but of Greatneſs, which never laſteth long. *Theodotus* the *Ætolian, Ptolomy's* Mercenary, which formerly defended *Cæloſyria* againſt *Antiochus,* now

weary

weary of his former Faithfulness (Mercenary like)
fells it to him, who took poffeffion of *Tirus* and
Ptolomais, with the *Ægyptian* Fleet there. *Antiochus*,
herewith emboldned, aims at *Egypt* it felf, ruled by
Agathocles and *Sofibius*, whilft *Ptolomy* himfelf minds
only his Pleafure. Thefe two make fecret preparation, but openly folicite Peace by themfelves and
feveral of their Allies; and *Antiochus* willing to reft
this Winter, agreeth on a Truce for four Months
to Treat of Peace, which he defigned only to lull
his Enemies afleep, who watched him better than
he did them. During the Truce, Embaffadours
from *Egypt* are heard, and both fides plead their
right to *Cœlofyria*, and propound Covenants, but
both would have it, or nothing. The Truce ended, *An-*
tiochus takes the Field, prefuming his ordinary Power will ferve againft his unprovided Enemies; but
was deceived, and well beaten for it at *Raphia*, lofing
Ten Thoufand Foot out of Seventy Thoufand, and
Four Hundred Horfe out of Six Thoufand, in which
Ptolomy exceeded, as *Antiochus* did in Elephants:
After which he feeks Peace, though what he had
gotten in *Syria* was fallen from him. *Antiochus* after this, followed the fuppreffion of *Achæus*, whom
he foon penn'd up in *Sardis*, which yet he could not
take in two Years, till a *Cretian*, obferved by Ravens
which continually pitched upon part of the Wall
where Carrion was caft into the Ditch, that there it
was unguarded; as indeed it was, being thought
unapproachable; yet here, though with difficulty,
the Town was won, and he driven into the Caftle,
out of which, alfo he was drawn by a *Cretian* trick of
one *Bolis* a *Cretian*, which knew all the difficult paffages of the Rocks, on which the Caftle ftood. *Pto-*
lomy defiring to deliver *Achæus* out of his danger,
hired this *Cretian*, who undertook it with *Camby-*
fus his Country-man, as very a *Cretian* as himfelf
(that is, as falfe a Knave) and brought him out, but
betrayed

betrayed him to *Antiochus*; who seeing him, could not refrain Tears, considering the Calamities incident to great Fortunes, but Condemned him to a cruel Death.

Antiochus some Years after, made an Expedition against the *Hyrcanians* and *Parthians,* a little Nation, subject to the *Median* Government, which was now in the hand of *Antiochus's* Lieutenant, whose Insolency provoked *Arsaces* a Noble-man to Rebel, and made himself King. He succeeded so well, that he withstood *Seleucus Callinicus,* and took him Prisoner, but entertained him nobly, and released him; his Posterity increased the Dominion. *Arsaces* the Second now Reigned, against whom *Antiochus* led such an Army as he could not encounter, till *Antiochus* had pass'd through the Country, and won *Tambrace* in *Hyrcania,* by which time he had gathered such Forces as enabled him to try Battel. After this he sought Peace, which *Antiochus* granted, making him a Friend whom he could not force to be a Subject. The like Expedition made against the *Bactrians* Governed by *Euthydemus,* with whom also he made Peace; and went over *Caucasus* to review the Old League with the *Indians.*

§. 3. *Ptolomæus Philopater,* so called by derision, as having made away Father and Mother, as it is thought, though he began to Reign young after the Battel at *Raphia,* gave himself over to Sensuality; and by the instigation of *Agathoclea* his Strumpet, Sister to *Agathocles,* murdered his Wife, set his Sister, which was *Arsinoe,* by whom he had *Ptolomæus Epiphanes,* which he left but five Years Old, unto the tuition of *Agathocles.* He Assembled the *Macedonians,* which were the Kings ordinary Forces in Pay. (Not all Born in *Macedon,* but of the Posterity of them which Planted in *Egypt* with *Ptolomæus Lagus,* and would not be called *Egyptians,* as neither would the Kings,) To these he made an

Oration

Oration with Tears, intreating their Fidelity to the King, whom he shewed in his Sister's Arms, and accused one *Tlepolemus* of Treason; but finding himself deceived, he departed; and upon his taking one of them upon suspicion of Treason against himself, they rose in Arms, took away the King, slew him, dragged the Strumpet his Sister naked through the Streets of *Alexandria,* as also her Mother the Bawd, and tore them in pieces. *Antiochus,* and *Philip* of *Macedon,* thought to make advantage of these troubles in *Egypt,* and to divide the Orphans Estate between them. But the *Romans* whom *Philopater* had obliged in the *Punick* War, being Solicited, were easily persuaded to protect the Child. The *Macedonian* was imployed at Home. *Antiochus* having recovered his losses in *Syria,* the *Jews* were civilly treated by him: And he suffered himself to be persuaded by the *Romans,* to forbear the *Egyptians.* He also sent to make League with the *Romans,* who applyed themselves to give him all satisfaction, though they secretly intended otherwise, till they had effected their design for *Macedon.* *Antiochus* dealt after the same manner with *Philip,* and with *Eumenes,* Son of *Attalus,* King of *Pergamus,* offering either of them a Daughter, and yet endeavour'd to destroy them. *Eumenes* excuseth his refusal, and tells his Brethren (who wondred at it) that in taking the Offer he should fall into the Quarrel against the *Romans,* who would surely make War upon him. The *Rhodians* also had the prudence to foresee that Storm, when they threatned to set upon his Fleet, if it did pass a certain Promontory in *Cilicia:* Thus seeking to keep him from joyning with *Philip* their Enemy, and molesting the South of *Asia* belonging to *Ptolomy,* the next Spring he passed over *Hellespont* into *Europe,* and re-edified, and peopled *Lysimachia.*

C c   §. 4. *Rome.*

§. 4. *Rome* having temporized with *Antiochus*, till the War in *Macedon* was ended, and moſt of *Greece* become little better than Clyents, *L. Cornelius* is ſent unto *Antiochus* in more plain Terms, urging his reſtoring to *Ptolomy* what he had lately taken from him, and the like alſo to *Philip*, and to let the free Cities in *Aſia* reſt quiet, and requiring a Reaſon for his bringing ſuch an Army into *Europe*. *Antiochus* wonders the *Romans* ſhould trouble themſelves with *Aſian* matters, more than he with *Italian*, and anſwers the reſt ſo as *Cornelius* replyed not; but upon falſe rumours of *Ptolomy*'s Death he haſteth thither, having Commiſſion for that purpoſe. *Antiochus* alſo haſteth thither, with all his Sea-Forces, to take poſſeſſion; but hearing *Ptolomy* was alive, he took another way; and after a dangerous Shipwrack recovered *Seleucia*, and ſo went to *Antiochia*, where he was ſecure for that Winter. *Rome* in the mean time is careful to ſecure *Greece* and *Macedon*, againſt the *Aſian* War, the Fame whereof coming to *Carthage*, gave *Hannibal*'s Enemies occaſion to contrive his Expulſion. He had of late put on the long Robe, being choſen Prætor, and reformed the Treaſurers who Robbed the Treaſury, and brought the Judges to be Annual, who had been for Life, which inflamed their Envy. *Rome* is informed his Faction was ſtrong, and will be in Arms ſuddenly; for preventing whereof three Embaſſadours, are ſent, pretending his well-wiſhers, as alſo other buſineſs about *Maſaniſſa*; for *Rome* is glad of ſuch an occaſion againſt him, though *P. Scipio* diſſuaded that diſhonourable courſe; and *Hannibal*, for all the pretence, knew their meaning, and having ſhewed himſelf in the Aſſembly, and in the Evening walking out with two Friends, took Horſe where he had appointed them, and that Night came to a Tower of his own, where he had a Ship always furniſhed for ſuch purpoſe, and ſo Sailed to

Tyre,

Tyre, and thence to *Antiochus* at *Ephesus*, who is exceedingly rejoyced at his coming. But what could this great General do in the *Asiatique* War? He could not make such Souldiers of base *Asiatiques*, as of hardy *Spaniards*, *Gauls* and *Africans*, &c. Nay, could he do it, yet the Pride of *Antiochus*'s Court, the Baseness of his Flatteries, and a Thousand Vexations would make his Virtues unprofitable, being a banished Desolate Man, wanting his Brethren to assist him. But *Antiochus* was more careful of Peace with *Rome*, sending to *Quintius*, to require the Faithful keeping of it, though the *Romans* intended nothing less, as the common talk at *Rome*, and *Quintius*'s stay in *Greece*, and seeking pretences not to Depart, did Argue. For being secure of *Philip*, *Greece* being at Peace, *Antiochus* still Solicites Peace. But the *Ætolians* are much convinced, that *Quintius* should still keep Possession of *Chalcis*, *Demetrias*, and *Acrocorinthus*. *Nabis*, Tyrant of *Lacedemon* kept *Argos* in Bondage, which concerns the *Romans* in Honour to make free, saith *Quintius*, which the *Ætolians* will undertake. Yet in a common Assembly of all the States, *Quintius* is intreated to do it, as being easie, when all the Confedrates were joined with him. After this, the *Romans* depart out of *Greece*, and *Titus Quintius* Triumpheth at *Rome*. *Quintius* and his Associates from *Rome*, and *Antiochus* his Embassadours make many Treaties to no purpose, but to give *Antiochus* leisure of two Years to prepare for War. The *Roman* Conditions were not less dishonourable for him to yield to, than unreasonable for them to Demand. For though, they which have been at War, and gotten no great advantage of each other, may demand restitution of things gotten, or lost; Yet between them, who never fell out, for wrong done, or received, there can no such Conditions for establishing Friendship be proposed: Seeing it is reasonable, that each should enjoy their own; and

neither

neither take Superiority over the other to preicribe Conditions, as Conquerours may do.

§. 5. *Rome,* after *Hannibal*'s departure out of *Italy,* was continually Infested with Infurrections of the *Infubrians, Boijans,* and other *Cifalpine Gauls,* with the *Ligurians* ; who having served together under *Mago,* and *Amilcar,* became such Friendly partakers of each others Fortune, that they seldom undertook any Enterprize, but together. The *Cifalpine Gauls,* or *Lumbards,* had been kept under by *Rome,* from the second *Punick* War, until *Hannibal* invaded *Italy,* and held out after by the assistance of the *Ligurians* ; a stout, subtle, hardy, poor People, induring hardness, and not discouraged by losses; obstinate in War, without respect of keeping Covenant, and continu'd Enemies and Friends more by Custom, as Savages do, than by Judgment. The *Roman* War with them, served to train their Men to Hardness, and Military patience. *Spain* also, after *Scipio*'s departure, put *Rome* to continual employment, slew a Proconsul. *Porcius Cato* Consul, had almost as much work there, as the Re-conquest of *Spain* : He began to disarm them, which made them desperate ; he cast down all their Walls, and brought the Country to that pass, that it was in no danger to be lost long after.

Hannibal being forced to leave *Carthage,* his Enemies promise themselves and their City all the happiness which obedience to *Rome* could afford ; but coming to try the Controversie before the Senate with King *Mafaniffa,* who had taken from them some Land, which he claimed anciently belonging to his Fore-fathers, they found how little regard they had to *Carthage.*

§. 6. The *Ætolians* discontented with the Peace made by the *Romans,* as finding their Merit undervalued, invite *Philip, Antiochus,* and *Nabis,* against the *Romans. Nabis* beginneth and besiegeth *Gytheum,* and wasteth waiteth *Achæa*. *Philopœmen* was now Prætor of *A-chæa*, to whose discretion all being referred, he began with a Sea-fight, wherein his skill failed; then he fell to his own Element to prove the Enemy at Land, where his skill in discerning the advantages of Ground, was excellent, and by an Ambush intrapped his Enemy and slew many. So likewise, he deceived *Nabis* by a counterfeit Fugitive, which told him *Philopœmen* designed to get between him and *Lacedemon*, which made him hasten Homeward, leaving some Troops to Guard his Camp, which was presently fired, and he pursued so hard that his People fled into a Wood, thinking to get Home in the Night; but the Ways being laid, hardly a quarter of them got into *Sparta*. While the *Romans* are busie in *Greece* to prepare War with *Antiochus*, their Embassadours with *Antiochus* Treat of Peace; and there meeting with *Hannibal*, and conferring often with him, *Antiochus* grew jealous, till he was informed by him of the Oath his Father had made him take, never to be Friends with the *Romans*. *Antiochus* rejecting the dear rated Peace offered by *Rome*, complies with the *Ætolians*, who thereupon in their *Panætolium*, or common Assembly of the Nation, decree to call *Antiochus* into *Greece*, to decide their Controversie with the *Romans*. The execution of the Decree was referred to the *Apocleti*, or Privy-Council, who suddenly surprized *Demetrias*, but failed of *Chalcis*; yet they got *Lacedemon* by killing *Nabis* their Friend, under pretence to give him aid in his weakness, after his Overthrow by *Philopœmen*; but while they were busie in rifling his Palace, the Citizens took Arms and slew them. *Philopœmen*, while *Lacedemon* was in this doubtful Estate, went to it, and called out the chief Citizens, persuading them to Incorporate the City unto *Achæa*, which they yielded unto.

§. 7. *Antiochus*, upon *Thoas*, the *Ætolians* Counsel, changed his purpose of sending *Hannibal* with a Fleet

against

against the *Romans* in *Africa*, and ordered him presently to pass over to *Greece*, which he performed,
but with no such numbers as were expected, having
only Forty serviceable Ships, Six Elephants, Ten
Thousand Foot, and Five Hundred Horse; which
smalness of number he excused, promising shortly to
fill all *Greece*. Being chosen their General, he went
first against *Chalcis*, thinking to gain them with
words, but could not till he returned with greater
Power; upon this, the rest of the Island of *Eubæa* yielded. Then Embassadours are sent to all Quarters to
persuade them to join with King *Antiochus*, who
came to procure their Freedom; they answer as had
the *Chalicidians*, Their Freedom could not be bettered.
They meet with *Quintius* at an *Achæan* Council, where
the *Ætolians* and *Antiocheans* extol one another, by
which *Quintius* took opportunity to shew their vanity,
and the Kings weakness both in Judgment and Power, and that he and the *Ætolians* did but delude each
other: So War was Proclaimed against them. Thus
as the turbulent *Ætolians* were only forward with
Antiochus against the *Romans*, so the *Achæans* do at
last declare for them; all the rest stand doubtful, except *Elamis*, who loved the *Ætolians*, and the *Eubæans* and *Bœotians* forced by *Antiochus*, with the
Magnetians and *Athamanians*. *Antiochus* confers
with these, and *Hannibal* long neglected, by reason
of the bragging *Ætolians*, is consulted, who spake plainly his mind: *That as for these Confederates, their
weakness and fear made them uncertain Friends, whereas if the Macedonian had been engaged, he was strong
and could not start, having once fallen off from Rome;
but if he dare not, let him keep at Work at Home; and
let the Gauls be provoked, and a strong Power sent into
Italy, while the King proceeds at Greece.* They are
pleased with the brave Speech of this great Spirit;
but nothing is done, except forcing *Thessaly*, where
yet *Larissa* withstood his Army, and was relieved by
                                                    the

the *Romans*, at whose sight he rose and went to *Chalcis*, to promote the Love of a trappanning Woman.

M. Acilius, Consul, comes into *Greece* with Ten Thousand Foot, Two Thousand Horse, and Fifteen Elephants, to whom *Ptolomy*, *Philip*, *Carthage* and *Masanissa* offer their assistance, but only *Philip* is accepted, and recompenced with *Athamania*, *Aminander* the King being expelled. All *Thessaly* willingly yielded, and *Antiochus* is perplexed, crying out he was betrayed, and called upon the *Ætolians*, who sent in some small Forces, with which and his own, he took the Passage of the Straits of *Thermopylæ*, out of which nevertheless he was beaten by the Consul *Porcius Cato*'s indefatigable labour, in finding out an unknown Passage up, where the *Ætolians* had six Hundred to keep the Place, whom he put to flight, and following them was led to *Antiochus*'s Camp, upon sight of whom all ran away, and *Antiochus* forsaketh *Greece*. In few days all that *Antiochus* had got was recovered, and *Heraclia* won from the *Ætolians* to their great Terrour, they having sent Post to *Antiochus* for Aid before they had been subdued by the *Romans*, who now left no Enemy behind against their Invading *Asia*. *Antiochus* upon that consideration, sent *Nicanor* with Money and promise of Forces; but upon loss of *Heraclia* they sue humbly to the Consul, who will scarcely hear them. In the end offering to yield to the *Romans*, upon discretion, he required such Conditions as they thought slavish; whereupon he offered to lay Chains upon them, but was over perswaded. So he went to besiege *Naupactus* while *Quintius* was settling *Peloponesus*, from whence he came to the Consul when the earnest Suit of the *Ætolians* had procured Truce, while they might send to *Rome*, which they did to no purpose; whereupon they Sue for Pardon. The Consul suddenly attempeth *Lamia*, and won it, while they prepare against him at *Naupactus*, and then goeth to *Amphyssa*.

C c 4 §. 8. *Cor-*

§ 8. *Cornelius Scipio* is chosen Consul, and upon *Publius Scipio Africanus*'s offer to be his Lieutenant, is appointed to *Asia*; who having Thirteen Thousand Foot, and an Hundred Horse, came into *Greece*, and took charge of that Army at *Amphyssa*, which presently was forsaken; but the Castle held out and was thought impregnable, which made *Publius Scipio* procure a Years Truce for them, much desiring to be in *Asia*. So that the *Scipio*'s set forward, and in *Macedon* find all desired assistance, and *Philip* to accompany them to the *Hellespont*, where they stay till the Navy to Transport them be ready. At the Sea this Spring *Polixenidas* banished *Rhodia*, but *Antiochus*'s faithful Admiral desiring to be revenged, hearing the *Rhodian* Fleet lay at *Samos*, sent the Admiral private Intelligence, that if his Banishment might be repealed, he would betray the Kings Fleet. After agreement between them, the *Rhodian* grew secure, so that *Polixenidas* coming suddenly upon him, took or sunk all but five. *Seleucus* Son of *Antiochus* besieged *Pergamus*, which was defended by *Attalus*, Brother of King *Eumenes*, who was assisted by *Diophanes*, bred up by *Philopœmen* with a Thousand Foot, and an Hundred Horse; He observing from the Walls how careless the Enemy was, went out with his *Achæans*, and encamped near the Enemy, who derided his boldness, and seeing him so quiet, became secure, but were soon surprized, and many slain: So that after such another defeat, *Seleucus* was forced to quit the Siege. *Antiochus* shortly after lost Forty Gallies near *Myonesus*, a Promontory in *Asia*, being Overthrown by the *Romans* and *Rhodians*, so that he had but Forty nine left. Upon this he called Home the Garrison from *Lysimachia*, and Mustred all his Forces, intending only his own defence, to which he desired a Supply of his Father in Law, the King of *Cappadocia*: But he hearing the Consul was Landed in *Asia*, sent to intreat Peace, offering to free what

                                    Towns

Towns he would name upon the Coaſt, yea to part
Aſia with them, and bear half their Charge. All
this the Conſul thought too little; he will have all
the Charges, and all the leſſer *Aſia* freed, and him
confined over Mount *Taurus* ; to which *Publius Sci-*
pio adviſeth the Kings Embaſſadour to perſuade his
Maſter, when he privately ſolicited his mediation
to the Conſul. His King eſteeming theſe demands
no leſs than if he had been Conquered, would not
liſten to them, having Seventy Thouſand Foot, and
Twelve Thouſand Horſe, Ninety two Elephants, and
many Armed Chariots after the Eaſtern manner,
with Sithes; nor did he fear him. For hearing *Pub-*
lius Scipio was ſick, he ſent him his Son, whom he had
taken Priſoner and uſed honourably ; which comforted the Father, who for requital wiſhed him not to
fight till he heard of his coming to the Camp. The
King hereupon removed to *Magneſia* on *Sypylus*, and
Fortified himſelf, being followed by the Conſul, who
offered him Battle, which he would not accept ; till
at laſt fearing to diſhearten his Men, when the Conſul took the Field and ſet his Men in order, he alſo
did the like, which made an admirable Show for numbers and variety, through the different manner every Nation uſed. It is ſhameful to relate, and incredible to believe, how little reſiſtance this brave Show
of *Aſiatiques* made, ſuffering themſelves to be ſlain like
ſo many Beaſts, to the Number of Fifty Thouſand Foot,
and Four Thouſand Horſe, beſides Priſoners, with only
the loſs of three Hundred *Roman* Foot, Twenty four
Horſe, and Twenty five of *Eumenes*'s Men. *Antio-*
chus ſends from *Apamea*, whither he was fled, an Embaſſadour with full Power to ſubmit to what the
Conſul would require, to which *Publius Scipio* obtained leave to Anſwer, becauſe it ſhould be mode-
rate. He requireth Fifteen Thouſand Talents
to be paid at ſet times ; That *Antiochus* ſhall a-
bandon all on this ſide *Taurus*, pay *Eumenes* four Hundred

dred Talents, and a proportion of Corn ; put in
Twenty Hoſtages, and deliver *Hannibal*, and *Thoas*
the *Ætolian*, unto the *Romans*. *Antiochus's* Embaſſadour comes to *Rome*, accompanied with King *Eumenes* and the *Rhodians*; and the Peace is Confirmed with
the diviſion of the Conqueſts among the *Roman* Allies
to their full ſatisfaction. *Cornelius Scipio* returning,
hath a Triumph exceeding any Ten before, and had
the Sirname *Aſiatique* for his Title, as the Merits
of his Victory, tho' the Virtue requiſite was ſhort
of that in *Publius Scipio*.

§. 9. *Marcus Fulvius*, and *Curius Manlius* the
Conſuls, have *Greece* and *Aſia* divided between them,
being more than one could look after at once, having the *Ætolians* to reduce unto the acknowledgment of the *Romans*, and their new Conqueſts in *A-
ſia* to be regulated. In the interim of the *Ætolians*
Truce, *Aminander* (whoſe Kingdom of *Athamania*
the *Romans* had permitted *Philip* to Poſſeſs) found
means to recover it, as the *Ætolians* did the *Am-
philochians* and *Aperantians*. *Fulvius* being come into *Greece*, beſieged the noble City *Ambracia*, which
much imported the *Ætolians* not to loſe, and yet
were not able to relieve it : So that the *Athenians* and
Rhodians interceed for Peace, which the Conſul
(finding the difficulty of winning the Town) condeſcended to. To *Rome* they go, and agree to divers
Articles, which make them more obnoxious to *Rome*
than any people of *Greece*. Conſul *Manlius* in *Aſia*,
viſited all that *Antiochus* had loſt on this ſide *Taurus*,
and loaded himſelf with the Booty, and at length
came to the *Gallo-Grecians* upon the River *Halis* ;
who took all they had, and went up to the Mountains *Olympus* and *Margæna*, hoping the Conſul either would not follow, or be eaſily repelled. But
in both they were deceived; being unfurniſhed with
Arrows or Slings, or defenſive Armour, and ſo in
the end were forced to throw themſelves off the
                                          Rocks,

Rocks, leaving to the *Romans* all that Wealth which they had gotten by long robbing their Neighbours. He forced *Ararathes* and others to submit, from whom he also drew, what he could get. Finally, having sworn the Peace of *Antiochus*, and tak an Oath of his Embassadours for him, to take h way Home by *Hellespont*, loaden with rich Spoils; and accordingly passing through *Thrace*, he was eased of the carriage of no small part, not without the instigation of *Philip*, grown very uneasie with the *Romans* for not respecting him according to his Deferts, as he thought. But the Consuls at their return to *Rome*, triumphed; and *Manlius* was charged with sending his Armies over *Taurus*, the fatal Bounds of *Rome*, according to the *Sybills* Prophesie : Yet *Lucullus* and *Pompey* led the *Roman* Army over those Hills with *Manlius*, when he deferred Triumph, there being an hot Inquisition in the City, by the Tribunes against the *Scipio*'s, as not having brought into the Treasury, what was gotten in their Victories. This indignity so offended *Publius Scipio*, that he left the City, and never returned, redeemed his Brethren, and his Goods were all confiscated. After this, *Manlius* brought into the Treasury as much as made the last Payment of the Money borrowed of Private Men in the *Punick* War. Thus began the Civil War, of the Tongue in the *Roman* pleading; Security from danger abroad, and sufficient employment kindling this fire at Home, which caught hold upon that great Worthy, to whose Virtue *Rome* was so much indebted. But these Factions did not long contain themselves within the heat of words; but when Men found themselves over-matched at the Weapon of the Tongue, whose Art in leading the multitude was grown to perfection, they turned to open Hands by Frays in Streets, and after by Battels in open Fields, which in three Generations after, overthrew the insolent Rule both of Senate and People.

CHAP.

CHAP. VI.

Of the second Macedonian *War.*

ANtiochus being Overthrown, *Philip, Eumenes,*
and all *Greece* feemed to be Free Men, and Govern by their own Laws ; but indeed were
abfolute Vaffals to *Rome,* which of the five Prerogatives of an abfolute Monarch, or Sovereign Power,
*viz. To make Laws, Magiftrates, Peace and War,
Coyn Money, and receive Appeals,* the *Romans* had
affumed four, efpecially the greateft, which is Appeals, and in the other three, interpofed her felf at
Pleafure. Yet *Eumenes* living far off, and the Neighbour
Nations not well fubdued, and obedient to *Rome,* he
was long unqueftioned of any thing ; as was alfo *Mafaniffa.* *Philip's* Temper was more noble, as he
which had not forgot his own former Greatnefs, Honour of his Family, and the high Reputation of his
Kingdom. His Magnanimity is conftrued Want of
Reverence to the *Roman* Greatnefs : fo that upon the
complaint of *Eumenes* and the States of *Theffaly,* he
muft depart, leaving even thofe places he had Conquered, by the Confent of *Rome. Lifimachia* the chief
City in *Thrace,* having been affiftant in *Philip's* U-
furpation, was deftroyed by the *Thracians,* and Re-
edified by *Antiochus,* after he had won *Cherfonefus,*
both which the *Romans* beftowed upon *Eumenes* :
To thefe *Ænus* and *Maronea* had belonged, both gotten by *Philip,* and Fortified for Guard of his Kingdom againft the Barbarous *Thracians,* which now *Eumenes* beggeth ; but the People of thefe places endeavour their own Freedom from both. This defign of the *Maronites* fo provoked *Philip,* that by
Caffander, one of his Men in *Maronea,* directed by
Onomaftus his Warden of the Sea Coaft, the *Thracians* were let into the Town, which was fackt by
them :

them : And when *Cassander* at the *Romans* demand, was to be sent to *Rome* to be examined about it, he was Poisoned by the Way, according to *Machivel*'s Rule. *Philip* hereby grew further into question at *Rome*, but sent *Demetrius* his Son, who had been Hostage there, and obtained the favour for him to answer. In the mean time the *Roman* Embassadour which had judged between him and his Neighbours, passing through *Greece*, hears of a Controversie between the *Achæans* and *Lacedemonians*, which *Lycortus* the *Achæan* Prætor, told *Appius Claudius* boldly, that it was strange, that the *Romans* should call their faithful Allies to account, as if they were Vassals. *Appius* answered like a *Roman* Lord, and threatned to force them, and shortly after, the Senate made void all Judgments of Death, or Banishment given by the *Achæans* against the *Lacedemonians* : And made it a question whether *Lacedemon* should not be made a free State, as of Old. Into this Slavery, had the *Romans* brought all the States near them, which had desired their Patronage, and made them groan under the Yoke. *Demetrius* returned to his Father with desired Peace ; more for his own sake than his Fathers, as they wrote to *Philip*, which made the Son insolent, and the Father to hate both them and him.

§. 2. *Messene*, which had been annexed to the *Achæan* Commonwealth against their Wills, grew bold upon the *Romans* Peremptory dealing with the *Achæans* designing to fall off, in hope to become a free State again : *Philopœmen* Prætor of *Achæa*, Levied Forces in haste to meet *Dinocrates* the *Messenian* Captain, and forced him to retire, till a fresh Supply coming from *Messene*, compelled him to retreat, in which labouring to make Way for his Horsemen, himself weak with former Sickness was dismounted, taken, and carried to *Messene*, where *Dinocrates* seeing him so generally affected, hastned his Death by an Hangman, which brought him a Cup of Poison.

Hannibal

Hannibal about the fame time was with *Prufias* King of *Bythinia*, to whom *T. Quintius* was fent to demand him, as the moft fpiteful Enemy of *Rome*; wherein the wretched King intending to give the *Romans* fatisfaction, fet a Guard about *Hannibal's* Lodgings, who feeing himfelf befet, took a Poifon, which he always carried about him, and fo Died; exclaiming againft the *Romans*, degenerating from the Virtue of their Anceftors, who would not confent to the Poifoning of *Pyrrhus* their Enemy, and againft the Treachery of *Prufias*, betraying his Gueft, contrary to the Honour of a King, and the Laws of Hofpitality, and Faith given. *Publius Scipio* died the fame Year, to accompany *Philopœmen* and *Hannibal*: Being as great Generals as ever the World had; but as Unfortunate as Famous. Had *Hannibal*, whofe Tragedy we have endeavoured only fome hints of, been Prince of *Carthage*, able to command fuch fupplies as the War he took in hand required, it is probable he had torn up the *Roman* Empire by the Roots. But the ftrong Cowardly Factions of Enemies at Home, made his great Virtue (wanting Publick Force to fuftain it) to diffolve it felf in his own and Countries Calamity.

From fuch Envy of Equals, or jealoufie of our Mafters, whether Kings, or Commonwealths, it is, that no Profeffion is more unprofperous than that of Generals; befides the Rapes, Slaughters, Devaftations, *&c.* which are fo hateful to God, *That were not the Mercies of God infinite* (as *Monluc* Marfhal of *France* confeffed) *it were in vain for thofe of his profeffion to hope for any portion thereof*, fuch Cruelties being permitted, or committed by them. And true it is, that as the Victories obtained by fo many of the greateft Commanders, are commonly afcribed either to Fortune, or to their Followers, or Cowardize of the vanquifhed, fo the moft, whofe Virtues have raifed them above all Envy, have in the end been

been rewarded either with Diſgrace, Baniſhment, or Death ; as Examples, both of the *Romans*, and *Grecians* Witneſs.

§. 3. *Philip* well perceiving the *Romans* aimed at his Kingdom, repented himſelf of his Obſequiouſneſs to them. Yet was in ill Condition to help himſelf, having been beaten by them ; his People unwilling to deal with them, and no Friends to aſſiſt him. Yet Neceſſity, the Mother of Invention, made him reſolved to remove the Inhabitants of his Maritime Towns to *Emathia*, and people them with *Thracians* that feared not the *Romans*. He alſo deſigned to draw the *Baſternæ*, an hardy Nation, beyond *Danubius*, into *Dardania*, and to root out the *Dardanians*, always troubleſome to *Macedon*: But this device took ſlow effect, and was hindred divers ways. His Subjects removed againſt their Will, broke into words, which his cruel Nature ſeeking to repreſs by putting many unto Death, increaſed to exclamation, which inflamed him barbarouſly to Maſſacre their Children. After this, the Furies enter his own Houſe, and Vengeance was poured upon him from Heaven in his own Children, as was thought by the jealouſie he had of *Demetrius* his Younger Son, and the fear *Pruſius* had of him for his Intereſt in the *Romans* Affections. Wicked Inſtruments are not wanting, who counterfeit a Letter from *Quintius* to *Philip*, intreating for *Demetrius*, with an intimation of his ambitious Deſire againſt his Brother *Pruſius* : One *Didas* alſo, to whom he was committed by *Philip*, pretending Friendſhip to him, founded him, and told the King that he meant to flye to the *Romans*, who would not fail him : So the Father, without any examination, commanded his unhappy Son to be Murdered ; and after, upon his Couſin *Antigonus* his ſearching, found out the Contrivance too late. Hereupon he intended to confer the Kingdom upon *Antigonus*, but Death prevented it.

§. 4. *Per-*

§. 4. _Perseus_ succeeded his Father, who had Reigned Forty two Years ; he thought it not expedient to imbroil himself so soon with the _Roman_ War, but to settle his Dominions, and therefore to prevent danger, slew _Antigonus._ Then to get his Subjects Affections, he sate in Judgment, and made them many publick Shows ; and to win the _Romans,_ he sent and renewed the League.

Masanissa, had heretofore taken the Country of _Emporia_ from _Carthage,_ and about this time he took other Land from them by force, about Seventy Towns and Castles, of which, when the _Carthaginians_ complained by their Embassadours, prostrate with Tears before the Senate, desiring Right, or Liberty to defend themselves against him, or at least to know how far _Masanissa_ should be allowed to proceed : And if none of these would be granted, that then the Senate it self would inflict upon them what they thought meet, rather than to keep them in continual fear of this _Numidian_ Hangman. See the fruits of their Envy against that valiant Family of the _Barchines,_ and of the _Roman_ Peace desired by _Hanno_ ; which hath made them Slaves to the Servants of the _Numidian,_ whose Fathers they had used to sell over _Africk_ and _Greece._ Their Answer was gentle, but without effect, and _Masanissa_ hath a mild rebuke. _Perseus_ is not yet brought into such a Yoke, but must be, for he is questioned for taking up Arms without their leave, though to subdue his own Rebels. After the same manner they dealt with _Greece_ : And of all others, with the _Achæans,_ who presumed most on their Favour : So that all saw, that the _Roman_ Patronage tended to nothing, but the bondage of _Greece._ This gave _Perseus_ hopes to find a Party there, as indeed he did, though it little availed him.

§. 5. _Eumenes_ King of _Pergamus_ hated _Perseus_ exceedingly, not only for an Hereditary quarrel with

Mace-

Macedon, but for that, he perceived the *Greeks* began to favour him more than himself, whom they seemed to neglect, for being over serviceable to *Rome*. For Redress hereof, he thought it not hard to induce the *Romans*, utterly to overthrow the *Macedonian* Kingdom, which the *Greeks* now adored; to which end, he took a second Journey to *Rome*, where he laboured to provoke the Fathers against *Perseus*; which needed not, though yet they heard him willingly, that their Pretence of War might have the fairer shew, as proceeding from the information of such a King, come on purpose so far as out of *Asia*. The *Rhodians* also were there with the *Macedonian* Embassadours, to answer, with matter of recrimination, that *Eumenes* had provoked the *Lycians* to Rebel against the *Rhodians*. Careless Audience was given to the *Rhodians*, for their Friendly Office in conveying *Laodice* the Daughter of *Antiochus* to *Perseus*; and their Answer is, that the *Lycians* were assigned to *Rhodes*, not as Vassals, but Associates: Thus their Subjects are become their Fellows. *Masanissa* and the *Ætolians*, whose Subjects were not increased by the *Romans*, or by the Cities and People bestowed upon them after *Antiochus*'s Overthrow, but their Friends, had cause to resent this Decree. The *Macedonian* Embassadours were heard, not so carelesly as angerly, being glad that *Harpatus*, the chief Embassadour, had by violent Speeches given them cause of anger. And though *Perseus* his faint Heart was not fit to threaten ; Yet now he might think to get more by a little Bravery than submission, seeing the Eyes of all *Greece* were set upon him for a Delivery from the *Roman* Servitude. And it seems *Perseus* was not very cautious of offending them, when he hired three or four Ruffians to Murder *Eumenes*, in his return from Worshiping at *Delphos*, whom they had left for Dead, though he recovered. The Report of his Death made *Attalus* his

Bro-

Brother to take upon him as King, and would have taken *Stratonica* his Wife (as a matter of State) had not *Eumenes's* coming home, put a stop to it: All which *Eumenes* only checked, with wishing him not to Marry with the Queen, till he was sure the King was Dead, who then bequeathed her to him. The Senate upon these occasions, Decree War, and send Embassadours to require satisfaction, or to denounce it, which *Perseus* slights, calling the *Romans* greedy, and insolent; commanding them to depart. This present heat was too much, he wanting constant resolution, which he neglected in hope of Peace.

S. 6. *Rome* had now fair occasion of War with *Macedon*, which though it had been long sought, yet the preparation for War was to seek, and the want of it helped to found the disposition of *Greece*, which they solicite by Embassadours with better terms than Threatnings, though they durst not but promise aid to them, whose Ruin they desired. The fear of *Greece*, grew from the timerous demeanour of *Perseus*, whom they secretly affected, but saw his want of resolution would betray them all that declared for them, if he could make his Peace, which even then he sought, when he was in the Field, and his Enemy not in sight. His Embassadours were scarce come Home, when *Licinius* the *Roman* Consul was at *Apollonia*; and yet *Perseus* is still in deliberation, though at last the stoutest and wisest Counsel prevailed, if it had been as well followed after he had brought his Forces together, which were Thirty nine Thousand Foot, and four Thousand Horse. Being come into *Thessaly*, which was the Enemies way, some Towns yield, and some he forc'd, and so came to *Sicurium*. *Licinius* is also come into *Thessaly*, with only two Legions, tyred in his passage through *Athamania*; and resteth by the River *Peneus*, Incamping there, and intending not to Fight
till

till his Auxiliaries were come ; that so he might
strongly force through *Tempe*, of whose Straits
Perseus was Master, to his great advantage, and might
have had more in taking the Straits of *Aous*. Eu-
menes, and *Attalus* his Brother, are come to the
Consul with four Thousand Foot, and one Thousand Horse. Yet the Consul keepeth in his Trenches, and is content to be insulted day by day,
by *Perseus*, till at last, he was forced to send out
Eumenes, *Attalus*, and his own Brother. In this
Skirmish *Perseus* slew two Hundred, and took as
many, with little loss, and might have distressed
the Consuls Camp, if his fear had not baffled his
Incouragement by this Success; For the Consul
was glad to Decamp at Midnight, to a stronger
Place beyond the River. Of all the advantages
he had, this weak spirited Man made no other
use, than to hope for Peace; though *Licinius* peremptorily told him he should look for none,
without an absolute yielding both Person and Kingdom. Not long after, attempting to force the Consuls Camp, he had the worst, and thereupon leaving a weak Guard in *Tempe*, he returned to *Macedon*. *Licinius* the Consul, and *Lucretius* the Admiral, ended their Year with cruel Oppression of
the Confederates; as did this Successours, *Hostilius*,
and *Hortensis* the Admiral, who more intended
quarrelling with Friends, than warring with Enemies; of the Oppressions by the two Admirals,
Complaint was made at *Rome*, and *Lucretius* deeply fined, and a Decree sent to *Greece*, Ordering
him to refuse all Impositions not warranted by the
Senate.

§. 7. *Perseus* in the two first Years of the
War, was grown stronger, being inlarged on the
Illyrian side, and his *Grecian* Friends grown bold-
er; and many of the *Roman* Friends keep out their
Admiral by force, for his Oppression; and the

Glory of the Enterprize against *Macedon*, defac'd
as their Army leffened greatly. *P. Martius* a new
Conful, cometh to help all, if he knew how; yet
he began hotly, and indeed the right way to
pafs through the Straits, not by Force against the
Guard that kept them, but by feeking untrodden
Ways over fuch fteep Mountains, as if Nature had
determined Armies fhould never pafs them, e-
fpecially with Elephants. *Perfeus* could not be ignorant of the *Romans* coming towards him, and
might have diftreffed them, if his Heart had ferved; but he only Guarded the ordinary Paffages
into *Tempe*; and when he faw the *Romans* entred,
he was fo far from forcing them upon their extreme
Wearinefs, that he fled, crying All was loft without a
Fight. So in hafte he left *Dium*, being the ftrong
Paffage into *Macedon*, and fent Poft to fet Fire on
his *Arfenal* at *Theffalonica*, and caft his Treafure at
Pella into the Sea, and called the Captains which
kept the Straits; but after his Fear was paft,
he put the two Firft to Death, to cover his Fear,
as if they had acted without his Command. *Martius* prefently took *Dium*, yet after one days March
into *Macedon*, want of Food forced him back to
Theffaly, fo unable was he to hold out, if he had
kept the Straits. So he forfook *Dium*, and took
the Way to *Phila*, to meet his defired Provifion,
and foolifhly gave over the Enterprize, either for
want of Courage, or Skill; which fo Incouraged
Perfeus, that he Fortified *Dium* again, and fo fru-
ftrated all the Confuls proceeding that Summer,
who only took *Heraclea*, five Miles off. The like
Succefs had the Admiral at Sea in Attempting
Theffalonica, *Caffandria*, and *Demetrias*, though affifted by *Eumenes*. While the Conful lay at *Heraclea*, he perfuaded the *Rhodian* Embaffadours to
Mediate for a Peace, which might argue his Fear,
though *Polybius* thinks it was to indanger the *Rhodians*.

Here

Here also *Polybius* brought him word of Supplies Decreed for him out of *Achæa*, which he refused, and also diffuaded fending any to *Appius Claudius*, as not needful, though *Claudius* on the Frontier of *Illyria* was in danger, and sent for it, and for want of it, was highly difpleafed with *Polybius*. *Eumenes* at this time grew cold in Affection to *Rome*, upon what occafion is doubtful; though it was generally thought, that upon difguft of fome ufage of *Martius* he went Home, from whence *Perfeus* fent to invite him by fome hope of Gain, and upon confideration of that, the Fire was like to take his own Houfe, next after *Perfeus*'s Houfe was burnt. The like courfe *Perfeus* took with *Gentius* King of *Illyria*, and gained him, and both fend to the *Rhodians*, defiring them to Mediate between *Perfeus* and *Rome*, which they promifed, thinking *Martius* alfo defired it: But when their Embaffadour moved for that Mediation, they were fo difdainfully taken up, that in all Humility they were glad to fubmit. *Gentius* having received Ten Talents, and more being coming, laid hands on the *Roman* Embaffadours, and committed them, whereupon *Perfeus* recalled his laft Treafure, feeing *Gentius* fo far ingaged. About that time came *Clondicus* with Ten Thoufand Horfe, and Ten Thoufand Foot of *Gauls*, or *Baftarnes*, procured by *Perfeus*; but for want of Covenanted Pay, prefently returned toward *Danubius*.

§. 8. *Lucius Æmilius Paulus* Conful the fecond time, had *Macedon* for his Province, but refufed to propound any thing for that Service to the Senate, till a view were taken of the State of the Army there, and how it ftood with the *Macedonian*; fo Supplies are made accordingly for him, and the Admiral, and *L. Anicius* to fucceed *Appius*

D d 3   *pius*

pius Claudius the Pretor. *Æmilius* at his departing, in his grave Oration , *Requested them which thought themselves wise enough to manage those Wars, either to go with him for his assistance, or govern their Tongues at Home, and not Censure upon hear-say: For he would frame his Actions to the advantage of the State ; not to the expectation of the Multitude.*

He was Honourably attended out of the City, and in five Days came to the Camp, when *Perseus* lay in *Dium*, and Fortified the Fords of *Enipeus* ; between which, and *Tempe*, for Ten Miles, which is along the Sea-shore and *Olympus*, is no fresh Water ; but *Æmilius* knew no Shore wants fresh Water after a little digging ; for want whereof *Martius* was glad to go to *Heraclea*. Yet the Passage over *Olympus* was as difficult now as then : So that *Æmilius* fell to enquire, and found a Passage over *Olympus*, but narrow, leading to *Perrabia*, difficult of Ascent, but slenderly Guarded ; either not found, or not attempted by *Martius* ; whose Men being tryed in getting over *Ossa*, would hardly adventure such another. But *Paulus* was a far more able Commander, and had Taught them better than to question a Generals Command, and made choice of five Thousand for the Enterprize, whom he committed to his two Adopted Sons, *Scipio Æmilianus*, and *Quintus Fabius Maximus*. These two, the better to conceal their Journey over the Mountains, Marched out another way, till Night came ; and the Consul made shew as if he would have set upon *Perseus*, and gain a Passage over *Enipeus* to divert him from the business intended ; so that *Scipio* and *Fabius* having forced the small Guard, got in three Days over, and were not discovered till the Guard, which fled, were come to the Camp.

                                    Then

Then was all in a Tumult, and the King, most
of all amazed, hasteth to *Pydna,* where he con-
sults whether he should Fortifie some Town, or
put all to the hazard of a Battle ; which latter,
though the worst, is resolved upon, and that which
the Consul wished. The King chose the place
near *Pydna,* whither the Consul came ; but made
a stand, till a place for the Camp were Intrenched, and the Souldiers refreshed after Marching,
though both sides thought it long, especially the
Romans feared, lest the King should remove farther off. That Evening was the Consul told by
a *Tribune,* of an Ecclipse of the Moon that Night,
and the Natural cause of it, who was contented
it should be Published in the Camp, to prevent
their Fear. Superstition captivates the Wise, where
the help of true Religion is wanting. *Æmilius,* as
soon as the Moon recovered her Light, Congratulated her with a Sacrifice ; for which *Plutarch*
calls him a Godly Man : And the next Morning
he made another to *Hercules,* about which, much
of the Day was spent before the *Grecian* partial
God gave a good sign to the Entrals of the Sacrifice ; so that on Day neither side had any great desire to Fight. Yet after ten of the Clock, upon
a light occasion of watring of Horses, two or
three of each side fell to Blows, and Parties came
in so fast, that both the Generals were forced to
put their Men in order of Battel, and after an
Oration, set them together : But *Perseus* used the
shift of a Coward, to leave his Men, and withdraw himself to *Pydna,* pretending Sacrifice, which
being unseasonable, proved him an Hypocritical
Coward. He sped accordingly, for returning he
found it little better than lost, but got the Honour to be present, that he might run away with
his Men, leaving Twenty Thousand Foot slain

in

in the Field, while he recovered *Pella*; from which
he fled in the Night for fear of his own People,
and came to *Amphipolis*; but was glad to be gon
by Sea with his Treasure to *Samothrace*. The
Head having forsaken the Body, little Sense was
left, or Strength to stand; all the Kingdom fell
presently into the Conquerours hand, while the
King taketh Sanctuary with his Treasure, Wife
and Children, in *Samothrace*, and after base Suit
to the Consul, endeavours to escape in a *Cretian* Ship; which having taken in much of his
Treasure, set Sail, and left him in the lurch; in
the end he was forced to yield himself, and all
into the Consuls hand, and so made the Conquest
compleat: Being before the Consul, he meanly
prostrated himself, so that he seemed to dishonour
the Victory, as obtained upon a Man of so base
a Condition. Thus ended the *Macedonian* Kingdom, after a War of Four Years, and the Glory
of the World was Translated to *Rome*.

§. 9. *Gentius* King of *Illyria* with fifteen Thousand
Men at *Lyssus*, ready to assist *Perseus* upon Receipt
of the Mony promised, was attack'd by *Anicius*
the *Roman* Prætor, who drove him into *Scodra* or
Sutary, where after a while he yielded himself and
all his Men to the *Roman* Prætor, who ended
that War in Thirty days.

§. 10. *Rome* swelling with the Pride of her Fortune, called the *Rhodian* Embassadours, whom they
threaten as Parties with *Macedon*, whose Cause they
had presumed to undertake: And though they
Congratulated the Victory, Deprecated their Folly, and their Citizens had put to Death, or sent
Prisoners to *Rome* all the chief Men of the *Macedonian* Faction; yet War had been Proclaimed
against them but for *Cato*, who said it would be
judged rather a Quarrel at their Wealth, than any
just

juft caufe ; confidering alfo what Friends they had
been to *Rome* in former Wars. *Macedon* was divided into four Quarters, and each prohibited Commerce with other. Their Laws abrogated, new
given, and all the Nobles fent into *Italy,* and the
Tribute leffened by half, which was the beft part
of the Liberty *Rome* ufed to give. *Greece* muft
now bear her Yoke ; and all that can be found, not
only Affociates with *Perfeus,* but good Patriots which
were not held ferviceable to *Rome,* were fent to *Rome*
and there clapt up, of which fort a Thoufand were
fent out of *Achæa,* and *Polybius* among them. This
was the Virtue of the *Roman* Oath and League. *E-*
pirus was more barbaroufly dealt with, and given to
the Souldiers to Plunder for their Pay, to fave the
Macedonian Treafure whole *:* So in one day feventy
Cities of the *Roman* Confederates were Plundered
by the Companies put into them in Peace, only to
Quarter ; and One Hundred and Fifty Thoufand
made Slaves, which act of *Æmilius* ftained his other
Virtues.

§. 11. *Antiochus* the Great dyed in the Thirty fixth
Year of his Reign; *Seleuchus* his Eldeft Son, fucceeded
Twelve Years, whom *Daniel* defcribed Three Hundred Years before, *Onias* being then High Prieft.
Mac. 3. The Firft Book of *Maccabees* ends *An.* 167
of the *Syrian* Kings ; the Second Book ends the 151
Year. *Antiochus Epiphanes* fucceedes his Brother in
Syria, An. 137 ; whofe death he procured. *Ptolome-*
us Epiphanes after twenty four Years left *Egypt* to his
Son *Ptolomeus Philometor,* fo called by the Rule of contraries ; for Murdering his Mother, he was hated by
his Subjects, and rebelled againft by his Brother *Pto-*
lomy Phifcon, who got poffeffion of *Alexandria,* upon
which contention *Antiochus Epiphanes* his Uncle thought
to poffefs that Kingdom, under pretence of protecting
the Young Prince. *Antiochus*'s proceedings herein and at
Jerufalem are Recorded, 1. *Mac.* 1. About the beginning

ginning of the *Macedonian* War, when beſides the
Spoil of *Egypt*, he took all *Cæloſyria*, and ſold the
High Prieſts place to *Jaſon*, thruſt out *Onias*, and
after ſold it to *Manelaus*, who procured *Onias*, being fled into the Sanctuary at *Daphus* by *Antioch*,
to be Murdered. 2 *Mac.* 4. *Onias* his taking protection of *Apollo* and *Diana*, ſeemed allowed by the
Author, which argues the Book to be Apocryphal.
His Second Expedition into *Egypt*, 2 *Mac.* 1. was
foreſhewn by prodigious Signs in the Air for forty
days together, and was occaſioned by the unexpected agreement of the Brethren, which incens'd him,
he deſigning they ſhould deſtroy one another. So he
entred *Egypt*, though the Young King intreated the
contrary by Embaſſadours, of whom he demanded *Cyprus* and *Peluſium*, and took *Memphis* and other
places. The *Egyptians* ſeek help from *Rome*, but
in vain, they being now deep in with the *Macedonian* War; the like they deſire of the *Greeks*, e-
ſpecially the *Achæans*, whoſe forwardneſs was hindred by the *Roman* Faction; yet at length the Senate being moved with compaſſion of the Embaſſadours lamentable behaviour and ſupplication, ſent
C. Popilius and others, with Command that *Antiochus*
ſhould leave *Egypt*; to which he ſubmitted according to the Prophet *Daniel*, or rather the Hiſtory
of *Daniel*.

§. 12. *Rome* we ſee is grown terrible: When the
greateſt Kings muſt bow to her Majeſty, how ſhall
inferiour Kings and States carry themſelves to be aſ-
ſured of Favour? *Eumenes* had been very officious,
and help'd to kindle the Fire which has burnt up the
Kingdom of *Macedon*. He therefore ſends *Attalus*
his Brother to Congratulate the Victory, and crave
Aid againſt the *Gallo-Greeks*: But *Attalus* had ſucceeded better, if he had requeſted his Brothers
Kingdom; which becauſe he hid not as they expected,

ed, the Fathers went from what they had promiſed of his having *Enus* and *Maronia* ; as for the *Gallo-Greeks* they have a Meſſage ſent them, rather to incourage than diſſuade them. The diſpleaſure of the Senate being ſo manifeſt, *Eumenes* will again viſit them, but the Fathers will not receive him, it being decreed that no King ſhall come within *Rome.* Yet *Pruſius* King of *Bythinia,* a little before had been welcomed after a better manner ; as he who gave theſe Mortal Gods the Title and Worſhip done to them, kiſſing the Threſhold, and calling them his Gods and Saviours, commending his Son *Nicomedes* to their Tuition. *Cotys* the *Thracian* excuſed his helping *Perſeus,* and intreats the diſcharge of his Son, taken with *Perſeus*'s Children, which is granted, with admonition of his good behaviour to *Rome.*

Maſaniſſa only kept his Reputation with theſe great Maſters, who ſtand by him in all Quarrels with *Carthage,* whoſe Ruin he muſt help forward, before his own turn be ſerved : His Congratulations are well accepted.

Perſeus and *Gentius* the unhappy Kings, have the laſt Act to play at *Rome,* in the Triumphs of *Æmilius* and *Anicius,* being led in Chains before their Chariot. *Perſeus* made application to *Æmilius,* not to be put to the diſgrace, and was ſcornfully anſwered that he might prevent it, meaning he might kill himſelf ; his end is uncertain, whether ſtarved or by over-watching. *Alexander* his Youngeſt Son became a Turner in *Rome ;* what conceit ſoever his Father had of him, when he gave him that Name in wantonneſs of Sovereignty, in which he commanded poor Men to be ſlain for getting up his Treaſure out of the Sea by Diving. He conſidered not, that the greateſt Oppreſſours and the moſt abject Wretches are all
ſub-

subject to one high Power, governing all alike
with absolute Command. But such is our Unhappiness, that instead of that blessed Counsel, *to do as
we would be done to,* which teacheth Moderation,
we entertain that arrogant Thought, *I will be like the
most high*; that is, I will do what pleaseth my self.
The very desire of ability to do Evil without controul, is a dangerous Temptation to the performance; God hath granted it to few, and very few
they are which use it not to their own damage;
as Princes, who rack their Sovereignity to the uttermost extent, teach others by the like strain to
root out their own Progeny. Nay, excellent Princes are often forced to flatter some base Minion
or Harlot which Governs some unworthy Fellow,
that Governs all, of which there are too many
Examples. *Æmilius's* Triumph so glorious by reason of a Kings Person, brought also such Riches
into the *Roman* Treasury, that till *Julius Cæsar's*
Death the State never needed to burden it self
with Tribute. The joy of this Triumph God abated with the loss of his Two Sons, one Five
days before, another Five days after it.

We have seen the beginning and end of the
three First Monarchies of the World, whose Founders thought they should never end: And the
Fourth, of the *Romans,* is already at the highest;
where we left it in the Field, wherein nothing is left
to shadow it from the Eyes of the World: But
after some time the Storms of Ambition shall tear
her Branches, her Leaves shall fall, her Limbs
wither, and a Rabble of barbarous Nations shall
cut her down. These great Conquerours have been
the Subject of our Ancient Histories, and Tragical Poets; shewing us their great undertakings,
not so much desiring Rule over others, which is
so full of Care, as hunting after Fame, which
Ploweth

Ploweth up the Air, and Soweth in the Wind. And certainly as Fame has often been dangerous to the Living, so is it of no use to the Dead; who if they did understand what is Reported of them, they would wish they had stolen out of the World without noise, rather than to hear the Report of their Treacheries, Murders, Rapines, giving the spoil of Innocent labouring Souls, to the idle and insolent.

Since the Fall of the *Roman* Empire (omitting the *Germans,* neither great, nor of long continuance) there hath been no State formidable in the East, but the *Turk;* nor in the West, except the *Spaniard,* who by so many Attempts hath sought to make himself Master of all *Europe* : As one who is powerful both by his *Indian* Treasure, and many Kingdoms he possessed in *Europe* : But as the *Turk* is now Counterpoised by the *Persian*; So if, for so many Millions spent by *English, French,* and *Netherlands,* in defensive War, and 'diversions against them, Two Hundred Sixty Thousand Pound were imployed for Two or Three Years, it is easie to demonstrate how they may be brought to live in Peace, and their swelling Streams be brought within the Banks. These are the only Nations of Eminency to be regarded of us; the one seeking to root out the Christian Religion, the other the sincere Profession of it.

If farther Reason be required of the continuance of this boundless Ambition of Mortal Men, than desire of Fame, we may say, That the Kings and Princes of the World have always laid before them the Actions, not the Ends of those great ones, the Glory of the one Transporting them,

never

never minding the Misery of the other till it seized upon him. They neglect the Advice of God, while they hope to live; but when Death comes, then they believe what it tells them, Death without speaking a word, perswades what God with promises and threats cannot do, though the one hates and destroys Man, whereas the other made and loves him. I have considered (saith *Solomon*) all Works that are under the Sun, and behold all is Vanity and vexation of Spirit: Who believes this till Death beats it into us? It was Death which forced the Conscience of *Charles* 5th. and made him enjoyn *Philip* his Son, to restore *Navarre*; and *Francis* the First, King of *France*, to command justice to be done upon the Murderers of the Protestants in *Merindol* and *Calabries*, till then neglected. Death alone can make Man know himself; the proud and insolent, that he is but abject, and can make him hate his fore-past Happiness: The rich Man he proves a naked Beggar, which hath interest in nothing but in the Gravel that fills his Mouth; and when he holds the Glass before the Eyes of the most Beautiful, they see and acknowledge their Deformity and Rottenefs. O eloquent, just and mighty Death! whom none could advise, thou hast perswaded; what none hath presumed, thou hast done; whom all the World have flattered, thou hast cast out of the World and despised: Thou hast drawn together all the extravagant Greatness, all the Pride, Cruelty and Ambition of Man, and covered it all over with two narrow Words, *Hic jacet.*

Lastly, Whereas this Book bearing this Title, The First Part of the general, *&c.* implying a Second, and a Third, which I intended, and have
                                                                    hewn

hewn out ; befides many other Difcouragements perfuading my Silence, it hath pleafed God to take that glorious Prince out of the World, for whom they were defigned : Whofe unfpeakable and never enough lamented lofs, hath taught me to fay with *Job*, *Verfa eft in luctum cithara mea, & organum meum in vocem flentium.*

F I N I S.

CPSIA information can be obtained
at www.ICGtesting.com
Printed in the USA
BVHW041527270820
587459BV00012B/232